M000294599

Mt. Vernon
Port Angeles
WASHINGTON
Aberdeen
Wenatchee
Longview
Walla Walla
Coeur d'Alene
Missoula
Helena
MONTANA
Bozeman
Minot
NORTH DAKOTA
SOUTH DAKOTA
Pendleton
Albany - Corvallis
OREGON
Bend
Coos Bay
Roseburg
Grants Pass
Klamath Falls
IDAHO
Idaho Falls
Pocatello
Twin Falls
WYOMING
Rock Springs
NEBRASKA
Grand Island
Arcata - Eureka
Elko
Logan
Carson City
NEVADA
UTAH
COLORADO
Hollister
CALIFORNIA
Hanford - Lemoore
St George
Farmington
Gallup
Stillwater
Chickasha
Duncan
Prescott
ARIZONA
El Centro -
Calexico - Brawley
NEW MEXICO
Clovis
Roswell
Alamogordo
Hobbs
Carlsbad
Sierra Vista
ALASKA
Fairbanks
Del Rio
Eagle Pass
HAWAII

America's 193 Micropolitan Areas

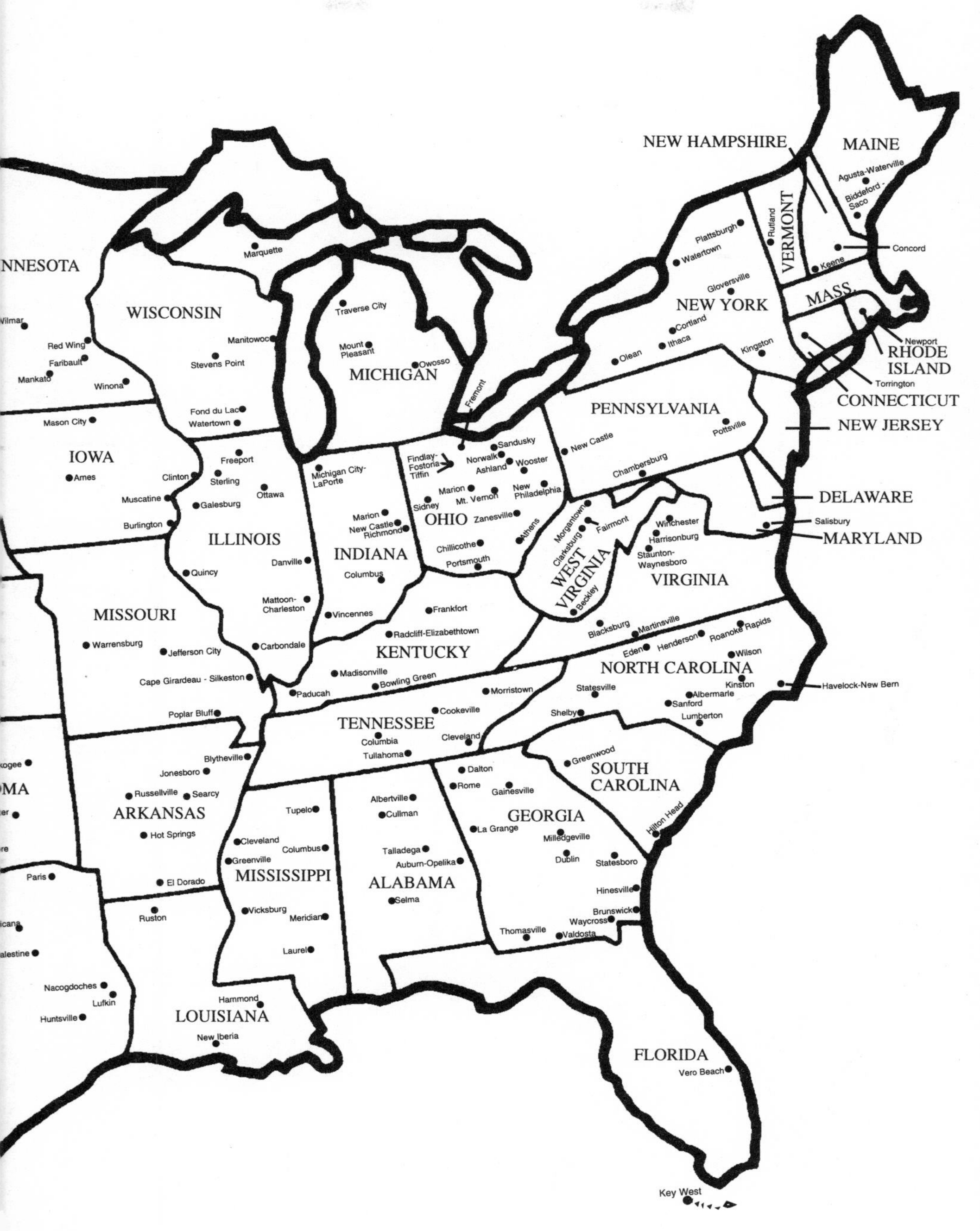

THE *NEW* RATING GUIDE TO

LIFE IN AMERICA'S SMALL CITIES

THE *NEW* RATING GUIDE TO

LIFE IN AMERICA'S SMALL CITIES

KEVIN HEUBUSCH

59 John Glenn Drive
Amherst, New York 14228-2197

Published 1997 by Prometheus Books

01 00 99 98 97   5 4 3 2 1

Library of Congress Cataloging-in-Publication Data

Heubusch, Kevin.

The new rating guide to life in America's small cities / by Kevin Heubusch.

p. cm.

"Second edition"—Pref.

Previous edition published as The rating guide to life in America's small cities / G. Scott Thomas. c1990.

ISBN 1–57392–170–X (cloth : alk. paper) — ISBN 1–57392–192–0 (pbk. : alk. paper)

1. Cities and towns—Ratings—United States. 2. Cities and towns—United States—Statistics. 3. Urban-rural migration—United States. 4. Quality of life—United States. I. Thomas, G. Scott. Rating guide to life in America's small cities. II. Title.

HT123.H49 1997

307.76′0973—dc21 97–35830

CIP

Printed in the United States of America on acid-free paper

Contents

Preface to the New Edition

Much has changed since Scott Thomas wrote the first edition of *The Rating Guide to Life in America's Small Cities* in 1990. We have seen a national recession and an uneven recovery, accelerated growth in the mountain states, and telecommunications advances that dramatically alter where we live and work. But one thing remains the same. Americans are continuing to "think small." And thinking small continues to lead people away from sprawling metropolitan areas to small cities throughout the country. Micropolitan America is alive and well.

Nowhere is this clearer than in fast-growing states out west. Many newcomers to Arizona, Utah, and Washington are stopping short of the metropolitan traffic jams to settle in nonmetropolitan areas. Washington state's large cities and suburbs grew 9.7 percent in the first half of the decade, but its nonmetropolitan communities proved even more popular. Population there grew 10.2 percent. The majority of newcomers to California opted out of the high costs and strain of that state's large cities. California's nonmetropolitan population grew 8.4 percent, while its metropolitan population grew just 5.5 percent.

Overall, the the share of the West's nonmetro population increased 9.3 percent in the first half of the 1990s, compared with 7.5 percent in metropolitan growth. The share of residents living outside of big cities and suburbs increased from 13.5 percent to 13.7 percent in just four years. Doesn't sound like much?

That's an additional 662,000 people in the West who chose to settle outside metropolitan areas rather than in them.

The growth in some small cities in the first half of the decade has been outstanding. The population of St. George, Utah, a town not listed in the first edition of this book, grew at a dizzying rate of 34 percent. Coeur d'Alene, Idaho, grew 25 percent, and Bend, Oregon, grew 22 percent. The population of the nation as a whole grew just 5.6 percent over the same period.

The popularity of small cities extends beyond the nation's fastest-growing states. Other small cities are proving to be vibrant communities in states experiencing otherwise slow growth. Traverse City, Michigan, grew 8.6 percent over the first half of the decade, while the state population grew just 2.1 percent. Vicksburg, Mississippi, grew 7.9 percent—twice the rate of Mississippi's overall growth.

All this running around has shaken up the original list of top-rated small cities. Three of the ten highest-rated small cities from the first edition are not included in the second edition. Number-one ranked San Luis Obispo, California; number three Fredericksburg, Virginia; and number six Hattiesburg, Mississippi, all proved so popular that they have outgrown this book's definition of a micropolitan area. Other cities jockeyed up and down the list with the changing times. Some cities have rebounded from the recession of the early 1990s with job growth, income gains, and new faces. Others have yet to see the rising tide reach their shores.

Some particulars: Bozeman, Montana, leapt from tenth place to second in recreation availability. Key West, Florida, stepped up to first. Shoppers in Carson City, Nevada, propelled that city from eighth in retail spending to first between editions. Vero Beach, Florida, now has the highest personal income among the nation's small cities.

Some of these changes have occurred as previous winners left the realm of small cities. All-in-all, fifty-two cities from the first edition are not back for the second edition. The majority of them—thirty-seven—grew in size until they became recognized by the federal government as official metropolitan centers. San Luis Obispo and Hattiesburg, for example, became the central cities in newly defined metropolitan areas. Other small cities such as Fredericksburg became encompassed by spreading metropolitan areas. Fredericksburg is now considered to be a city in the Washington, D.C.-Virginia-Maryland metropolitan area.

The remainder of the cities that have not returned declined in population until they were too small to be considered a city for the purposes of this book. Louisiana lost four entries for this reason—the most of any state.

But busy in the background, more than two dozen towns and cities that were too small when the first edition was published have since grown in popularity and population. Twenty-seven cities are new to this edition. Georgia alone added five new cities, more than any other state.

Documenting this decade's worth of change is a wealth of new data. The new numbers tell where we're moving, what we're earning, and how much school we've completed. They detail the cost, size, and heating and cooling requirements of our houses. They count the retail stores in town, and measure the volume of their annual sales.

This book uses these new data to their fullest value, presenting them at the most local level. You'll find out not the average income in *Nevada*, but the average income of the 40,463 residents in *Elko*, Nevada. Want to know how long your commute might be in Pocatello, Idaho? It's here. Only have one car for two workers? There's bus service in Pocatello. And it's pretty reliable. Pocatello has one of the most popular bus systems among small cities.

Sometimes just the name of a town is enough to prick up your ears: Coos Bay, Longview, Watertown. It's a hint that maybe you're longing for a change of pace and of place. I hope you'll find the following pages both a resource and an inspiration in considering your move to micropolitan America.

I echo Scott's wishes from the first edition: Happy Hunting!

—Kevin Heubusch

Introduction: Micropolitan America

Big is better. That's the American credo. Our milk comes in gallons, our hamburgers by the quarter pound. We aspire to drive big cars, own big houses, and hold big jobs. Maybe it's because we live in a big country that we have come to believe that size and quality are inextricably linked. The bigger something is, the more impressed we are.

The same is true of cities. Metropolitan giants like New York City, Los Angeles, and Chicago dazzle the nation with their wealth, glamour, and power. We give our big cities big nicknames: the Big Apple, the Big Easy, the City of Big Shoulders. They are big magnets. Eighty percent of the country now lives in metropolitan areas.

It would seem only logical that a big city would provide the best possible quality of life. Why else would millions upon millions of people have crowded into our cities? Big *is* better, isn't it?

Not necessarily. Consider these examples of metropolitan unrest:

• Fewer than 1 in 3 New York City residents say they are very satisfied with their quality of life, according to a 1996 study conducted by the Regional Plan Association. New Yorkers are the most likely among residents of the entire New York-New Jersey-Connecticut region to cite a lack of community, poor public schools, and high crime as big problems. Urban residents in the area are far more likely than nonurban residents to say they would move if they could.

• Sixty-one percent of registered voters in New Orleans report that the city's quality of life has deteriorated, according to a 1996 study by the Survey Research Center at the University of New Orleans. Fewer than 25 percent of residents in neighboring Jefferson Parish say the same of their communities.

A similar poll conducted by the *Los Angeles Times* several years earlier also found that 6 in 10 Los Angeles residents also considered their city's quality of life to have deteriorated.

• The biggest cities provide the poorest environment for children. From pollution to crime and poverty, big cities are failed by federal organizations and child advocacy groups alike. A recent report by Zero Population Growth, an organization concerned with the impact of population growth, ranked 207 large U.S. cities according to fourteen factors that most directly affect the well-being of children. The twenty cities that ranked lowest had an average population of 438,000. The twenty highest-scoring cities had smaller populations by far, with an average of 146,000 residents.

The traditional outlet for urban stress has been the dream of moving to a tranquil suburb, where the big worries are crabgrass and the wait at the first tee, not crime and the one-and-a-half-mile backup on the expressway. But many of these islands of serenity have been flooded by encroaching, sprawling urbanization. "My suburb has become a city, without any of the amenities," columnist Judy Mann complained in the *Washington Post.* "We have traffic jams that rival New York's. Half-hour commutes have become 45-minute and hour-long commutes."

Close-in suburbs such as Mann's have become saturated. Some are increasingly being abandoned. "Older suburbs in the Washington area are becoming a lot more like older cities," says land-use consultant Douglas R. Porter, quoted in the *Washington Post.* "If they are not careful, they could end up with slums." A county redevelopment manager says of one long-established Washington, D.C., suburb, "Rents are down, property values are down, there are a lot of vacancies. It is a reason for concern."

Other suburbs are becoming prohibitively expensive. Housing costs in the Chicago suburb of Schaumburg, Illinois, are 37 percent above the national average, according to the American Chamber of Commerce Researchers Association. Driving thirty miles out to Joliet only brings housing costs down to 16 percent above average.

High prices and "urbanized" suburbs send many residents to the outermost fringes of metro areas. In many such fast-growing metros, it doesn't take long for the sprawl to catch up. Alan Post, who moved out to the edges of the Washington, D.C., area for some elbow room and quiet is now faced with the prospect of a four-lane highway through his subdivision. "It's going to cut right through the middle of our back yards," he says. "I moved out here to get away from all that."

The Newest Frontier

The process of elimination provides the answer for Americans seeking quality lives without excessive stress, expense, and four-lane highways running through the rhododendrons. Big cities are out, and suburbs have followed them. If farm life is not for you, what's left? Small cities.

City dwellers have always scorned small towns for being isolated, placid, and decidedly unmetropolitan. But such contempt played better in the days before the obvious deterioration of urban life and rapid advances in telecommunications. The recent growth in nonmetropolitan areas is solidly based on long-term economic changes that favor areas removed from central cities, as well as "the strong conviction of many Americans that small-town life is better than big-city life," write Kenneth M. Johnson and Calvin L. Beale in *American Demographics* magazine.

Most home buyers now want to move as far from big cities as possible. *Professional Builder,* the national magazine for contractors, asked Americans in 1996 where they would prefer to purchase a new home. Fewer than 2 percent picture their dream home in a central city; only 20 percent say they would prefer a close-in suburb. Instead, 37 percent want to buy in outlying suburbs, and the largest share, 39 percent, want to buy their new home in a rural area. (Three percent of respondents chose "other.")

Add the figures for the suburban fringe and rural America, and you have 76 percent of respondents who want to get out of urban areas. And it's an increase from 64 percent who gave the same answer in the 1988 survey. *New York Times* correspondent John Herbers recorded this trend as it was taking shape in his 1986 book, *The New Heartland.* Herbers saw middle-class residents of large cities and their suburbs yearning for space and independence and looking for those qualities beyond metropolitan boundaries. "It is an alternative to both the big cities and their massive suburbs, one that a sizable number of people have chosen," he wrote. "And nothing on the horizon strongly indicates an end to this trend."

This book seeks to provide essential facts to those residents of cities and suburbs who are contemplating life in a smaller, quieter, safer, and less costly community. The following pages focus on 193 small cities spread throughout the country that are large enough to provide the community and services of an urban area, but are removed from the congestion and difficulties of metro areas. Each "micropolitan" area consists of a small central city and its county. Just three rules and two notes define a micropolitan:

1. The central city must have at least 15,000 residents.

2. The county must have at least 40,000 residents (including the population of the central city).

3. No micropolitan area may be part of an officially designated metropolitan area, as defined by the federal government in July 1994.

Note 1. A micro is not limited to a single central city in a single county.

Some cities near county lines are considered to reside in each county. Likewise, if one county contains two qualifying cities, the micro area includes both cities as central cities.

Note 2. Some states have independent cities that are not located within counties. Any independent city of 15,000 or more residents qualifies as a micropolis. If the city is larger than fifteen square miles, the micro consists of the independent city only. If the city is smaller, the micropolitan area consists of the city and its adjacent county.

Approximately 14 million people live in micropolitan America—5.4 percent of the nation's population. Small cities account for 10 percent or more of the population in thirteen states. Idaho and New Mexico have the highest share of residents who live in micros: nearly 27 percent. Other states strong in small cities include Maine and Montana (23 percent), New Hampshire and Oregon (17 percent), and Mississippi (16 percent). Ohio has both the largest number of micropolitan residents and the highest number of micros: 1.1 million people living in fourteen small cities across the state. Six states (and the District of Columbia) have no micros: Colorado, Delaware, Hawaii, Massachusetts, New Jersey, and South Dakota.

Small Cities Today

Some big cities are better than others. Some small cities are better than others.

This book is designed to help you find the best small city for your needs, using a statistical system to grade the quality of life in each. But before determining the differences between micropolitan communities, it is useful to learn what they have in common:

Youth. Most small cities have young populations. Nearly 60 percent of all micros have median ages below the national average. Many of these are college towns or the sites of military bases.

Friendliness. What city dwellers avoid, small-city residents don't fear: eye contact. "I experienced culture shock," says Abby Ostein, describing her move from Seattle to micropolitan Ithaca, New York. "My students waved to me on the street. My neighbors stopped by the front porch to introduce themselves."

Less stress. The pace eases up when commutes are easier, personal safety is higher, and streets are less crowded. James Rouse, a noted urban planner and developer, contends that large cities are so huge that they prevent people from feeling in control of their lives. "I believe this out-of-scaleness promotes loneliness, irresponsibility, superficial values," he says. "People grow best in small communities where the institutions, which are the dominant force in our lives, are within the scale of their comprehension and within reach of their sense of responsibility and capacity to manage."

Less education. The residents of micropolitan areas generally have less education than the national norm. Only 74 percent of small-city adults have received their high school diploma, compared with 78 percent of adults nationwide. Fourteen percent of adults in micropolitans have a college degree, compared with a national average of 21 percent. The notable exceptions to this trend are university towns.

Less racial and ethnic diversity. Most small cities do not offer the mix of racial and ethnic groups that large cities usually feature. Only 28 percent of the nation's micropolitan areas have a larger share of black residents than does the nation as a whole. Just 11 percent have a share of Hispanic residents higher than the national average.

Lower incomes. Paychecks are definitely lighter in small cities. Per capita incomes match the national average in just 5 percent of micropolitans. Keep in mind, though, that the cost of living is usually lower in small cities. In many cases, the disparity in income is not as great as it seems.

Closeness to nature. It can be a frustrating, time-consuming trip to escape from a metro area to your favorite campground or lake. Small cities are often very close to such attractions. "Wages are lower here, but you have to weigh what's important," Vermont speech therapist Steve Libby told *USA Today.* "Do I want to live near the Metropolitan Museum of Art, or do I want to live somewhere where I can take my kids to see butterflies?"

Closeness to metro areas. Many city dwellers think of the typical small city as being an isolated backwater. The reality is much different. Most micropolitan areas are close enough to a big city for day trips or even commuting. Fifty-five percent are within fifty miles of the center of a metropolitan area.

After studying this list of qualities—some good, some not so good—you might decide that the balance tips in favor of micropolitan life. But how do you find the small city that is right for you?

The main body of this book is divided into ten sections, each section measuring a different aspect of life in micropolitan America. Sections include subjects such as economics, health care, education, and crime. Five categories in each section measure the general topic in a specific way, assigning points to every micro on a scale of 0 to 20. The best performances receive the highest points.

The scoring system thus allows you to easily consider each micro on a single topic. Of a possible 100 points in transportation, how many did the micro receive? And the system allows you to conveniently compare several micros that may each have caught your eye.

The obvious last step is to add the ten section totals, resulting in a score for each community's overall quality of life. Such final totals can be found at the back of the book, along with "report cards" that summarize the scores.

The data used in the categories are the most current publicly available from the federal government and several private sources as of May 1997. Much of the data is for 1994—it can take time to collect, process, and publish the statistics for a nation of 260 million people. In many cases, surveys of the detailed geographic areas used in this book are not conducted annually. For instance, only once every five years does the Census Bureau set out to collect the highly specific data on the number, type, size, and income of retail establishments in each county in the country. Who can blame them? There is no other agency, private or public, equipped to undertake and make publicly available such comprehensive studies.

Author Sherwood Anderson, who was unsparingly critical of small-town America in his early writings, came to a change of heart just before his death. "The big world outside now is so filled with confusion," he wrote in 1940, "it seemed to me that our only hope, in the present muddle, was to try thinking small."

The statistics and scores in this book are intended to inspire exactly that. Study the ten sections; check out the report cards. You might find that "thinking small" will lead you to a happy home in micropolitan America.

America's 193 Micropolitan Areas

	component	population
Alabama		
Albertville	Marshall County	76,802
Auburn-Opelika	Lee County	91,869
Cullman	Cullman County	71,615
Selma	Dallas County	47,991
Talladega	Talladega County	76,034
Alaska		
Fairbanks	Fairbanks North Star Borough	84,711
Arizona		
Prescott	Yavapai County	127,942
Sierra Vista	Cochise County	107,446
Arkansas		
Blytheville	Mississippi County	50,923
El Dorado	Union County	46,255
Hot Springs	Garland County	79,792
Jonesboro	Craighead County	73,447
Russellville	Pope County	50,211
Searcy	White County	59,554
California		
Arcata-Eureka	Humboldt County	121,715
El Centro-Calexico-Brawley	Imperial County	137,090
Hanford-Lemoore	Kings County	110,867
Hollister	San Benito County	41,082
Connecticut		
Torrington	Litchfield County	178,523
Florida		
Key West	Monroe County	81,796
Vero Beach	Indian River County	95,618
Georgia		
Brunswick	Glynn County	65,037
Dalton	Whitfield County	76,859
Dublin	Laurens County	42,264
Gainesville	Hall County	105,204

Hinesville	Liberty County	58,895
La Grange	Troup County	57,560
Milledgeville	Baldwin County	41,334
Rome	Floyd County	83,268
Statesboro	Bulloch County	47,810
Thomasville	Thomas County	40,246
Valdosta	Lowndes County	82,310
Waycross	Ware, Pierce Counties	50,044
Idaho		
Coeur d'Alene	Kootenai County	87,345
Idaho Falls	Bonneville County	79,181
Pocatello	Bannock, Power Counties	79,127
Twin Falls	Twin Falls County	58,619
Illinois		
Carbondale	Jackson County	61,444
Danville	Vermilion County	87,799
Freeport	Stephenson County	49,015
Galesburg	Knox County	56,287
Mattoon-Charleston	Coles County	52,231
Ottawa	La Salle County	109,415
Quincy	Adams County	67,769
Sterling	Whiteside County	60,381
Indiana		
Columbus	Bartholomew County	67,042
Marion	Grant County	73,858
Michigan City-La Porte	La Porte County	110,008
New Castle	Henry County	49,018
Richmond	Wayne County	72,557
Vincennes	Knox County	40,240
Iowa		
Ames	Story County	74,478
Burlington	Des Moines County	42,879
Clinton	Clinton County	50,983
Mason City	Cerro Gordo County	46,518
Muscatine	Muscatine County	41,292
Kansas		
Hutchinson	Reno County	62,653

Manhattan	Riley, Pottawatomie Counties	86,818
Salina	Saline County	49,301
Kentucky		
Bowling Green	Warren County	83,027
Frankfort	Franklin County	45,603
Madisonville	Hopkins County	46,283
Paducah	McCracken County	64,708
Radcliff-Elizabethtown	Hardin County	90,401
Louisiana		
Hammond	Tangipahoa County	91,337
New Iberia	Iberia County	70,820
Ruston	Lincoln County	43,112
Maine		
Augusta-Waterville	Kennebec County	117,111
Biddeford-Saco	York County	169,410
Maryland		
Salisbury	Wicomico County	78,469
Michigan		
Marquette	Marquette County	70,156
Mount Pleasant	Isabella County	55,545
Owosso	Shiawassee County	71,729
Traverse City	Grand Traverse, Leelenau Counties	87,728
Minnesota		
Faribault	Rice County	51,524
Mankato	Blue Earth, Nicolett Counties	83,118
Red Wing	Goodhue County	42,039
Willmar	Kandiyohi County	40,563
Winona	Winona County	48,351
Mississippi		
Cleveland	Bolivar County	41,596
Columbus	Lowndes County	60,759
Greenville	Washington County	66,786
Laurel	Jones County	63,000
Meridian	Lauderdale County	76,377
Tupelo	Lee County	70,760
Vicksburg	Warren County	49,076

Missouri		
Cape Girardeau-Sikeston	Cape Girardeau, New Madrid, Scott Counties	125,289
Jefferson City	Cole, Callaway Counties	101,396
Poplar Bluff	Butler County	40,146
Warrensburg	Johnson County	46,024
Montana		
Bozeman	Gallatin County	57,811
Helena	Lewis and Clark County	51,604
Missoula	Missoula County	85,689
Nebraska		
Grand Island	Hall County	50,747
Nevada		
Carson City	Carson City (independent city)	45,117
Elko	Elko County	40,463
New Hampshire		
Concord	Merrimack County	121,939
Keene	Cheshire County	70,800
New Mexico		
Alamogordo	Otero County	54,306
Carlsbad	Eddy County	52,795
Clovis	Curry County	47,910
Farmington	San Juan County	99,279
Gallup	McKinley County	65,493
Hobbs	Lea County	57,079
Roswell	Chaves County	60,986
New York		
Cortland	Cortland County	49,287
Gloversville	Fulton County	54,419
Ithaca	Tompkins County	96,309
Kingston	Ulster County	168,442
Olean	Cattaraugus County	85,472
Plattsburgh	Clinton County	86,525
Watertown	Jefferson County	115,327
North Carolina		
Albemarle	Stanly County	53,756

Eden	Rockingham County	87,496
Havelock-New Bern	Craven County	83,930
Henderson	Vance County	40,457
Kinston	Lenoir County	58,656
Lumberton	Robeson County	110,754
Roanoke Rapids	Halifax County	57,275
Sanford	Lee County	44,907
Shelby	Cleveland County	88,482
Statesville	Iredell County	100,706
Wilson	Wilson County	67,050
North Dakota		
Minot	Ward County	57,903
Ohio		
Ashland	Ashland County	50,594
Athens	Athens County	60,409
Chillicothe	Ross County	73,250
Findlay-Fostoria-Tiffin	Seneca, Hancock Counties	128,164
Fremont	Sandusky County	62,738
Marion	Marion County	65,272
Mount Vernon	Knox County	50,108
New Philadelphia	Tuscarawas County	86,585
Norwalk	Huron County	58,016
Portsmouth	Scioto County	81,113
Sandusky	Erie County	78,046
Sidney	Shelby County	46,648
Wooster	Wayne County	106,176
Zanesville	Muskingum County	83,685
Oklahoma		
Ardmore	Carter County	43,729
Chickasha	Grady County	43,068
Duncan	Stephens County	43,195
McAlester	Pittsburg County	42,721
Muskogee	Muskogee County	69,295
Stillwater	Payne County	63,436
Oregon		
Albany-Corvallis	Benton, Linn Counties	74,450
Bend	Deschutes County	91,089
Coos Bay	Coos County	62,731

America's 193 Micropolitan Areas (continued)

Grants Pass	Josephine County	69,421
Klamath Falls	Klamath County	60,534
Pendleton	Umatilla County	63,197
Roseburg	Douglas County	98,355
Pennsylvania		
Chambersburg	Franklin County	125,959
New Castle	Lawrence County	96,639
Pottsville	Schuylkill County	154,063
Rhode Island		
Newport	Newport County	83,689
South Carolina		
Greenwood	Greenwood County	61,401
Hilton Head Island	Beaufort County	97,230
Tennessee		
Cleveland	Bradley County	77,543
Columbia	Maury County	63,936
Cookeville	Putnam County	55,870
Morristown	Hamblen County	52,376
Tullahoma	Coffee, Franklin Counties	78,851
Texas		
Corsicana	Navarro County	40,326
Del Rio	Val Verde County	42,764
Eagle Pass	Maverick County	44,297
Huntsville	Walker County	53,706
Lufkin	Angelina County	74,826
Nacogdoches	Nacogdoches County	56,072
Palestine	Anderson County	49,850
Paris	Lamar County	44,924
Utah		
Logan	Cache County	75,888
St. George	Washington County	65,231
Vermont		
Rutland	Rutland County	62,495

Virginia		
Blacksburg-Radford-Christiansburg	Montgomery, Pulaski Counties and Radford (independent city)	125,725
Harrisonburg	Rockingham County and Harrisonburg (independent city)	94,398
Martinsville	Henry County and Martinsville (independent city)	72,479
Staunton-Waynesboro	Augusta County and Staunton-Waynesboro (independent cities)	102,491
Winchester	Frederick County and Winchester (independent city)	74,486
Washington		
Aberdeen	Grays Harbor County	66,701
Longview	Cowlitz County	87,463
Mount Vernon	Skagit County	91,762
Port Angeles	Clallam County	61,784
Walla Walla	Walla Walla County	52,734
Wenatchee	Chelan County	56,275
West Virginia		
Beckley	Raleigh County	78,132
Clarksburg	Harrison County	70,770
Fairmont	Marion County	58,109
Morgantown	Monongalia County	78,013
Wisconsin		
Fond du Lac	Fond du Lac County	92,834
Manitowoc	Manitowoc County	82,077
Stevens Point	Portgage County	64,123
Watertown	Jefferson, Dodge Counties	150,906
Wyoming		
Rock Springs	Sweetwater County	40,792

Source: Population Division, U.S. Bureau of the Census, Washington, D.C. Data are for 1994.

Micropolitan Populations: State by State

State	Total Population	Micropolitan Population	% Micropolitan
Alabama	4,220,178	364,311	8.6
Alaska	602,723	84,711	14.1
Arizona	4,078,567	235,388	5.8
Arkansas	2,453,351	360,182	14.7
California	31,408,473	410,754	1.3
Connecticut	3,274,599	178,523	5.5
Florida	13,957,508	177,414	1.3
Georgia	7,057,510	750,831	10.6
Idaho	1,134,492	304,272	26.8
Illinois	11,759,259	544,341	4.6
Indiana	5,754,670	412,723	7.2
Iowa	2,830,779	256,150	9.0
Kansas	2,550,897	198,772	7.8
Kentucky	3,827,891	330,022	8.6
Louisiana	4,316,281	205,269	4.8
Maine	1,239,342	286,521	23.1
Maryland	4,999,864	78,469	1.6
Michigan	9,491,836	285,158	3.0
Minnesota	4,567,695	265,595	5.8
Mississippi	2,670,425	428,354	16.0
Missouri	5,279,423	312,855	5.9
Montana	856,242	195,104	22.8
Nebraska	1,624,272	50,747	3.1
Nevada	1,452,026	85,580	5.9
New Hampshire	1,135,382	192,739	17.0
New Mexico	1,655,172	437,848	26.5
New York	18,152,701	655,781	3.6
North Carolina	7,069,739	793,469	11.2
North Dakota	639,145	57,903	9.1
Ohio	11,104,005	1,030,804	9.3
Oklahoma	3,256,890	305,444	9.4
Oregon	3,087,141	519,777	16.8
Pennsylvania	12,061,661	376,661	3.1
Rhode Island	994,313	83,689	8.4
South Carolina	3,642,903	158,631	4.4
Tennessee	5,176,214	328,576	6.3
Texas	18,413,094	406,765	2.2
Utah	1,908,543	141,119	7.4

Micropolitan Populations: State by State (continued)

Vermont	580,204	62,495	10.8
Virginia	6,551,380	469,579	7.2
Washington	5,338,173	416,719	7.8
West Virginia	1,823,623	285,024	15.6
Wisconsin	5,083,152	389,940	7.7
Wyoming	476,061	40,792	8.6
United States	260,350,000	13,955,801	5.4

Source: Population Division, U.S. Bureau of the Census, Washington, D.C. Data are for 1994.

Glossary of Important Terms

Average. The theoretical "typical" number among a group of numbers. The average is calculated by totaling all the numbers in the group and dividing them by the number of units they represent. For instance, three communities have 32, 29, and 11 doctors respectively. Each community has an average of 24 doctors—the total number of doctors divided by the number of communities.

Because averages are calculations, they often vary from *medians* (see below). Averages are sometimes used instead of medians when many numbers are involved, or when only the total number for all units is available. For these reasons in this book figures for the entire United States are given as averages. Also called *mean*.

Category. A single statistical measure used in assessing a broader section of a community. For example, the category of housing age is one measure in the overall rating of the housing market. There are five categories in each of this book's ten sections.

Central city. The major community in a region; the city or cities that give the area its name. Augusta and Waterville are the central cities of the Augusta-Waterville, Maine, micropolitan area. Aberdeen is the central city of the Aberdeen, Washington, micropolitan area. Also called *core city*.

East. The geographical region that includes Connecticut, Delaware, District of Columbia, Maine, Maryland, Massachusetts, New Hampshire, New Jersey, New York, Pennsylvania, Rhode Island, Vermont, and West Virginia.

Median. The actual middle number in a group of numbers when arranged from highest to lowest. To use the above example, three communities have 32, 29, and 11 doctors respectively. The median number of doctors for the communities is 29. (The median is different from the *average*—see above.)

Metro center. The dominant city in an officially designated metropolitan area. Only one city may be the metro center (Albany is the metro center of the Albany-Schenectady-Troy, New York, metro area). Tulsa is the metro center of the Tulsa, Oklahoma, metro area.

Metropolitan Statistical Area. A large city and its suburbs, or a combination of neighboring large cities and their suburbs, recognized by the federal government as "socially and economically interrelated." There are 328 such areas in the country. Also called *metro area*.

Micropolitan area. A small city and its surrounding territory, or a combination of neighboring small cities and their surrounding territory. The statistical requirements of a micropolitan are given in the introduction of this book. There are 193 micropolitan areas. Also called *micropolitan, micro,* or *micropolis.*

Midwest. A region that includes Illinois, Indiana, Iowa, Kansas, Michigan, Minnesota, Missouri, Nebraska, North Dakota, Ohio, South Dakota, and Wisconsin.

Per capita. Any figure expressed as a rate per person. A region with 2,000 residents that spends $50,000 on parks and recreation programs spends $25 per capita on these programs.

Rate. A number expressed as a ratio, such as 1:100,000. In this book, rates are used to adjust for differences in city populations. Using a rate provides a common base for comparison. For instance, a city has 100 retail stores for 5,000 residents. A second city has 120 stores for 7,500 residents. The first community has fewer stores overall, but a higher rate of stores per residents—20 stores per 100,000 residents, compared with the second city's rate of 16 stores per 100,000 residents.

Section. A broad component of a community's quality of life, such as housing or health care. This book identifies ten sections: Climate/Environment, Diversions, Economics, Education, Community Assets, Health Care, Housing, Public Safety, Transportation, and Urban Proximity.

South. A region that includes Alabama, Arkansas, Florida, Georgia, Kentucky, Louisiana, Mississippi, North Carolina, Oklahoma, South Carolina, Tennessee, Texas, and Virginia.

Spacing. The interval that equally divides a range of values. For example, several communities are awarded points on the number of local retail stores available to them. The highest number of stores is 40; the lowest is 0. The maximum number of points that a community can earn is 20. The space is thus one point for every two stores.

West. A region that includes Alaska, Arizona, California, Colorado, Hawaii, Idaho, Montana, Nevada, New Mexico, Oregon, Utah, Washington, and Wyoming.

1

Climate/Environment

"The weather is always doing something," Mark Twain once noted slyly. "[It is] always getting up new designs and trying them on people to see how they will go."

And it always has a ready audience. In fact, our intense interest in weather sometimes shows no bounds. Forecasts of snow in Washington, D.C., a city always prepared to greet a little dusting with a lot of hysteria, has resulted in television news reporters standing live on downtown corners, reporting, "As you can see, there is no snow coming down yet."

Our interest in the weather forecast has spawned around-the-clock weather programming, special four-color weather sections in national newspapers, and Internet web sites complete with radar images and international weather data. Some web sites set a camera in the window allowing you to see local conditions yourself. One site includes the helpful note, "If your screen is black, then it's night here."

But the weather undeniably plays a key part in our daily lives, from our mood to our health, from our kitchen gardens to the nation's agricultural crops. Just witness the 1997 floods in North Dakota to measure the terrible damage that the weather can inflict.

This section provides an overall picture of what the weather is usually up to in each micropolitan area. Four categories rank each city according to the desirability of their climates. A fifth category assesses potential environmental hazards in each area.

The variety of climates among the small cities is impressive. But that's unsurprising, because the United States is a nation of meteorological extremes. Its southwestern deserts are often intolerably hot; California's Death Valley once reached 134 degrees. The country's northern reaches are capable of unbearable cold, with record lows of minus 80 in Alaska and minus 70 in Montana. Oregon climatologists estimate that rainfall in some remote parts of the coastal mountains in that state may top 200 inches per year—more than sixteen feet! Through the winter, the Great Lakes region often lies buried under mountainous snowdrifts. Watertown, New York, once received five feet of snow in three days. Usually unfazed, the city had to call for the National Guard. Nor does the South escape extremes. Oppressive humidity intensifies the impact of its high summer temperatures.

As willing as people are to watch what the weather is "trying out on us," as Mark Twain would say, they have also shown themselves willing to try out a vast array of hazardous chemicals on the weather. Unfortunately, we are finding that our finely balanced environment is easily altered.

The Great Lakes and most of our major rivers have been polluted and acid rain falls on eastern forests. Many of our cities are draped in smog. The Environmental Protection Agency (EPA) officially identified 1,206 uncontrolled hazardous waste sites in need of priority cleanup in 1995. Serious pollution at these sites threatens the ground water, surface water, soil, or air in the surrounding area. These sites are prevalent in manufacturing areas and, to a lesser degree, in military installations throughout the country.

Small cities are largely free of the airborne pollutants mainly produced by power plants, factories, and auto exhaust. Most major air pollution is restricted to urban areas with heavy concentrations of factories and cars. Thirty-three metro areas exceeded EPA safe standards for levels of carbon monoxide in 1993 and 1994. Nationwide, the EPA estimates that approximately 80 million people lived in areas that failed clean air quality standards for at least one of six critical pollutants in 1995. Residents ran the risk of being exposed to the pollutants, depending on where they lived and worked.

Good news is forthcoming in small ways, however. Major efforts to identify the causes, effects, and remedies to pollution are showing results. The EPA reports that emissions of the six major airborne pollutants decreased between 1986 and 1995. Emissions of carbon monoxide and sulfur dioxide are down 37 percent; lead emissions have decreased 78 percent.

Big cities, where the levels are highest and the monitoring is greatest, showed encouraging reductions. The level of at least one airborne pollutant decreased significantly in 204 metro areas between 1986 and 1995. The number of "unhealthful" days due to air pollution decreased 58 percent in large cities nationwide over the same period. Decreases are also beginning in the production of sulfur dioxide, a product of energy plants that is largely responsible for acid rain. In 1995, the first year of the EPA's Acid Rain Program, selected factories reduced emissions of sulfur dioxide by 5.6 million tons or nearly half of 1980 levels.

Ranking micropolitan America. The ideal small city would avoid climatic extremes as much as possible while still offering a change of seasons. The area would offer the clean environment lacking in many large cities. Each micropolitan is rated in five categories:

1. Summer Comfort: Is the summer warm, without being stiflingly hot?
2. Winter Lows: How comfortable is the winter season? Does the weather get brisk, but remain above the freezing point?
3. Temperature Variability: Is there a reasonable fluctuation in temperature over the year, or does the thermometer plummet from hot summer highs to frigid winter lows?
4. Precipitation: Can you measure local average rainfall in inches, or in feet?
5. Potential Environmental Dangers: Is the area free of serious pollution, or does it have some sites in need of cleanup?

Summer Comfort

A long, hot summer is the rule for much of America. The southern interior is typically blanketed by a steamy mixture of high temperatures and high humidity. Residents of the southwestern desert may claim that the very low humidity makes their 100+ temperatures quite reasonable, but this is very open to debate.

If you want to escape the heat, look north and to the coasts. This category measures each area's summer comfort level by taking the difference between the average high temperature in July and the arbitrary temperature of 80 degrees, chosen as a pleasantly warm reading.

The breezes from nearby Lake Ontario keep Watertown, New York, comfortable all summer long. Its mean maximum temperature for July is 79.9 degrees. The temperature usually climbs past 90 degrees only twice in the month. Watertown has never had a day hotter than 97 degrees.

Two California small cities have the greatest summer deviations from 80 degrees. Pacific breezes and the moderating effect of the ocean keep summers cool in Arcata-Eureka, California. In fact, you could miss summer altogether in Arcata-Eureka. The average daily temperature in July is just 57 degrees. Miles from the ocean in the California interior, El Centro-Calexico-Brawley has greatest deviation on the hot side. The average daily high in July is 108.4 degrees.

The most moderate cities in summer are concentrated in the eastern Midwest states. The greatest deviations occur in the hot South, the Western interior states, and the cool Pacific coast.

Source: Climatography of the United States, no. 81, National Oceanic and Atmospheric Administration, Silver Spring, Maryland. Data are daily averages for the years 1950 through 1980.

Scoring: Twenty points for a deviation of 0.5 degrees or less; no points for 19.6 degrees or more. The spacing is every one degree.

Summer Comfort: Highs and Lows

	Deviation of July Mean Maximum from 80 Degrees
Lowest	
1. Watertown, N.Y.	– 0.1
2. Ithaca, N.Y.	0.3
3. Beckley, W.Va.	– 0.4
Manitowoc, Wisc.	– 0.4
5. Cortland, N.Y.	0.5
Plattsburgh, N.Y.	0.5
7. Newport, R.I.	0.6
Augusta-Waterville, Maine	– 0.6
9. Albany-Corvallis, Ore.	0.7
Traverse City, Mich.	0.7
Median	
96. Sanford, N.C.	8.4
97. Statesville, N.C.	8.4
Highest	
184. Chickasha, Okla.	15.3
185. Carlsbad, N.Mex.	15.6
186. Duncan, Okla.	16.0
187. Ardmore, Okla.	16.1
188. Corsicana, Tex.	16.3
189. Searcy, Ark.	16.6
190. Del Rio, Tex.	17.7
191. Eagle Pass, Tex.	19.1
192. Hanford-Lemoore, Calif.	23.1
193. El Centro-Calexico-Brawley, Calif.	28.4

Summer Comfort Area by Area

(Deviation of July mean maximum temperature from 80 degrees and rating points)

Micro median	8.4	
Alabama		
Albertville	10.4	(10)
Auburn-Opelika	10.6	(9)
Cullman	9.4	(11)
Selma	12.8	(7)
Talladega	10.6	(9)
Alaska		
Fairbanks	– 7.7	(12)
Arizona		
Prescott	8.1	(12)
Sierra Vista	13.5	(7)
Arkansas		
Blytheville	12.7	(7)
El Dorado	12.6	(7)
Hot Springs	13.3	(7)
Jonesboro	12.3	(8)
Russellville	13.7	(6)
Searcy	16.6	(3)
California		
Arcata-Eureka	–12.0	(8)
El Centro-Calexico-Brawley	28.4	(0)
Hanford-Lemoore	23.1	(0)
Hollister	– 9.9	(10)
Connecticut		
Torrington	3.5	(17)
Florida		
Key West	8.9	(11)
Vero Beach	9.9	(10)
Georgia		
Brunswick	11.6	(8)
Dalton	9.2	(11)
Dublin	11.6	(8)
Gainesville	7.1	(13)
Hinesville	12.2	(8)
La Grange	10.4	(10)
Milledgeville	10.8	(9)
Rome	9.7	(10)
Statesboro	12.2	(8)
Thomasville	11.8	(8)
Valdosta	10.0	(10)
Waycross	12.8	(7)
Idaho		
Coeur d'Alene	6.0	(14)
Idaho Falls	6.4	(14)
Pocatello	8.6	(11)
Twin Falls	11.3	(9)
Illinois		
Carbondale	9.7	(10)
Danville	6.9	(13)
Freeport	3.7	(16)
Galesburg	5.3	(15)
Mattoon-Charleston	6.5	(14)
Ottawa	6.6	(13)
Quincy	7.0	(13)
Sterling	5.3	(15)
Indiana		
Columbus	6.4	(14)
Marion	4.7	(15)
Michigan City-La Porte	4.5	(16)
New Castle	5.5	(15)
Richmond	4.3	(16)
Vincennes	8.5	(12)

Iowa

Ames	5.0	(15)
Burlington	6.9	(13)
Clinton	5.1	(15)
Mason City	3.2	(17)
Muscatine	6.1	(14)

Kansas

Hutchinson	14.1	(6)
Manhattan	11.7	(8)
Salina	12.7	(7)

Kentucky

Bowling Green	9.2	(11)
Frankfort	7.5	(13)
Madisonville	9.4	(11)
Paducah	10.6	(9)
Radcliff-Elizabethtown	7.9	(12)

Louisiana

Hammond	12.4	(8)
New Iberia	11.2	(9)
Ruston	12.7	(7)

Maine

Augusta-Waterville	– 0.6	(19)
Biddeford-Saco	– 1.1	(19)

Maryland

Salisbury	6.1	(14)

Michigan

Marquette	– 4.7	(15)
Mount Pleasant	3.2	(17)
Owosso	2.4	(18)
Traverse City	0.7	(19)

Minnesota

Faribault	4.0	(16)
Mankato	4.5	(16)
Red Wing	3.0	(17)
Willmar	3.1	(17)
Winona	4.5	(16)

Mississippi

Cleveland	12.8	(7)
Columbus	12.7	(7)
Greenville	12.7	(7)
Laurel	12.2	(8)
Meridian	12.5	(8)
Tupelo	12.5	(8)
Vicksburg	11.4	(9)

Missouri

Cape Girardeau-Sikeston	10.5	(10)
Jefferson City	10.9	(9)
Poplar Bluff	11.2	(9)
Warrensburg	10.6	(9)

Montana

Bozeman	– 1.6	(18)
Helena	3.6	(16)
Missoula	4.8	(15)

Nebraska

Grand Island	8.8	(11)

Nevada

Carson City	9.1	(11)
Elko	10.4	(10)

New Hampshire

Concord	2.6	(17)
Keene	3.5	(17)

New Mexico

Alamogordo	15.2	(5)
Carlsbad	15.6	(4)
Clovis	11.1	(9)
Farmington	12.7	(7)
Gallup	8.5	(12)
Hobbs	13.3	(7)
Roswell	13.7	(6)

New York

Cortland	0.5	(20)

Gloversville	0.9	(19)
Ithaca	0.3	(20)
Kingston	4.1	(16)
Olean	3.5	(17)
Plattsburgh	0.5	(20)
Watertown	– 0.1	(20)
North Carolina		
Albemarle	8.7	(11)
Eden	7.9	(12)
Havelock-New Bern	8.3	(12)
Henderson	8.9	(11)
Kinston	9.5	(11)
Lumberton	9.4	(11)
Roanoke Rapids	9.9	(10)
Sanford	8.4	(12)
Shelby	8.8	(11)
Statesville	8.4	(12)
Wilson	8.8	(11)
North Dakota		
Minot	1.7	(18)
Ohio		
Ashland	2.8	(17)
Athens	5.7	(14)
Chillicothe	6.6	(13)
Findlay-Fostoria-Tiffin	3.3	(17)
Fremont	4.3	(16)
Marion	3.3	(17)
Mount Vernon	4.6	(15)
New Philadelphia	4.9	(15)
Norwalk	3.4	(17)
Portsmouth	6.4	(14)
Sandusky	2.7	(17)
Sidney	3.4	(17)
Wooster	1.8	(18)
Zanesville	3.7	(16)
Oklahoma		
Ardmore	16.1	(4)
Chickasha	15.3	(5)
Duncan	16.0	(4)
McAlester	14.0	(6)
Muskogee	14.1	(6)
Stillwater	13.9	(6)
Oregon		
Albany-Corvallis	0.7	(19)
Bend	2.1	(18)
Coos Bay	–13.2	(7)
Grants Pass	10.4	(10)
Klamath Falls	4.7	(15)
Pendleton	8.9	(11)
Roseburg	14.2	(6)
Pennsylvania		
Chambersburg	5.1	(15)
New Castle	4.5	(16)
Pottsville	4.6	(15)
Rhode Island		
Newport	0.6	(19)
South Carolina		
Greenwood	10.5	(10)
Hilton Head Island	9.9	(10)
Tennessee		
Cleveland	9.3	(11)
Columbia	9.8	(10)
Cookeville	3.7	(16)
Morristown	7.6	(12)
Tullahoma	8.3	(12)
Texas		
Corsicana	16.3	(4)
Del Rio	17.7	(2)
Eagle Pass	19.1	(1)
Huntsville	15.1	(5)
Lufkin	13.8	(6)
Nacogdoches	14.5	(6)
Palestine	14.9	(5)
Paris	14.3	(6)

Utah		
Logan	7.2	(13)
St. George	13.2	(7)
Vermont		
Rutland	1.5	(19)
Virginia		
Blacksburg-Radford-Christiansburg	2.6	(17)
Harrisonburg	6.3	(14)
Martinsville	7.9	(12)
Staunton-Waynesboro	5.1	(15)
Winchester	6.5	(14)
Washington		
Aberdeen	–11.0	(9)
Longview	– 2.8	(17)
Mount Vernon	– 5.5	(15)
Port Angeles	–11.3	(9)
Walla Walla	9.5	(11)
Wenatchee	7.9	(12)
West Virginia		
Beckley	– 0.4	(20)
Clarksburg	5.1	(15)
Fairmont	3.7	(16)
Morgantown	3.6	(16)
Wisconsin		
Fond du Lac	1.9	(18)
Manitowoc	– 0.4	(20)
Stevens Point	1.5	(19)
Watertown	4.0	(16)
Wyoming		
Rock Springs	6.5	(14)

Winter Lows

It's a scientifically proven fact that cold weather is good for you.

Well, maybe it's not actually scientifically proven, but some of us (especially in the Northeast and Midwest) insist that an annual dose of cold weather is good for the health. It keeps you strong, and the change of seasons keeps you alert.

This section rates the winter temperatures in each area by measuring the deviation between the mean daily temperature in January, usually the coldest month of the year, and 40 degrees. Mean daily temperature is the average thermometer reading for the day; in other words, the sum of the high and low temperatures divided by two. A mean temperature of 40 degrees might equal a high of 50 degrees and a low of 30—cool enough to guarantee a change of seasons, but warm enough to keep the likelihood of snow to a minimum. Areas with the least deviation score the highest. Those that stray too far in either direction score the lowest.

Henderson, North Carolina, has an average daily temperature of exactly 40 degrees in January. The thermometer dips to a low of 29.6 degrees at night, but rebounds to 50.4 degrees during the day.

January days in Fairbanks, Alaska, don't warm up above 0 degrees, much less above freezing point. The average daily low is minus 18.5 degrees, with a high of minus 5.7. The city with the greatest deviation on the warm side is Key West, Florida. The only ice in Key West in January is crushed ice in the daiquiris. Nightly lows are a balmy 65.6 degrees, and daytime temperatures rise only slightly to 71.8.

Cities with mean daily temperatures closest to 40 degrees are in the South and West. Cities with the greatest deviation are in the most northern Midwest and the most southern South.

Source: Climatography of the United States, no. 81, National Oceanic and Atmospheric Administration, Silver Spring, Maryland. Data are daily averages for 1950 through 1980.

Scoring: Twenty points for a deviation of less than one degree; no points for 29.5 degrees or more. The spacing is every 1.5 degrees.

Winter Lows: Highs and Lows

	Deviation of January Mean Daily Temperature from 40 Degrees
Lowest	
1. Henderson, N.C.	0.0
2. Aberdeen, Wash.	– 0.1
Duncan, Okla.	– 0.1
Grants Pass, Ore.	– 0.1
5. Cullman, Ala.	0.2
6. St. George, Utah	0.3
7. Gainesville, Ga.	0.5
8. Paris, Tex.	0.6
9. Sanford, N.C.	0.7
Hot Springs, Ark.	– 0.7
Median	
96. Beckley, W.Va.	– 9.9
97. Waycross, Ga.	10.1
Highest	
184. Stevens Point, Wisc.	–27.0
185. Winona, Minn.	–27.3
186. Marquette, Mich.	–27.9
187. Faribault, Minn.	–28.6
188. Key West, Fla.	28.7
189. Mankato, Minn.	–29.0
Red Wing, Minn.	–29.0
191. Willmar, Minn.	–31.0
192. Minot, N.Dak.	–33.7
193. Fairbanks, Alaska	–52.1

Winter Lows: Area by Area

(Deviation of January mean daily temperature from 40 degrees and rating points)

Micro median	10.0	
Alabama		
Albertville	1.0	(19)
Auburn-Opelika	4.6	(17)
Cullman	0.2	(20)
Selma	8.1	(15)
Talladega	3.4	(18)
Alaska		
Fairbanks	–52.1	(0)
Arizona		
Prescott	– 3.8	(18)
Sierra Vista	5.1	(17)
Arkansas		
Blytheville	– 2.3	(19)
El Dorado	3.1	(18)
Hot Springs	– 0.7	(20)
Jonesboro	– 3.4	(18)
Russellville	– 1.3	(19)
Searcy	– 0.9	(20)
California		
Arcata-Eureka	7.3	(15)
El Centro-Calexico-Brawley	13.9	(11)
Hanford-Lemoore	4.9	(17)
Hollister	8.9	(14)
Connecticut		
Torrington	–13.8	(11)
Florida		
Key West	28.7	(1)
Vero Beach	21.9	(6)
Georgia		
Brunswick	13.2	(11)
Dalton	– 0.9	(20)
Dublin	6.5	(16)
Gainesville	0.5	(20)
Hinesville	11.0	(13)
La Grange	4.5	(17)
Milledgeville	3.7	(18)
Rome	1.7	(19)
Statesboro	8.0	(15)
Thomasville	11.3	(13)
Valdosta	8.5	(14)
Waycross	10.1	(13)
Idaho		
Coeur d'Alene	–11.8	(12)
Idaho Falls	–21.3	(6)
Pocatello	–16.2	(9)
Twin Falls	–12.4	(12)
Illinois		
Carbondale	– 8.3	(15)
Danville	–14.3	(11)
Freeport	–21.7	(6)
Galesburg	–19.1	(7)
Mattoon-Charleston	–14.4	(11)
Ottawa	–17.1	(9)
Quincy	–16.4	(9)
Sterling	–20.3	(7)
Indiana		
Columbus	–12.4	(12)
Marion	–16.4	(9)
Michigan City-La Porte	–17.2	(9)
New Castle	–15.3	(10)
Richmond	–14.4	(11)
Vincennes	–11.5	(12)

Iowa

Ames	–22.9	(5)
Burlington	–19.0	(7)
Clinton	–20.5	(6)
Mason City	–26.8	(2)
Muscatine	–19.3	(7)

Kansas

Hutchinson	–11.1	(13)
Manhattan	–12.9	(12)
Salina	–12.7	(12)

Kentucky

Bowling Green	– 6.1	(16)
Frankfort	– 9.1	(14)
Madisonville	– 5.8	(16)
Paducah	– 5.7	(16)
Radcliff-Elizabethtown	– 5.5	(16)

Louisiana

Hammond	11.0	(13)
New Iberia	11.9	(12)
Ruston	4.4	(17)

Maine

Augusta-Waterville	–20.4	(7)
Biddeford-Saco	–18.5	(8)

Maryland

Salisbury	– 4.9	(17)

Michigan

Marquette	–27.9	(2)
Mount Pleasant	–19.2	(7)
Owosso	–18.3	(8)
Traverse City	–20.3	(7)

Minnesota

Faribault	–28.6	(1)
Mankato	–29.0	(1)
Red Wing	–29.0	(1)
Willmar	–31.0	(0)
Winona	–27.3	(2)

Mississippi

Cleveland	1.9	(19)
Columbus	2.4	(19)
Greenville	3.0	(18)
Laurel	6.6	(16)
Meridian	5.4	(17)
Tupelo	1.2	(19)
Vicksburg	6.7	(16)

Missouri

Cape Girardeau-Sikeston	– 6.6	(16)
Jefferson City	–10.5	(13)
Poplar Bluff	– 5.9	(16)
Warrensburg	–11.0	(13)

Montana

Bozeman	–19.9	(7)
Helena	–21.9	(6)
Missoula	–18.7	(8)

Nebraska

Grand Island	–19.4	(7)

Nevada

Carson City	– 6.5	(16)
Elko	–15.0	(10)

New Hampshire

Concord	–20.1	(7)
Keene	–18.4	(8)

New Mexico

Alamogordo	2.5	(18)
Carlsbad	3.2	(18)
Clovis	– 3.0	(18)
Farmington	–10.7	(13)
Gallup	–11.2	(13)
Hobbs	2.9	(18)
Roswell	1.4	(19)

New York

Cortland	–18.4	(8)

Gloversville	−19.9	(7)
Ithaca	−17.8	(8)
Kingston	−15.6	(10)
Olean	−15.7	(10)
Plattsburgh	−23.4	(5)
Watertown	−21.6	(6)
North Carolina		
Albemarle	0.9	(20)
Eden	− 2.0	(19)
Havelock-New Bern	4.0	(17)
Henderson	0.0	(20)
Kinston	1.8	(19)
Lumberton	2.5	(18)
Roanoke Rapids	1.1	(19)
Sanford	0.7	(20)
Shelby	− 0.8	(20)
Statesville	− 1.4	(19)
Wilson	1.3	(19)
North Dakota		
Minot	−33.7	(0)
Ohio		
Ashland	−15.4	(10)
Athens	−11.0	(13)
Chillicothe	−10.3	(13)
Findlay-Fostoria-Tiffin	−15.8	(10)
Fremont	−14.3	(11)
Marion	−15.6	(10)
Mount Vernon	−14.6	(10)
New Philadelphia	−12.9	(12)
Norwalk	−14.8	(10)
Portsmouth	− 8.0	(15)
Sandusky	−14.3	(11)
Sidney	−14.6	(10)
Wooster	−15.2	(10)
Zanesville	−12.7	(12)
Oklahoma		
Ardmore	2.5	(18)
Chickasha	− 2.2	(19)
Duncan	− 0.1	(20)
McAlester	− 1.9	(19)
Muskogee	− 2.3	(19)
Stillwater	− 4.7	(17)
Oregon		
Albany-Corvallis	− 1.0	(19)
Bend	− 9.2	(14)
Coos Bay	5.0	(17)
Grants Pass	− 0.1	(20)
Klamath Falls	−10.2	(13)
Pendleton	− 7.2	(15)
Roseburg	1.2	(19)
Pennsylvania		
Chambersburg	−11.4	(13)
New Castle	−12.9	(12)
Pottsville	−12.7	(12)
Rhode Island		
Newport	−11.8	(12)
South Carolina		
Greenwood	1.7	(19)
Hilton Head Island	9.1	(14)
Tennessee		
Cleveland	− 1.3	(19)
Columbia	− 2.4	(19)
Cookeville	− 7.7	(15)
Morristown	− 3.2	(18)
Tullahoma	− 1.7	(19)
Texas		
Corsicana	4.5	(17)
Del Rio	10.8	(13)
Eagle Pass	11.0	(13)
Huntsville	8.4	(15)
Lufkin	8.6	(14)
Nacogdoches	6.2	(16)
Palestine	3.5	(18)
Paris	0.6	(20)

Utah		
Logan	–15.3	(10)
St. George	0.3	(20)
Vermont		
Rutland	–19.4	(7)
Virginia		
Blacksburg-Radford-Christiansburg	– 9.1	(14)
Harrisonburg	– 8.1	(15)
Martinsville	– 4.2	(17)
Staunton-Waynesboro	– 7.6	(15)
Winchester	– 7.8	(15)
Washington		
Aberdeen	– 0.1	(20)
Longview	– 1.2	(19)
Mount Vernon	– 2.3	(19)
Port Angeles	– 1.0	(19)
Walla Walla	– 6.7	(16)
Wenatchee	–12.3	(12)
West Virginia		
Beckley	– 9.9	(14)
Clarksburg	–10.2	(13)
Fairmont	–10.2	(13)
Morgantown	–10.3	(13)
Wisconsin		
Fond du Lac	–24.2	(4)
Manitowoc	–21.7	(6)
Stevens Point	–27.0	(2)
Watertown	–22.5	(5)
Wyoming		
Rock Springs	–18.4	(8)

Temperature Variability

A lazy, warm summer; a brisk, cold winter—the change in seasons is refreshing. Many cities, however, carry this concept to extremes. In some parts of the country the thermometer plunges from oppressive summer heat to bone-chilling winter cold, dragging you back and forth with it.

This category ranks each area according to the volatility of its climate. The average low temperature for January, the coldest month in most of the country, is subtracted from the average high for July, typically the warmest month.

Key West, Florida, has the smallest swing between hot and cold. Its July mean maximum temperature is 88.9 degrees; its January mean minimum is 65.6, a difference of just 23.3 degrees. The moderating effect of the ocean waters are the reason for Key West's moderate climate.

The mountains that virtually surround Fairbanks, Alaska, have the opposite effect. They bar maritime air masses from the city. The result is an erratic climate, with an average high of 72.3 degrees in July and a numbing average low of minus 18.5 degrees in January. The swing is 90.8 degrees between these extremes.

Coastal regions in the West and South have the smallest temperature variations. The greatest variations occur in Midwestern cities away from the Great Lakes.

Source: Climatography of the United States, no. 81, National Oceanic and Atmospheric Administration, Silver Spring, Maryland. Data are daily averages for 1950 through 1980.

Scoring: Twenty points for a range of less than 36 degrees; no points for 83.5 degrees or more. The spacing is every 2.5 degrees.

Temperature Variability: Highs and Lows

	Difference in Degrees between July Mean Maximum and January Mean Minimum Temperatures
Lowest	
1. Key West, Fla.	23.3
2. Coos Bay, Ore.	28.1
3. Arcata-Eureka, Calif.	31.0
4. Hollister, Calif.	31.9
5. Aberdeen, Wash.	34.6
6. Port Angeles, Wash.	35.5
7. Vero Beach, Fla.	38.3
8. Searcy, Ark.	41.0
9. Mount Vernon, Wash.	42.9
10. Longview, Wash.	44.4
Median	
96. Zanesville, Ohio	65.1
97. Clarksburg, W.Va.	65.2
Highest	
184. Grand Island, Nebr.	78.9
185. Mason City, Iowa	79.7
186. Red Wing, Minn.	81.9
187. Winona, Minn.	82.5
188. Faribault, Minn.	82.6
189. Ardmore, Okla.	83.0
190. Willmar, Minn.	83.5
191. Minot, N.Dak.	84.0
192. Mankato, Minn.	84.1
193. Fairbanks, Alaska	90.8

Temperature Variability Area by Area

(Difference in degrees between July mean maximum and January mean minimum temperatures and rating points)

Micro median	65.2	
Alabama		
Albertville	59.4	(10)
Auburn-Opelika	56.9	(11)
Cullman	58.4	(11)
Selma	55.0	(12)
Talladega	58.4	(11)
Alaska		
Fairbanks	90.8	(0)
Arizona		
Prescott	66.2	(7)
Sierra Vista	66.7	(7)
Arkansas		
Blytheville	64.0	(8)
El Dorado	60.2	(10)
Hot Springs	64.8	(8)
Jonesboro	64.4	(8)
Russellville	66.7	(7)
Searcy	41.0	(17)
California		
Arcata-Eureka	31.0	(20)
El Centro-Calexico-Brawley	70.1	(6)
Hanford-Lemoore	62.1	(9)
Hollister	31.9	(20)
Connecticut		
Torrington	66.3	(7)
Florida		
Key West	23.3	(20)
Vero Beach	38.3	(19)
Georgia		
Brunswick	49.4	(14)
Dalton	60.1	(10)
Dublin	57.1	(11)
Gainesville	56.3	(11)
Hinesville	52.9	(13)
La Grange	57.3	(11)
Milledgeville	59.4	(10)
Rome	58.9	(10)
Statesboro	55.5	(12)
Thomasville	52.8	(13)
Valdosta	52.6	(13)
Waycross	55.7	(12)
Idaho		
Coeur d'Alene	64.2	(8)
Idaho Falls	76.1	(3)
Pocatello	73.5	(4)
Twin Falls	72.3	(5)
Illinois		
Carbondale	67.6	(7)
Danville	70.1	(6)
Freeport	73.9	(4)
Galesburg	73.2	(5)
Mattoon-Charleston	69.1	(6)
Ottawa	72.0	(5)
Quincy	71.9	(5)
Sterling	74.3	(4)
Indiana		
Columbus	68.3	(7)
Marion	69.6	(6)
Michigan City-La Porte	69.6	(6)
New Castle	69.9	(6)
Richmond	67.4	(7)
Vincennes	69.2	(6)

Area	Score	Rank
Iowa		
Ames	77.1	(3)
Burlington	75.1	(4)
Clinton	74.2	(4)
Mason City	79.7	(2)
Muscatine	74.0	(4)
Kansas		
Hutchinson	75.8	(4)
Manhattan	75.2	(4)
Salina	75.9	(4)
Kentucky		
Bowling Green	64.6	(8)
Frankfort	66.6	(7)
Madisonville	64.8	(8)
Paducah	65.7	(8)
Radcliff-Elizabethtown	63.0	(9)
Louisiana		
Hammond	52.7	(13)
New Iberia	49.4	(14)
Ruston	58.9	(10)
Maine		
Augusta-Waterville	68.4	(7)
Biddeford-Saco	67.0	(7)
Maryland		
Salisbury	59.8	(10)
Michigan		
Marquette	71.2	(5)
Mount Pleasant	70.1	(6)
Owosso	68.3	(7)
Traverse City	67.6	(7)
Minnesota		
Faribault	82.6	(1)
Mankato	84.1	(0)
Red Wing	81.9	(1)
Willmar	83.5	(0)
Winona	82.5	(1)

Area	Score	Rank
Mississippi		
Cleveland	60.4	(10)
Columbus	61.1	(9)
Greenville	59.7	(10)
Laurel	56.7	(11)
Meridian	58.3	(11)
Tupelo	61.3	(9)
Vicksburg	54.4	(12)
Missouri		
Cape Girardeau-Sikeston	66.1	(7)
Jefferson City	72.9	(5)
Poplar Bluff	67.1	(7)
Warrensburg	71.3	(5)
Montana		
Bozeman	68.9	(6)
Helena	75.5	(4)
Missoula	71.1	(5)
Nebraska		
Grand Island	78.9	(2)
Nevada		
Carson City	68.6	(6)
Elko	77.2	(3)
New Hampshire		
Concord	73.6	(4)
Keene	72.6	(5)
New Mexico		
Alamogordo	67.3	(7)
Carlsbad	66.4	(7)
Clovis	68.5	(6)
Farmington	74.9	(4)
Gallup	74.8	(4)
Hobbs	65.3	(8)
Roswell	66.3	(7)
New York		
Cortland	67.0	(7)

Gloversville	69.4	(6)
Ithaca	66.5	(7)
Kingston	69.3	(6)
Olean	67.9	(7)
Plattsburgh	72.8	(5)
Watertown	71.0	(5)
North Carolina		
Albemarle	59.4	(10)
Eden	60.0	(10)
Havelock-New Bern	54.7	(12)
Henderson	59.3	(10)
Kinston	58.8	(10)
Lumberton	58.2	(11)
Roanoke Rapids	59.7	(10)
Sanford	57.6	(11)
Shelby	61.3	(9)
Statesville	61.9	(9)
Wilson	58.3	(11)
North Dakota		
Minot	84.0	(0)
Ohio		
Ashland	66.0	(7)
Athens	67.4	(7)
Chillicothe	65.5	(8)
Findlay-Fostoria-Tiffin	66.4	(7)
Fremont	66.0	(7)
Marion	67.4	(7)
Mount Vernon	68.2	(7)
New Philadelphia	67.8	(7)
Norwalk	66.5	(7)
Portsmouth	63.0	(9)
Sandusky	64.0	(8)
Sidney	65.9	(8)
Wooster	65.0	(8)
Zanesville	65.1	(8)
Oklahoma		
Ardmore	83.0	(1)
Chickasha	69.9	(6)
Duncan	67.9	(7)
McAlester	66.5	(7)
Muskogee	66.8	(7)
Stillwater	70.4	(6)
Oregon		
Albany-Corvallis	47.8	(15)
Bend	61.1	(9)
Coos Bay	28.1	(20)
Grants Pass	57.6	(11)
Klamath Falls	63.8	(8)
Pendleton	62.6	(9)
Roseburg	60.3	(10)
Pennsylvania		
Chambersburg	64.7	(8)
New Castle	66.3	(7)
Pottsville	65.1	(8)
Rhode Island		
Newport	62.0	(9)
South Carolina		
Greenwood	59.8	(10)
Hilton Head Island	51.6	(13)
Tennessee		
Cleveland	60.1	(10)
Columbia	62.4	(9)
Cookeville	61.4	(9)
Morristown	61.5	(9)
Tullahoma	59.8	(10)
Texas		
Corsicana	62.7	(9)
Del Rio	59.4	(10)
Eagle Pass	61.0	(9)
Huntsville	56.8	(11)
Lufkin	55.8	(12)
Nacogdoches	59.7	(10)
Palestine	59.8	(10)
Paris	64.1	(8)

Utah		
Logan	70.9	(6)
St. George	66.3	(7)
Vermont		
Rutland	70.4	(6)
Virginia		
Blacksburg-Radford-Christiansburg	62.0	(9)
Harrisonburg	65.0	(8)
Martinsville	64.0	(8)
Staunton-Waynesboro	63.6	(8)
Winchester	63.1	(9)
Washington		
Aberdeen	34.6	(20)
Longview	44.4	(16)
Mount Vernon	42.9	(17)
Port Angeles	35.5	(20)
Walla Walla	62.4	(9)
Wenatchee	66.7	(7)
West Virginia		
Beckley	58.0	(11)
Clarksburg	65.2	(8)
Fairmont	62.4	(9)
Morgantown	62.2	(9)
Wisconsin		
Fond du Lac	74.7	(4)
Manitowoc	69.1	(6)
Stevens Point	78.0	(3)
Watertown	75.1	(4)
Wyoming		
Rock Springs	75.3	(4)

Precipitation

A little rain is good for the garden. It keeps the creeks flowing in the summer, and the city water reservoir adequately full.

But too much precipitation, be it rain, sleet, or snow, can dampen the spirits. It means incessant gray skies and being stuck in the house. Likewise, very little precipitation results in a dry landscape where the gardening is limited and water supplies are low. Certainly some people thrive best in the rainy Northwest, and others prefer the climate of the arid deserts. But on the whole, they are select breeds.

This category ranks each area according to the annual precipitation it receives including both rain and the water value of any frozen precipitation such as sleet or snow. The average for the nation's small cities is thirty-eight inches per year, and this amount is used as a convenient benchmark. Each area is rated according to its deviation from this "normal" amount.

New Castle, Pennsylvania, and Warrensburg, Missouri, tie for first. Each city receives 37.8 inches of precipitation each year, just 0.2 inches from the normal.

If you're not familiar with the Pacific Northwest coast, there's something you should know. It rains a lot. It rains a whole lot. And among small cities, it rains the most in Aberdeen, Washington. The area receives a total of 82.3 inches of precipitation each year, almost all of it rain.

The micropolitan area that receives the least precipitation is El Centro-Calexico-Brawley, California. Located in the interior of Southern California, and shielded from the ocean by mountain ranges, the area receives just 2.4 inches of rain in a year.

Midwestern and Southern small cities have precipitation amounts closest to the norm, partly reflecting the significant share of small cities in these regions. Cities with the greatest deviation are located in the West, especially in the desert Southwest.

Source: Climatography of the United States, no. 81, National Oceanic and Atmospheric Administration, Silver Spring, Maryland. Data are daily averages for 1950 through 1980.

Scoring: Twenty points for a deviation of 0.5 inches or less; no points for more than 29. The spacing is every 1.5 inches.

Precipitation: Highs and Lows

	Deviation of Average Annual Precipitation from 38 Inches
Lowest	
1. New Castle, Pa.	0.2
Warrensburg, Mo.	0.2
3. Quincy, Ill.	– 0.3
Chillicothe, Ohio	0.3
Winchester, Va.	0.3
6. Zanesville, Ohio	0.4
7. Danville, Ill.	0.5
Arcata-Eureka, Calif.	0.5
9. Richmond, Ind.	0.7
10. Ashland, Ohio	– 0.8
Marquette, Mich.	– 0.8
Highest	
184. Gallup, N.Mex.	–28.3
Roswell, N.Mex.	–28.3
186. Elko, Nev.	–28.7
187. Wenatchee, Wash.	–29.2
188. Rock Springs, Wyo.	–29.6
Farmington, N.Mex.	–29.6
190. St. George, Utah	–30.1
191. Hanford-Lemoore, Calif.	–30.2
192. El Centro-Calexico-Brawley, Calif.	–35.7
193. Aberdeen, Wash.	44.3

Note: Median not applicable because deviations are based on the average precipitation for all small cities.

Precipitation Area by Area

(Deviation of average annual precipitation from 38 inches and rating points)

Alabama

Albertville	16.1	(9)
Auburn-Opelika	18.5	(8)
Cullman	16.7	(9)
Selma	15.5	(10)
Talladega	16.0	(9)

Alaska

Fairbanks	–27.1	(2)

Arizona

Prescott	–18.4	(8)
Sierra Vista	–19.4	(7)

Arkansas

Blytheville	11.4	(12)
El Dorado	11.1	(12)
Hot Springs	18.5	(8)
Jonesboro	9.2	(14)
Russellville	9.6	(13)
Searcy	13.8	(11)

California

Arcata-Eureka	0.5	(20)
El Centro-Calexico-Brawley	–35.7	(0)
Hanford-Lemoore	–30.2	(0)
Hollister	–16.6	(9)

Connecticut

Torrington	5.2	(16)

Florida

Key West	1.4	(19)
Vero Beach	13.4	(11)

Georgia

Brunswick	12.7	(11)
Dalton	18.5	(8)
Dublin	7.5	(15)
Gainesville	17.8	(8)
Hinesville	10.1	(13)
La Grange	16.6	(9)
Milledgeville	8.5	(14)
Rome	16.2	(9)
Statesboro	7.3	(15)
Thomasville	13.8	(11)
Valdosta	8.6	(14)
Waycross	11.8	(12)

Idaho

Coeur d'Alene	–12.2	(12)
Idaho Falls	–28.2	(1)
Pocatello	–27.1	(2)
Twin Falls	–27.9	(1)

Illinois

Carbondale	4.6	(17)
Danville	0.5	(20)
Freeport	– 1.2	(19)
Galesburg	– 2.0	(19)
Mattoon-Charleston	– 1.0	(19)
Ottawa	– 3.2	(18)
Quincy	– 0.3	(20)
Sterling	– 3.2	(18)

Indiana

Columbus	2.3	(18)
Marion	– 1.3	(19)
Michigan City-La Porte	3.5	(18)
New Castle	1.0	(19)
Richmond	0.7	(19)
Vincennes	4.3	(17)

Iowa

Ames	– 6.3	(16)
Burlington	– 2.9	(18)
Clinton	– 2.3	(18)
Mason City	– 5.9	(16)
Muscatine	– 3.5	(18)

Kansas

Hutchinson	– 8.8	(14)
Manhattan	– 5.1	(16)
Salina	– 9.0	(14)

Kentucky

Bowling Green	12.0	(12)
Frankfort	4.9	(17)
Madisonville	8.3	(14)
Paducah	7.8	(15)
Radcliff-Elizabethtown	13.1	(11)

Louisiana

Hammond	25.3	(3)
New Iberia	19.3	(7)
Ruston	14.2	(10)

Maine

Augusta-Waterville	4.5	(17)
Biddeford-Saco	5.5	(16)

Maryland

Salisbury	7.4	(15)

Michigan

Marquette	– 0.8	(19)
Mount Pleasant	– 7.8	(15)
Owosso	– 9.2	(14)
Traverse City	– 8.3	(14)

Minnesota

Faribault	– 7.0	(15)
Mankato	– 9.9	(13)
Red Wing	– 7.7	(15)
Willmar	–10.3	(13)
Winona	– 5.3	(16)

Mississippi

Cleveland	19.0	(7)
Columbus	18.8	(7)
Greenville	15.3	(10)
Laurel	18.3	(8)
Meridian	15.3	(10)
Tupelo	18.1	(8)
Vicksburg	14.4	(10)

Missouri

Cape Girardeau-Sikeston	8.8	(14)
Jefferson City	– 1.9	(19)
Poplar Bluff	7.8	(15)
Warrensburg	0.2	(20)

Montana

Bozeman	–11.3	(12)
Helena	–28.1	(1)
Missoula	–24.7	(3)

Nebraska

Grand Island	–14.7	(10)

Nevada

Carson City	–27.2	(2)
Elko	–28.7	(1)

New Hampshire

Concord	– 1.5	(19)
Keene	2.3	(18)

New Mexico

Alamogordo	–26.8	(2)
Carlsbad	–27.3	(2)
Clovis	–21.5	(6)
Farmington	–29.6	(0)
Gallup	–28.3	(1)
Hobbs	–23.2	(4)
Roswell	–28.3	(1)

New York

Cortland	3.2	(18)
Gloversville	4.0	(17)
Ithaca	– 2.7	(18)
Kingston	2.2	(18)
Olean	– 6.9	(15)
Plattsburgh	– 4.3	(17)
Watertown	2.5	(18)

North Carolina

Albemarle	9.3	(14)
Eden	5.3	(16)
Havelock-New Bern	15.1	(10)
Henderson	6.2	(16)
Kinston	13.6	(11)
Lumberton	8.0	(15)
Roanoke Rapids	10.0	(13)
Sanford	7.6	(15)
Shelby	11.4	(12)
Statesville	8.5	(14)
Wilson	9.1	(14)

North Dakota

Minot	–20.1	(6)

Ohio

Ashland	– 0.8	(19)
Athens	1.1	(19)
Chillicothe	0.3	(20)
Findlay-Fostoria-Tiffin	– 4.7	(17)
Fremont	– 2.7	(18)
Marion	– 2.3	(18)
Mount Vernon	– 1.5	(19)
New Philadelphia	1.6	(19)
Norwalk	– 2.4	(18)
Portsmouth	3.3	(18)
Sandusky	– 4.1	(17)
Sidney	– 2.7	(18)
Wooster	– 2.3	(18)
Zanesville	0.4	(20)

Oklahoma

Ardmore	– 4.6	(17)
Chickasha	– 9.0	(14)
Duncan	– 7.3	(15)
McAlester	4.5	(17)
Muskogee	2.0	(19)
Stillwater	– 5.7	(16)

Oregon

Albany-Corvallis	4.6	(17)
Bend	–26.5	(2)
Coos Bay	23.4	(4)
Grants Pass	– 5.7	(16)
Klamath Falls	–24.3	(4)
Pendleton	–25.8	(3)
Roseburg	– 4.6	(17)

Pennsylvania

Chambersburg	2.6	(18)
New Castle	0.2	(20)
Pottsville	6.3	(16)

Rhode Island

Newport	10.5	(13)

South Carolina

Greenwood	8.9	(14)
Hilton Head Island	12.2	(12)

Tennessee

Cleveland	14.6	(10)
Columbia	15.9	(9)
Cookeville	20.5	(6)
Morristown	4.3	(17)
Tullahoma	18.6	(7)

Texas

Corsicana	– 1.4	(19)
Del Rio	–20.9	(6)
Eagle Pass	–17.1	(8)
Huntsville	6.2	(16)
Lufkin	3.5	(18)
Nacogdoches	4.2	(17)
Palestine	3.7	(17)
Paris	7.0	(15)

Utah

Logan	–20.6	(6)
St. George	–30.1	(0)

Vermont

Rutland	– 3.1	(18)

Virginia		
Blacksburg-Radford-Christiansburg	2.0	(19)
Harrisonburg	– 2.7	(18)
Martinsville	7.0	(15)
Staunton-Waynesboro	– 2.1	(18)
Winchester	0.3	(20)
Washington		
Aberdeen	44.3	(0)
Longview	8.1	(14)
Mount Vernon	8.4	(14)
Port Angeles	–12.6	(11)
Walla Walla	–19.6	(7)
Wenatchee	–29.2	(0)
West Virginia		
Beckley	4.1	(17)
Clarksburg	3.1	(18)
Fairmont	5.3	(16)
Morgantown	3.5	(18)
Wisconsin		
Fond du Lac	– 9.2	(14)
Manitowoc	– 9.2	(14)
Stevens Point	– 7.1	(15)
Watertown	– 5.8	(16)
Wyoming		
Rock Springs	–29.6	(0)

Note: Micro median not applicable because deviations are based on the average precipitation for all small cities.

Potential Environmental Dangers

Many people may be fortunate enough not to see the effects of pollution, but for those who witness dead fish in the rivers, trees defoliated from acid rain, and the heavy smog of factory and car emissions, it is obvious that man can carelessly endanger the environment. Pollution is generally much worse in large cities, but not all micropolitan areas have escaped the problem.

This category ranks each area according to its rate of both potentially dangerous waste sites and sites with substandard air quality. Included are locations targeted for cleanup by the Environmental Protection Agency (EPA), the Defense Department, and the states. Each area's total number of sites is projected to a rate per 1,000 square miles.

Fortunately, 128 small cities do not have problems so serious as to be made national priorities. But Newport, Rhode Island, has a rate of 19.2 sites per 1,000 square miles. Contamination at a local Navy installation, as well as unacceptably high levels of ozone throughout the entire region of Rhode Island, place small Newport last in the category. Cleanup of the waste site is under way, however, and the state is required to meet clean air goals set by the EPA by 1999.

Areas without hazardous waste and air quality problems are located throughout the country. The majority with potentially hazardous sites are located throughout the Midwest and South, usually in manufacturing areas, areas adjacent to military installments, or near large cities.

Sources: National Priorities List for Uncontrolled Hazardous Waste Sites, and *National Air Quality and Emissions Trends Report, 1995,* Environmental Protection Agency, Research Triangle Park, North Carolina. Data on hazardous waste sites are for 1997; data on air quality are for 1994–95.

Scoring: Twenty points for zero potentially dangerous sites; no points for a rate of 5.8 sites or more per 1,000 square miles. The spacing is every 0.3 sites.

Potential Environmental Dangers: Highs and Lows

Lowest

A total of 128 areas tie for first place, with no hazardous waste sites and no sites with substandard air quality. See the complete area-by-area list.

	Hazardous Waste Sites and Sites with Substandard Air Quality per 1,000 Square Miles
Highest	
184. Grand Island, Nebr.	3.7
185. Pottsville, Pa.	3.9
186. Paducah, Ky.	4.0
187. Columbus, Ind.	4.9
188. Michigan City-La Porte, Ind.	5.0
189. Hilton Head Island, S.C.	5.1
Manitowoc, Wisc.	5.1
191. Chambersburg, Pa.	6.5
192. Brunswick, Ga.	7.1
193. Newport, R.I.	19.2

Potential Environmental Dangers Area by Area

(Hazardous waste sites and sites with substandard air quality per 1,000 square miles and rating points)

Micro median	0.0	
Alabama		
Albertville	0.0	(20)
Auburn-Opelika	0.0	(20)
Cullman	0.0	(20)
Selma	0.0	(20)
Talladega	1.4	(15)
Alaska		
Fairbanks	0.5	(18)
Arizona		
Prescott	0.0	(20)
Sierra Vista	0.3	(19)
Arkansas		
Blytheville	0.0	(20)
El Dorado	1.0	(16)
Hot Springs	0.0	(20)
Jonesboro	0.0	(20)
Russellville	0.0	(20)
Searcy	0.0	(20)
California		
Arcata-Eureka	0.3	(19)
El Centro-Calexico-Brawley	0.2	(19)
Hanford-Lemoore	3.6	(8)
Hollister	0.0	(20)
Connecticut		
Torrington	1.1	(16)
Florida		
Key West	0.0	(20)
Vero Beach	2.0	(13)
Georgia		
Brunswick	7.1	(0)
Dalton	0.0	(20)
Dublin	0.0	(20)
Gainesville	0.0	(20)
Hinesville	0.0	(20)
La Grange	0.0	(20)
Milledgeville	0.0	(20)
Rome	0.0	(20)
Statesboro	0.0	(20)
Thomasville	0.0	(20)
Valdosta	0.0	(20)
Waycross	0.0	(20)
Idaho		
Coeur d'Alene	0.0	(20)
Idaho Falls	0.5	(18)
Pocatello	1.6	(14)
Twin Falls	0.0	(20)
Illinois		
Carbondale	0.0	(20)
Danville	0.0	(20)
Freeport	0.0	(20)
Galesburg	1.4	(15)
Mattoon-Charleston	0.0	(20)
Ottawa	2.6	(11)
Quincy	1.2	(16)
Sterling	0.0	(20)
Indiana		
Columbus	4.9	(3)
Marion	2.4	(12)
Michigan City-La Porte	5.0	(3)
New Castle	0.0	(20)
Richmond	2.5	(11)
Vincennes	1.9	(13)

Iowa		
Ames	0.0	(20)
Burlington	0.0	(20)
Clinton	1.4	(15)
Mason City	1.8	(14)
Muscatine	2.3	(12)
Kansas		
Hutchinson	0.8	(17)
Manhattan	0.0	(20)
Salina	0.0	(20)
Kentucky		
Bowling Green	0.0	(20)
Frankfort	0.0	(20)
Madisonville	0.0	(20)
Paducah	4.0	(6)
Radcliff-Elizabethtown	1.6	(14)
Louisiana		
Hammond	0.0	(20)
New Iberia	0.0	(20)
Ruston	0.0	(20)
Maine		
Augusta-Waterville	2.3	(12)
Biddeford-Saco	2.0	(13)
Maryland		
Salisbury	0.0	(20)
Michigan		
Marquette	0.5	(18)
Mount Pleasant	0.0	(20)
Owosso	0.0	(20)
Traverse City	1.2	(16)
Minnesota		
Faribault	2.0	(13)
Mankato	0.8	(17)
Red Wing	0.0	(20)
Willmar	0.0	(20)
Winona	0.0	(20)
Mississippi		
Cleveland	0.0	(20)
Columbus	0.0	(20)
Greenville	0.0	(20)
Laurel	0.0	(20)
Meridian	0.0	(20)
Tupelo	0.0	(20)
Vicksburg	0.0	(20)
Missouri		
Cape Girardeau-Sikeston	1.8	(14)
Jefferson City	0.0	(20)
Poplar Bluff	0.0	(20)
Warrensburg	0.0	(20)
Montana		
Bozeman	0.4	(18)
Helena	0.6	(18)
Missoula	1.2	(16)
Nebraska		
Grand Island	3.7	(7)
Nevada		
Carson City	0.0	(20)
Elko	0.1	(19)
New Hampshire		
Concord	0.0	(20)
Keene	0.0	(20)
New Mexico		
Alamogordo	0.0	(20)
Carlsbad	0.0	(20)
Clovis	0.7	(17)
Farmington	0.2	(19)
Gallup	0.2	(19)
Hobbs	0.0	(20)
Roswell	0.0	(20)
New York		
Cortland	2.0	(13)

Gloversville	2.0	(13)
Ithaca	0.0	(20)
Kingston	0.9	(17)
Olean	1.5	(15)
Plattsburgh	1.0	(16)
Watertown	0.8	(17)
North Carolina		
Albemarle	0.0	(20)
Eden	0.0	(20)
Havelock-New Bern	1.4	(15)
Henderson	0.0	(20)
Kinston	0.0	(20)
Lumberton	0.0	(20)
Roanoke Rapids	0.0	(20)
Sanford	0.0	(20)
Shelby	2.2	(12)
Statesville	1.7	(14)
Wilson	0.0	(20)
North Dakota		
Minot	0.0	(20)
Ohio		
Ashland	0.0	(20)
Athens	0.0	(20)
Chillicothe	0.0	(20)
Findlay-Fostoria-Tiffin	0.0	(20)
Fremont	0.0	(20)
Marion	0.0	(20)
Mount Vernon	0.0	(20)
New Philadelphia	3.5	(8)
Norwalk	0.0	(20)
Portsmouth	0.0	(20)
Sandusky	0.0	(20)
Sidney	0.0	(20)
Wooster	0.0	(20)
Zanesville	1.5	(15)
Oklahoma		
Ardmore	0.0	(20)
Chickasha	0.0	(20)
Duncan	0.0	(20)
McAlester	0.0	(20)
Muskogee	0.0	(20)
Stillwater	0.0	(20)
Oregon		
Albany-Corvallis	0.7	(17)
Bend	0.0	(20)
Coos Bay	0.0	(20)
Grants Pass	1.2	(16)
Klamath Falls	0.3	(19)
Pendleton	0.3	(19)
Roseburg	0.0	(20)
Pennsylvania		
Chambersburg	6.5	(0)
New Castle	0.0	(20)
Pottsville	3.9	(7)
Rhode Island		
Newport	19.2	(0)
South Carolina		
Greenwood	0.0	(20)
Hilton Head Island	5.1	(3)
Tennessee		
Cleveland	0.0	(20)
Columbia	0.0	(20)
Cookeville	0.0	(20)
Morristown	0.0	(20)
Tullahoma	0.0	(20)
Texas		
Corsicana	0.0	(20)
Del Rio	0.0	(20)
Eagle Pass	0.0	(20)
Huntsville	0.0	(20)
Lufkin	0.0	(20)
Nacogdoches	0.0	(20)
Palestine	0.0	(20)
Paris	0.0	(20)

Utah		
Logan	0.0	(20)
St. George	0.0	(20)
Vermont		
Rutland	0.0	(20)
Virginia		
Blacksburg-Radford-Christiansburg	0.0	(20)
Harrisonburg	0.0	(20)
Martinsville	0.0	(20)
Staunton-Waynesboro	0.0	(20)
Winchester	2.4	(12)
Washington		
Aberdeen	0.0	(20)
Longview	0.0	(20)
Mount Vernon	0.0	(20)
Port Angeles	0.0	(20)
Walla Walla	0.0	(20)
Wenatchee	0.0	(20)
West Virginia		
Beckley	0.0	(20)
Clarksburg	0.0	(20)
Fairmont	3.2	(9)
Morgantown	2.8	(10)
Wisconsin		
Fond du Lac	1.4	(15)
Manitowoc	5.1	(3)
Stevens Point	0.0	(20)
Watertown	0.0	(20)
Wyoming		
Rock Springs	0.0	(20)

The Results

The Albany-Corvallis area takes first place in the climate/environment section, earning 87 of a possible 100 points. Situated in the broad valley between the coast and Cascade Mountain ranges, about fifty miles from the Pacific Ocean, the region experiences varied but moderate weather.

Summer highs typically peak at 81 degrees. In an average year, the thermometer tops 90 degrees thirteen times. January days range from a low just above freezing to a high in the mid-forties. The temperature drops below freezing an average of fifty-five days in the year. Average snowfall is just 5.7 inches for the entire year. Overall, the area receives 42.7 inches of precipitation each year, close to the normal for all small cities of 38 inches.

Pollution is not a major concern in the Albany-Corvallis area. Each of the center cities has one site listed on the *National Priorities List,* giving the area a rate of 0.7 sites per 1,000 square miles. Cleanup at the Corvallis site is partially completed.

Micros in the Pacific Northwest take the top three slots in the climate/environment section. The majority of the top-twenty list is dominated by small cities in the states where the Midwest, the South, and the Northeast meet: Ohio, Pennsylvania, West Virginia, Virginia, North Carolina, and Tennessee.

The extreme weather that characterizes Fairbanks also lands the area in last place with just 32 points. Winters are harsh in Fairbanks, with average January daytime temperatures below zero and nighttime lows approaching minus 20. The city averages 222 days each year with a temperature below freezing. Fairbanks's extreme northern location doesn't cheer the winter with plenty of sunlight, either. On January 1, the city greets the new year with just four hours of daylight.

Fairbanks's summers are far more reasonable, with an average July high in the low 70s. But Fairbanks is given to extremes in the summer months also. Record highs have reached into the mid 90s. Add Fairbanks's record high of 96 degrees to its record low of minus 62 and you have a record temperature range of 158 degrees!

Fairbanks is not free from major pollution, but its rate of 0.5 sites per 1,000 square miles is low. Three sites, two of them military installations, are identified for cleanup on the *National Priorities List.* The city has also been targeted by the EPA to lower its amount of carbon monoxide emissions.

Cities in the northern Midwest, interior Western states, and desert Southwest score the lowest in the section. Brunswick, Georgia, is the sole exception; its high number of classified hazardous waste sites are responsible.

Climate/Environment Scores: Highs and Lows

		Total Rating Points
Highest		
1.	Albany-Corvallis, Ore.	87
2.	Longview, Wash.	86
3.	Mount Vernon, Wash.	85
4.	Arcata-Eureka, Calif.	82
	Beckley, W.Va.	82
6.	Blacksburg-Radford-Christiansburg, Va.	79
	Port Angeles, Wash.	79
8.	Sanford, N.C.	78
9.	Eden, N.C.	77
	Henderson, N.C.	77
11.	Morristown, Tenn.	76
	Portsmouth, Ohio	76
	Salisbury, Md.	76
	Staunton-Waynesboro, Va.	76
15.	Albemarle, N.C.	75
	Harrisonburg, Va.	75
	Lumberton, N.C.	75
	New Castle, Pa.	75
	Wilson, N.C.	75
20.	Chillicothe, Ohio	74
	Clarksburg, W.Va.	74
	Wooster, Ohio	74
Median		
96.	Auburn-Opelika, Ala.	65
97.	Freeport, Ill.	65
Lowest		
184.	Brunswick, Ga.	44
	Minot, N.Dak.	44
186.	Elko, Nev.	43
	Farmington, N.Mex.	43
188.	Idaho Falls, Idaho	42
189.	Pocatello, Idaho	40
190.	Grand Island, Nebr.	37
191.	El Centro-Calexico-Brawley, Calif.	36
192.	Hanford-Lemoore, Calif.	34
193.	Fairbanks, Alaska	32

Climate/Environment Performance Comparison

	Albany-Corvallis, Oregon	Micro median	Fairbanks, Alaska
Total Points in Section	87	65	32
Rank in Section	1		193
Summer Comfort			
Deviation of July mean maximum from 80 degrees	0.7	8.4	– 7.7
Summer Comfort points	(19)		(12)
Winter Lows			
Deviation of January mean daily temperature from 40 degrees	– 1.0	10.0	–52.1
Winter Lows points	(19)		(0)
Temperature Variability			
Difference in degrees between July mean maximum and January mean minimum	47.8	65.2	90.8
Temperature Variability points	(15)		(0)
Precipitation			
Deviation of average annual precipitation from 38 inches	4.6	*	–27.1
Precipitation points	(17)		(2)
Potential Environmental Dangers			
Hazardous waste sites and sites with substandard air quality per 1,000 square miles	0.7	0.0	0.5
Potential Dangers points	(17)		(18)

*Not applicable. See accompanying text.

Climate/Environment Scores Area by Area

(Total climate/environment rating points)

Micro median	65
Alabama	
Albertville	68
Auburn-Opelika	65
Cullman	71
Selma	64
Talladega	62
Alaska	
Fairbanks	32
Arizona	
Prescott	65
Sierra Vista	57
Arkansas	
Blytheville	66
El Dorado	63
Hot Springs	63
Jonesboro	68
Russellville	65
Searcy	71
California	
Arcata-Eureka	82
El Centro-Calexico-Brawley	36
Hanford-Lemoore	34
Hollister	73
Connecticut	
Torrington	67
Florida	
Key West	71
Vero Beach	59
Georgia	
Brunswick	44
Dalton	69
Dublin	70
Gainesville	72
Hinesville	67
La Grange	67
Milledgeville	71
Rome	68
Statesboro	70
Thomasville	65
Valdosta	71
Waycross	64
Idaho	
Coeur d'Alene	66
Idaho Falls	42
Pocatello	40
Twin Falls	47
Illinois	
Carbondale	69
Danville	70
Freeport	65
Galesburg	61
Mattoon-Charleston	70
Ottawa	56
Quincy	63
Sterling	64
Indiana	
Columbus	54
Marion	61
Michigan City-La Porte	52
New Castle	70
Richmond	64
Vincennes	60
Iowa	
Ames	59
Burlington	62
Clinton	58
Mason City	51
Muscatine	55
Kansas	
Hutchinson	54
Manhattan	60
Salina	57
Kentucky	
Bowling Green	67
Frankfort	71
Madisonville	69
Paducah	54
Radcliff-Elizabethtown	62
Louisiana	
Hammond	57
New Iberia	62
Ruston	64
Maine	
Augusta-Waterville	62
Biddeford-Saco	63
Maryland	
Salisbury	76
Michigan	
Marquette	59
Mount Pleasant	65
Owosso	67
Traverse City	63
Minnesota	
Faribault	46
Mankato	47
Red Wing	54
Willmar	50
Winona	55

Mississippi

Cleveland	63
Columbus	62
Greenville	65
Laurel	63
Meridian	66
Tupelo	64
Vicksburg	67

Missouri

Cape Girardeau-Sikeston	61
Jefferson City	66
Poplar Bluff	67
Warrensburg	67

Montana

Bozeman	61
Helena	45
Missoula	47

Nebraska

Grand Island	37

Nevada

Carson City	55
Elko	43

New Hampshire

Concord	67
Keene	68

New Mexico

Alamogordo	52
Carlsbad	51
Clovis	56
Farmington	43
Gallup	49
Hobbs	57
Roswell	53

New York

Cortland	66
Gloversville	62
Ithaca	73
Kingston	67
Olean	64
Plattsburgh	63
Watertown	66

North Carolina

Albemarle	75
Eden	77
Havelock-New Bern	66
Henderson	77
Kinston	71
Lumberton	75
Roanoke Rapids	72
Sanford	78
Shelby	64
Statesville	68
Wilson	75

North Dakota

Minot	44

Ohio

Ashland	73
Athens	73
Chillicothe	74
Findlay-Fostoria-Tiffin	71
Fremont	72
Marion	72
Mount Vernon	71
New Philadelphia	61
Norwalk	72
Portsmouth	76
Sandusky	73
Sidney	73
Wooster	74
Zanesville	71

Oklahoma

Ardmore	60
Chickasha	64
Duncan	66
McAlester	69
Muskogee	71
Stillwater	65

Oregon

Albany-Corvallis	87
Bend	63
Coos Bay	68
Grants Pass	73
Klamath Falls	59
Pendleton	57
Roseburg	72

Pennsylvania

Chambersburg	54
New Castle	75
Pottsville	58

Rhode Island

Newport	53

South Carolina

Greenwood	73
Hilton Head Island	52

Tennessee

Cleveland	70
Columbia	67
Cookeville	66
Morristown	76
Tullahoma	68

Texas

Corsicana	69
Del Rio	51
Eagle Pass	51
Huntsville	67
Lufkin	70

Nacogdoches 69
Palestine 70
Paris 69

Utah
Logan 55
St. George 54

Vermont
Rutland 70

Virginia
Blacksburg-Radford-Christiansburg 79
Harrisonburg 75
Martinsville 72
Staunton-Waynesboro 76
Winchester 70

Washington
Aberdeen 69
Longview 86
Mount Vernon 85
Port Angeles 79
Walla Walla 63
Wenatchee 51

West Virginia
Beckley 82
Clarksburg 74
Fairmont 63
Morgantown 66

Wisconsin
Fond du Lac 55
Manitowoc 49
Stevens Point 59
Watertown 61

Wyoming
Rock Springs 46

2

Diversions

One of the most popular U.S. exports can't be weighed, priced, or checked at customs. It's the expression "okay." It's a distinctively U.S. word, as "American" as blue jeans. Informal and expedient, it lacks all the elaboration and formality of Old World languages.

Now we seem to be shipping another verbal export: the word "stress." The *New York Times* notes that the word is popping up around the world. It's pronounced "STRESS-a" in Russian, "ess-TRESS" in Spanish, and "su-tor-es-u" in Japanese. When the French get harried, they say, "je stresse."

America has always been a country in a hurry, and for some years now we've been busy charting our rising levels of stress and our declining hours of leisure. One in three Americans agrees with statements such as "I just don't have time for fun anymore," according to the 1991 Hilton Time Values Project.

The American's Use of Time Project, based at the University of Maryland, has tracked the squeeze on leisure time and the rise in stress since 1965. The share of Americans aged sixty-four and younger who report feeling stress increased from 24 percent in 1965 to 38 percent in 1992. Sixty-one percent of adults said that they never had spare time on their hands in 1995—a dramatic increase from 48 percent thirty years earlier.

But that rapid rise in stress may be slowing down, suggest director of the study John Robinson and colleague Geoffrey Godbey. In the June 1996 issue of

American Demographics magazine, Robinson and Godbey report that respondents to the 1995 American's Use of Time survey seemed just a little bit calmer than previous respondents. The share of working-age adults who report always feeling rushed declined from 38 percent in 1992 to 34 percent in 1995. The share of people who say they have less free time than in the past was just 45 percent—well below the 54 percent who answered the same question when posed by survey company Roper Starch Worldwide in 1990. Perhaps most significant, note Robinson and Godbey, working Americans are no more likely now than twenty years ago to say that they are worn out at the end of the day. "Either life is really beginning to slow down, or we're learning how to cope," say Robinson and Godbey.

This section ranks the range and availability of relaxing and diverting pursuits for those "slow" or "coping" times. These include going out to dinner, going to the movies, or going to the park. Because the need for relaxation has increased while leisure time has shrunk, it is important that a city have a variety of local restaurants, movie theaters, or video rental stores.

And that selection should be wide, because when Americans set out to rest and relax, they cover ground. For starters, we spent a collective 295,473 days at the park in 1993, according to the U.S. Forest Service. (One visitor "day" equals twelve hours spent in a national park, forest, or recreation area.) That included 2,700 days studying nature, 17,000 days hunting it, and 79,000 days picnicking and swimming in it. Luckily there is room enough for all of us. Federal and state parklands, forests, and wildlife reserves cover more than 86 million acres.

Approximately 71.2 million of us took in a major league baseball game in 1993. Forty-two million of us went to the horse races in 1994 (down from 73.3 million in 1985), and 36.4 million fans attended an NCAA college football game. The number of professional rodeos peaked at 798 in 1991, but broncos bucked in 782 rodeos in 1994.

Nearly 71 million people walked for exercise at least twice 1994, making it the most popular recreational activity that year, according to the National Sporting Goods Association. Sixty million swimmers placed swimming in second and 50 million cyclists brought bicycle riding in third.

More than 42 million adults played softball in 1994; 24 million golfers played 464,800,000 rounds of golf. We spent $14.1 billion on recreational boats. It's unclear from the data whether this includes the beer and ice.

We spent $19.3 billion on audio, video, computer, and musical equipment in 1994; $43.9 billion on books, magazines, and newspapers; and $5.2 billion on spectator sports. We spent $4.6 billion getting the television repaired. We rented $6.6 billion in video tapes, spent $6.5 billion at the movies, $3 billion at the bowling alley, and $5.9 billion at amusement parks. We paid $4.2 billion in fitness club memberships, and spent $3.2 billion in greens fees at public golf courses.

Closer to home and garden, 28 percent of households participated in "insect control" in 1994, according to the National Gardening Association. That's down from 39 percent in 1990. Other gardening activities remain popular. But it seems we've been letting the lawn go, or hiring someone else to tend it. The share of households participating in lawn work fell from 66 percent to 54 percent between 1990 and 1994.

On the cultural front, 27 percent of us visited an art museum in 1992, according to the National Endowment for the Arts. Five percent of us made it to the ballet, 13 percent to a classical music concert, and 11 percent to a jazz concert. More than half of us read "literature," 17 percent of us sat through a musical, and 14 percent went to a play.

Other times, we just can't sit still. Americans took 434.3 million pleasure trips in 1994, up from 301.2 in 1985, according to the U.S. Travel Data Center. The increase in getaway trips outpaced population growth by 35 percentage points during the period.

We're not getting as far on our jaunts as we used to, however. The average trip covered 821 miles in 1994, down steadily from 1985 when Americans roamed an average of 1,010 miles in search of pleasure. The number of nights spent per trip also declined, from an average of 5.6 in 1985 to 3.7 in 1994. This returns us to the issue of declining leisure time. People may feel the need to escape their hectic routines more often, but they seem to have less time to stay away.

Ranking micropolitan America. The ideal micropolitan area would offer a convenient mix of urban forms of entertainment and open-air spaces close at hand. There must be equal chances to see a movie, land a fish, go shopping, and linger in the park. Each small city is rated in the following five categories:

1. Amusement Place Availability: Does the area have an adequate selection of theaters, bowling alleys, golf courses, arcades, and the like?
2. Shopping Availability: When you head downtown or to the mall will you find a large array of stores, or will the pickings be slim?
3. Food and Drink: How's the selection of local restaurants and taverns?
4. Population Density: Is there room enough for your favorite outdoor activity, or is the micropolitan in a relatively urban area?
5. Local Recreation Funding: Is the local government willing to spend money on parks, swimming pools, and recreation programs?

Amusement Place Availability

Tuesday is a day off for many of Key West's working musicians. But that doesn't mean that residents and visitors can't hear a little music. Just stop by Grunt's (named for the fish) around nine or ten o'clock in the evening, as local musicians drop in to play—not work—on their night off. Like Key West, many of the country's small cities provide a variety of ways to play and relax seven days a week.

This category ranks each micro by its rate of what the government calls "amusement/recreation establishments": places like movie theaters, bowling alleys, golf courses, race tracks, amusement parks, skating rinks, and arcades. Key West features 172 such establishments, or 210 per 100,000 residents. The popular vacation spot has many tourists to entertain. The national average is 51 per 100,000.

Hinesville, Georgia stands at the other end of the entertainment spectrum from Key West. Hinesville, is a military town on the edge of Fort Stewart, not a vacation spot. The town offers only 14 amusement and recreation establishments per 100,000 residents. Other southern micros join Hinesville at the low end of the list.

Source: County Business Patterns, 1996, U.S. Bureau of the Census, Washington, D.C. Data are for 1994.

Scoring: Twenty points for 110 or more establishments per 100,000 residents; no points for fewer than 15. The spacing is every 5 establishments per 100,000 residents.

Amusement Place Availability: Highs and Lows

	Amusement and Recreation Establishments per 100,000 Residents
Highest	
1. Key West, Fla.	210.3
2. Bozeman, Mont.	145.3
3. Hilton Head Island, S.C.	114.2
4. Wenatchee, Wash.	112.0
5. Bend, Ore.	99.9
6. Rutland, Vt.	99.2
7. Helena, Mont.	96.9
Traverse City, Mich.	96.9
9. Newport, R.I.	96.8
10. Carson City, Nev.	90.0
Median	
96. Stillwater, Okla.	45.7
97. Gainesville, Fla.	45.6
Lowest	
184. Gallup, N.Mex.	24.4
185. Warrensburg, Mo.	23.9
186. Searcy, Ark.	23.5
187. Selma, Ala.	22.9
188. Eagle Pass, Tex.	22.6
189. Cullman, Ala.	19.5
190. Milledgeville, Ga.	19.4
191. McAlester, Okla.	16.4
192. El Centro-Calexico-Brawley, Calif.	16.0
193. Hinesville, Ga.	13.6

Amusement Place Availability Area by Area

(Amusement and recreation establishments per 100,000 residents and rating points)

Area	Establishments	Points
Micro median	45.7	
Alabama		
Albertville	43.0	(6)
Auburn-Opelika	28.3	(3)
Cullman	19.5	(1)
Selma	22.9	(2)
Talladega	27.6	(3)
Alaska		
Fairbanks	86.2	(15)
Arizona		
Prescott	41.4	(6)
Sierra Vista	33.5	(4)
Arkansas		
Blytheville	29.5	(3)
El Dorado	41.1	(6)
Hot Springs	87.7	(15)
Jonesboro	46.3	(7)
Russellville	39.8	(5)
Searcy	23.5	(2)
California		
Arcata-Eureka	56.7	(9)
El Centro-Calexico-Brawley	16.0	(1)
Hanford-Lemoore	26.2	(3)
Hollister	38.9	(5)
Connecticut		
Torrington	65.0	(11)
Florida		
Key West	210.3	(20)
Vero Beach	60.7	(10)
Georgia		
Brunswick	47.7	(7)
Dalton	49.4	(7)
Dublin	26.0	(3)
Gainesville	45.6	(7)
Hinesville	13.6	(0)
La Grange	50.4	(8)
Milledgeville	19.4	(1)
Rome	43.2	(6)
Statesboro	33.5	(4)
Thomasville	37.3	(5)
Valdosta	37.7	(5)
Waycross	28.0	(3)
Idaho		
Coeur d'Alene	75.6	(13)
Idaho Falls	50.5	(8)
Pocatello	49.3	(7)
Twin Falls	75.1	(13)
Illinois		
Carbondale	48.8	(7)
Danville	44.4	(6)
Freeport	34.7	(4)
Galesburg	71.1	(12)
Mattoon-Charleston	57.4	(9)
Ottawa	60.3	(10)
Quincy	54.6	(8)
Sterling	36.4	(5)
Indiana		
Columbus	47.7	(7)
Marion	40.6	(6)
Michigan City-La Porte	46.4	(7)
New Castle	34.7	(4)
Richmond	52.4	(8)
Vincennes	32.3	(4)

Area	Score	(Rank)
Iowa		
Ames	65.8	(11)
Burlington	58.3	(9)
Clinton	68.7	(11)
Mason City	79.5	(13)
Muscatine	41.2	(6)
Kansas		
Hutchinson	38.3	(5)
Manhattan	42.6	(6)
Salina	46.7	(7)
Kentucky		
Bowling Green	55.4	(9)
Frankfort	48.2	(7)
Madisonville	38.9	(5)
Paducah	51.0	(8)
Radcliff-Elizabethtown	31.0	(4)
Louisiana		
Hammond	27.4	(3)
New Iberia	43.8	(6)
Ruston	27.8	(3)
Maine		
Augusta-Waterville	68.3	(11)
Biddeford-Saco	69.7	(11)
Maryland		
Salisbury	39.5	(5)
Michigan		
Marquette	59.9	(9)
Mount Pleasant	45.0	(7)
Owosso	44.6	(6)
Traverse City	96.9	(17)
Minnesota		
Faribault	62.1	(10)
Mankato	55.3	(9)
Red Wing	73.7	(12)
Willmar	54.2	(8)
Winona	33.1	(4)
Mississippi		
Cleveland	31.3	(4)
Columbus	46.1	(7)
Greenville	41.9	(6)
Laurel	41.3	(6)
Meridian	41.9	(6)
Tupelo	38.2	(5)
Vicksburg	57.1	(9)
Missouri		
Cape Girardeau-Sikeston	43.9	(6)
Jefferson City	45.4	(7)
Poplar Bluff	47.3	(7)
Warrensburg	23.9	(2)
Montana		
Bozeman	145.3	(20)
Helena	96.9	(17)
Missoula	84.0	(14)
Nebraska		
Grand Island	67.0	(11)
Nevada		
Carson City	90.9	(16)
Elko	66.7	(11)
New Hampshire		
Concord	63.1	(10)
Keene	60.7	(10)
New Mexico		
Alamogordo	35.0	(5)
Carlsbad	43.6	(6)
Clovis	39.7	(5)
Farmington	33.2	(4)
Gallup	24.4	(2)
Hobbs	42.0	(6)
Roswell	39.4	(5)
New York		
Cortland	67.0	(11)

Gloversville	47.8	(7)
Ithaca	55.0	(9)
Kingston	64.7	(10)
Olean	42.1	(6)
Plattsburgh	46.2	(7)
Watertown	46.0	(7)
North Carolina		
Albemarle	35.3	(5)
Eden	33.1	(4)
Havelock-New Bern	40.5	(6)
Henderson	42.0	(6)
Kinston	47.7	(7)
Lumberton	30.7	(4)
Roanoke Rapids	41.9	(6)
Sanford	53.4	(8)
Shelby	40.7	(6)
Statesville	60.6	(10)
Wilson	47.7	(7)
North Dakota		
Minot	77.7	(13)
Ohio		
Ashland	67.2	(11)
Athens	44.7	(6)
Chillicothe	42.3	(6)
Findlay-Fostoria-Tiffin	51.5	(8)
Fremont	49.4	(7)
Marion	42.9	(6)
Mount Vernon	43.9	(6)
New Philadelphia	43.9	(6)
Norwalk	29.3	(3)
Portsmouth	40.7	(6)
Sandusky	84.6	(14)
Sidney	36.4	(5)
Wooster	38.6	(5)
Zanesville	58.6	(9)
Oklahoma		
Ardmore	52.6	(8)
Chickasha	25.5	(3)
Duncan	32.4	(4)
McAlester	16.4	(1)
Muskogee	30.3	(4)
Stillwater	45.7	(7)
Oregon		
Albany-Corvallis	45.2	(7)
Bend	99.9	(17)
Coos Bay	47.8	(7)
Grants Pass	57.6	(9)
Klamath Falls	51.2	(8)
Pendleton	52.2	(8)
Roseburg	48.8	(7)
Pennsylvania		
Chambersburg	43.7	(6)
New Castle	44.5	(6)
Pottsville	36.3	(5)
Rhode Island		
Newport	96.8	(17)
South Carolina		
Greenwood	50.5	(8)
Hilton Head Island	114.2	(20)
Tennessee		
Cleveland	54.2	(8)
Columbia	57.9	(9)
Cookeville	55.5	(9)
Morristown	53.5	(8)
Tullahoma	40.6	(6)
Texas		
Corsicana	29.8	(3)
Del Rio	28.1	(3)
Eagle Pass	22.6	(2)
Huntsville	29.8	(3)
Lufkin	37.4	(5)
Nacogdoches	33.9	(4)
Palestine	34.1	(4)
Paris	42.3	(6)

Utah		
Logan	58.0	(9)
St. George	53.7	(8)
Vermont		
Rutland	99.2	(17)
Virginia		
Blacksburg-Radford-Christiansburg	36.6	(5)
Harrisonburg	53.0	(8)
Martinsville	37.3	(5)
Staunton-Waynesboro	42.0	(6)
Winchester	71.2	(12)
Washington		
Aberdeen	81.0	(14)
Longview	57.2	(9)
Mount Vernon	55.6	(9)
Port Angeles	59.9	(9)
Walla Walla	39.8	(5)
Wenatchee	112.0	(20)
West Virginia		
Beckley	37.1	(5)
Clarksburg	41.0	(6)
Fairmont	53.3	(8)
Morgantown	47.4	(7)
Wisconsin		
Fond du Lac	54.9	(8)
Manitowoc	42.6	(6)
Stevens Point	48.3	(7)
Watertown	53.0	(8)
Wyoming		
Rock Springs	63.7	(10)

Shopping Availability

Large cities have always been synonymous with thriving retail centers. Say "Fifth Avenue" to a person anywhere in America and you will likely receive the response, "New York." Likewise, Michigan Avenue—the "Magnificent Mile"—means Chicago, and Atlanta is known for Peachtree Street.

Small cities may not have the same high profile, but their Main Streets are every bit as important to their regions as Peachtree is to northwest Georgia. And don't forget the ubiquitous shopping malls. Many a small city resident shops at Bloomingdales without traveling to New York City.

This category measures each area's retail services by projecting its total number of stores into a rate per 100,000 residents. The national rate is 600.8 retail outlets per 100,000 residents. The median for micros is 655.0.

Key West, Florida, leads the pack. The popular tourist destination offers 116 clothing stores, 60 grocery stores, 57 furniture and homefurnishing stores, 42 sporting goods stores, and 31 jewelry stores. Its grand total is 1,007 retail establishments, or a rate of 1,232 per 100,000 residents.

Hinesville, Georgia, offers the fewest retail outlets. Its total number is 202 stores, a rate of 343 stores per 100,000 residents.

Source: County Business Patterns, 1996, U.S. Bureau of the Census, Washington, D.C. Data are for 1994.

Scoring: Twenty points for 1,030 stores or more per 100,000; no points for 459.9 or less. The spacing is every 30 stores per 100,000.

Shopping Availability: Highs and Lows

	Retail Establishments per 100,000 Residents
Highest	
1. Key West, Fla.	1,232.3
2. Bozeman, Mont.	1,084.6
3. Traverse City, Mich.	1,065.8
4. Rutland, Vt.	1,036.9
5. Brunswick, Ga.	1,033.3
6. Wenatchee, Wash.	998.7
7. Hilton Head Island, S.C.	945.2
8. Grand Island, Nebr.	943.9
9. Bend, Ore.	940.8
10. Paducah, Ky.	939.6
Median	
96. Klamath Falls, Ore.	655.8
97. La Grange, Ga.	655.0
Lowest	
184. New Iberia, La.	499.9
185. Sidney, Ohio	493.1
186. Ruston, La.	487.1
187. Warrensburg, Mo.	475.8
188. Logan, Utah	470.4
189. Owosso, Mich.	454.5
190. Huntsville, Tex.	417.1
191. Hollister, Calif.	411.4
192. Hanford-Lemoore, Calif.	376.1
193. Hinesville, Ga.	343.0

Shopping Availability Area by Area

(Retail establishments per 100,000 residents and rating points)

Area	Per 100,000	Points
Micro median	655.4	
Alabama		
Albertville	871.1	(14)
Auburn-Opelika	548.6	(3)
Cullman	580.9	(5)
Selma	600.1	(5)
Talladega	557.6	(4)
Alaska		
Fairbanks	573.7	(4)
Arizona		
Prescott	734.7	(10)
Sierra Vista	581.7	(5)
Arkansas		
Blytheville	614.7	(6)
El Dorado	726.4	(9)
Hot Springs	830.9	(13)
Jonesboro	757.0	(10)
Russellville	728.9	(9)
Searcy	626.3	(6)
California		
Arcata-Eureka	787.9	(11)
El Centro-Calexico-Brawley	513.5	(2)
Hanford-Lemoore	376.1	(0)
Hollister	411.4	(0)
Connecticut		
Torrington	640.8	(7)
Florida		
Key West	1,232.3	(20)
Vero Beach	759.3	(10)
Georgia		
Brunswick	1,033.3	(20)
Dalton	746.8	(10)
Dublin	823.4	(13)
Gainesville	637.8	(6)
Hinesville	343.0	(0)
La Grange	655.0	(7)
Milledgeville	665.3	(7)
Rome	731.4	(10)
Statesboro	648.4	(7)
Thomasville	785.2	(11)
Valdosta	838.3	(13)
Waycross	751.3	(10)
Idaho		
Coeur d'Alene	811.7	(12)
Idaho Falls	717.3	(9)
Pocatello	634.4	(6)
Twin Falls	779.6	(11)
Illinois		
Carbondale	670.5	(8)
Danville	564.9	(4)
Freeport	595.7	(5)
Galesburg	685.8	(8)
Mattoon-Charleston	681.6	(8)
Ottawa	699.2	(8)
Quincy	659.6	(7)
Sterling	564.7	(4)
Indiana		
Columbus	692.1	(8)
Marion	618.8	(6)
Michigan City-La Porte	664.5	(7)
New Castle	556.9	(4)
Richmond	632.6	(6)
Vincennes	713.2	(9)
Iowa		
Ames	678.1	(8)
Burlington	774.3	(11)
Clinton	659.0	(7)

Mason City	874.9	(14)
Muscatine	639.3	(6)
Kansas		
Hutchinson	731.0	(10)
Manhattan	579.4	(5)
Salina	807.3	(1)
Kentucky		
Bowling Green	766.0	(11)
Frankfort	629.3	(6)
Madisonville	635.2	(6)
Paducah	939.6	(16)
Radcliff-Elizabethtown	566.4	(4)
Louisiana		
Hammond	551.8	(4)
New Iberia	499.9	(2)
Ruston	487.1	(1)
Maine		
Augusta-Waterville	676.3	(8)
Biddeford-Saco	763.2	(11)
Maryland		
Salisbury	713.7	(9)
Michigan		
Marquette	687.0	(8)
Mount Pleasant	590.5	(5)
Owosso	454.5	(0)
Traverse City	1,065.8	(20)
Minnesota		
Faribault	605.5	(5)
Mankato	664.1	(7)
Red Wing	744.5	(10)
Willmar	779.0	(11)
Winona	639.1	(6)
Mississippi		
Cleveland	552.9	(4)
Columbus	730.8	(10)
Greenville	584.0	(5)
Laurel	582.5	(5)
Meridian	769.9	(11)
Tupelo	887.5	(15)
Vicksburg	707.1	(9)
Missouri		
Cape Girardeau-Sikeston	773.4	(11)
Jefferson City	587.8	(5)
Poplar Bluff	729.8	(9)
Warrensburg	475.8	(1)
Montana		
Bozeman	1,084.6	(20)
Helena	775.1	(11)
Missoula	884.6	(15)
Nebraska		
Grand Island	943.9	(17)
Nevada		
Carson City	740.3	(10)
Elko	509.1	(2)
New Hampshire		
Concord	684.8	(8)
Keene	673.7	(8)
New Mexico		
Alamogordo	537.7	(3)
Carlsbad	560.7	(4)
Clovis	622.0	(6)
Farmington	596.3	(5)
Gallup	563.4	(4)
Hobbs	613.2	(6)
Roswell	591.9	(5)
New York		
Cortland	708.1	(9)
Gloversville	542.1	(3)
Ithaca	623.0	(6)
Kingston	678.0	(8)

Olean	693.8	(8)
Plattsburgh	755.9	(10)
Watertown	642.5	(7)
North Carolina		
Albemarle	636.2	(6)
Eden	609.2	(5)
Havelock-New Bern	652.9	(7)
Henderson	694.6	(8)
Kinston	748.4	(10)
Lumberton	503.8	(2)
Roanoke Rapids	614.6	(6)
Sanford	795.0	(12)
Shelby	587.7	(5)
Statesville	647.4	(7)
Wilson	709.9	(9)
North Dakota		
Minot	801.3	(12)
Ohio		
Ashland	531.7	(3)
Athens	591.0	(5)
Chillicothe	520.1	(3)
Findlay-Fostoria-Tiffin	656.2	(7)
Fremont	561.1	(4)
Marion	554.6	(4)
Mount Vernon	518.9	(2)
New Philadelphia	695.3	(8)
Norwalk	589.5	(5)
Portsmouth	548.6	(3)
Sandusky	789.3	(11)
Sidney	493.1	(2)
Wooster	505.8	(2)
Zanesville	703.8	(9)
Oklahoma		
Ardmore	724.9	(9)
Chickasha	506.2	(2)
Duncan	632.0	(6)
McAlester	589.9	(5)
Muskogee	624.9	(6)
Stillwater	676.3	(8)

Oregon		
Albany-Corvallis	558.0	(4)
Bend	940.8	(17)
Coos Bay	728.5	(9)
Grants Pass	666.9	(7)
Klamath Falls	655.8	(7)
Pendleton	666.2	(7)
Roseburg	645.6	(7)
Pennsylvania		
Chambersburg	562.9	(4)
New Castle	578.4	(4)
Pottsville	595.9	(5)
Rhode Island		
Newport	873.5	(14)
South Carolina		
Greenwood	708.5	(9)
Hilton Head Island	945.2	(17)
Tennessee		
Cleveland	633.2	(6)
Columbia	614.7	(6)
Cookeville	782.2	(11)
Morristown	702.6	(9)
Tullahoma	656.9	(7)
Texas		
Corsicana	629.9	(6)
Del Rio	584.6	(5)
Eagle Pass	539.5	(3)
Huntsville	417.1	(0)
Lufkin	566.6	(4)
Nacogdoches	595.7	(5)
Palestine	507.5	(2)
Paris	663.3	(7)
Utah		
Logan	470.4	(1)
St. George	669.9	(7)

Vermont		
Rutland	1,036.9	(20)
Virginia		
Blacksburg-Radford-Christiansburg	571.1	(4)
Harrisonburg	657.9	(7)
Martinsville	631.9	(6)
Staunton-Waynesboro	611.8	(6)
Winchester	800.2	(12)
Washington		
Aberdeen	740.6	(10)
Longview	656.3	(7)
Mount Vernon	877.3	(14)
Port Angeles	736.4	(10)
Walla Walla	546.1	(3)
Wenatchee	998.7	(18)
West Virginia		
Beckley	605.4	(5)
Clarksburg	706.5	(9)
Fairmont	564.5	(4)
Morgantown	689.6	(8)
Wisconsin		
Fond du Lac	596.8	(5)
Manitowoc	578.7	(4)
Stevens Point	625.4	(6)
Watertown	546.0	(3)
Wyoming		
Rock Springs	686.4	(8)

Food and Drink

Cities, whether large or small, are proof of man's essentially social nature, and the existence of restaurants and bars provides further evidence.

This category measures the availability of eating and drinking establishments in each micro. Using the same method employed to rate shopping availability, this category projects the number of eating and drinking establishments into a rate per 100,000 residents.

Key West, Florida, must provide dining for its large tourist population as well as its residents. The micro takes first place, with nearly 400 restaurants and bars per 100,000 population. That's far above the national rate of 172.5. The median rate for micropolitans is 168.9.

Pack your lunch in Hinesville, Georgia. The micro has the lowest rate, with 73 eating and drinking establishments per 100,000 residents.

Tourist locales and western states offer the most opportunities to dine out. Southern micros offer the fewest.

Source: County Business Patterns, 1996, U.S. Bureau of the Census, Washington, D.C. Data are for 1994.

Scoring: Twenty points for 290 or more establishments per 100,000; no points for 99.9 or less. The spacing is every 10 establishments.

Food and Drink: Highs and Lows

	Eating and Drinking Establishments per 100,000 Residents
Highest	
1. Key West, Fla.	399.8
2. Bozeman, Mont.	307.9
3. Wenatchee, Wash.	296.8
4. Newport, R.I.	296.3
5. Missoula, Mont.	278.9
6. Mason City, Iowa	268.7
7. Hilton Head Island, S.C.	267.4
8. Rutland, Vt.	267.2
9. Aberdeen, Wash.	266.9
10. Grand Island, Nebr.	262.1
Median	
96. Concord, N.H.	168.1
97. Fairbanks, Alaska	167.6
Lowest	
184. Logan, Utah	110.7
185. Lumberton, N.C.	110.2
186. Talladega, Ala.	109.2
187. Cullman, Ala.	108.9
188. Selma, Ala.	106.3
189. Hanford-Lemoore, Calif.	105.5
190. Eagle Pass, Tex.	97.1
191. Palestine, Tex.	96.3
192. Cleveland, Miss.	84.1
193. Hinesville, Ga.	73.0

Food and Drink Area by Area

(Eating and drinking establishments per 100,000 residents and rating points)

Area	Rate	Points
Micro median	167.9	
Alabama		
Albertville	171.9	(8)
Auburn-Opelika	141.5	(5)
Cullman	108.9	(1)
Selma	106.3	(1)
Talladega	109.2	(1)
Alaska		
Fairbanks	167.6	(7)
Arizona		
Prescott	229.0	(13)
Sierra Vista	204.8	(11)
Arkansas		
Blytheville	125.7	(3)
El Dorado	144.8	(5)
Hot Springs	206.8	(11)
Jonesboro	136.2	(4)
Russellville	165.3	(7)
Searcy	139.4	(4)
California		
Arcata-Eureka	221.8	(13)
El Centro-Calexico-Brawley	124.7	(3)
Hanford-Lemoore	105.5	(1)
Hollister	148.5	(5)
Connecticut		
Torrington	180.9	(9)
Florida		
Key West	399.8	(20)
Vero Beach	164.2	(7)
Georgia		
Brunswick	246.0	(15)
Dalton	152.2	(6)
Dublin	151.4	(6)
Gainesville	164.4	(7)
Hinesville	73.0	(0)
La Grange	151.1	(6)
Milledgeville	140.3	(5)
Rome	163.3	(7)
Statesboro	154.8	(6)
Thomasville	151.6	(6)
Valdosta	172.5	(8)
Waycross	143.9	(5)
Idaho		
Coeur d'Alene	226.7	(13)
Idaho Falls	179.3	(8)
Pocatello	199.7	(10)
Twin Falls	187.7	(9)
Illinois		
Carbondale	206.7	(11)
Danville	183.4	(9)
Freeport	199.9	(10)
Galesburg	231.0	(14)
Mattoon-Charleston	227.8	(13)
Ottawa	244.9	(15)
Quincy	183.0	(9)
Sterling	182.2	(9)
Indiana		
Columbus	165.6	(7)
Marion	176.0	(8)
Michigan City-La Porte	177.3	(8)
New Castle	151.0	(6)
Richmond	164.0	(7)
Vincennes	159.0	(6)
Iowa		
Ames	208.1	(11)
Burlington	223.9	(13)
Clinton	219.7	(12)

Mason City	268.7	(17)
Muscatine	210.7	(12)
Kansas		
Hutchinson	204.3	(11)
Manhattan	142.8	(5)
Salina	217.0	(12)
Kentucky		
Bowling Green	179.5	(8)
Frankfort	173.2	(8)
Madisonville	118.8	(2)
Paducah	213.3	(12)
Radcliff-Elizabethtown	111.7	(2)
Louisiana		
Hammond	131.4	(4)
New Iberia	111.6	(2)
Ruston	113.7	(2)
Maine		
Augusta-Waterville	170.8	(8)
Biddeford-Saco	238.5	(14)
Maryland		
Salisbury	141.5	(5)
Michigan		
Marquette	206.7	(11)
Mount Pleasant	174.6	(8)
Owosso	121.3	(3)
Traverse City	234.8	(14)
Minnesota		
Faribault	168.9	(7)
Mankato	179.3	(8)
Red Wing	176.0	(8)
Willmar	184.9	(9)
Winona	184.1	(9)
Mississippi		
Cleveland	84.1	(0)
Columbus	133.3	(4)
Greenville	110.8	(2)
Laurel	114.3	(2)
Meridian	158.4	(6)
Tupelo	172.4	(8)
Vicksburg	126.3	(3)
Missouri		
Cape Girardeau-Sikeston	181.2	(9)
Jefferson City	156.8	(6)
Poplar Bluff	154.4	(6)
Warrensburg	160.8	(7)
Montana		
Bozeman	307.9	(20)
Helena	253.9	(16)
Missoula	278.9	(18)
Nebraska		
Grand Island	262.1	(17)
Nevada		
Carson City	234.9	(14)
Elko	160.6	(7)
New Hampshire		
Concord	168.1	(7)
Keene	146.9	(5)
New Mexico		
Alamogordo	147.3	(5)
Carlsbad	134.5	(4)
Clovis	125.2	(3)
Farmington	132.0	(4)
Gallup	132.8	(4)
Hobbs	162.9	(7)
Roswell	160.7	(7)
New York		
Cortland	257.7	(16)
Gloversville	185.6	(9)
Ithaca	236.7	(14)
Kingston	207.8	(11)

Olean	235.2	(14)
Plattsburgh	197.6	(10)
Watertown	203.8	(11)

North Carolina

Albemarle	137.7	(4)
Eden	116.6	(2)
Havelock-New Bern	143.0	(5)
Henderson	133.5	(4)
Kinston	144.9	(5)
Lumberton	110.2	(2)
Roanoke Rapids	111.7	(2)
Sanford	182.6	(9)
Shelby	125.4	(3)
Statesville	164.8	(7)
Wilson	144.7	(5)

North Dakota

Minot	226.2	(13)

Ohio

Ashland	170.0	(8)
Athens	200.3	(11)
Chillicothe	136.5	(4)
Findlay-Fostoria-Tiffin	217.7	(12)
Fremont	170.6	(8)
Marion	170.1	(8)
Mount Vernon	179.6	(8)
New Philadelphia	207.9	(11)
Norwalk	182.7	(9)
Portsmouth	173.8	(8)
Sandusky	253.7	(16)
Sidney	154.3	(6)
Wooster	146.0	(5)
Zanesville	197.2	(10)

Oklahoma

Ardmore	150.9	(6)
Chickasha	134.7	(4)
Duncan	162.1	(7)
McAlester	154.5	(6)
Muskogee	173.2	(8)
Stillwater	179.7	(8)

Oregon

Albany-Corvallis	161.2	(7)
Bend	233.8	(14)
Coos Bay	250.3	(16)
Grants Pass	204.5	(11)
Klamath Falls	201.5	(11)
Pendleton	215.2	(12)
Roseburg	206.4	(11)

Pennsylvania

Chambersburg	146.9	(5)
New Castle	176.9	(8)
Pottsville	164.9	(7)

Rhode Island

Newport	296.3	(20)

South Carolina

Greenwood	172.6	(8)
Hilton Head Island	267.4	(17)

Tennessee

Cleveland	143.1	(5)
Columbia	140.8	(5)
Cookeville	164.7	(7)
Morristown	152.7	(6)
Tullahoma	148.4	(5)

Texas

Corsicana	124.0	(3)
Del Rio	149.7	(5)
Eagle Pass	97.1	(0)
Huntsville	115.4	(2)
Lufkin	124.3	(3)
Nacogdoches	126.6	(3)
Palestine	96.3	(0)
Paris	164.7	(7)

Utah

Logan	110.7	(2)
St. George	165.6	(7)

Vermont		
Rutland	267.2	(17)
Virginia		
Blacksburg-Radford-Christiansburg	163.8	(7)
Harrisonburg	146.2	(5)
Martinsville	122.8	(3)
Staunton-Waynesboro	128.8	(3)
Winchester	188.0	(9)
Washington		
Aberdeen	266.9	(17)
Longview	202.4	(11)
Mount Vernon	237.6	(14)
Port Angeles	220.1	(13)
Walla Walla	157.4	(6)
Wenatchee	296.8	(20)
West Virginia		
Beckley	133.1	(4)
Clarksburg	165.3	(7)
Fairmont	153.2	(6)
Morgantown	207.7	(11)
Wisconsin		
Fond du Lac	195.0	(10)
Manitowoc	202.2	(11)
Stevens Point	224.6	(13)
Watertown	216.0	(12)
Wyoming		
Rock Springs	191.2	(10)

Population Density

Perhaps the best reason to escape a metropolitan area for a micropolitan community is to get yourself some room. This is particularly true if you enjoy camping, fishing, hiking, and other outdoor activities that require a bit of wilderness.

Harried residents of New York City can find relaxation in the green expanse of Central Park, but they'll find little real solitude. Nearly 24,000 people lived in each square mile of the New York metro area in 1994. In comparison, just ninety-four people live in each square mile in America's small cities. And those who have begun their weekend getaway by leaving Manhattan on a Friday afternoon may well envy the residents of Rutland, Vermont, who are just miles from two national forests in the Green Mountains.

This category estimates each micro's outdoor recreation potential by considering its population density. The Elko, Nevada, area offers the best choice of wide open spaces, with an average of only 2.4 people living in each of its 17,182 square miles.

Newport, Rhode Island, was once a thriving seaport. It became a popular resort town as robber barons, yachtsmen, and society figures flocked there each summer to live in their massive "cottages." Newport has twice as many residents as Elko and has less than 1 percent of the space. Newport ranks the highest population density of any small city, with 805 residents per square mile.

The deserts and plains of the West obviously offer the best opportunities for outdoor solitude. Southern and Eastern micropolitan areas are generally the most crowded.

Source: Population Division, U.S. Bureau of the Census, Washington, D.C. Population estimates are for 1994.

Scoring: Twenty points for fewer than 10 people per square mile; no points for more than 295. The spacing is every 15 people per square mile.

Population Density: Highs and Lows

	Persons per Square Mile
Lowest	
1. Elko, Nev.	2.4
2. Rock Springs, Wyo.	3.9
3. Alamogordo, N.Mex.	8.2
4. Roswell, N.Mex.	10.0
5. Klamath Falls, Ore.	10.2
6. Fairbanks, Alaska	11.5
7. Gallup, N.Mex.	12.0
8. Carlsbad, N.Mex.	12.6
9. Hobbs, N.Mex.	13.0
10. Del Rio, Tex.	13.5
Median	
96. Lufkin, Tex.	93.3
97. Muscatine, Iowa	94.1
Highest	
184. Frankfort, Ky.	216.1
185. Cleveland, Tenn.	235.7
186. Paducah, Ky.	257.8
187. Dalton, Ga.	265.0
188. Gainesville, Ga.	267.0
189. New Castle, Pa.	267.7
190. Sandusky, Ohio	306.1
191. Carson City, Nev.	313.3
192. Morristown, Tenn.	325.3
193. Newport, R.I.	804.7

Population Density Area by Area

(Persons per square mile and rating points)

Micro median	93.7	
Alabama		
Albertville	135.5	(11)
Auburn-Opelika	150.9	(10)
Cullman	96.9	(14)
Selma	48.9	(17)
Talladega	102.7	(13)
Alaska		
Fairbanks	11.5	(19)
Arizona		
Prescott	15.7	(19)
Sierra Vista	17.4	(19)
Arkansas		
Blytheville	56.7	(16)
El Dorado	44.5	(17)
Hot Springs	117.7	(12)
Jonesboro	103.3	(13)
Russellville	61.8	(16)
Searcy	57.6	(16)
California		
Arcata-Eureka	34.1	(18)
El Centro-Calexico-Brawley	32.8	(18)
Hanford-Lemoore	79.8	(15)
Hollister	29.6	(18)
Connecticut		
Torrington	194.0	(7)
Florida		
Key West	82.0	(15)
Vero Beach	190.1	(7)
Georgia		
Brunswick	154.1	(10)
Dalton	265.0	(2)
Dublin	52.0	(17)
Gainesville	267.0	(2)
Hinesville	113.5	(13)
La Grange	139.0	(11)
Milledgeville	159.6	(10)
Rome	162.3	(9)
Statesboro	70.0	(15)
Thomasville	73.4	(15)
Valdosta	163.3	(9)
Waycross	40.2	(17)
Idaho		
Coeur d'Alene	70.2	(15)
Idaho Falls	42.4	(17)
Pocatello	31.4	(18)
Twin Falls	30.5	(18)
Illinois		
Carbondale	104.5	(13)
Danville	97.7	(14)
Freeport	86.9	(14)
Galesburg	78.6	(15)
Mattoon-Charleston	102.8	(13)
Ottawa	96.4	(14)
Quincy	79.1	(15)
Sterling	88.1	(14)
Indiana		
Columbus	164.7	(9)
Marion	178.4	(8)
Michigan City-La Porte	184.0	(8)
New Castle	124.7	(12)
Richmond	179.6	(8)
Vincennes	78.0	(15)
Iowa		
Ames	130.0	(11)
Burlington	103.1	(13)
Clinton	73.4	(15)

Mason City 81.9 (15)
Muscatine 94.1 (14)

Kansas
Hutchinson 49.9 (17)
Manhattan 59.7 (16)
Salina 68.5 (16)

Kentucky
Bowling Green 152.3 (10)
Frankfort 216.1 (6)
Madisonville 84.0 (15)
Paducah 257.8 (3)
Radcliff-Elizabethtown 144.0 (11)

Louisiana
Hammond 115.6 (12)
New Iberia 123.2 (12)
Ruston 91.5 (14)

Maine
Augusta-Waterville 134.9 (11)
Biddeford-Saco 170.9 (9)

Maryland
Salisbury 208.1 (6)

Michigan
Marquette 38.5 (18)
Mount Pleasant 96.8 (14)
Owosso 133.1 (11)
Traverse City 107.8 (13)

Minnesota
Faribault 103.5 (13)
Mankato 69.0 (16)
Red Wing 55.4 (16)
Willmar 51.0 (17)
Winona 77.2 (15)

Mississippi
Cleveland 47.5 (17)
Columbus 121.0 (12)
Greenville 92.2 (14)
Laurel 90.8 (14)
Meridian 108.5 (13)
Tupelo 157.2 (10)
Vicksburg 83.6 (15)

Missouri
Cape Girardeau-Sikeston 74.7 (15)
Jefferson City 82.4 (15)
Poplar Bluff 57.5 (16)
Warrensburg 55.4 (16)

Montana
Bozeman 23.1 (19)
Helena 14.9 (19)
Missoula 33.0 (18)

Nebraska
Grand Island 92.9 (14)

Nevada
Carson City 313.3 (0)
Elko 2.4 (20)

New Hampshire
Concord 130.4 (11)
Keene 100.0 (13)

New Mexico
Alamogordo 8.2 (20)
Carlsbad 12.6 (19)
Clovis 34.1 (18)
Farmington 18.0 (19)
Gallup 12.0 (19)
Hobbs 13.0 (19)
Roswell 10.0 (19)

New York
Cortland 98.6 (14)
Gloversville 109.7 (13)
Ithaca 202.3 (7)

Area	Density	Rank
Kingston	149.5	(10)
Olean	65.2	(16)
Plattsburgh	83.3	(15)
Watertown	90.7	(14)

North Carolina

Area	Density	Rank
Albemarle	136.1	(11)
Eden	154.3	(10)
Havelock-New Bern	120.6	(12)
Henderson	159.3	(10)
Kinston	146.6	(10)
Lumberton	116.7	(12)
Roanoke Rapids	79.0	(15)
Sanford	174.7	(9)
Shelby	190.7	(7)
Statesville	175.4	(8)
Wilson	180.7	(8)

North Dakota

Area	Density	Rank
Minot	28.8	(18)

Ohio

Area	Density	Rank
Ashland	119.3	(12)
Athens	119.1	(12)
Chillicothe	106.3	(13)
Findlay-Fostoria-Tiffin	118.5	(12)
Fremont	153.4	(10)
Marion	161.6	(9)
Mount Vernon	95.1	(14)
New Philadelphia	152.4	(10)
Norwalk	117.7	(12)
Portsmouth	132.5	(11)
Sandusky	306.1	(0)
Sidney	114.1	(13)
Wooster	191.3	(7)
Zanesville	125.8	(12)

Oklahoma

Area	Density	Rank
Ardmore	53.1	(17)
Chickasha	39.1	(18)
Duncan	49.3	(17)
McAlester	32.7	(18)
Muskogee	85.1	(14)
Stillwater	92.5	(14)

Oregon

Area	Density	Rank
Albany-Corvallis	58.1	(16)
Bend	30.2	(18)
Coos Bay	39.2	(18)
Grants Pass	42.3	(17)
Klamath Falls	10.2	(19)
Pendleton	19.7	(19)
Roseburg	19.5	(19)

Pennsylvania

Area	Density	Rank
Chambersburg	163.2	(9)
New Castle	267.7	(2)
Pottsville	197.8	(7)

Rhode Island

Area	Density	Rank
Newport	804.7	(0)

South Carolina

Area	Density	Rank
Greenwood	134.7	(11)
Hilton Head Island	165.6	(9)

Tennessee

Area	Density	Rank
Cleveland	235.7	(4)
Columbia	104.3	(13)
Cookeville	139.3	(11)
Morristown	325.3	(0)
Tullahoma	80.3	(15)

Texas

Area	Density	Rank
Corsicana	37.7	(18)
Del Rio	13.5	(19)
Eagle Pass	34.6	(18)
Huntsville	68.2	(16)
Lufkin	93.3	(14)
Nacogdoches	59.2	(16)
Palestine	46.5	(17)
Paris	49.0	(17)

Utah		
Logan	65.1	(16)
St. George	26.9	(18)
Vermont		
Rutland	67.1	(16)
Virginia		
Blacksburg-Radford-Christiansburg	174.9	(9)
Harrisonburg	108.6	(13)
Martinsville	184.4	(8)
Staunton-Waynesboro	101.9	(13)
Winchester	175.7	(8)
Washington		
Aberdeen	34.8	(18)
Longview	76.8	(15)
Mount Vernon	52.9	(17)
Port Angeles	35.4	(18)
Walla Walla	41.5	(17)
Wenatchee	19.3	(19)
West Virginia		
Beckley	128.7	(12)
Clarksburg	170.1	(9)
Fairmont	187.4	(8)
Morgantown	216.1	(6)
Wisconsin		
Fond du Lac	128.4	(12)
Manitowoc	138.6	(11)
Stevens Point	79.6	(15)
Watertown	104.9	(13)
Wyoming		
Rock Springs	3.9	(20)

Local Recreation Funding

An area may be rich in wilderness, beachfront, and downtown greenspaces. For residents to enjoy local hiking, swimming, and picnicking, however, local government must commit to establishing and maintaining parks and recreation areas.

This category ranks each area according to its annual per capita expenditures on parks and recreation facilities. Included is all money spent by county and city governments on playgrounds, picnic areas, beaches, pools, golf courses, piers, and marinas. State and federal spending on state and federal parks and wilderness areas is not included.

Rock Springs, Wyoming, shows the greatest commitment to local recreation resources. Not content with the score of federal and state forests and recreation areas within 100 miles, local government allocated $172 for every man, woman, and child in the Rock Springs area. That's more than three times the national average of $53 per resident.

Portsmouth, Ohio, places the lightest emphasis on government support for recreation. The micro spends just $1 per resident on parks and recreation. Portsmouth residents turn to a wealth of nearby state and federal parks and forests for their outdoor recreation.

Western cities show the greatest commitment to funding their parks and recreation areas. Southern cities allocate the least funds per resident.

Source: Census of Governments: Compendium of Government Finances, U.S. Bureau of the Census, Washington, D.C. Data, published in 1997, are for fiscal year 1991–92.

Scoring: Twenty points for $100 or more per capita; no points for fewer than $5. The spacing is every $5 per capita.

Local Recreation Funding: Highs and Lows

	Annual Per Capita Recreation-Related Spending by Local Governments
Highest	**$**
1. Rock Springs, Wyo.	172
2. Vero Beach, Fla.	120
3. Longview, Wash.	107
4. St. George, Utah	93
5. Roswell, N.Mex.	86
6. Elko, Nev.	84
7. Walla Walla, Wash.	80
8. Farmington, N.Mex.	79
Red Wing, Minn.	79
10. Carson City, Nev.	74
New Philadelphia, Ohio	74
Median	
96. Hollister, Calif.	27
97. Manhattan, Kans.	27
Lowest	
183. Athens, Ohio	7
Hammond, La.	7
Zanesville, Ohio	7
186. Chillicothe, Ohio	6
Mount Vernon, Ohio	6
Owosso, Mich.	6
Pottsville, Pa.	6
190. Fairmont, W.Va.	5
Jonesboro, Ark.	5
192. Chickasha, Okla.	4
193. Portsmouth, Ohio	1

Local Recreation Funding Area by Area

(Annual per capita spending by local governments on parks and recreation in dollars and rating points)

Area	Dollars	Points
Micro median	27	
Alabama		
Albertville	28	(5)
Auburn-Opelika	33	(6)
Cullman	25	(5)
Selma	17	(3)
Talladega	26	(5)
Alaska		
Fairbanks	71	(14)
Arizona		
Prescott	54	(10)
Sierra Vista	36	(7)
Arkansas		
Blytheville	9	(1)
El Dorado	9	(1)
Hot Springs	43	(8)
Jonesboro	5	(1)
Russellville	8	(1)
Searcy	9	(1)
California		
Arcata-Eureka	33	(6)
El Centro-Calexico-Brawley	32	(6)
Hanford-Lemoore	45	(9)
Hollister	27	(5)
Connecticut		
Torrington	33	(6)
Florida		
Key West	66	(13)
Vero Beach	120	(20)
Georgia		
Brunswick	49	(9)
Dalton	45	(9)
Dublin	27	(5)
Gainesville	43	(8)
Hinesville	9	(1)
La Grange	33	(6)
Milledgeville	36	(7)
Rome	28	(5)
Statesboro	70	(14)
Thomasville	32	(6)
Valdosta	22	(4)
Waycross	11	(2)
Idaho		
Coeur d'Alene	36	(7)
Idaho Falls	63	(12)
Pocatello	37	(7)
Twin Falls	20	(4)
Illinois		
Carbondale	50	(10)
Danville	18	(3)
Freeport	20	(4)
Galesburg	51	(10)
Mattoon-Charleston	34	(6)
Ottawa	18	(3)
Quincy	45	(9)
Sterling	43	(8)
Indiana		
Columbus	60	(12)
Marion	30	(6)
Michigan City-La Porte	14	(2)
New Castle	11	(2)
Richmond	49	(9)
Vincennes	28	(5)

Iowa

Ames	48	(9)
Burlington	45	(9)
Clinton	40	(8)
Mason City	46	(9)
Muscatine	67	(13)

Kansas

Hutchinson	30	(6)
Manhattan	27	(5)
Salina	60	(12)

Kentucky

Bowling Green	39	(7)
Frankfort	12	(2)
Madisonville	52	(10)
Paducah	13	(2)
Radcliff-Elizabethtown	18	(3)

Louisiana

Hammond	7	(1)
New Iberia	45	(9)
Ruston	24	(4)

Maine

Augusta-Waterville	31	(6)
Biddeford-Saco	18	(3)

Maryland

Salisbury	61	(12)

Michigan

Marquette	27	(5)
Mount Pleasant	20	(4)
Owosso	6	(1)
Traverse City	36	(7)

Minnesota

Faribault	34	(6)
Mankato	64	(12)
Red Wing	79	(15)
Willmar	29	(5)
Winona	64	(12)

Mississippi

Cleveland	10	(2)
Columbus	13	(2)
Greenville	18	(3)
Laurel	18	(3)
Meridian	21	(4)
Tupelo	42	(8)
Vicksburg	16	(3)

Missouri

Cape Girardeau-Sikeston	24	(4)
Jefferson City	25	(5)
Poplar Bluff	12	(2)
Warrensburg	10	(2)

Montana

Bozeman	21	(4)
Helena	20	(4)
Missoula	24	(4)

Nebraska

Grand Island	29	(5)

Nevada

Carson City	74	(14)
Elko	84	(16)

New Hampshire

Concord	29	(5)
Keene	22	(4)

New Mexico

Alamogordo	32	(6)
Carlsbad	40	(8)
Clovis	22	(4)
Farmington	79	(15)
Gallup	69	(13)
Hobbs	53	(10)
Roswell	86	(17)

New York

Cortland	22	(4)

Gloversville	8	(1)
Ithaca	48	(9)
Kingston	25	(5)
Olean	21	(4)
Plattsburgh	22	(4)
Watertown	23	(4)

North Carolina

Albemarle	13	(2)
Eden	18	(3)
Havelock-New Bern	19	(3)
Henderson	18	(3)
Kinston	37	(7)
Lumberton	14	(2)
Roanoke Rapids	26	(5)
Sanford	26	(5)
Shelby	18	(3)
Statesville	30	(6)
Wilson	34	(6)

North Dakota

Minot	52	(10)

Ohio

Ashland	35	(7)
Athens	7	(1)
Chillicothe	6	(1)
Findlay-Fostoria-Tiffin	18	(3)
Fremont	18	(3)
Marion	12	(2)
Mount Vernon	6	(1)
New Philadelphia	74	(14)
Norwalk	11	(2)
Portsmouth	1	(0)
Sandusky	36	(7)
Sidney	20	(4)
Wooster	18	(3)
Zanesville	7	(1)

Oklahoma

Ardmore	26	(5)
Chickasha	4	(0)
Duncan	10	(2)
McAlester	14	(2)
Muskogee	21	(4)
Stillwater	49	(9)

Oregon

Albany-Corvallis	31	(6)
Bend	38	(7)
Coos Bay	24	(4)
Grants Pass	34	(6)
Klamath Falls	28	(5)
Pendleton	28	(5)
Roseburg	42	(8)

Pennsylvania

Chambersburg	12	(2)
New Castle	11	(2)
Pottsville	6	(1)

Rhode Island

Newport	32	(6)

South Carolina

Greenwood	20	(4)
Hilton Head Island	49	(9)

Tennessee

Cleveland	17	(3)
Columbia	25	(5)
Cookeville	20	(4)
Morristown	22	(4)
Tullahoma	18	(3)

Texas

Corsicana	15	(3)
Del Rio	14	(2)
Eagle Pass	21	(4)
Huntsville	40	(8)
Lufkin	17	(3)
Nacogdoches	13	(2)
Palestine	16	(3)
Paris	9	(1)

Utah		
Logan	43	(8)
St. George	93	(18)
Vermont		
Rutland	14	(2)
Virginia		
Blacksburg-Radford-Christiansburg	31	(6)
Harrisonburg	21	(4)
Martinsville	11	(2)
Staunton-Waynesboro	18	(3)
Winchester	31	(6)
Washington		
Aberdeen	33	(6)
Longview	107	(20)
Mount Vernon	42	(8)
Port Angeles	47	(9)
Walla Walla	80	(16)
Wenatchee	45	(9)
West Virginia		
Beckley	10	(2)
Clarksburg	15	(3)
Fairmont	5	(1)
Morgantown	24	(4)
Wisconsin		
Fond du Lac	31	(6)
Manitowoc	43	(8)
Stevens Point	43	(8)
Watertown	43	(8)
Wyoming		
Rock Springs	172	(20)

The Results

People begin strolling toward Mallory Square in Key West, Florida, about thirty minutes before sunset. They gather in small groups, gazing toward the Gulf of Mexico. Street entertainers and vendors go about their business as the crowd grows. An outsider would find no meaning in any of this activity. Until dark—when the people on the docks break into applause as the flaming red sun sinks below the watery horizon. Then they head back to town as the nightlife begins.

"Key West is intensely unlike any other place in the Union," boasts a brochure. The nightly sunset ceremony is just one example of the city's uniquely fun-loving character. More than one million tourists come here each year to dive for sunken treasure, go deep-sea fishing, lie on the long sandy beaches, and eat at the sidewalk cafes.

The Key West area earns first place in the diversions section, with 88 of a possible 100 points. The completion of the Overseas Highway in 1938, connecting this small coral island to the Florida mainland, opened the way for tourists to flock down the Keys. Key West responded by blossoming with amusement places, shops, restaurants, and bars to serve them. There remains plenty of space under the palms for outdoor activities, particularly water sports.

Up in the Pacific Northwest, about as far from Key West as you could go in the continental United States, Wenatchee, Washington, comes in second place in the diversion section. It trails Key West by just 2 points, with a total of 86 points. Like its location, outdoor life in Wenatchee is also miles from that of Key West. At the foot of the Wenatchee Mountains, the city is a popular destination for hikers and skiers. Other Western small cities dominate the top of the diversions list, especially those that are popular vacation spots and college towns.

Residents of the Hinesville, Georgia, area are more likely to greet the dawn with roll call than to salute the sunset with applause. Hinesville is a military town on the edge of Fort Stewart and Wright Army Air Field. The army base covers approximately half the land area of the micropolitan, and provides many on-base services, such as shopping and health care, for army families.

Hinesville residents, civilian and military, often make the short trip to nearby Savannah, Georgia, for an abundance of entertainment and shopping. They are likely to head for the local Georgia and South Carolina coasts for recreation. As a result, Hinesville scores just 14 points in the diversion section. Seven other southern cities join Hinesville on the bottom-ten list of entertainment availability.

Diversion Scores: Highs and Lows

Highest	Total Rating Points
1. Key West, Fla.	88
2. Wenatchee, Wash.	86
3. Bozeman, Mont.	83
4. Bend, Ore.	73
5. Hilton Head Island, S.C.	72
Rutland, Vt.	72
7. Traverse City, Mich.	71
8. Missoula, Mont.	69
9. Mason City, Iowa	68
Rock Springs, Wyo.	68
11. Helena, Mont.	67
12. Minot, N.Dak.	66
13. Aberdeen, Wash.	65
14. Grand Island, Nebr.	64
15. Longview, Wash.	62
Mount Vernon, Wash.	62
17. Brunswick, Ga.	61
Red Wing, Minn.	61
19. Coeur d'Alene, Idaho	60
20. Fairbanks, Alaska	59
Galesburg, Ill.	59
Hot Springs, Ark.	59
Port Angeles, Wash.	59
Salina, Kans.	59

Median	Total Rating Points
96. Meridian, Miss.	40
97. Poplar Bluff, Mo.	40

Lowest	Total Rating Points
183. Eden, N.C.	24
Martinsville, Va.	24
Radcliff-Elizabethtown, Ky.	24
Ruston, La.	24
Shelby, N.C.	24
189. Lumberton, N.C.	22
New Castle, Pa.	22
Wooster, Ohio	22
192. Owosso, Mich.	21
193. Hinesville, Ga.	14

Diversions Performance Comparison

	Key West, Florida	Micro median	Hinesville, Georgia
Total Points in Section	88	40	14
Rank in Section	1		193
Amusement Place Availability			
Establishments per 100,000 residents	210.3	45.7	13.6
Amusement Place points	(20)		(0)
Shopping Availability			
Establishments per 100,000 residents	1,232.3	655.4	343.0
Shopping points	(20)		(0)
Food and Drink Establishments Availability			
Establishments per 100,000 residents	399.8	167.9	73.0
Food and Drink points	(20)		(0)
Population Density			
Persons per square miles	82.0	93.7	113.5
Population Density points	(15)		(13)
Local Recreation Funding			
Annual per capita spending by local governments	$66	$27	$9
Local Recreation Funding points	(13)		(1)

Diversion Scores Area by Area

(Total diversion rating points)

Micro median	40
Alabama	
Albertville	44
Auburn-Opelika	27
Cullman	26
Selma	28
Talladega	26
Alaska	
Fairbanks	59
Arizona	
Prescott	58
Sierra Vista	46
Arkansas	
Blytheville	29
El Dorado	38
Hot Springs	59
Jonesboro	35
Russellville	38
Searcy	29
California	
Arcata-Eureka	57
El Centro-Calexico-Brawley	30
Hanford-Lemoore	28
Hollister	33
Connecticut	
Torrington	40
Florida	
Key West	88
Vero Beach	54
Georgia	
Brunswick	61
Dalton	34
Dublin	44
Gainesville	30
Hinesville	14
La Grange	38
Milledgeville	30
Rome	37
Statesboro	46
Thomasville	43
Valdosta	39
Waycross	37
Idaho	
Coeur d'Alene	60
Idaho Falls	54
Pocatello	48
Twin Falls	55
Illinois	
Carbondale	49
Danville	36
Freeport	37
Galesburg	59
Mattoon-Charleston	49
Ottawa	50
Quincy	48
Sterling	40
Indiana	
Columbus	43
Marion	34
Michigan City-La Porte	32
New Castle	28
Richmond	38
Vincennes	39
Iowa	
Ames	50
Burlington	55
Clinton	53
Mason City	68
Muscatine	51
Kansas	
Hutchinson	49
Manhattan	37
Salina	59
Kentucky	
Bowling Green	45
Frankfort	29
Madisonville	38
Paducah	41
Radcliff-Elizabethtown	24
Louisiana	
Hammond	24
New Iberia	31
Ruston	24
Maine	
Augusta-Waterville	44
Biddeford-Saco	48
Maryland	
Salisbury	37
Michigan	
Marquette	51
Mount Pleasant	38
Owosso	21
Traverse City	71

Area	Score
Minnesota	
Faribault	41
Mankato	52
Red Wing	61
Willmar	50
Winona	46
Mississippi	
Cleveland	27
Columbus	35
Greenville	30
Laurel	30
Meridian	40
Tupelo	46
Vicksburg	39
Missouri	
Cape Girardeau-Sikeston	45
Jefferson City	38
Poplar Bluff	40
Warrensburg	28
Montana	
Bozeman	83
Helena	67
Missoula	69
Nebraska	
Grand Island	64
Nevada	
Carson City	54
Elko	56
New Hampshire	
Concord	41
Keene	40
New Mexico	
Alamogordo	39
Carlsbad	41
Clovis	36
Farmington	47
Gallup	42
Hobbs	48
Roswell	53
New York	
Cortland	54
Gloversville	33
Ithaca	45
Kingston	44
Olean	48
Plattsburgh	46
Watertown	43
North Carolina	
Albemarle	28
Eden	24
Havelock-New Bern	33
Henderson	31
Kinston	39
Lumberton	22
Roanoke Rapids	34
Sanford	43
Shelby	24
Statesville	38
Wilson	35
North Dakota	
Minot	66
Ohio	
Ashland	41
Athens	35
Chillicothe	27
Findlay-Fostoria-Tiffin	42
Fremont	32
Marion	29
Mount Vernon	31
New Philadelphia	49
Norwalk	31
Portsmouth	28
Sandusky	48
Sidney	30
Wooster	22
Zanesville	41
Oklahoma	
Ardmore	45
Chickasha	27
Duncan	36
McAlester	32
Muskogee	36
Stillwater	46
Oregon	
Albany-Corvallis	40
Bend	73
Coos Bay	54
Grants Pass	50
Klamath Falls	50
Pendleton	51
Roseburg	52
Pennsylvania	
Chambersburg	26
New Castle	22
Pottsville	25
Rhode Island	
Newport	57
South Carolina	
Greenwood	40
Hilton Head Island	72
Tennessee	
Cleveland	26
Columbia	38
Cookeville	42
Morristown	27
Tullahoma	36

Texas	
Corsicana	33
Del Rio	34
Eagle Pass	27
Huntsville	29
Lufkin	29
Nacogdoches	30
Palestine	26
Paris	38

Utah	
Logan	36
St. George	58

Vermont	
Rutland	72

Virginia	
Blacksburg-Radford-Christiansburg	31
Harrisonburg	37
Martinsville	24
Staunton-Waynesboro	31
Winchester	47

Washington	
Aberdeen	65
Longview	62
Mount Vernon	62
Port Angeles	59
Walla Walla	47
Wenatchee	86

West Virginia	
Beckley	28
Clarksburg	34
Fairmont	27
Morgantown	36

Wisconsin	
Fond du Lac	41
Manitowoc	40
Stevens Point	49
Watertown	44

Wyoming	
Rock Springs	68

3

Economics

Shoppers vote with their wallets. Voters vote for their wallets. Politicians know this well.

Running against presidential incumbent Jimmy Carter in 1980, Ronald Reagan shrewdly asked, "Are you better off than you were four years ago?" During the 1992 elections, Bill Clinton's campaign staff reportedly hung a sign in Clinton headquarters aimed at incumbent George Bush. "It's the economy, stupid," the sign said.

Nearly every day we think about paying the bills, affording a new car or a vacation, saving toward retirement, or financing a child's college education. Having enough money for security tops the list of our greatest worries in survey after survey.

Economic anxiety ebbs and flows through the population depending on the overall economy, but it never disappears. And in the 1990s, economic anxiety has been riding high. Median household income refused to budge upward through the early years of the decade. For many households, it declined, despite full-time employment.

This section measures the economy of each micropolitan area by checking personal income and the change in personal income. It measures the health of the local retail and manufacturing segments and it charts the change in population as an indicator of the job market.

It was 1995 before the country's median household income had its first increase of the decade. Income in 1995 increased 2.4 percent over the previous year to reach $34,076, but that remained 4 percent below the levels of 1989, adjusted for inflation.

Men's earnings have taken the hardest hit, largely because men's earnings have been the highest. An adult man entering the work force full time between 1991 and 1993 earned an average weekly wage of $459—$39 less per week than four years earlier, adjusted for inflation. The share of adult men hired to full-time jobs that paid less than $400 per week rose from 53.6 percent in 1987–89 to 55.4 percent in 1991–93. A middle-class lifestyle in the 1990s increasingly requires two earners in the house.

But not all U.S. households have seen their incomes stall or slide. In the nation's most affluent households, incomes have been steadily rising. Between 1985 and 1995, the wealthiest 20 percent of households increased their incomes 17.3 percent, in constant dollars. The wealthiest 5 percent of households saw their income leap a spectacular 34.7 percent. That's a dizzying climb compared to the experience of the bottom 60 percent of households, where growth ranged from 0.5 percent to 1.7 percent over the same period.

Hard times for much of the country are taking their toll on more than pocketbooks. An increasing number of Americans no longer believe they can get ahead, according to the General Social Survey conducted by National Opinion Research Center. The share of Americans who agree that their family currently has a good chance to improve its standard of living fell from 70 percent in the mid-1980s to 61 percent in 1994. The share that disagreed more than doubled, reaching 25 percent. And while nearly two-thirds of respondents in 1994 said their standard of living was better than their parents', fewer than half expect their children to be able to say the same.

America's small cities can't promise large wages to cure your economic worries once and for all. Only one in five small cities has a median personal income comparable to the national average of $21,696 in 1994. Only ten micros have a personal income that tops the national average. But personal income in micropolitan America is growing more quickly than the national average. Residents in small cities saw their income increase an average of 5.8 percent between 1990 and 1994, compared with the national average of 2.9 percent.

And it can require less money to live in some small cities, too. Residents of micropolitan Danville, Illinois, were spending nineteen cents less per dollar than residents in the Chicago suburb of Schaumburg in 1996, according to the American Chamber of Commerce Research Association. Housing, health, and miscellaneous services usually exhibit the greatest differences. The $67 trip to the dentist in Schaumburg costs $43.50 in Danville. In New York state, the $8 movie in Manhattan costs $6 in micropolitan Cortland.

Ranking micropolitan America. The ideal small city would offer its residents well-paying jobs in a healthy local economy that is growing. Each area is tested in five categories:

1. Per Capita Income: Does the average person make a good wage, or is he or she struggling to get by?

2. Income Change: Are incomes rising adequately, or is pay stagnant or declining?

3. Manufacturing Productivity: How healthy is the industrial sector of the local economy?

4. Retail Sales: How about the commercial sector? Are local stores doing a strong business?

5. Population Change: Is a healthy economy sustaining the population and attracting new people to town, or are residents being forced to leave in search of work?

Per Capita Income

The kids may call it "Zero" Beach because its lights aren't as bright as Fort Lauderdale, but Vero Beach, Florida, has at least one major distinction. The city has the highest per capita personal income of U.S. small cities. The community boasts a personal income of $29,000 for each resident. That's $7,000 above the national average, and $11,000 above the micropolitan median.

Vero Beach has been busy attracting snow birds and retirees since the mid-1980s. The micro offers a popular alternative to the more congested, expensive Florida beach communities. And in defense of Vero Beach's poor entertainment reputation among thrill-seeking youth, check its amusement-availability rating in chapter 2. It scores comfortably above the national average.

Eagle Pass, Texas, has the lowest per capita income of the 193 micropolitans. This city on the Rio Grande is a port of entry for immigrants from Mexico. The population of Eagle Pass has grown rapidly in the 1990s, but the typically low income of newcomers has not.

Cities with the highest incomes are concentrated on the East Coast and in the Midwest. Southern cities dominate the list of the lowest incomes.

Source: Bureau of Economic Analysis, Washington, D.C. Data, published in 1997, are for 1994.

Scoring: Twenty points for a per capita income of $28,000 or more; no points for less than $9,000. The spacing is every $1,000 per capita.

Personal Income: Highs and Lows

	Per Capita Personal Income
Highest	**$**
1. Vero Beach, Fla.	28,977
2. Torrington, Conn.	25,912
3. Key West, Fla.	25,160
4. Concord, N.H.	24,734
5. Carson City, Nev.	24,422
6. Newport, R.I.	22,465
7. Columbus, Ind.	22,464
8. Salina, Kans.	22,125
9. Elko, Nev.	21,785
10. Muscatine, Iowa	21,742
Median	
96. Havelock-New Bern, N.C.	17,825
97. Vincennes, Ind.	17,818
Lowest	
184. Palestine, Tex.	14,067
185. McAlester, Okla.	13,969
186. Cleveland, Miss.	13,956
187. Hanford-Lemoore, Calif.	13,622
188. Athens, Ohio	13,506
189. Huntsville, Tex.	13,051
190. Del Rio, Tex.	11,830
191. Hinesville, Ga.	10,998
192. Gallup, N.Mex.	10,694
193. Eagle Pass, Tex.	8,306

Per Capita Income Area by Area

(Per capita personal annual income in dollars and rating points)

Micro median	17,822	
Alabama		
Albertville	17,222	(9)
Auburn-Opelika	15,538	(7)
Cullman	17,060	(9)
Selma	15,053	(7)
Talladega	14,341	(6)
Alaska		
Fairbanks	19,318	(11)
Arizona		
Prescott	14,764	(6)
Sierra Vista	16,543	(8)
Arkansas		
Blytheville	16,049	(8)
El Dorado	19,262	(11)
Hot Springs	18,916	(10)
Jonesboro	18,916	(10)
Russellville	16,475	(8)
Searcy	14,336	(6)
California		
Arcata-Eureka	18,105	(10)
El Centro-Calexico-Brawley	14,302	(6)
Hanford-Lemoore	13,622	(5)
Hollister	17,263	(9)
Connecticut		
Torrington	25,912	(17)
Florida		
Key West	25,160	(17)
Vero Beach	28,977	(20)
Georgia		
Brunswick	20,927	(12)
Dalton	20,460	(12)
Dublin	16,825	(8)
Gainesville	20,133	(12)
Hinesville	10,998	(2)
La Grange	17,671	(9)
Milledgeville	17,898	(9)
Rome	19,143	(11)
Statesboro	14,319	(6)
Thomasville	18,702	(10)
Valdosta	16,834	(8)
Waycross	15,674	(7)
Idaho		
Coeur d'Alene	18,886	(10)
Idaho Falls	18,933	(10)
Pocatello	16,413	(8)
Twin Falls	17,219	(9)
Illinois		
Carbondale	15,091	(7)
Danville	18,098	(10)
Freeport	20,833	(12)
Galesburg	18,304	(10)
Mattoon-Charleston	18,151	(10)
Ottawa	19,201	(11)
Quincy	19,409	(11)
Sterling	18,747	(10)
Indiana		
Columbus	22,464	(14)
Marion	18,545	(10)
Michigan City-La Porte	18,583	(10)
New Castle	18,885	(10)
Richmond	18,418	(10)
Vincennes	17,818	(9)
Iowa		
Ames	19,443	(11)
Burlington	19,801	(11)
Clinton	18,834	(10)

Mason City	20,120	(12)
Muscatine	21,742	(13)
Kansas		
Hutchinson	18,935	(10)
Manhattan	16,077	(8)
Salina	22,125	(14)
Kentucky		
Bowling Green	18,756	(10)
Frankfort	19,796	(11)
Madisonville	18,172	(10)
Paducah	20,614	(12)
Radcliff-Elizabethtown	15,300	(7)
Louisiana		
Hammond	14,566	(6)
New Iberia	16,053	(8)
Ruston	16,255	(8)
Maine		
Augusta-Waterville	19,652	(11)
Biddeford-Saco	19,813	(11)
Maryland		
Salisbury	19,030	(11)
Michigan		
Marquette	17,406	(9)
Mount Pleasant	16,151	(8)
Owosso	18,402	(10)
Traverse City	21,413	(13)
Minnesota		
Faribault	17,818	(9)
Mankato	18,975	(10)
Red Wing	20,278	(12)
Willmar	18,372	(10)
Winona	18,823	(10)
Mississippi		
Cleveland	13,956	(5)
Columbus	16,515	(8)
Greenville	15,100	(7)
Laurel	16,059	(8)
Meridian	17,782	(9)
Tupelo	19,164	(11)
Vicksburg	18,917	(10)
Missouri		
Cape Girardeau-Sikeston	17,687	(9)
Jefferson City	18,856	(10)
Poplar Bluff	16,225	(8)
Warrensburg	14,386	(6)
Montana		
Bozeman	18,320	(10)
Helena	19,402	(11)
Missoula	18,446	(10)
Nebraska		
Grand Island	19,581	(11)
Nevada		
Carson City	24,422	(16)
Elko	21,785	(13)
New Hampshire		
Concord	24,734	(16)
Keene	21,629	(13)
New Mexico		
Alamogordo	14,298	(6)
Carlsbad	16,083	(8)
Clovis	15,273	(7)
Farmington	14,670	(6)
Gallup	10,694	(2)
Hobbs	15,254	(7)
Roswell	15,675	(7)
New York		
Cortland	16,797	(8)
Gloversville	17,694	(9)
Ithaca	17,760	(9)

Area	Income	Rank
Kingston	19,894	(11)
Olean	15,686	(7)
Plattsburgh	16,663	(8)
Watertown	16,103	(8)
North Carolina		
Albemarle	16,799	(8)
Eden	17,785	(9)
Havelock-New Bern	17,825	(9)
Henderson	16,332	(8)
Kinston	18,036	(10)
Lumberton	14,644	(6)
Roanoke Rapids	15,016	(7)
Sanford	20,704	(12)
Shelby	17,282	(9)
Statesville	19,245	(11)
Wilson	19,454	(11)
North Dakota		
Minot	18,640	(10)
Ohio		
Ashland	17,265	(9)
Athens	13,506	(5)
Chillicothe	16,271	(8)
Findlay-Fostoria-Tiffin	19,647	(11)
Fremont	18,509	(10)
Marion	17,767	(9)
Mount Vernon	17,265	(9)
New Philadelphia	16,989	(8)
Norwalk	18,610	(10)
Portsmouth	14,811	(6)
Sandusky	21,205	(13)
Sidney	19,471	(11)
Wooster	19,055	(11)
Zanesville	17,575	(9)
Oklahoma		
Ardmore	17,002	(9)
Chickasha	14,589	(6)
Duncan	15,799	(7)
McAlester	13,969	(5)
Muskogee	14,699	(6)
Stillwater	15,570	(7)
Oregon		
Albany-Corvallis	18,777	(10)
Bend	20,341	(12)
Coos Bay	17,225	(9)
Grants Pass	16,263	(8)
Klamath Falls	16,419	(8)
Pendleton	16,748	(8)
Roseburg	16,900	(8)
Pennsylvania		
Chambersburg	19,216	(11)
New Castle	17,061	(9)
Pottsville	18,031	(10)
Rhode Island		
Newport	22,465	(14)
South Carolina		
Greenwood	17,649	(9)
Hilton Head Island	21,691	(13)
Tennessee		
Cleveland	18,309	(10)
Columbia	17,800	(9)
Cookeville	17,962	(9)
Morristown	17,611	(9)
Tullahoma	17,545	(9)
Texas		
Corsicana	17,532	(9)
Del Rio	11,830	(3)
Eagle Pass	8,306	(0)
Huntsville	13,051	(5)
Lufkin	17,274	(9)
Nacogdoches	15,986	(7)
Palestine	14,067	(6)
Paris	18,127	(10)

Utah		
Logan	15,447	(7)
St. George	14,489	(6)
Vermont		
Rutland	19,464	(11)
Virginia		
Blacksburg-Radford-Christiansburg	15,100	(7)
Harrisonburg	18,993	(10)
Martinsville	18,281	(10)
Staunton-Waynesboro	18,917	(10)
Winchester	19,699	(11)
Washington		
Aberdeen	17,547	(9)
Longview	19,159	(11)
Mount Vernon	20,177	(12)
Port Angeles	19,446	(11)
Walla Walla	17,360	(9)
Wenatchee	21,176	(13)
West Virginia		
Beckley	16,797	(8)
Clarksburg	17,797	(9)
Fairmont	16,785	(8)
Morgantown	19,602	(11)
Wisconsin		
Fond du Lac	21,183	(13)
Manitowoc	19,147	(11)
Stevens Point	18,004	(10)
Watertown	18,012	(10)
Wyoming		
Rock Springs	20,666	(12)

Income Change

Any community with visions of future greatness must base those dreams on economic expansion. That is particularly true of small cities. Should they be unable to offer the reasonable expectation of a stable, comfortable life, micropolitan areas will lose their brightest residents to their metropolitan neighbors.

This category measures each area's change in income between 1990 and 1994, the latest year for which personal income data are available at the micropolitan level. The period covers the recession of the early 1990s and the beginning of the recovery. Economic recovery has been uneven both throughout the country and among different types of households. Most sectors of the population have experienced a mild improvement in income. National per capita personal income rose just 2.9 percent between 1990 to 1994, adjusted for inflation. Most small-city residents fared better, however. The median increase for micropolitans was 5.8 percent.

Per capita incomes in Jonesboro, Arkansas, leapt ahead of the national average. Per capita income rose 24.2 percent during the four-year period, catching up to and then surpassing the national average income. Other micros in southern states such as Mississippi and Louisiana join Jonesboro in the top-ten list.

Income declined in more than a dozen micros between 1990 and 1994. In many of these small cities, the declines represent the loss of well-paying manufacturing jobs. In El Centro-Calexico-Brawley, California, the decline partially reflects an influx of immigrants with few initial job skills and low earning potential.

Southern micros show the most promising income growth rates. Northeastern states are most likely to be experiencing slow growth or decline in income.

Source: Bureau of Economic Analysis, Washington, D.C. Data, published in 1997, are for 1994.

Scoring: Twenty points for an increase in income of 19 percent or more; no points for a decrease. The space is every 1 percent rise in income.

Income Change: Highs and Lows

	Change in Per Capita Personal Income, 1990–94 (adjusted for inflation)
Highest	%
1. Jonesboro, Ark.	24.2
2. Cleveland, Miss.	18.2
3. Blytheville, Ark.	18.1
4. Hinesville, Ga.	17.9
5. Ruston, La.	16.0
6. Lumberton, N.C.	15.2
7. Morgantown, W.Va.	15.1
8. Greenville, Miss.	15.0
9. Vicksburg, Miss.	14.7
10. Hammond, La.	14.1
Median	
96. Eden, N.C.	5.8
97. Frankfort, Ky.	5.8
Lowest	
184. Augusta-Waterville, Maine	– 1.0
185. Biddeford-Saco, Maine	– 1.2
186. Roswell, N.Mex.	– 1.3
187. Staunton-Waynesboro, Va.	– 2.1
188. Martinsville, Va.	– 2.7
189. Kingston, N.Y.	– 3.4
190. Torrington, Conn.	– 3.9
191. Hanford-Lemoore, Calif.	– 4.6
192. Hollister, Calif.	– 9.1
193. El Centro-Calexico-Brawley, Calif.	–17.0

Income Change Area by Area

(Percent change in per capita personal income, 1990–94, adjusted for inflation, and rating points)

Area	Change	Points
Micro median	5.8	
Alabama		
Albertville	6.4	(7)
Auburn-Opelika	3.0	(4)
Cullman	8.3	(9)
Selma	10.0	(11)
Talladega	3.8	(4)
Alaska		
Fairbanks	– 0.6	(0)
Arizona		
Prescott	2.5	(3)
Sierra Vista	2.3	(3)
Arkansas		
Blytheville	18.1	(19)
El Dorado	9.0	(10)
Hot Springs	5.7	(6)
Jonesboro	24.2	(20)
Russellville	6.0	(7)
Searcy	5.6	(6)
California		
Arcata-Eureka	1.4	(2)
El Centro-Calexico-Brawley	–17.0	(0)
Hanford-Lemoore	– 4.6	(0)
Hollister	– 9.1	(0)
Connecticut		
Torrington	– 3.9	(0)
Florida		
Key West	4.1	(5)
Vero Beach	2.4	(3)
Georgia		
Brunswick	6.0	(7)
Dalton	8.2	(9)
Dublin	7.9	(8)
Gainesville	8.2	(9)
Hinesville	17.9	(18)
La Grange	2.7	(3)
Milledgeville	9.6	(10)
Rome	8.5	(9)
Statesboro	5.8	(6)
Thomasville	12.7	(13)
Valdosta	6.4	(7)
Waycross	8.4	(9)
Idaho		
Coeur d'Alene	7.2	(8)
Idaho Falls	2.2	(3)
Pocatello	4.7	(5)
Twin Falls	1.9	(2)
Illinois		
Carbondale	5.4	(6)
Danville	5.7	(6)
Freeport	3.0	(4)
Galesburg	4.8	(5)
Mattoon-Charleston	6.7	(7)
Ottawa	6.8	(7)
Quincy	5.6	(6)
Sterling	2.3	(3)
Indiana		
Columbus	11.2	(12)
Marion	6.1	(7)
Michigan City-La Porte	4.9	(5)
New Castle	9.2	(10)
Richmond	6.8	(7)
Vincennes	9.2	(10)

Iowa		
Ames	11.6	(12)
Burlington	5.3	(6)
Clinton	5.5	(6)
Mason City	6.4	(7)
Muscatine	8.6	(9)
Kansas		
Hutchinson	4.5	(5)
Manhattan	6.9	(7)
Salina	3.0	(4)
Kentucky		
Bowling Green	11.0	(12)
Frankfort	5.8	(6)
Madisonville	1.1	(2)
Paducah	7.4	(8)
Radcliff-Elizabethtown	4.4	(5)
Louisiana		
Hammond	14.1	(15)
New Iberia	8.6	(9)
Ruston	16.0	(17)
Maine		
Augusta-Waterville	– 1.0	(0)
Biddeford-Saco	– 1.2	(0)
Maryland		
Salisbury	1.8	(2)
Michigan		
Marquette	10.2	(11)
Mount Pleasant	5.7	(6)
Owosso	7.7	(8)
Traverse City	10.7	(11)
Minnesota		
Faribault	3.9	(4)
Mankato	9.6	(10)
Red Wing	8.5	(9)
Willmar	4.2	(5)
Winona	7.6	(8)
Mississippi		
Cleveland	18.2	(19)
Columbus	4.1	(5)
Greenville	15.0	(16)
Laurel	12.6	(13)
Meridian	9.3	(10)
Tupelo	10.9	(11)
Vicksburg	14.7	(15)
Missouri		
Cape Girardeau-Sikeston	5.9	(6)
Jefferson City	3.2	(4)
Poplar Bluff	10.3	(11)
Warrensburg	2.9	(3)
Montana		
Bozeman	10.8	(11)
Helena	8.1	(9)
Missoula	8.5	(9)
Nebraska		
Grand Island	6.9	(7)
Nevada		
Carson City	3.3	(4)
Elko	6.0	(7)
New Hampshire		
Concord	6.9	(7)
Keene	4.4	(5)
New Mexico		
Alamogordo	4.1	(5)
Carlsbad	1.9	(2)
Clovis	3.4	(4)
Farmington	6.6	(7)
Gallup	7.4	(8)
Hobbs	2.9	(3)
Roswell	– 1.3	(0)
New York		
Cortland	4.5	(5)

Area		
Gloversville	4.9	(5)
Ithaca	2.7	(3)
Kingston	– 3.4	(0)
Olean	– 0.3	(0)
Plattsburgh	3.5	(4)
Watertown	– 0.4	(0)
North Carolina		
Albemarle	– 0.8	(0)
Eden	5.8	(6)
Havelock-New Bern	10.9	(11)
Henderson	4.8	(5)
Kinston	9.4	(10)
Lumberton	15.2	(16)
Roanoke Rapids	4.9	(5)
Sanford	11.5	(12)
Shelby	3.4	(4)
Statesville	6.3	(7)
Wilson	7.7	(8)
North Dakota		
Minot	10.3	(11)
Ohio		
Ashland	6.2	(7)
Athens	7.0	(8)
Chillicothe	8.6	(9)
Findlay-Fostoria-Tiffin	4.1	(5)
Fremont	2.1	(3)
Marion	7.6	(8)
Mount Vernon	8.5	(9)
New Philadelphia	3.6	(4)
Norwalk	2.9	(3)
Portsmouth	6.2	(7)
Sandusky	8.7	(9)
Sidney	4.2	(5)
Wooster	7.4	(8)
Zanesville	8.2	(9)
Oklahoma		
Ardmore	4.9	(5)
Chickasha	3.9	(4)
Duncan	3.5	(4)
McAlester	1.0	(2)
Muskogee	2.2	(3)
Stillwater	4.6	(5)
Oregon		
Albany-Corvallis	8.3	(9)
Bend	2.2	(3)
Coos Bay	2.9	(3)
Grants Pass	1.6	(2)
Klamath Falls	3.6	(4)
Pendleton	4.6	(5)
Roseburg	2.9	(3)
Pennsylvania		
Chambersburg	3.3	(4)
New Castle	2.1	(3)
Pottsville	2.4	(3)
Rhode Island		
Newport	– 0.6	(0)
South Carolina		
Greenwood	5.2	(6)
Hilton Head Island	1.8	(2)
Tennessee		
Cleveland	6.5	(7)
Columbia	8.6	(9)
Cookeville	10.0	(11)
Morristown	9.4	(10)
Tullahoma	7.1	(8)
Texas		
Corsicana	9.6	(10)
Del Rio	3.5	(4)
Eagle Pass	6.5	(7)
Huntsville	2.0	(3)
Lufkin	4.2	(5)
Nacogdoches	7.4	(8)
Palestine	6.9	(7)
Paris	8.9	(9)

Utah		
Logan	10.7	(11)
St. George	8.3	(9)
Vermont		
Rutland	4.4	(5)
Virginia		
Blacksburg-Radford-Christiansburg	2.1	(3)
Harrisonburg	4.7	(5)
Martinsville	– 2.7	(0)
Staunton-Waynesboro	– 2.1	(0)
Winchester	– 0.5	(0)
Washington		
Aberdeen	0.5	(1)
Longview	1.8	(2)
Mount Vernon	0.5	(1)
Port Angeles	– 0.9	(0)
Walla Walla	0.4	(1)
Wenatchee	7.9	(8)
West Virginia		
Beckley	7.3	(8)
Clarksburg	9.3	(10)
Fairmont	3.1	(4)
Morgantown	15.1	(16)
Wisconsin		
Fond du Lac	7.6	(8)
Manitowoc	7.7	(8)
Stevens Point	6.9	(7)
Watertown	6.0	(7)
Wyoming		
Rock Springs	9.3	(10)

Manufacturing Productivity

For decades, manufacturing employment has been on the decline. Almost all employment growth in recent memory has occurred in the service sector. But for many Americans, a job in manufacturing remains the key to a better wage, because manufacturing jobs almost always pay more than service jobs. "Manufacturing is the traditional route for the relatively low-educated or low-skilled into the middle class," says Steven Malin, an economist for the Conference Board. As such, it can promote a strong and stable local economy.

This category estimates the strength of each area's manufacturing base. It begins with a statistic known as "value added by manufacture," which is the price of a finished item minus all of the costs to produce it (such as labor, materials, and electricity). The Census Bureau, which conducts a comprehensive inventory of manufacturers every five years, considers this the best measure of manufacturing strength.

For our purposes, this figure is then divided by the number of production workers in the plant, creating a per capita rating that can be easily compared among cities. The average for all U.S. manufacturing industries is $122,387.

Manufacturing represents less than 3 percent of employment in Fairbanks, Alaska, but that small share is surprisingly powerful. Fairbanks has the highest value added by manufacture, at $446,667 per worker. The strength of Fairbanks's manufacturing is reflected in a second measure, also. Production workers earn an average annual wage of $32,000, compared with the national average production worker's wage of $24,185.

Helena, Montana, has the lowest value added by manufacture rating, at $36,667. This is less than half the median of small cities.

Small cities with high per capita value added by manufacture are located throughout the country, but they predominate in Northeastern and Midwestern industrial regions. The South has the largest share of small cities with low ratings.

Source: 1992 Census of Manufacturers, Economics and Statistics Administration, U.S. Bureau of the Census, Washington, D.C. These data, published in 1996, are for 1992.

Scoring: Twenty points for value added by manufacture of $227,500 or more; no points for less than $37,500. The spacing is every $10,000.

Manufacturing Productivity: Highs and Lows

	Value Added per Production Worker
Highest	**$**
1. Fairbanks, Alaska	446,667
2. Rock Springs, Wyo.	427,200
3. Newport, R.I.	227,692
4. Muscatine, Iowa	207,333
5. Wilson, N.C.	203,952
6. Ames, Iowa	198,625
7. Gallup, N.Mex.	195,008
8. Clinton, Iowa	184,805
9. Eden, N.C.	174,041
10. Plattsburgh, N.Y.	170,000
Median	
96. Norwalk, Ohio	90,695
97. Chambersburg, Pa.	90,483
Lowest	
184. Cullman, Ala.	55,872
185. Albertville, Ala.	55,088
186. Albemarle, N.C.	54,882
187. Gloversville, N.Y.	53,030
188. Cleveland, Miss.	52,636
189. Henderson, N.C.	50,320
190. Alamogordo, N.Mex.	39,167
191. Eagle Pass, Tex.	37,500
192. Palestine, Tex.	37,286
193. Helena, Mont.	36,667

Manufacturing Productivity Area by Area

(Manufacture value added in dollars per production worker and rating points)

Area	Value added	Rating
Micro median	90,589	
Alabama		
Albertville	55,088	(2)
Auburn-Opelika	100,937	(7)
Cullman	55,872	(2)
Selma	62,837	(3)
Talladega	70,770	(4)
Alaska		
Fairbanks	446,667	(20)
Arizona		
Prescott	81,550	(5)
Sierra Vista	108,000	(8)
Arkansas		
Blytheville	105,779	(7)
El Dorado	84,682	(5)
Hot Springs	64,520	(3)
Jonesboro	67,167	(3)
Russellville	82,333	(5)
Searcy	79,941	(5)
California		
Arcata-Eureka	114,143	(8)
El Centro-Calexico-Brawley	75,000	(4)
Hanford-Lemoore	98,083	(7)
Hollister	124,222	(9)
Connecticut		
Torrington	117,520	(9)
Florida		
Key West	99,000	(7)
Vero Beach	109,750	(8)
Georgia		
Brunswick	123,167	(9)
Dalton	96,254	(6)
Dublin	75,850	(4)
Gainesville	81,211	(5)
Hinesville	108,250	(8)
La Grange	73,239	(4)
Milledgeville	61,576	(3)
Rome	81,775	(5)
Statesboro	75,765	(4)
Thomasville	98,067	(7)
Valdosta	97,511	(7)
Waycross	70,821	(4)
Idaho		
Coeur d'Alene	91,833	(6)
Idaho Falls	124,900	(9)
Pocatello	169,421	(14)
Twin Falls	71,966	(4)
Illinois		
Carbondale	76,000	(4)
Danville	130,689	(10)
Freeport	95,763	(6)
Galesburg	73,026	(4)
Mattoon-Charleston	135,533	(10)
Ottawa	100,036	(7)
Quincy	94,768	(6)
Sterling	89,083	(6)
Indiana		
Columbus	116,464	(8)
Marion	88,321	(6)
Michigan City-La Porte	97,444	(6)
New Castle	82,280	(5)
Richmond	91,688	(6)
Vincennes	72,571	(4)
Iowa		
Ames	198,625	(17)
Burlington	111,087	(8)
Clinton	184,805	(15)

Mason City	88,250	(6)
Muscatine	207,333	(17)
Kansas		
Hutchinson	85,559	(5)
Manhattan	126,000	(9)
Salina	101,560	(7)
Kentucky		
Bowling Green	101,560	(7)
Frankfort	121,387	(9)
Madisonville	65,000	(3)
Paducah	152,708	(12)
Radcliff-Elizabethtown	106,846	(7)
Louisiana		
Hammond	62,550	(3)
New Iberia	69,947	(4)
Ruston	84,636	(5)
Maine		
Augusta-Waterville	76,653	(4)
Biddeford-Saco	74,225	(4)
Maryland		
Salisbury	86,703	(5)
Michigan		
Marquette	68,600	(4)
Mount Pleasant	93,923	(6)
Owosso	70,480	(4)
Traverse City	97,526	(7)
Minnesota		
Faribault	109,267	(8)
Mankato	94,653	(6)
Red Wing	97,970	(7)
Willmar	60,100	(3)
Winona	84,184	(5)
Mississippi		
Cleveland	52,636	(2)
Columbus	105,724	(7)
Greenville	89,111	(6)
Laurel	69,657	(4)
Meridian	81,837	(5)
Tupelo	69,038	(4)
Vicksburg	112,724	(8)
Missouri		
Cape Girardeau-Sikeston	137,000	(10)
Jefferson City	131,909	(10)
Poplar Bluff	71,350	(4)
Warrensburg	61,462	(3)
Montana		
Bozeman	79,714	(5)
Helena	36,667	(0)
Missoula	83,313	(5)
Nebraska		
Grand Island	75,455	(4)
Nevada		
Carson City	89,182	(6)
Elko	83,500	(5)
New Hampshire		
Concord	88,196	(6)
Keene	102,750	(7)
New Mexico		
Alamogordo	39,167	(1)
Carlsbad	83,106	(5)
Clovis	89,000	(6)
Farmington	89,875	(6)
Gallup	195,008	(16)
Hobbs	140,000	(11)
Roswell	79,611	(5)
New York		
Cortland	90,190	(6)
Gloversville	53,030	(2)

Ithaca	100,115	(7)
Kingston	81,500	(5)
Olean	119,786	(9)
Plattsburgh	170,000	(14)
Watertown	95,688	(6)
North Carolina		
Albemarle	54,882	(2)
Eden	174,041	(14)
Havelock-New Bern	89,029	(6)
Henderson	50,320	(2)
Kinston	110,540	(8)
Lumberton	68,289	(4)
Roanoke Rapids	62,955	(3)
Sanford	84,584	(5)
Shelby	81,694	(5)
Statesville	73,220	(4)
Wilson	203,952	(17)
North Dakota		
Minot	98,200	(7)
Ohio		
Ashland	76,154	(4)
Athens	98,889	(7)
Chillicothe	125,000	(9)
Findlay-Fostoria-Tiffin	108,722	(8)
Fremont	138,115	(11)
Marion	126,180	(9)
Mount Vernon	114,654	(8)
New Philadelphia	91,316	(6)
Norwalk	90,695	(6)
Portsmouth	96,467	(6)
Sandusky	115,417	(8)
Sidney	103,667	(7)
Wooster	111,873	(8)
Zanesville	81,841	(5)
Oklahoma		
Ardmore	127,739	(10)
Chickasha	145,571	(11)
Duncan	101,462	(7)
McAlester	63,000	(3)
Muskogee	114,514	(8)
Stillwater	120,333	(9)
Oregon		
Albany-Corvallis	131,071	(10)
Bend	74,303	(4)
Coos Bay	79,783	(5)
Grants Pass	72,714	(4)
Klamath Falls	80,241	(5)
Pendleton	63,300	(3)
Roseburg	89,016	(6)
Pennsylvania		
Chambersburg	90,483	(6)
New Castle	91,512	(6)
Pottsville	75,023	(4)
Rhode Island		
Newport	227,692	(20)
South Carolina		
Greenwood	84,095	(5)
Hilton Head Island	78,625	(5)
Tennessee		
Cleveland	131,439	(10)
Columbia	125,753	(9)
Cookeville	102,559	(7)
Morristown	64,266	(3)
Tullahoma	77,783	(5)
Texas		
Corsicana	93,625	(6)
Del Rio	67,539	(4)
Eagle Pass	37,500	(1)
Huntsville	72,800	(4)
Lufkin	74,897	(4)
Nacogdoches	78,281	(5)
Palestine	37,286	(0)
Paris	146,600	(11)

Utah		
Logan	86,177	(5)
St. George	88,000	(6)
Vermont		
Rutland	83,769	(5)
Virginia		
Blacksburg-Radford-Christiansburg	95,148	(6)
Harrisonburg	128,032	(10)
Martinsville	58,206	(3)
Staunton-Waynesboro	137,482	(10)
Winchester	112,833	(8)
Washington		
Aberdeen	101,186	(7)
Longview	111,234	(8)
Mount Vernon	134,645	(10)
Port Angeles	112,211	(8)
Walla Walla	111,000	(8)
Wenatchee	103,278	(7)
West Virginia		
Beckley	76,800	(4)
Clarksburg	69,067	(4)
Fairmont	75,750	(4)
Morgantown	135,438	(10)
Wisconsin		
Fond du Lac	91,351	(6)
Manitowoc	82,315	(5)
Stevens Point	122,071	(9)
Watertown	116,596	(8)
Wyoming		
Rock Springs	427,200	(20)

Retail Sales

One way to quickly gauge the economic health of an unfamiliar community is to glance at its shopping areas. One city may have a busy Main Street or a new mall on the highway out of town; the second may be characterized by vacant storefronts or old shopping centers in disrepair. The message is clear.

This category ranks each area according to its annual volume of retail trade. The total amount of money taken in by all stores is divided by the number of local residents. The average for the entire country is $7,431 of retail spending for every man, woman, and child.

Stores in Carson City, Nevada, do the briskest business. Per capita sales amount to $12,656 annually in the state capital. The largest share of sales goes to the city's thirty-five auto dealerships, who sold $147 million in cars in 1992, the latest year for which data are available. Car sales accounted for 28 percent of all retail sales in the city that year, or $3,443 for every man, woman, and child. Food stores followed car dealerships in sales volume, with a 24 percent share, or $3,011 per resident. Residents spent over $900 per person in restaurants and taverns; but just $134 apiece on clothing and accessories.

Residents of small cities with low per capita retail sales do their shopping outside of town. Hinesville, Georgia, has the lowest rating, with just $3,388 spent per resident in retail stores. Many of Hinesville's large share of military families shop on the army base. Other residents make the short drive to Savannah. In Hollister, California, residents spend just $4,108 at the local stores. They are more likely to shop in the larger nearby cities of Watsonville, Salinas, and San Jose.

Strong retail centers are evenly distributed around the country. Most of their weak counterparts are in the Midwest.

Source: 1992 Census of Retail, Economics and Statistics Administration, U.S. Census Bureau, Washington, D.C. The bureau collects comprehensive statistics on local retail trade every five years. This data is for 1992.

Scoring: Twenty points for per capita sales of $11,600 or more, no points for sales less than $4,000. The spacing is every $400.

Retail Sales: Highs and Lows

	Annual Per Capita Retail Sales
Highest	**$**
1. Carson City, Nev.	12,656
2. Traverse City, Mich.	11,733
3. Paducah, Ky.	11,596
4. Albertville, Ala.	11,549
5. Key West, Fla.	10,673
6. Grand Island, Nebr.	10,615
7. Missoula, Mont.	10,484
8. Bend, Ore.	10,482
9. Tupelo, Miss.	10,288
10. Keene, N.H.	10,267
Median	
96. Port Angeles, Wash.	7,264
97. Stevens Point, Wisc.	7,259
Lowest	
184. Ashland, Ohio	5,349
185. Sidney, Ohio	5,146
186. Logan, Utah	5,135
187. Chickasha, Okla.	4,845
188. Mount Vernon, Ohio	4,835
189. Cleveland, Miss.	4,596
190. Warrensburg, Mo.	4,465
191. Hanford-Lemoore, Calif.	4,322
192. Hollister, Calif.	4,108
193. Hinesville, Ga.	3,388

Retail Sales Area by Area

(Per capita annual retail sales in dollars and rating points)

Micro median	7,262	
Alabama		
Albertville	11,549	(19)
Auburn-Opelika	7,024	(8)
Cullman	6,889	(8)
Selma	5,886	(5)
Talladega	5,402	(4)
Alaska		
Fairbanks	8,433	(12)
Arizona		
Prescott	7,455	(9)
Sierra Vista	5,426	(4)
Arkansas		
Blytheville	5,818	(5)
El Dorado	6,872	(8)
Hot Springs	9,066	(13)
Jonesboro	9,181	(13)
Russellville	7,793	(10)
Searcy	6,553	(7)
California		
Arcata-Eureka	7,280	(9)
El Centro-Calexico-Brawley	6,572	(7)
Hanford-Lemoore	4,344	(1)
Hollister	4,099	(1)
Connecticut		
Torrington	7,169	(8)
Florida		
Key West	10,673	(17)
Vero Beach	8,577	(12)
Georgia		
Brunswick	9,634	(15)
Dalton	9,399	(14)
Dublin	7,926	(10)
Gainesville	7,897	(10)
Hinesville	3,388	(0)
La Grange	6,922	(8)
Milledgeville	6,809	(8)
Rome	7,371	(9)
Statesboro	7,264	(9)
Thomasville	7,609	(10)
Valdosta	8,949	(13)
Waycross	7,227	(9)
Idaho		
Coeur d'Alene	9,311	(14)
Idaho Falls	9,308	(14)
Pocatello	7,316	(9)
Twin Falls	10,070	(16)
Illinois		
Carbondale	7,072	(8)
Danville	6,028	(6)
Freeport	6,880	(8)
Galesburg	7,264	(9)
Mattoon-Charleston	7,090	(8)
Ottawa	7,706	(10)
Quincy	7,696	(10)
Sterling	6,198	(6)
Indiana		
Columbus	8,098	(11)
Marion	6,995	(8)
Michigan City-La Porte	7,387	(9)
New Castle	6,547	(7)
Richmond	8,284	(11)
Vincennes	7,481	(9)
Iowa		
Ames	7,423	(9)
Burlington	8,232	(11)
Clinton	6,967	(8)

Mason City	9,621	(15)
Muscatine	7,126	(8)
Kansas		
Hutchinson	7,437	(9)
Manhattan	5,741	(5)
Salina	9,690	(15)
Kentucky		
Bowling Green	9,813	(15)
Frankfort	7,489	(9)
Madisonville	6,890	(8)
Paducah	11,596	(19)
Radcliff-Elizabethtown	8,479	(12)
Louisiana		
Hammond	7,802	(10)
New Iberia	6,931	(8)
Ruston	6,001	(6)
Maine		
Augusta-Waterville	8,868	(13)
Biddeford-Saco	6,785	(7)
Maryland		
Salisbury	9,701	(15)
Michigan		
Marquette	7,041	(8)
Mount Pleasant	7,284	(9)
Owosso	6,590	(7)
Traverse City	11,733	(20)
Minnesota		
Faribault	6,408	(7)
Mankato	7,830	(10)
Red Wing	6,780	(7)
Willmar	8,186	(11)
Winona	6,772	(7)
Mississippi		
Cleveland	4,596	(2)
Columbus	7,266	(9)
Greenville	6,439	(7)
Laurel	5,803	(5)
Meridian	8,318	(11)
Tupelo	10,288	(16)
Vicksburg	7,420	(9)
Missouri		
Cape Girardeau-Sikeston	7,952	(10)
Jefferson City	6,997	(8)
Poplar Bluff	8,483	(12)
Warrensburg	4,465	(2)
Montana		
Bozeman	9,898	(15)
Helena	8,338	(11)
Missoula	10,484	(17)
Nebraska		
Grand Island	10,615	(17)
Nevada		
Carson City	12,656	(20)
Elko	6,967	(8)
New Hampshire		
Concord	8,662	(12)
Keene	10,267	(16)
New Mexico		
Alamogordo	5,395	(4)
Carlsbad	6,198	(6)
Clovis	7,039	(8)
Farmington	7,519	(9)
Gallup	7,549	(9)
Hobbs	6,288	(6)
Roswell	6,279	(6)
New York		
Cortland	7,725	(10)
Gloversville	5,662	(5)
Ithaca	6,520	(7)

Kingston	6,728	(7)
Olean	5,699	(5)
Plattsburgh	8,186	(11)
Watertown	7,693	(10)
North Carolina		
Albemarle	6,277	(6)
Eden	5,847	(5)
Havelock-New Bern	7,185	(8)
Henderson	8,127	(11)
Kinston	8,275	(11)
Lumberton	6,634	(7)
Roanoke Rapids	6,602	(7)
Sanford	10,233	(16)
Shelby	6,320	(6)
Statesville	7,224	(9)
Wilson	7,537	(9)
North Dakota		
Minot	9,185	(13)
Ohio		
Ashland	5,349	(4)
Athens	5,466	(4)
Chillicothe	6,097	(6)
Findlay-Fostoria-Tiffin	5,717	(5)
Fremont	6,087	(6)
Marion	7,208	(9)
Mount Vernon	4,835	(3)
New Philadelphia	7,272	(9)
Norwalk	5,965	(5)
Portsmouth	5,944	(5)
Sandusky	8,174	(11)
Sidney	5,146	(3)
Wooster	5,689	(5)
Zanesville	7,148	(8)
Oklahoma		
Ardmore	7,626	(10)
Chickasha	4,845	(3)
Duncan	6,340	(6)
McAlester	6,314	(6)
Muskogee	6,482	(7)
Stillwater	6,170	(6)
Oregon		
Albany-Corvallis	6,050	(6)
Bend	10,482	(17)
Coos Bay	7,500	(9)
Grants Pass	7,743	(10)
Klamath Falls	7,551	(9)
Pendleton	6,927	(8)
Roseburg	6,101	(6)
Pennsylvania		
Chambersburg	6,460	(7)
New Castle	5,820	(5)
Pottsville	5,855	(5)
Rhode Island		
Newport	7,373	(9)
South Carolina		
Greenwood	8,035	(11)
Hilton Head Island	10,180	(16)
Tennessee		
Cleveland	7,634	(10)
Columbia	7,485	(9)
Cookeville	9,115	(13)
Morristown	8,839	(13)
Tullahoma	7,545	(9)
Texas		
Corsicana	6,903	(8)
Del Rio	5,635	(5)
Eagle Pass	6,203	(6)
Huntsville	5,579	(4)
Lufkin	6,928	(8)
Nacogdoches	7,291	(9)
Palestine	5,426	(4)
Paris	7,116	(8)

Utah		
Logan	5,135	(3)
St. George	8,225	(11)
Vermont		
Rutland	8,472	(12)
Virginia		
Blacksburg-Radford-Christiansburg	7,211	(9)
Harrisonburg	7,782	(10)
Martinsville	6,908	(8)
Staunton-Waynesboro	6,552	(7)
Winchester	9,498	(14)
Washington		
Aberdeen	6,669	(7)
Longview	7,892	(10)
Mount Vernon	9,751	(15)
Port Angeles	7,264	(9)
Walla Walla	5,585	(4)
Wenatchee	9,330	(14)
West Virginia		
Beckley	8,138	(11)
Clarksburg	8,533	(12)
Fairmont	6,992	(8)
Morgantown	7,357	(9)
Wisconsin		
Fond du Lac	7,454	(9)
Manitowoc	5,756	(5)
Stevens Point	7,259	(9)
Watertown	5,538	(4)
Wyoming		
Rock Springs	8,510	(12)

Population Change

St. George, Utah, is located on Interstate 15, in the very southwestern corner of Utah. Ask anyone the way: it's the fastest-growing small city in the country, located on a road that runs between two of the fastest-growing big cities in the country—Provo-Orem, Utah, and Las Vegas, Nevada. The population of St. George increased 34 percent between 1990 and 1994. Compare that to the national average of 4 percent.

Population growth usually indicates a healthy economy—people usually follow the jobs. And by this measure, the Mountain States are booming. Their story in the 1990s is one of steady and rapid population growth. But it's no longer silver and iron mining that draws newcomers to St. George. The city became a popular destination for retirees in the 1980s. In the 1990s, working-age families were drawn by the healthy job market, furthering the boom in construction, service, and retail businesses.

Manufacturing towns through the Midwest and South are seeing the largest population drain as residents follow on the heels of jobs that have left town. Five micropolitans saw their populations decrease by 1 percent or more in the early 1990s. Blytheville, Arkansas, experienced the most dramatic drop by far—11.5 percent between 1990 and 1994.

Slow population growth may not guarantee an ailing economy, however. A small city with modest population influx may simply indicate a stable economy without a boom or a bust. And if you're looking for a quieter life, maybe a fast-growing micro is not for you. San Louis Obispo, California, the top-rated micro in the first edition of this book, grew so quickly that it grew right into its own metropolitan city.

Fast-growing micros are located in the Mountain States and along the Mexican border (due to high immigration). Micros that are experiencing slow growth or population loss are scattered throughout the East, South, and Midwest.

Source: Population Division, U.S. Bureau of the Census, Washington, D.C. Data are for 1990–94.

Scoring: Twenty points for population growth of 28 percent or higher; no points for a population loss. The spacing is every 1.5 percent.

Population Change: Highs and Lows

	Percent Change in Population, 1990–94
Highest	
1. St. George, Utah	34.3
2. El Centro-Calexico-Brawley, Calif.	25.4
3. Coeur d'Alene, Idaho	25.1
4. Eagle Pass, Tex.	21.8
5. Bend, Ore.	21.5
6. Elko, Nev.	20.9
7. Prescott, Ariz.	18.8
8. Columbia, Tenn.	16.6
9. Mount Vernon, Wash.	15.4
10. Bozeman, Mont.	14.6
Median	
96. Morristown, Tenn.	3.8
97. Grand Island, Nebr.	3.7
Lowest	
184. Marion, Ind.	– 0.4
185. Danville, Ill.	– 0.5
Mason City, Iowa	– 0.5
187. Cleveland, Miss.	– 0.7
188. Martinsville, Va.	– 0.9
189. El Dorado, Ark.	– 1.0
Marquette, Mich.	– 1.0
191. Greenville, Miss.	– 1.7
192. Newport, R.I.	– 4.0
193. Blytheville, Ark.	–11.5

Population Change Area by Area

(Percent change in population, 1990–94, and rating points)

Area	Change	Points
Micro median	3.8	
Alabama		
Albertville	8.4	(6)
Auburn-Opelika	5.4	(4)
Cullman	5.9	(4)
Selma	– 0.3	(0)
Talladega	2.6	(2)
Alaska		
Fairbanks	9.0	(7)
Arizona		
Prescott	18.8	(13)
Sierra Vista	10.1	(7)
Arkansas		
Blytheville	–11.5	(0)
El Dorado	– 1.0	(0)
Hot Springs	8.7	(6)
Jonesboro	6.5	(5)
Russellville	9.4	(7)
Searcy	8.9	(6)
California		
Arcata-Eureka	2.2	(2)
El Centro-Calexico-Brawley	25.4	(17)
Hanford-Lemoore	9.3	(7)
Hollister	11.9	(8)
Connecticut		
Torrington	2.5	(2)
Florida		
Key West	4.8	(4)
Vero Beach	6.0	(5)
Georgia		
Brunswick	4.1	(3)
Dalton	6.1	(5)
Dublin	5.7	(4)
Gainesville	10.2	(7)
Hinesville	11.7	(8)
La Grange	3.7	(3)
Milledgeville	4.6	(4)
Rome	2.5	(2)
Statesboro	10.9	(8)
Thomasville	3.3	(3)
Valdosta	8.3	(6)
Waycross	2.6	(2)
Idaho		
Coeur d'Alene	25.1	(17)
Idaho Falls	9.7	(7)
Pocatello	8.2	(6)
Twin Falls	9.4	(7)
Illinois		
Carbondale	0.6	(1)
Danville	– 0.5	(0)
Freeport	2.0	(2)
Galesburg	– 0.2	(0)
Mattoon-Charleston	1.1	(2)
Ottawa	2.3	(2)
Quincy	2.5	(2)
Sterling	0.3	(1)
Indiana		
Columbus	5.3	(4)
Marion	– 0.4	(0)
Michigan City-La Porte	2.7	(2)
New Castle	1.8	(2)
Richmond	0.8	(1)
Vincennes	0.9	(1)
Iowa		
Ames	0.3	(1)
Burlington	0.6	(1)
Clinton	– 0.1	(0)

Mason City	– 0.5	(0)
Muscatine	3.5	(3)
Kansas		
Hutchinson	0.4	(1)
Manhattan	4.3	(3)
Salina	4.2	(3)
Kentucky		
Bowling Green	6.8	(5)
Frankfort	3.3	(3)
Madisonville	0.3	(1)
Paducah	2.9	(2)
Radcliff-Elizabethtown	1.3	(1)
Louisiana		
Hammond	6.6	(5)
New Iberia	3.7	(3)
Ruston	3.3	(3)
Maine		
Augusta-Waterville	1.0	(1)
Biddeford-Saco	2.9	(2)
Maryland		
Salisbury	5.6	(4)
Michigan		
Marquette	– 1.0	(0)
Mount Pleasant	1.7	(2)
Owosso	2.8	(2)
Traverse City	8.6	(6)
Minnesota		
Faribault	4.8	(4)
Mankato	1.2	(1)
Red Wing	3.3	(3)
Willmar	4.6	(4)
Winona	1.1	(1)
Mississippi		
Cleveland	– 0.7	(0)
Columbus	2.4	(2)
Greenville	– 1.7	(0)
Laurel	1.6	(2)
Meridian	1.1	(1)
Tupelo	7.9	(6)
Vicksburg	2.5	(2)
Missouri		
Cape Girardeau-Sikeston	2.7	(2)
Jefferson City	5.2	(4)
Poplar Bluff	3.6	(3)
Warrensburg	8.3	(6)
Montana		
Bozeman	14.6	(10)
Helena	8.7	(6)
Missoula	8.9	(6)
Nebraska		
Grand Island	3.7	(3)
Nevada		
Carson City	11.5	(8)
Elko	20.9	(14)
New Hampshire		
Concord	1.4	(1)
Keene	1.0	(1)
New Mexico		
Alamogordo	4.6	(4)
Carlsbad	8.6	(6)
Clovis	13.5	(10)
Farmington	8.4	(6)
Gallup	7.9	(6)
Hobbs	2.4	(2)
Roswell	5.4	(4)
New York		
Cortland	0.7	(1)
Gloversville	0.4	(1)
Ithaca	2.4	(2)

Kingston	1.9	(2)
Olean	1.5	(2)
Plattsburgh	0.6	(1)
Watertown	4.0	(3)
North Carolina		
Albemarle	3.8	(3)
Eden	1.7	(2)
Havelock-New Bern	2.8	(2)
Henderson	4.0	(3)
Kinston	2.4	(2)
Lumberton	5.3	(4)
Roanoke Rapids	3.1	(3)
Sanford	8.5	(6)
Shelby	4.4	(3)
Statesville	8.4	(6)
Wilson	1.5	(2)
North Dakota		
Minot	0.0	(1)
Ohio		
Ashland	6.5	(5)
Athens	1.4	(1)
Chillicothe	5.7	(4)
Findlay-Fostoria-Tiffin	2.3	(2)
Fremont	1.3	(1)
Marion	1.6	(2)
Mount Vernon	5.6	(4)
New Philadelphia	3.0	(3)
Norwalk	3.2	(3)
Portsmouth	1.0	(1)
Sandusky	1.7	(2)
Sidney	3.9	(3)
Wooster	4.6	(4)
Zanesville	2.0	(2)
Oklahoma		
Ardmore	1.9	(2)
Chickasha	3.2	(3)
Duncan	2.1	(2)
McAlester	5.3	(4)
Muskogee	1.8	(2)
Stillwater	3.1	(3)
Oregon		
Albany-Corvallis	6.4	(5)
Bend	21.5	(15)
Coos Bay	4.1	(3)
Grants Pass	10.8	(8)
Klamath Falls	4.9	(4)
Pendleton	6.7	(5)
Roseburg	3.9	(3)
Pennsylvania		
Chambersburg	4.0	(3)
New Castle	0.4	(1)
Pottsville	1.0	(1)
Rhode Island		
Newport	– 4.0	(0)
South Carolina		
Greenwood	3.1	(3)
Hilton Head Island	12.5	(9)
Tennessee		
Cleveland	5.2	(4)
Columbia	16.6	(12)
Cookeville	8.8	(6)
Morristown	3.8	(3)
Tullahoma	5.0	(4)
Texas		
Corsicana	1.0	(1)
Del Rio	10.4	(7)
Eagle Pass	21.8	(15)
Huntsville	5.5	(4)
Lufkin	7.1	(5)
Nacogdoches	2.4	(2)
Palestine	3.8	(3)
Paris	2.2	(2)

Utah		
Logan	8.1	(6)
St. George	34.3	(20)
Vermont		
Rutland	0.6	(1)
Virginia		
Blacksburg-Radford-Christiansburg	1.1	(1)
Harrisonburg	7.0	(5)
Martinsville	– 0.9	(0)
Staunton-Waynesboro	4.9	(4)
Winchester	10.1	(7)
Washington		
Aberdeen	3.9	(3)
Longview	6.5	(5)
Mount Vernon	15.4	(11)
Port Angeles	9.9	(7)
Walla Walla	8.9	(6)
Wenatchee	7.7	(6)
West Virginia		
Beckley	1.7	(2)
Clarksburg	2.0	(2)
Fairmont	1.5	(2)
Morgantown	3.3	(3)
Wisconsin		
Fond du Lac	3.1	(3)
Manitowoc	2.1	(2)
Stevens Point	4.4	(3)
Watertown	4.5	(4)
Wyoming		
Rock Springs	5.1	(4)

The Results

Local economies are diverse, as this section plainly shows. A city with a strong retail base due to tourist trade, for instance, is unlikely to have a major industrial component. For this reason, no single small city runs away with a high score in this section. The cities with the highest scores, however, reflect healthy economies that are well-balanced among growth, income, and the strength of the retail and manufacturing trades.

Rock Springs, Wyoming, bills itself as True West. The town was founded in 1868 along the tracks of the newly completed Union Pacific Railroad, and local legend has it that outlaw Butch Cassidy got his nickname here working in a local butcher shop. And Rock Springs made its fortune in mining.

Rock Springs scores first in the economics section, with a total of 58 points. Industry remains the driving force behind the area's above-average income, income growth, and retail sales. Over half the area work force is employed in industry. The local coal, petroleum, electricity, and trona industries win Rock Springs the maximum score in manufacturing productivity. (Trona is a natural resource converted into soda ash, a main component in the manufacture of glass, aluminum, paper, detergents, and more. The Rock Springs area produces about 95 percent of the nation's baking soda.) Five other Western small cities share the top-ten list with Rock Springs.

An equal number of Southern small cities populate the bottom-ten list. Albemarle, North Carolina, scores lowest in this section, with just 14 points. Per capita income in Albemarle is below the national average and it declined slightly between 1990 and 1994. Neither the retail nor the manufacturing trades are particularly strong. But just because the city scores low in this section does not mean it is dwindling away. Population growth between 1990 and 1994 matches the micropolitan median and is comparable to the national average.

Economic Scores: Highs and Lows

	Total Rating Points
Highest	
1. Rock Springs, Wyo.	58
2. Traverse City, Mich.	57
3. Coeur d'Alene, Idaho	55
4. Carson City, Nev.	54
5. Paducah, Ky.	53
6. St. George, Utah	52
7. Bend, Ore.	51
Bozeman, Mont.	51
Jonesboro, Ark.	51
Sanford, N.C.	51
11. Ames, Iowa	50
Fairbanks, Alaska	50
Key West, Fla.	50
Muscatine, Iowa	50
15. Bowling Green, Ky.	49
Columbus, Ind.	49
Morgantown, W.Va.	49
Mount Vernon, Wash.	49
19. Columbia, Tenn.	48
Tupelo, Miss.	48
Vero Beach, Fla.	48
Wenatchee, Wash.	48
Median	
96. Dublin, Ga.	34
97. El Centro-Calexico-Brawley, Calif.	34

	Total Rating Points
Lowest	
183. Gloversville, N.Y.	22
Roswell, N.Mex.	22
185. Martinsville, Va.	21
186. Alamogordo, N.Mex.	20
Hanford-Lemoore, Calif.	20
Huntsville, Tex.	20
McAlester, Okla.	20
Palestine, Tex.	20
Talladega, Ala.	20
Warrensburg, Mo.	20
193. Albemarle, N.C.	19

Economics Performance Comparison

	Rock Springs, Wyoming	Micro median	Albemarle, North Carolina
Total Points in Section	58	34	19
Rank in Section	1		193
Income			
Per capita personal income	$ 20,666	$17,822	$16,799
Income points	(12)		(8)
Income Change			
Percent change in per-capita personal income, 1990–94	9.3	5.8	– 0.8
Income change points	(10)		(0)
Manufacturing Productivity			
Manufacture value added per production worker	$427,200	$90,589	$54,882
Manufacturing points	(20)		(2)
Per Capita Retail Sales			
Annual retail sales per resident	$ 8,510	$ 7,262	$ 6,277
Retail sales points	(12)		(6)
Population Change			
Percent change in population, 1990–94	5.1	3.8	3.8
Population change points	(4)		(3)

Economic Scores Area by Area

(Total economic rating points)

Area	Points
Micro media	34
Alabama	
Albertville	43
Auburn-Opelika	30
Cullman	32
Selma	26
Talladega	20
Alaska	
Fairbanks	50
Arizona	
Prescott	36
Sierra Vista	30
Arkansas	
Blytheville	39
El Dorado	34
Hot Springs	38
Jonesboro	51
Russellville	37
Searcy	30
California	
Arcata-Eureka	31
El Centro-Calexico-Brawley	34
Hanford-Lemoore	20
Hollister	27
Connecticut	
Torrington	36
Florida	
Key West	50
Vero Beach	48
Georgia	
Brunswick	46
Dalton	46
Dublin	34
Gainesville	43
Hinesville	36
La Grange	27
Milledgeville	34
Rome	36
Statesboro	33
Thomasville	43
Valdosta	41
Waycross	31
Idaho	
Coeur d'Alene	55
Idaho Falls	43
Pocatello	42
Twin Falls	38
Illinois	
Carbondale	26
Danville	32
Freeport	32
Galesburg	28
Mattoon-Charleston	37
Ottawa	37
Quincy	35
Sterling	26
Indiana	
Columbus	49
Marion	31
Michigan City-La Porte	32
New Castle	34
Richmond	35
Vincennes	33
Iowa	
Ames	50
Burlington	37
Clinton	39
Mason City	40
Muscatine	50
Kansas	
Hutchinson	30
Manhattan	32
Salina	43
Kentucky	
Bowling Green	49
Frankfort	38
Madisonville	24
Paducah	53
Radcliff-Elizabethtown	32
Louisiana	
Hammond	39
New Iberia	32
Ruston	39
Maine	
Augusta-Waterville	29
Biddeford-Saco	24
Maryland	
Salisbury	37
Michigan	
Marquette	32
Mount Pleasant	31
Owosso	31
Traverse City	57
Minnesota	
Faribault	32
Mankato	37
Red Wing	38
Willmar	33
Winona	31

Mississippi

Cleveland	28
Columbus	31
Greenville	36
Laurel	32
Meridian	36
Tupelo	48
Vicksburg	44

Missouri

Cape Girardeau-Sikeston	37
Jefferson City	36
Poplar Bluff	38
Warrensburg	20

Montana

Bozeman	51
Helena	37
Missoula	47

Nebraska

Grand Island	42

Nevada

Carson City	54
Elko	47

New Hampshire

Concord	42
Keene	42

New Mexico

Alamogordo	20
Carlsbad	27
Clovis	35
Farmington	34
Gallup	41
Hobbs	29
Roswell	22

New York

Cortland	30
Gloversville	22
Ithaca	28
Kingston	25
Olean	23
Plattsburgh	38
Watertown	27

North Carolina

Albemarle	19
Eden	36
Havelock-New Bern	36
Henderson	29
Kinston	41
Lumberton	37
Roanoke Rapids	25
Sanford	51
Shelby	27
Statesville	37
Wilson	47

North Dakota

Minot	42

Ohio

Ashland	29
Athens	25
Chillicothe	36
Findlay-Fostoria-Tiffin	31
Fremont	31
Marion	37
Mount Vernon	33
New Philadelphia	30
Norwalk	27
Portsmouth	25
Sandusky	43
Sidney	29
Wooster	36
Zanesville	33

Oklahoma

Ardmore	36
Chickasha	27
Duncan	26
McAlester	20
Muskogee	26
Stillwater	30

Oregon

Albany-Corvallis	40
Bend	51
Coos Bay	29
Grants Pass	32
Klamath Falls	30
Pendleton	29
Roseburg	26

Pennsylvania

Chambersburg	31
New Castle	24
Pottsville	23

Rhode Island

Newport	43

South Carolina

Greenwood	34
Hilton Head Island	45

Tennessee

Cleveland	41
Columbia	48
Cookeville	46
Morristown	38
Tullahoma	35

Texas

Corsicana	34
Del Rio	23
Eagle Pass	29
Huntsville	20
Lufkin	31

Nacogdoches	31
Palestine	20
Paris	40

Utah

Logan	32
St. George	52

Vermont

Rutland	34

Virginia

Blacksburg-Radford-Christiansburg	26
Harrisonburg	40
Martinsville	21
Staunton-Waynesboro	31
Winchester	40

Washington

Aberdeen	27
Longview	36
Mount Vernon	49
Port Angeles	35
Walla Walla	28
Wenatchee	48

West Virginia

Beckley	33
Clarksburg	37
Fairmont	26
Morgantown	49

Wisconsin

Fond du Lac	39
Manitowoc	31
Stevens Point	38
Watertown	33

Wyoming

Rock Springs	58

4

Education

Few national topics have become as intensely debated as the state of U.S. education. Public secondary-school education is a founding principle of the country, and the country schoolhouse is a national icon. Education has been front-page news before in this century—just think of desegregation—but only in the past fifteen to twenty years has the nation's concern over the quality of the educational system become a national priority.

Up until the first half of the century, secondary schooling served as adequate for most Americans. Fewer than one in four Americans had completed four years of high school in 1940. Fewer than 5 percent had spent the same amount of time in college. The postwar economic boom and the GI Bill sent young Americans to college and kept younger students in high school. Americans began garnering degrees like never before. By 1980, nearly three-quarters of the population had completed their high school education. Nearly 20 percent of the population held a college degree.

But quantity did not necessarily equate to quality. In 1983, the National Commission on Excellence in Education released a report entitled *A Nation at Risk.* Summed up simply, the report contended that the nation's schools were badly failing to prepare students for the working world. The report focused intense attention on the nation's schools, scholars, and future work force, and moved the condition of U.S. students to the fore of national debate.

Nearly fifteen years later, the results of greater scrutiny, higher expectations, and new standards are hard to grade. A 1996 report prepared by *Education Week* and funded by the Pew Charitable Trusts evaluated state education systems on seventy-five measures, including class size, environment, funding, and teacher qualifications. Results varied dramatically, almost wildly. No state received consistently good grades in all the measures. Some states strong in math were weak in reading. Others that led the nation in reading comprehension fell far below national goals. "No state can boast of a school system adequate to its needs," says Ronald Wolk, editor of the report. Most states earned C's in key areas such as academic standards, adequate and equitable funding, and supportive school culture.

But still, many states showed improvement. For example, West Virginia and Kentucky were cited as having made great strides in their school systems. Among other gains, per capita spending on education in West Virginia now rivals that of much more affluent states. And nationwide, high school students are increasingly meeting key recommendations made in *A Nation at Risk,* including completing a greater number of core and advanced courses.

Meanwhile, educational attainment continues to rise. The share of the population with a high school degree reached 82 percent in 1995; the share of Americans with a college degree rose to 23 percent. The population holds more educational degrees than ever before.

But then again, the population needs those degrees like never before. The educational baseline has been upped in the working world. Many a high school grad has found that his or her diploma is no promise of a living wage. Further, workers with only a high school diploma can expect the least increase in their earning power over their working life. Young working men with a high school degree already earn salaries equivalent to 73 percent of the wages of senior workers with similar degrees, according to *Forecast* newsletter.

Unfortunately for many young adults—especially those dependent on diminishing federal aid—the cost of a college degree is moving beyond their means. Morton Owen Shapiro, dean at the University of Southern California and a specialist in the economics of higher education, calculates that tuition at public colleges, adjusted for inflation, has risen 4 percent to 4.5 percent each year since the late 1970s. "We have greater inequality of educational attainment by age twenty-four than at any time in the last twenty-five years," said Shapiro, quoted in the *New York Times* in 1997. "Lower-income kids are having a terrible time in higher education."

Those students who do meet the cost of a sheepskin find that the document is earning less now than a decade ago. Starting salaries of bachelor's degree candidates fell in constant dollars between 1980 and 1995 in sixteen of eighteen fields monitored by the National Association of Colleges and Employers.

Small cities are by no means immune to these national trends, but many are pockets of high-quality school systems in otherwise troubling state trends. This is especially true of school systems in university towns. The public schools of Ithaca, New York, home of Cornell University and Ithaca College, share little in common beyond the state flag with the overcrowded, underfunded public schools of New York City. Ithaca even boasts one of the nation's few publicly funded alternative high schools.

Every parent wants a good education for his or her child, and a wise city understands that a well-educated population is good for the entire community. Higher degrees result in higher incomes, higher tax bases, and a work force capable of drawing attractive, high-wage industries. Communities with high levels of education also show greater levels of civic participation. Adults with college degrees are more likely than average to belong to community organizations, to be well informed on local issues, and to vote, according to a 1996 study by the National Center for Education Statistics. Half of the adults with a bachelor's degree volunteer in on-going community service, compared with one-third of the adults who hold only a high school diploma.

Ranking micropolitan America. The ideal micropolis would place a strong emphasis on education, encouraging its students to graduate from high school and go on to college. The adult population would have an average or above-average share of high school and college graduates. Each small city is evaluated in five categories.

1. High School Education: Are most of the community's adults themselves high school graduates who understand the value of a diploma? Does the work force have basic high school level skills?
2. High School Dropouts: Does the community do a good job of encouraging students to stay in school, or is there a high dropout rate?
3. College Education: Does the micro have a good share of college grads, or are college degrees rare?
4. College Influence: Is there a university or college in town that adds its facilities and inspiration to local support for education?
5. Local Education Funding: Does local support for education extend beyond sentiment to adequate government funding?

High School Education

Often the people who best appreciate the value of a high school diploma are those who have one. It stands to reason that communities with a high share of high school graduates are more likely than communities with a low share to make good schools a priority. Such communities may also be more likely to encourage students to complete high school.

This category ranks each micro according to the percent of residents aged twenty-five and older who have completed four years of high school or more. More than 3 in 4 adults nationwide had a high school diploma in 1990. That's up from 2 in 3 ten years before. The highest gains are among minorities.

Ames, Iowa, has the largest share of high school grads. More than 9 in 10 adults aged twenty-five and older have a high school diploma. A walk around town will reveal much of the reason. Ames is home to Iowa State University. Other college towns follow close behind Ames.

Eagle Pass, Texas, could not present more of a contrast. Just 36 percent of adults have a high school education. The unusually low share of high school grads is accounted for by the high number of immigrants entering the United States through the port of entry at Eagle Pass.

Most of the small cities with the highest share of high school grads lie west of the Mississippi, while many of the cities with the lowest share of high school grads lie south of the Mason-Dixon line.

Source: Census of the Population, U.S. Bureau of the Census, Washington, D.C. The data are for 1990.

Scoring: Twenty points for 89 percent or higher; no points for less than 51 percent. The spacing is every 2 percentage points.

High School Education: Highs and Lows

	Percent of Adults with a High School Education
Highest	
1. Ames, Iowa	91.0
2. Bozeman, Mont.	90.4
3. Fairbanks, Alaska	89.8
4. Logan, Utah	89.3
5. Manhattan, Kans.	89.2
6. Helena, Mont.	87.4
7. Ithaca, N.Y.	87.2
8. Missoula, Mont.	85.4
9. Traverse City, Mich.	84.9
10. St. George, Utah	84.5
Median	
96. Marion, Ohio	73.8
97. Wooster, Ohio	73.6
Lowest	
184. Gallup, N.Mex.	58.5
185. Henderson, N.C.	57.1
186. Lumberton, N.C.	57.0
187. Poplar Bluff, Mo.	56.8
188. Del Rio, Tex.	56.1
189. Martinsville, Va.	56.0
190. Cleveland, Miss.	54.9
191. Roanoke Rapids, N.C.	53.9
192. El Centro-Calexico-Brawley, Calif.	53.2
193. Eagle Pass, Tex.	35.7

High School Education Area by Area

(Percent of residents aged twenty-five years and older having completed four years of high school or more and rating points)

Micro median	73.7	
Alabama		
Albertville	61.5	(6)
Auburn-Opelika	73.2	(12)
Cullman	58.8	(4)
Selma	59.6	(5)
Talladega	60.7	(5)
Alaska		
Fairbanks	89.8	(20)
Arizona		
Prescott	78.9	(14)
Sierra Vista	75.7	(13)
Arkansas		
Blytheville	60.0	(5)
El Dorado	65.9	(8)
Hot Springs	70.2	(10)
Jonesboro	67.5	(9)
Russellville	66.5	(8)
Searcy	62.6	(6)
California		
Arcata-Eureka	80.5	(15)
El Centro-Calexico-Brawley	53.2	(2)
Hanford-Lemoore	65.6	(8)
Hollister	68.4	(9)
Connecticut		
Torrington	80.9	(15)
Florida		
Key West	79.7	(15)
Vero Beach	76.5	(13)
Georgia		
Brunswick	74.3	(12)
Dalton	59.8	(5)
Dublin	61.0	(6)
Gainesville	65.1	(8)
Hinesville	82.1	(16)
La Grange	60.8	(5)
Milledgeville	64.7	(7)
Rome	63.9	(7)
Statesboro	67.6	(9)
Thomasville	63.3	(7)
Valdosta	69.8	(10)
Waycross	60.8	(5)
Idaho		
Coeur d'Alene	81.1	(16)
Idaho Falls	84.0	(17)
Pocatello	81.9	(16)
Twin Falls	75.4	(13)
Illinois		
Carbondale	78.8	(14)
Danville	72.8	(11)
Freeport	76.7	(13)
Galesburg	76.6	(13)
Mattoon-Charleston	76.1	(13)
Ottawa	73.1	(12)
Quincy	75.1	(13)
Sterling	73.3	(12)
Indiana		
Columbus	76.9	(13)
Marion	71.8	(11)
Michigan City-La Porte	73.9	(12)
New Castle	71.4	(11)
Richmond	71.2	(11)
Vincennes	74.5	(12)
Iowa		
Ames	91.0	(20)
Burlington	78.9	(14)

Clinton 77.4 (14)
Mason City 81.3 (16)
Muscatine 75.0 (13)

Kansas
Hutchinson 77.4 (14)
Manhattan 89.2 (20)
Salina 82.4 (16)

Kentucky
Bowling Green 70.9 (10)
Frankfort 76.0 (13)
Madisonville 62.5 (6)
Paducah 73.1 (12)
Radcliff-Elizabethtown 75.3 (13)

Louisiana
Hammond 60.7 (5)
New Iberia 59.3 (5)
Ruston 74.5 (12)

Maine
Augusta-Waterville 78.9 (14)
Biddeford-Saco 79.5 (15)

Maryland
Salisbury 72.1 (11)

Michigan
Marquette 81.8 (16)
Mount Pleasant 79.7 (15)
Owosso 78.7 (14)
Traverse City 84.9 (17)

Minnesota
Faribault 78.7 (14)
Mankato 82.3 (16)
Red Wing 78.0 (14)
Willmar 76.3 (13)
Winona 77.7 (14)

Mississippi
Cleveland 54.9 (2)
Columbus 69.0 (10)
Greenville 58.8 (4)
Laurel 64.3 (7)
Meridian 69.7 (10)
Tupelo 67.8 (9)
Vicksburg 67.7 (9)

Missouri
Cape Girardeau-Sikeston 66.6 (8)
Jefferson City 74.9 (12)
Poplar Bluff 56.8 (3)
Warrensburg 80.7 (15)

Montana
Bozeman 90.4 (20)
Helena 87.4 (19)
Missoula 85.4 (18)

Nebraska
Grand Island 79.3 (15)

Nevada
Carson City 82.7 (16)
Elko 78.5 (14)

New Hampshire
Concord 83.2 (17)
Keene 80.8 (15)

New Mexico
Alamogordo 81.6 (16)
Carlsbad 67.3 (9)
Clovis 75.8 (13)
Farmington 69.2 (10)
Gallup 58.5 (4)
Hobbs 63.8 (7)
Roswell 67.3 (9)

New York
Cortland 76.8 (13)
Gloversville 70.5 (10)
Ithaca 87.2 (19)

Kingston	76.6	(13)
Olean	74.5	(12)
Plattsburgh	74.2	(12)
Watertown	76.4	(13)

North Carolina

Albemarle	62.1	(6)
Eden	59.2	(5)
Havelock-New Bern	75.9	(13)
Henderson	57.1	(4)
Kinston	62.9	(6)
Lumberton	57.0	(4)
Roanoke Rapids	53.9	(2)
Sanford	72.4	(11)
Shelby	63.5	(7)
Statesville	66.5	(8)
Wilson	62.2	(6)

North Dakota

Minot	82.8	(16)

Ohio

Ashland	76.0	(13)
Athens	74.6	(12)
Chillicothe	67.6	(9)
Findlay-Fostoria-Tiffin	79.3	(15)
Fremont	76.6	(13)
Marion	73.8	(12)
Mount Vernon	75.2	(13)
New Philadelphia	71.9	(11)
Norwalk	74.1	(12)
Portsmouth	63.8	(7)
Sandusky	76.2	(13)
Sidney	72.9	(11)
Wooster	73.6	(12)
Zanesville	71.1	(11)

Oklahoma

Ardmore	70.3	(10)
Chickasha	69.0	(10)
Duncan	70.8	(10)
McAlester	64.3	(7)
Muskogee	68.3	(9)
Stillwater	82.2	(16)

Oregon

Albany-Corvallis	81.5	(16)
Bend	83.2	(17)
Coos Bay	75.5	(13)
Grants Pass	75.2	(13)
Klamath Falls	76.2	(13)
Pendleton	75.1	(13)
Roseburg	74.5	(12)

Pennsylvania

Chambersburg	69.4	(10)
New Castle	73.0	(12)
Pottsville	68.4	(9)

Rhode Island

Newport	82.8	(16)

South Carolina

Greenwood	64.1	(7)
Hilton Head Island	83.4	(17)

Tennessee

Cleveland	64.4	(7)
Columbia	65.2	(8)
Cookeville	63.2	(7)
Morristown	61.6	(6)
Tullahoma	64.4	(7)

Texas

Corsicana	64.6	(7)
Del Rio	56.1	(3)
Eagle Pass	35.7	(0)
Huntsville	73.3	(12)
Lufkin	65.3	(8)
Nacogdoches	69.7	(10)
Palestine	67.7	(9)
Paris	67.3	(9)

Utah		
Logan	89.3	(20)
St. George	84.5	(17)
Vermont		
Rutland	79.4	(15)
Virginia		
Blacksburg-Radford-Christiansburg	68.9	(9)
Harrisonburg	68.1	(9)
Martinsville	56.0	(3)
Staunton-Waynesboro	70.0	(10)
Winchester	69.7	(10)
Washington		
Aberdeen	74.0	(12)
Longview	77.3	(14)
Mount Vernon	81.0	(16)
Port Angeles	79.7	(15)
Walla Walla	79.1	(15)
Wenatchee	74.3	(12)
West Virginia		
Beckley	63.2	(7)
Clarksburg	70.6	(10)
Fairmont	71.4	(11)
Morgantown	75.4	(13)
Wisconsin		
Fond du Lac	77.5	(14)
Manitowoc	75.4	(13)
Stevens Point	79.7	(15)
Watertown	74.5	(12)
Wyoming		
Rock Springs	81.5	(16)

High School Dropouts

Over the course of an academic year, 5 percent of all the students enrolled in the tenth, eleventh, and twelfth grades combined drop out of school. In the 1993–94 school year, that totalled 382,000 teenagers who quit school. Nationwide, over 13 percent of young adults are high school dropouts.

Small cities have a lower average share of dropouts—below 11 percent. Many have rates below 5 and 6 percent. But small cities with high dropout rates share all the big-city problems associated with low levels of education. In particular, many cities must replace disappearing well-paying manufacturing jobs that had once employed workers with lower levels of education. To attract new, higher-tech industries, cities must be able to offer a well-educated work force.

This category estimates the dropout problem in each area by calculating the share of teens aged sixteen to nineteen that is neither students nor high school graduates. Those enlisted in the military are excluded.

Ames, Iowa, has the lowest percent of high school dropouts. Fewer than 2 percent of high-school-aged youth there have quit school. Education is a central focus in Ames because, as mentioned previously, the micro is home to Iowa State University. It has a high share of high school and college grads and invests well in its school system.

Nearly 24 percent of older teens have dropped out of school in Dalton, Georgia. Many teens there leave school to work in the carpet mills.

University towns and towns with above-average incomes have the lowest dropout rates. Dropout rates are highest throughout the South.

Source: Census of the Population, U.S. Bureau of the Census, Washington, D.C. The data are for 1990.

Scoring: Twenty points for a dropout rate below 2 percent; no points for a rate of 21 percent or higher. The spacing is 1 percentage point.

High School Dropouts: Highs and Lows

	Percent of Residents Aged 16 to 19 Not Enrolled in School and Not High School Graduates
Lowest	
1. Ames, Iowa	1.8
2. Carbondale, Ill.	2.3
3. Minot, N.Dak.	2.6
4. Ithaca, N.Y.	2.7
5. Bozeman, Mont.	3.1
Marquette, Mich.	3.1
7. Stevens Point, Wisc.	3.2
8. Mattoon-Charleston, Ill.	3.3
9. Mankato, Minn.	3.4
10. Athens, Ohio	3.7
Median	
96. Fairbanks, Alaska	10.6
97. Valdosta, Ga.	10.7
Highest	
184. Cleveland, Tenn.	18.5
185. Dublin, Ga.	18.6
186. New Iberia, La.	18.8
187. Martinsville, Va.	19.2
188. Eagle Pass, Tex.	19.7
189. Brunswick, Ga.	19.8
190. Grants Pass, Ore.	20.3
191. Gainesville, Ga.	21.9
192. Albertville, Ala.	22.3
193. Dalton, Ga.	23.7

High School Dropouts Area by Area

(Percent of residents aged 16 to 19 not enrolled in school and not high school graduates and rating points)

Micro median	10.6	
Alabama		
Albertville	22.3	(0)
Auburn-Opelika	5.2	(16)
Cullman	16.2	(5)
Selma	7.7	(14)
Talladega	15.6	(6)
Alaska		
Fairbanks	10.6	(11)
Arizona		
Prescott	12.3	(9)
Sierra Vista	15.7	(6)
Arkansas		
Blytheville	15.9	(6)
El Dorado	11.1	(10)
Hot Springs	15.7	(6)
Jonesboro	9.7	(12)
Russellville	8.3	(13)
Searcy	8.8	(13)
California		
Arcata-Eureka	9.1	(12)
El Centro-Calexico-Brawley	11.7	(10)
Hanford-Lemoore	15.7	(6)
Hollister	11.3	(10)
Connecticut		
Torrington	8.8	(13)
Florida		
Key West	14.6	(7)
Vero Beach	18.4	(3)
Georgia		
Brunswick	19.8	(2)
Dalton	23.7	(0)
Dublin	18.6	(3)
Gainesville	21.9	(0)
Hinesville	16.9	(5)
La Grange	13.1	(8)
Milledgeville	11.8	(10)
Rome	13.9	(8)
Statesboro	5.0	(16)
Thomasville	14.3	(7)
Valdosta	10.7	(11)
Waycross	14.9	(7)
Idaho		
Coeur d'Alene	8.8	(13)
Idaho Falls	11.9	(10)
Pocatello	10.2	(11)
Twin Falls	14.1	(7)
Illinois		
Carbondale	2.3	(19)
Danville	13.2	(8)
Freeport	8.8	(13)
Galesburg	8.6	(13)
Mattoon-Charleston	3.3	(18)
Ottawa	12.3	(9)
Quincy	7.2	(14)
Sterling	9.0	(12)
Indiana		
Columbus	12.4	(9)
Marion	10.4	(11)
Michigan City-La Porte	11.5	(10)
New Castle	9.5	(12)
Richmond	13.2	(8)
Vincennes	6.5	(15)
Iowa		
Ames	1.8	(20)
Burlington	8.4	(13)

Clinton	6.7	(15)
Mason City	4.3	(17)
Muscatine	8.2	(13)
Kansas		
Hutchinson	11.9	(10)
Manhattan	4.0	(17)
Salina	6.9	(15)
Kentucky		
Bowling Green	6.8	(15)
Frankfort	14.3	(7)
Madisonville	16.8	(5)
Paducah	11.0	(10)
Radcliff-Elizabethtown	9.9	(12)
Louisiana		
Hammond	14.2	(7)
New Iberia	18.8	(3)
Ruston	4.7	(17)
Maine		
Augusta-Waterville	9.6	(12)
Biddeford-Saco	8.3	(13)
Maryland		
Salisbury	12.6	(9)
Michigan		
Marquette	3.1	(18)
Mount Pleasant	3.8	(18)
Owosso	10.1	(11)
Traverse City	7.4	(14)
Minnesota		
Faribault	6.1	(15)
Mankato	3.4	(18)
Red Wing	6.2	(15)
Willmar	6.8	(15)
Winona	4.5	(17)
Mississippi		
Cleveland	11.7	(10)
Columbus	10.3	(11)
Greenville	16.8	(5)
Laurel	10.0	(11)
Meridian	10.8	(11)
Tupelo	15.4	(6)
Vicksburg	10.9	(11)
Missouri		
Cape Girardeau-Sikeston	10.8	(11)
Jefferson City	10.8	(11)
Poplar Bluff	16.6	(5)
Warrensburg	3.8	(18)
Montana		
Bozeman	3.1	(18)
Helena	10.0	(11)
Missoula	4.2	(17)
Nebraska		
Grand Island	10.8	(11)
Nevada		
Carson City	10.3	(11)
Elko	16.5	(5)
New Hampshire		
Concord	8.2	(13)
Keene	8.7	(13)
New Mexico		
Alamogordo	9.2	(12)
Carlsbad	9.7	(12)
Clovis	11.6	(10)
Farmington	15.6	(6)
Gallup	11.7	(10)
Hobbs	17.5	(4)
Roswell	12.1	(9)

New York		
Cortland	5.5	(16)
Gloversville	9.5	(12)
Ithaca	2.7	(19)
Kingston	7.9	(14)
Olean	9.7	(12)
Plattsburgh	9.1	(12)
Watertown	12.2	(9)
North Carolina		
Albemarle	11.8	(10)
Eden	16.0	(5)
Havelock-New Bern	12.3	(9)
Henderson	18.1	(3)
Kinston	15.7	(6)
Lumberton	15.9	(6)
Roanoke Rapids	12.6	(9)
Sanford	12.1	(9)
Shelby	13.6	(8)
Statesville	18.1	(3)
Wilson	12.2	(9)
North Dakota		
Minot	2.6	(19)
Ohio		
Ashland	7.7	(14)
Athens	3.7	(18)
Chillicothe	8.6	(13)
Findlay-Fostoria-Tiffin	6.1	(15)
Fremont	7.4	(14)
Marion	10.1	(11)
Mount Vernon	5.2	(16)
New Philadelphia	11.4	(10)
Norwalk	6.9	(15)
Portsmouth	9.7	(12)
Sandusky	9.1	(12)
Sidney	12.3	(9)
Wooster	12.8	(9)
Zanesville	7.1	(14)

Oklahoma		
Ardmore	10.4	(11)
Chickasha	11.1	(10)
Duncan	9.7	(12)
McAlester	9.7	(12)
Muskogee	11.6	(10)
Stillwater	4.6	(17)
Oregon		
Albany-Corvallis	8.6	(13)
Bend	8.6	(13)
Coos Bay	12.8	(9)
Grants Pass	20.3	(1)
Klamath Falls	15.4	(6)
Pendleton	15.0	(6)
Roseburg	15.0	(6)
Pennsylvania		
Chambersburg	11.9	(10)
New Castle	8.6	(13)
Pottsville	11.4	(10)
Rhode Island		
Newport	6.4	(15)
South Carolina		
Greenwood	9.4	(12)
Hilton Head Island	11.2	(10)
Tennessee		
Cleveland	18.5	(3)
Columbia	14.7	(7)
Cookeville	9.0	(12)
Morristown	16.4	(5)
Tullahoma	14.2	(7)
Texas		
Corsicana	11.3	(10)
Del Rio	13.3	(8)
Eagle Pass	19.7	(2)
Huntsville	8.6	(13)
Lufkin	15.3	(6)

Nacogdoches	6.8	(15)
Palestine	16.5	(5)
Paris	9.7	(12)
Utah		
Logan	5.9	(16)
St. George	5.7	(16)
Vermont		
Rutland	7.1	(14)
Virginia		
Blacksburg-Radford-Christiansburg	4.0	(17)
Harrisonburg	8.1	(13)
Martinsville	19.2	(2)
Staunton-Waynesboro	11.2	(10)
Winchester	12.7	(9)
Washington		
Aberdeen	16.5	(5)
Longview	12.9	(9)
Mount Vernon	13.1	(8)
Port Angeles	14.6	(7)
Walla Walla	10.4	(11)
Wenatchee	15.0	(6)
West Virginia		
Beckley	12.0	(9)
Clarksburg	11.1	(10)
Fairmont	7.7	(14)
Morgantown	4.4	(17)
Wisconsin		
Fond du Lac	6.4	(15)
Manitowoc	5.5	(16)
Stevens Point	3.2	(18)
Watertown	6.4	(15)
Wyoming		
Rock Springs	6.6	(15)

College Education

A college education should expose young adults to new ideas and wide horizons. It should increase their understanding of the world around them and the issues that affect their communities and their country. And it should also give them the skills and credentials to achieve better-paying jobs in a marketplace that increasingly requires a bachelor's degree.

This category records the share of adults aged twenty-five and older who are college graduates. The national average in 1990 was 21 percent, up from 16 percent ten years previously. Women and minorities show the greatest gains in college degrees.

Ithaca, New York, is the small city with the big vocabulary. The home of Cornell University and Ithaca College is also home to professors and many alumni. Forty-two percent of Ithaca residents are college grads—twice the national average.

Eagle Pass, Texas, has the lowest share of college graduates. Again, the high concentration of immigrants from Mexico at this port-of-entry town is the reason.

University towns across the country have the highest share of college grads. Industrial cities in the South and Midwest have the lowest share.

Source: Census of the Population, U.S. Bureau of the Census, Washington, D.C. The data are for 1990.

Scoring: Twenty points for 36 percent or higher; no points for less than 7.5 percent. The spacing is every 1.5 percentage points.

College Education: Highs and Lows

	Percent of Residents Who Are College Graduates
Highest	
1. Ithaca, N.Y.	41.7
2. Ames, Iowa	38.4
3. Bozeman, Mont.	33.8
4. Newport, R.I.	30.1
Stillwater, Okla.	30.1
6. Logan, Utah	30.0
7. Manhattan, Kans.	29.7
8. Carbondale, Ill.	29.5
9. Morgantown, W.Va.	28.1
10. Helena, Mont.	27.8
Median	
96. Sandusky, Ohio	13.8
97. Rome, Ga.	13.7
Lowest	
184. New Iberia, La.	9.0
New Philadelphia, Ohio	9.0
186. Eden, N.C.	8.8
Martinsville, Va.	8.8
188. Poplar Bluff, Mo.	8.6
Roanoke Rapids, N.C.	8.6
190. Portsmouth, Ohio	8.5
191. Pottsville, Pa.	8.1
192. Cullman, Ala.	7.8
193. Eagle Pass, Tex.	7.3

College Education Area by Area

(Percent of residents aged twenty-five years and older who are college graduates and rating points)

Area	Percent	Points
Micro median	13.8	
Alabama		
Albertville	11.5	(3)
Auburn-Opelika	25.3	(12)
Cullman	7.8	(1)
Selma	12.2	(4)
Talladega	10.2	(2)
Alaska		
Fairbanks	25.2	(12)
Arizona		
Prescott	17.7	(7)
Sierra Vista	16.1	(6)
Arkansas		
Blytheville	10.5	(3)
El Dorado	12.7	(4)
Hot Springs	14.2	(5)
Jonesboro	16.4	(6)
Russellville	14.7	(5)
Searcy	10.9	(3)
California		
Arcata-Eureka	20.0	(9)
El Centro-Calexico-Brawley	9.7	(2)
Hanford-Lemoore	9.0	(2)
Hollister	14.4	(5)
Connecticut		
Torrington	25.0	(12)
Florida		
Key West	20.3	(9)
Vero Beach	19.1	(8)
Georgia		
Brunswick	19.9	(9)
Dalton	12.0	(4)
Dublin	12.0	(4)
Gainesville	15.4	(6)
Hinesville	13.4	(4)
La Grange	13.6	(5)
Milledgeville	13.3	(4)
Rome	13.7	(5)
Statesboro	19.9	(9)
Thomasville	13.4	(4)
Valdosta	16.3	(6)
Waycross	9.3	(2)
Idaho		
Coeur d'Alene	16.0	(6)
Idaho Falls	23.2	(11)
Pocatello	19.0	(8)
Twin Falls	13.3	(4)
Illinois		
Carbondale	29.5	(15)
Danville	11.1	(3)
Freeport	13.6	(5)
Galesburg	12.7	(4)
Mattoon-Charleston	18.7	(8)
Ottawa	10.5	(3)
Quincy	13.7	(5)
Sterling	9.9	(2)
Indiana		
Columbus	16.9	(7)
Marion	11.2	(3)
Michigan City-La Porte	11.7	(3)
New Castle	9.2	(2)
Richmond	11.3	(3)
Vincennes	11.1	(3)
Iowa		
Ames	38.4	(20)
Burlington	12.7	(4)

Clinton	12.9	(4)
Mason City	15.5	(6)
Muscatine	13.0	(4)
Kansas		
Hutchinson	14.9	(5)
Manhattan	29.7	(15)
Salina	17.7	(7)
Kentucky		
Bowling Green	19.2	(8)
Frankfort	21.3	(10)
Madisonville	9.6	(2)
Paducah	14.3	(5)
Radcliff-Elizabethtown	12.9	(4)
Louisiana		
Hammond	12.9	(4)
New Iberia	9.0	(2)
Ruston	26.2	(13)
Maine		
Augusta-Waterville	18.1	(8)
Biddeford-Saco	19.0	(8)
Maryland		
Salisbury	18.5	(8)
Michigan		
Marquette	20.3	(9)
Mount Pleasant	21.5	(10)
Owosso	10.3	(2)
Traverse City	22.5	(11)
Minnesota		
Faribault	19.3	(8)
Mankato	22.6	(11)
Red Wing	14.1	(5)
Willmar	15.7	(6)
Winona	19.7	(9)
Mississippi		
Cleveland	15.2	(6)
Columbus	18.6	(8)
Greenville	14.3	(5)
Laurel	12.2	(4)
Meridian	13.3	(4)
Tupelo	15.0	(6)
Vicksburg	19.1	(8)
Missouri		
Cape Girardeau-Sikeston	13.9	(5)
Jefferson City	19.5	(9)
Poplar Bluff	8.6	(1)
Warrensburg	21.4	(10)
Montana		
Bozeman	33.8	(18)
Helena	27.8	(14)
Missoula	27.7	(14)
Nebraska		
Grand Island	14.6	(5)
Nevada		
Carson City	16.3	(6)
Elko	13.3	(4)
New Hampshire		
Concord	25.4	(12)
Keene	23.9	(11)
New Mexico		
Alamogordo	15.0	(6)
Carlsbad	10.9	(3)
Clovis	13.7	(5)
Farmington	12.3	(4)
Gallup	11.1	(3)
Hobbs	11.5	(3)
Roswell	14.3	(5)
New York		
Cortland	18.2	(8)
Gloversville	11.4	(3)
Ithaca	41.7	(20)

Kingston	21.6	(10)
Olean	12.8	(4)
Plattsburgh	16.5	(7)
Watertown	13.6	(5)
North Carolina		
Albemarle	9.4	(2)
Eden	8.8	(1)
Havelock-New Bern	15.1	(6)
Henderson	9.5	(2)
Kinston	11.5	(3)
Lumberton	11.0	(3)
Roanoke Rapids	8.6	(1)
Sanford	14.3	(5)
Shelby	11.1	(3)
Statesville	11.8	(3)
Wilson	14.4	(5)
North Dakota		
Minot	19.0	(8)
Ohio		
Ashland	13.0	(4)
Athens	23.4	(11)
Chillicothe	9.2	(2)
Findlay-Fostoria-Tiffin	14.7	(5)
Fremont	10.7	(3)
Marion	9.9	(2)
Mount Vernon	12.8	(4)
New Philadelphia	9.0	(2)
Norwalk	9.4	(2)
Portsmouth	8.5	(1)
Sandusky	13.8	(5)
Sidney	11.2	(3)
Wooster	13.9	(5)
Zanesville	10.1	(2)
Oklahoma		
Ardmore	13.4	(4)
Chickasha	13.2	(4)
Duncan	14.7	(5)
McAlester	10.3	(3)
Muskogee	14.1	(5)
Stillwater	30.1	(16)
Oregon		
Albany-Corvallis	23.3	(11)
Bend	18.9	(8)
Coos Bay	12.3	(4)
Grants Pass	12.0	(4)
Klamath Falls	12.4	(4)
Pendleton	13.3	(4)
Roseburg	11.7	(3)
Pennsylvania		
Chambersburg	12.4	(4)
New Castle	11.8	(3)
Pottsville	8.1	(1)
Rhode Island		
Newport	30.1	(16)
South Carolina		
Greenwood	16.0	(6)
Hilton Head Island	26.5	(13)
Tennessee		
Cleveland	11.9	(3)
Columbia	12.1	(4)
Cookeville	16.8	(7)
Morristown	11.2	(3)
Tullahoma	14.3	(5)
Texas		
Corsicana	12.7	(4)
Del Rio	13.0	(4)
Eagle Pass	7.3	(0)
Huntsville	19.0	(8)
Lufkin	13.2	(4)
Nacogdoches	20.0	(9)
Palestine	9.5	(2)
Paris	13.0	(4)

Utah		
Logan	30.0	(16)
St. George	17.7	(7)
Vermont		
Rutland	20.6	(9)
Virginia		
Blacksburg-Radford-Christiansburg	24.4	(12)
Harrisonburg	18.5	(8)
Martinsville	8.8	(1)
Staunton-Waynesboro	14.5	(5)
Winchester	16.1	(6)
Washington		
Aberdeen	11.0	(3)
Longview	11.3	(3)
Mount Vernon	16.3	(6)
Port Angeles	16.1	(6)
Walla Walla	18.8	(8)
Wenatchee	16.7	(7)
West Virginia		
Beckley	10.7	(3)
Clarksburg	13.5	(5)
Fairmont	12.5	(4)
Morgantown	28.1	(14)
Wisconsin		
Fond du Lac	13.3	(4)
Manitowoc	12.1	(4)
Stevens Point	19.1	(8)
Watertown	12.5	(4)
Wyoming		
Rock Springs	13.3	(4)

College Influence

Urbanites who expect a low level of culture in small cities are in for a surprise should they arrive in many of the county's micropolitans. Their waiter at lunch may be a Ph.D. student in philosophy. The two women at lunch next to them may not be housewives out shopping, but professors discussing a contemporary writer the urbanites may not have even heard of, much less read.

Small cities benefit in many ways from a local college. Colleges enliven the local cultural and social life with concerts, lectures, and sporting events. They provide an opportunity for local high school graduates to better afford college by attending while remaining at home. This category measures the influence of local colleges and universities by calculating the share of residents who are enrolled in college.

Carbondale, Illinois, and Ames, Iowa, may be the cities with the best-educated waitstaff. They certainly have the highest share of young adults enrolled in college. Just over 32 percent of residents in those micros are college students.

Norwalk, Ohio, is just an hour's drive from the museums, theaters, and music of Cleveland. But Norwalk boasts little higher-education influence at home. Only 3 percent of its residents are college students.

Midwestern college towns lead the list of top towns for college influence. Industrial cities throughout the South and Midwest dominate the bottom-ten list.

Source: Census of the Population, U.S. Bureau of the Census, Washington, D.C. The data are for 1990.

Scoring: Twenty points for college enrollment of 32 percent or higher; no points for less than 3.5 percent. The spacing is every 1.5 percentage points.

College Influence: Highs and Lows

	Percent of Residents Enrolled in College
Highest	
1. Ames, Iowa	32.3
Carbondale, Ill.	32.3
3. Athens, Ohio	29.7
4. Ithaca, N.Y.	29.4
5. Mount Pleasant, Mich.	28.2
6. Ruston, La.	27.9
7. Stillwater, Okla.	27.6
8. Blacksburg-Radford-Christiansburg, Va.	27.3
9. Auburn-Opelika, Ala.	25.4
10. Manhattan, Kans.	25.1
Median	
96. Paris, Tex.	5.6
97. Roswell, N.Mex.	5.5
Lowest	
184. Albertville, Ala.	3.8
Martinsville, Va.	3.8
Roanoke Rapids, N.C.	3.8
187. Dalton, Ga.	3.7
Grants Pass, Ore.	3.7
189. New Castle, Ind.	3.6
190. Pottsville, Pa.	3.4
191. New Iberia, La.	3.3
New Philadelphia, Ohio	3.3
193. Norwalk, Ohio	3.2

College Influence Area by Area

(Percent of population enrolled in college and rating points)

Area	Percent	Points
Micro median	5.6	
Alabama		
Albertville	3.8	(1)
Auburn-Opelika	25.4	(15)
Cullman	4.6	(1)
Selma	4.6	(1)
Talladega	4.5	(1)
Alaska		
Fairbanks	10.0	(5)
Arizona		
Prescott	6.8	(3)
Sierra Vista	6.8	(3)
Arkansas		
Blytheville	4.8	(1)
El Dorado	3.9	(1)
Hot Springs	4.2	(1)
Jonesboro	10.1	(5)
Russellville	8.3	(4)
Searcy	8.9	(4)
California		
Arcata-Eureka	11.6	(6)
El Centro-Calexico-Brawley	6.7	(3)
Hanford-Lemoore	5.9	(2)
Hollister	6.1	(2)
Connecticut		
Torrington	5.7	(2)
Florida		
Key West	4.9	(1)
Vero Beach	4.1	(1)
Georgia		
Brunswick	4.0	(1)
Dalton	3.7	(1)
Dublin	3.9	(1)
Gainesville	4.5	(1)
Hinesville	5.9	(2)
La Grange	4.7	(1)
Milledgeville	9.6	(5)
Rome	6.6	(3)
Statesboro	22.5	(13)
Thomasville	3.9	(1)
Valdosta	9.4	(4)
Waycross	4.1	(1)
Idaho		
Coeur d'Alene	6.2	(2)
Idaho Falls	5.7	(2)
Pocatello	10.6	(5)
Twin Falls	4.8	(1)
Illinois		
Carbondale	32.3	(20)
Danville	5.1	(2)
Freeport	5.5	(2)
Galesburg	6.4	(2)
Mattoon-Charleston	21.3	(12)
Ottawa	4.6	(1)
Quincy	6.0	(2)
Sterling	5.3	(2)
Indiana		
Columbus	4.6	(1)
Marion	6.2	(2)
Michigan City-La Porte	5.0	(2)
New Castle	3.6	(1)
Richmond	5.5	(2)
Vincennes	12.6	(7)
Iowa		
Ames	32.3	(20)
Burlington	5.4	(2)
Clinton	5.2	(2)
Mason City	6.2	(2)
Muscatine	4.6	(1)

Kansas		
Hutchinson	6.3	(2)
Manhattan	25.1	(15)
Salina	5.0	(2)
Kentucky		
Bowling Green	12.1	(6)
Frankfort	6.4	(2)
Madisonville	4.6	(1)
Paducah	4.6	(1)
Radcliff-Elizabethtown	5.8	(2)
Louisiana		
Hammond	7.3	(3)
New Iberia	3.3	(0)
Ruston	27.9	(17)
Maine		
Augusta-Waterville	6.7	(3)
Biddeford-Saco	4.8	(1)
Maryland		
Salisbury	8.9	(4)
Michigan		
Marquette	11.2	(6)
Mount Pleasant	28.2	(17)
Owosso	5.1	(2)
Traverse City	6.8	(3)
Minnesota		
Faribault	13.7	(7)
Mankato	20.2	(12)
Red Wing	3.9	(1)
Willmar	6.2	(2)
Winona	16.4	(9)
Mississippi		
Cleveland	9.0	(4)
Columbus	6.3	(2)
Greenville	4.1	(1)
Laurel	5.2	(2)

Meridian	5.3	(2)
Tupelo	4.1	(1)
Vicksburg	5.5	(2)
Missouri		
Cape Girardeau-Sikeston	7.5	(3)
Jefferson City	7.0	(3)
Poplar Bluff	4.0	(1)
Warrensburg	21.2	(12)
Montana		
Bozeman	20.4	(12)
Helena	5.6	(2)
Missoula	13.8	(7)
Nebraska		
Grand Island	4.7	(1)
Nevada		
Carson City	7.6	(3)
Elko	5.0	(2)
New Hampshire		
Concord	6.3	(2)
Keene	9.3	(4)
New Mexico		
Alamogordo	6.9	(3)
Carlsbad	4.3	(1)
Clovis	8.6	(4)
Farmington	5.6	(2)
Gallup	5.0	(2)
Hobbs	5.2	(2)
Roswell	5.5	(2)
New York		
Cortland	13.7	(7)
Gloversville	4.1	(1)
Ithaca	29.4	(18)
Kingston	7.7	(3)
Olean	6.9	(3)
Plattsburgh	10.7	(5)
Watertown	4.1	(1)

North Carolina

Albemarle	5.1	(2)
Eden	4.4	(1)
Havelock-New Bern	6.0	(2)
Henderson	4.8	(1)
Kinston	5.3	(2)
Lumberton	5.3	(2)
Roanoke Rapids	3.8	(1)
Sanford	4.8	(1)
Shelby	5.2	(2)
Statesville	4.3	(1)
Wilson	5.8	(2)

North Dakota

Minot	9.5	(5)

Ohio

Ashland	6.4	(2)
Athens	29.7	(18)
Chillicothe	4.4	(1)
Findlay-Fostoria-Tiffin	6.0	(2)
Fremont	4.4	(1)
Marion	4.3	(1)
Mount Vernon	7.9	(3)
New Philadelphia	3.3	(0)
Norwalk	3.2	(0)
Portsmouth	4.8	(1)
Sandusky	4.1	(1)
Sidney	4.4	(1)
Wooster	5.6	(2)
Zanesville	5.1	(2)

Oklahoma

Ardmore	4.2	(1)
Chickasha	5.1	(2)
Duncan	4.1	(1)
McAlester	3.8	(1)
Muskogee	4.9	(1)
Stillwater	27.6	(17)

Oregon

Albany-Corvallis	14.5	(8)
Bend	5.4	(2)
Coos Bay	4.5	(1)
Grants Pass	3.7	(1)
Klamath Falls	5.6	(2)
Pendleton	4.8	(1)
Roseburg	4.0	(1)

Pennsylvania

Chambersburg	3.9	(1)
New Castle	5.6	(2)
Pottsville	3.4	(0)

Rhode Island

Newport	8.6	(4)

South Carolina

Greenwood	6.8	(3)
Hilton Head Island	5.6	(2)

Tennessee

Cleveland	6.5	(3)
Columbia	3.9	(1)
Cookeville	12.9	(7)
Morristown	4.4	(1)
Tullahoma	5.2	(2)

Texas

Corsicana	5.6	(2)
Del Rio	5.0	(2)
Eagle Pass	5.1	(2)
Huntsville	19.6	(11)
Lufkin	5.4	(2)
Nacogdoches	21.8	(13)
Palestine	5.5	(2)
Paris	5.6	(2)

Utah

Logan	18.2	(10)
St. George	7.1	(3)

Vermont

Rutland	6.6	(3)

Virginia		
Blacksburg-Radford-Christiansburg	27.3	(16)
Harrisonburg	15.3	(8)
Martinsville	3.8	(1)
Staunton-Waynesboro	4.4	(1)
Winchester	4.9	(1)
Washington		
Aberdeen	4.3	(1)
Longview	4.4	(1)
Mount Vernon	4.6	(1)
Port Angeles	4.5	(1)
Walla Walla	11.1	(6)
Wenatchee	4.3	(1)
West Virginia		
Beckley	4.6	(1)
Clarksburg	4.4	(1)
Fairmont	6.8	(3)
Morgantown	22.7	(13)
Wisconsin		
Fond du Lac	5.6	(2)
Manitowoc	4.6	(1)
Stevens Point	14.7	(8)
Watertown	5.7	(2)
Wyoming		
Rock Springs	6.5	(3)

Local Education Funding

Providing a solid secondary-school education is the best investment a community can make in its youngest members. The importance of education—and the considerable costs—are reflected in many a budget sheet. Schools are the largest single item on a small city expenditure sheet and, according to the Census Bureau, local governments dedicate 36 percent of their annual budget to education.

This category measures each area's investment in education by dividing total spending on education by the total number of residents. Spending includes any meals, health, and recreation programs administered by schools.

Education spending in Rock Springs, Wyoming, amounts to 44 percent of government spending. That equals $1,806 per resident—twice the national average. One visible result is a below-average rate of high school dropouts.

Southern cities spend the least per capita on education. Cookeville, Tennessee, leads the way among micropolitans. Cookeville allocates 27 percent of total spending to education, or $460 per resident.

Cities that spend the most on education are distributed through the northern states, from New York to Oregon. Southeastern states dominate the list of lowest-spending micros.

Source: Census of Governments: Compendium of Government Finances, U.S. Bureau of the Census, Washington, D.C. Data, published in 1997, are for fiscal year 1991–92.

Scoring: Twenty points for spending of $1,500 or more per resident; no points for less than $550. The spacing is every $50 per resident.

Local Education Funding: Highs and Lows

	Annual Per Capita Education-Related Spending by Local Governments
Highest	**$**
1. Rock Springs, Wyo.	1,806
2. Kingston, N.Y.	1,575
3. Olean, N.Y.	1,552
4. Bend, Ore.	1,536
5. El Centro-Calexico-Brawley, Calif.	1,490
6. Burlington, Iowa	1,440
7. Watertown, N.Y.	1,369
8. Gloversville, N.Y.	1,356
9. Traverse City, Mich.	1,333
10. Coos Bay, Ore.	1,299
Willmar, Minn.	1,299
Median	
96. Prescott, Ariz.	860
97. Havelock-New Bern, N.C.	858
Lowest	
184. Jonesboro, Ark.	601
185. Hinesville, Ga.	596
Madisonville, Ky.	596
187. Auburn-Opelika, Ala.	593
188. Mount Pleasant, Mich.	589
189. Talladega, Ala.	587
190. Cleveland, Tenn.	553
191. Carbondale, Ill.	531
192. Cullman, Ala.	507
193. Cookeville, Tenn.	460

Local Education Funding Area by Area

(Annual per capita education-related spending by local governments in dollars and rating points)

Micro median	859	
Alabama		
Albertville	618	(2)
Auburn-Opelika	593	(1)
Cullman	507	(0)
Selma	731	(4)
Talladega	587	(1)
Alaska		
Fairbanks	1,270	(15)
Arizona		
Prescott	860	(7)
Sierra Vista	1,091	(11)
Arkansas		
Blytheville	765	(5)
El Dorado	746	(4)
Hot Springs	620	(2)
Jonesboro	601	(2)
Russellville	699	(3)
Searcy	700	(4)
California		
Arcata-Eureka	1,109	(12)
El Centro-Calexico-Brawley	1,490	(19)
Hanford-Lemoore	1,106	(12)
Hollister	1,111	(12)
Connecticut		
Torrington	1,155	(13)
Florida		
Key West	714	(4)
Vero Beach	764	(5)
Georgia		
Brunswick	798	(5)
Dalton	880	(7)
Dublin	897	(7)
Gainesville	703	(4)
Hinesville	596	(1)
La Grange	767	(5)
Milledgeville	625	(2)
Rome	909	(8)
Statesboro	721	(4)
Thomasville	895	(7)
Valdosta	717	(4)
Waycross	783	(5)
Idaho		
Coeur d'Alene	963	(9)
Idaho Falls	991	(9)
Pocatello	875	(7)
Twin Falls	1,094	(11)
Illinois		
Carbondale	531	(0)
Danville	807	(6)
Freeport	903	(8)
Galesburg	800	(6)
Mattoon-Charleston	690	(3)
Ottawa	810	(6)
Quincy	773	(5)
Sterling	767	(5)
Indiana		
Columbus	1,076	(11)
Marion	966	(9)
Michigan City-La Porte	834	(6)
New Castle	935	(8)
Richmond	825	(6)
Vincennes	677	(3)
Iowa		
Ames	703	(4)
Burlington	1,440	(18)

Clinton	929	(8)
Mason City	1,106	(12)
Muscatine	962	(9)
Kansas		
Hutchinson	1,069	(11)
Manhattan	625	(2)
Salina	816	(6)
Kentucky		
Bowling Green	617	(2)
Frankfort	605	(2)
Madisonville	596	(1)
Paducah	666	(3)
Radcliff-Elizabethtown	629	(2)
Louisiana		
Hammond	731	(4)
New Iberia	888	(7)
Ruston	614	(2)
Maine		
Augusta-Waterville	991	(9)
Biddeford-Saco	987	(9)
Maryland		
Salisbury	918	(8)
Michigan		
Marquette	812	(6)
Mount Pleasant	589	(1)
Owosso	903	(8)
Traverse City	1,333	(16)
Minnesota		
Faribault	877	(7)
Mankato	801	(6)
Red Wing	1,180	(13)
Willmar	1,299	(15)
Winona	816	(6)
Mississippi		
Cleveland	787	(5)
Columbus	705	(4)
Greenville	687	(3)
Laurel	871	(7)
Meridian	826	(6)
Tupelo	885	(7)
Vicksburg	701	(4)
Missouri		
Cape Girardeau-Sikeston	657	(3)
Jefferson City	659	(3)
Poplar Bluff	715	(4)
Warrensburg	642	(2)
Montana		
Bozeman	947	(8)
Helena	835	(6)
Missoula	928	(8)
Nebraska		
Grand Island	982	(9)
Nevada		
Carson City	1,232	(14)
Elko	1,244	(14)
New Hampshire		
Concord	867	(7)
Keene	987	(9)
New Mexico		
Alamogordo	662	(3)
Carlsbad	885	(7)
Clovis	872	(7)
Farmington	1,245	(14)
Gallup	1,138	(12)
Hobbs	886	(7)
Roswell	814	(6)
New York		
Cortland	1,144	(12)
Gloversville	1,356	(17)
Ithaca	1,189	(13)

Kingston	1,575	(20)
Olean	1,552	(20)
Plattsburgh	1,294	(15)
Watertown	1,369	(17)

North Carolina

Albemarle	861	(7)
Eden	825	(6)
Havelock-New Bern	858	(7)
Henderson	1,198	(13)
Kinston	1,036	(10)
Lumberton	1,034	(10)
Roanoke Rapids	997	(9)
Sanford	1,066	(11)
Shelby	928	(8)
Statesville	842	(6)
Wilson	904	(8)

North Dakota

Minot	683	(3)

Ohio

Ashland	803	(6)
Athens	738	(4)
Chillicothe	758	(5)
Findlay-Fostoria-Tiffin	766	(5)
Fremont	901	(8)
Marion	872	(7)
Mount Vernon	742	(4)
New Philadelphia	810	(6)
Norwalk	762	(5)
Portsmouth	873	(7)
Sandusky	1,069	(11)
Sidney	787	(5)
Wooster	848	(6)
Zanesville	875	(7)

Oklahoma

Ardmore	883	(7)
Chickasha	740	(4)
Duncan	743	(4)
McAlester	804	(6)
Muskogee	875	(7)
Stillwater	693	(3)

Oregon

Albany-Corvallis	1,085	(11)
Bend	1,536	(20)
Coos Bay	1,299	(15)
Grants Pass	920	(8)
Klamath Falls	1,081	(11)
Pendleton	1,196	(13)
Roseburg	1,137	(12)

Pennsylvania

Chambersburg	725	(4)
New Castle	814	(6)
Pottsville	717	(4)

Rhode Island

Newport	922	(8)

South Carolina

Greenwood	780	(5)
Hilton Head Island	856	(7)

Tennessee

Cleveland	553	(1)
Columbia	727	(4)
Cookeville	460	(0)
Morristown	604	(2)
Tullahoma	651	(3)

Texas

Corsicana	1,051	(11)
Del Rio	1,124	(12)
Eagle Pass	1,261	(15)
Huntsville	620	(2)
Lufkin	981	(9)
Nacogdoches	713	(4)
Palestine	734	(4)
Paris	1,006	(10)

Utah		
Logan	823	(6)
St. George	1,056	(11)
Vermont		
Rutland	958	(9)
Virginia		
Blacksburg-Radford-Christiansburg	654	(3)
Harrisonburg	670	(3)
Martinsville	718	(4)
Staunton-Waynesboro	691	(3)
Winchester	1,024	(10)
Washington		
Aberdeen	1,076	(11)
Longview	1,088	(11)
Mount Vernon	1,203	(14)
Port Angeles	911	(8)
Walla Walla	1,283	(15)
Wenatchee	984	(9)
West Virginia		
Beckley	845	(6)
Clarksburg	853	(7)
Fairmont	919	(8)
Morgantown	748	(4)
Wisconsin		
Fond du Lac	1,169	(13)
Manitowoc	732	(4)
Stevens Point	890	(7)
Watertown	838	(6)
Wyoming		
Rock Springs	1,806	(20)

The Results

Ithaca, New York, gives new meaning to the term "higher education." Cornell University and Ithaca College perch atop steep hills overlooking Cayuga Lake and downtown Ithaca. The Cornell bell tower is a local emblem and its chimes ring the quarter hour out over town.

Cornell University, some of whose colleges are state funded, is the only Ivy League school based in a micropolitan area. More than 19,000 students attend classes on a 745-acre campus set among woods, gorges, and waterfalls. Seventeen campus libraries house 5.8 million books.

Ithaca College began in 1892 as a music conservatory in four rented rooms. The fully accredited, private college now enrolls more than 5,000 students and boasts an extensive campus. The Ithaca area also benefits from the wide variety of courses offered at Tompkins-Cortland Community College.

This impressive arsenal of higher-learning institutions is the primary reason Ithaca scores first in the education section. Large colleges and universities play prominent roles in seventeen cities on the top-twenty education list. Not only are the schools' resources available to the community, but the large share of resident professors, instructors, and students contribute to an environment that has a strong emphasis on learning and arts.

One result is a tempting climate for the college-educated. Brad Edmondson is a Cornell grad who, like many others felt so at home in Ithaca that he stayed. "At first I stayed for the cheap movies, and the beautiful parks and forests," he says. But he and his friends easily put down roots. Now he finds Ithaca a great place to raise his son and daughter. But there is an unexpected side-effect: as he warns in the *Utne Reader* magazine: "When you live in a college town, people on the street stay the same age as you get older."

A second result of Ithaca's educational climate is a strong emphasis on public schools. The dedication shows: The city has a very low high-school dropout rate and above-average school funding. Natural benefits that follow include small, high-tech industries, local theater companies, and a year-round calendar of cultural events.

Unlike Ithaca, the main industry in Martinsville, Virginia, is not education. Martinsville is a manufacturing town, featuring a variety of industries that include furniture factories and textile mills. Martinsville invests in its schools at a level comparable to most micropolitans, but nearly 1 in 5 teens leaves high school early to begin working in the plants. Martinsville ties for last place with Cullman, Alabama, scoring just 11 points.

Cullman, Alabama, too, is a manufacturing city. Nearly 1 in 3 adults aged sixteen and older are employed as machine operators or in precision production alone. Fifty-nine percent of the population has a high school degree and 16 percent of youth are high school dropouts.

Education Scores: Highs and Lows

	Total Rating Points
Highest	
1. Ithaca, N.Y.	89
2. Ames, Iowa	84
3. Bozeman, Mont.	76
4. Manhattan, Kans.	69
Stillwater, Okla.	69
6. Carbondale, Ill.	68
Logan, Utah	68
8. Missoula, Mont.	64
9. Athens, Ohio	63
Fairbanks, Alaska	63
Mankato, Minn.	63
12. Morgantown, W.Va.	61
Mount Pleasant, Mich.	61
Ruston, La.	61
Traverse City, Mich.	61
16. Bend, Ore.	60
Kingston, N.Y.	60
18. Albany-Corvallis, Ore.	59
Newport, R.I.	59
20. Rock Springs, Wyo.	58
Median	
96. Farmington, N.Mex.	36
97 Key West, Fla.	36
Lowest	
184. Cleveland, Tenn.	17
Dalton, Ga.	17
Morristown, Tenn.	17
New Iberia, La.	17
188. Madisonville, Ky.	15
Talladega, Ala.	15
190. Poplar Bluff, Mo.	14
191. Albertville, Ala.	12
192. Cullman, Ala.	11
Martinsville, Va.	11

Education Performance Comparison

	Ithaca, New York	Micro median	Cullman, Alabama	Martinsville, Virginia
Total Points in Section	89	36	11	11
Rank in Section	1		192 (tie)	192 (tie)
High School Education				
Percent of adults with a high school education	87.2	73.7	58.8	56.0
High School Education points	(19)		(4)	(3)
High School Dropouts				
Percent of teenagers not in school and not a high school graduate	2.7	10.6	16.2	19.2
High School Dropout points	(19)		(5)	(2)
College Education				
Percent of adults who are college graduates	41.7	13.8	7.8	8.8
College Education points	(20)		(1)	(1)
College Influence				
Percent of residents enrolled in college	29.4	5.6	4.6	3.8
College Influence points	(18)		(1)	(1)
Local Education Funding				
Annual per capita spending by local governments	$1,189	$859	$507	$718
Education Funding points	(13)		(0)	(4)

Education Scores Area by Area

(Total education rating points)

Area	Points
Micro media	36
Alabama	
Albertville	12
Auburn-Opelika	56
Cullman	11
Selma	28
Talladega	15
Alaska	
Fairbanks	63
Arizona	
Prescott	40
Sierra Vista	39
Arkansas	
Blytheville	20
El Dorado	27
Hot Springs	24
Jonesboro	34
Russellville	33
Searcy	30
California	
Arcata-Eureka	54
El Centro-Calexico-Brawley	36
Hanford-Lemoore	30
Hollister	38
Connecticut	
Torrington	55
Florida	
Key West	36
Vero Beach	30
Georgia	
Brunswick	29
Dalton	17
Dublin	21
Gainesville	19
Hinesville	28
La Grange	24
Milledgeville	28
Rome	31
Statesboro	51
Thomasville	26
Valdosta	35
Waycross	20
Idaho	
Coeur d'Alene	46
Idaho Falls	49
Pocatello	47
Twin Falls	36
Illinois	
Carbondale	68
Danville	30
Freeport	41
Galesburg	38
Mattoon-Charleston	54
Ottawa	31
Quincy	39
Sterling	33
Indiana	
Columbus	41
Marion	36
Michigan City-La Porte	33
New Castle	34
Richmond	30
Vincennes	40
Iowa	
Ames	84
Burlington	51
Clinton	43
Mason City	53
Muscatine	40
Kansas	
Hutchinson	42
Manhattan	69
Salina	46
Kentucky	
Bowling Green	41
Frankfort	34
Madisonville	15
Paducah	31
Radcliff-Elizabethtown	33
Louisiana	
Hammond	23
New Iberia	17
Ruston	61
Maine	
Augusta-Waterville	46
Biddeford-Saco	46
Maryland	
Salisbury	40
Michigan	
Marquette	55
Mount Pleasant	61
Owosso	37
Traverse City	61
Minnesota	
Faribault	51
Mankato	63
Red Wing	48
Willmar	51
Winona	55

Mississippi

Cleveland	27
Columbus	35
Greenville	18
Laurel	31
Meridian	33
Tupelo	29
Vicksburg	34

Missouri

Cape Girardeau-Sikeston	30
Jefferson City	38
Poplar Bluff	14
Warrensburg	57

Montana

Bozeman	76
Helena	52
Missoula	64

Nebraska

Grand Island	41

Nevada

Carson City	50
Elko	39

New Hampshire

Concord	51
Keene	52

New Mexico

Alamogordo	40
Carlsbad	32
Clovis	39
Farmington	36
Gallup	31
Hobbs	23
Roswell	31

New York

Cortland	56
Gloversville	43
Ithaca	89
Kingston	60
Olean	51
Plattsburgh	51
Watertown	45

North Carolina

Albemarle	27
Eden	18
Havelock-New Bern	37
Henderson	23
Kinston	27
Lumberton	25
Roanoke Rapids	22
Sanford	37
Shelby	28
Statesville	21
Wilson	30

North Dakota

Minot	51

Ohio

Ashland	39
Athens	63
Chillicothe	30
Findlay-Fostoria-Tiffin	42
Fremont	39
Marion	33
Mount Vernon	40
New Philadelphia	29
Norwalk	34
Portsmouth	28
Sandusky	42
Sidney	29
Wooster	34
Zanesville	36

Oklahoma

Ardmore	33
Chickasha	30
Duncan	32
McAlester	29
Muskogee	32
Stillwater	69

Oregon

Albany-Corvallis	59
Bend	60
Coos Bay	42
Grants Pass	27
Klamath Falls	36
Pendleton	37
Roseburg	34

Pennsylvania

Chambersburg	29
New Castle	36
Pottsville	24

Rhode Island

Newport	59

South Carolina

Greenwood	33
Hilton Head Island	49

Tennessee

Cleveland	17
Columbia	24
Cookeville	33
Morristown	17
Tullahoma	24

Texas

Corsicana	34
Del Rio	29
Eagle Pass	19
Huntsville	46

Lufkin 29
Nacogdoches 51
Palestine 22
Paris 37

Utah
Logan 68
St. George 54

Vermont
Rutland 50

Virginia
Blacksburg-Radford-Christiansburg 57
Harrisonburg 41
Martinsville 11
Staunton-Waynesboro 29
Winchester 36

Washington
Aberdeen 32
Longview 38
Mount Vernon 45
Port Angeles 37
Walla Walla 55
Wenatchee 35

West Virginia
Beckley 26
Clarksburg 33
Fairmont 40
Morgantown 61

Wisconsin
Fond du Lac 48
Manitowoc 38
Stevens Point 56
Watertown 39

Wyoming
Rock Springs 58

5

Community Assets

Many residents of metropolitan areas shudder at the very thought of moving to a city with a population of less than 1 million. They fear they would somehow be cut off from modern life. The otherwise admirable *Places Rated Almanac* condescendingly imagines the tribulations of a transplanted urbanite in a small city:

> You trot down to the public library in your new town, only to find a well-worn selection of fiction, mostly published in the fifties, and a few back issues of *Family Circle* and *Field & Stream.* You search for a theater or musical event and find your only choice is a concert stop by touring country-and-western performer Clyde McFritter and His Heavy Haulers.

This scenario paints small-city living with a wide brush, to say the least. There are small university towns with extensive libraries and regular schedules of cultural events that are the envy of many metro areas. Other micropolitans support the kinds of thriving artistic communities that sprawling suburban metro areas often lack. Key West, Florida, is still home to a literary community that has included Ernest Hemingway, Tennessee Williams, Wallace Stevens, and John Dos Passos.

Nor are residents in smaller cities out of touch with current events. Cable television broadcasts sessions of Congress on C-SPAN and the latest headline news on the Cable News Network. The local newsstand carries the national newsmagazines and *USA Today.* And don't forget that most micropolitans are relatively near large cities, whose television stations and newspapers are also available to them. Other residents may simply read the national dailies each morning via the Internet.

"I have friends in New York who think there's nothing out there 'til you get to Hollywood," said the late Charles Kuralt, CBS's famous "On the Road" correspondent. "And boy, is that wrong. That's the big change: this explosion of information."

Intellectual sparks fly best in community settings, and they often lead residents to become more involved in their towns. Sociologists Michael Irwin, Charles Tolbert, and Thomas Lyson find that the most stable communities are those where residents invest themselves in local institutions. Irwin, Tolbert, and Lyson created a "civic engagement index" to measure the wealth of local organizations and community involvement. Sixteen of their top twenty nonmetro communities are small cities featured in this book. Litchfield County, Connecticut, (the Torrington micropolitan area) tops their list.

Charles Kuralt also cites the willingness of small-city residents to get involved. "Let something go wrong, and you can be sure somebody will form a committee, somebody will hire a hall," he says. "The next thing you know, people are at work on the problem." People often have a greater sense of ownership in smaller communities.

Community involvement can be fostered by a variety of factors, from church membership to newspaper readership. Adults who read the paper, for instance, are the most likely residents to belong to a local organization, attend religious services regularly, and volunteer for community service, according to the National Center for Education Statistics (NCES). In a 1996 study entitled *Adult Civic Involvement in the United States,* the NCES found that 75 percent of adults who report that they read, listen to, or watch the national news nearly every day are involved in one or more community activities, compared with 65 percent of adults who do not follow the news regularly. Eighty-five percent of well-informed residents vote, attend public meetings, or volunteer for political work, compared with 63 percent of non-newshounds.

This section evaluates both the community involvement and the intellectual climate of each area, taking into account local newspaper circulation, broadcast outlets, museums and libraries, and membership organizations, social service groups, and owner-occupied housing.

Kuralt's New York friends are certainly college graduates. Very likely they prefer their city because it affords an easy opportunity to meet other educated people, and they feel it raises the level of sophistication in their community. They might be surprised to learn that Ithaca, New York, and Ames, Iowa, are among the small cities with a share of college graduates equivalent to Manhattan.

Ranking micropolitan America. The perfect small city would have plenty of access to information on current events, and plenty of opportunity to get involved with the community. You would be able to, as the saying goes, "Think globally, act locally."

1. Homeownership: Does a reasonable share of owner-occupied housing promise stable neighborhoods that invest in the long-term?

2. Newspaper Strength: How heavily read is the local paper?

3. Broadcast Outlets: Does the area have a good mixture of radio, television, and cable stations, or are there few sources of local news and programming?

4. Arts and Learning Institutions: How's the supply of local museums, colleges, libraries, and even zoos?

5. Community Groups and Services: Is there plenty of opportunity to get involved in civic life through membership groups? Does the community indicate a willingness to help with local social services?

Homeownership

Communities with higher levels of homeownership often indicate higher levels of neighborhood stability and investment than those where many of the homes are rented. That's not to slight those of us who have rented our roofs for years. Plenty of renters maintain nice lawns and gardens and are a benefit to their neighborhood, but homeowners have the highest stake in the future of their houses and their neighborhoods.

Homeowners are the most likely to keep the castle and grounds looking nice, and to plan for long-term improvement. They often protect and advance the quality of life on their street through participation in homeowner organizations. And more so than absent landlords, homeowners maintain and improve their residences, raising property values on the whole block.

This category ranks micropolitans according to the share of houses that are occupied by the people who own them. The national average is 64 percent; the median for micropolitans is 70 percent. A dozen micros have shares of 75 percent or higher.

Older, stable cities have the highest rates. Pottsville, Pennsylvania, tops them all, with 78.1 percent of homes occupied by their owners. College towns, with their large share of transient students, fill up the bottom of the list. But Hinesville, Georgia, adjacent to Fort Stewart military base, has the lowest rate. Just 43.5 percent of homes in Hinesville are owner-occupied.

Source: Census of Housing, U.S. Census Bureau, Washington, D.C. These data, published in 1993, are for 1990.

Scoring: Twenty points for a share of 78 percent or higher; no points for less than 49.5 percent. The spacing is every 1.5 percent.

Homeownership: Highs and Lows

	Percent of Owner-Occupied Housing
Highest	
1. Pottsville, Pa.	78.1
2. Cullman, Ala.	77.8
3. Owosso, Mich.	77.7
4. Albemarle, N.C.	76.6
5. Red Wing, Minn.	76.5
6. Laurel, Miss.	76.4
7. Traverse City, Mich.	76.2
8. New Castle, Pa.	76.1
9. Chickasha, Okla.	75.8
10. Beckley, W.Va.	75.5
Fairmont, Ohio	75.5
Faribault, Minn.	75.5
Median	
96. Portsmouth, Ohio	69.7
97. Corsicana, Tex.	69.5
Lowest	
184. Huntsville, Tex.	57.4
185. Ames, Iowa	56.0
186. Ithaca, N.Y.	55.3
187. Stillwater, Okla.	54.5
188. Blytheville, Ark.	54.4
189. Hanford-Lemoore, Calif.	52.9
190. Carbondale, Ill.	52.7
191. Manhattan, Kans.	51.4
192. Fairbanks, Alaska	49.0
193. Hinesville, Ga.	43.5

Homeownership Area by Area

(Percent of housing that is owner-occupied and rating points)

Micro median 69.6

Alabama

Albertville	74.2	(17)
Auburn-Opelika	58.1	(6)
Cullman	77.8	(19)
Selma	62.2	(9)
Talladega	75.2	(18)

Alaska

Fairbanks	49.0	(0)

Arizona

Prescott	72.1	(16)
Sierra Vista	63.6	(10)

Arkansas

Blytheville	54.4	(4)
El Dorado	73.8	(17)
Hot Springs	70.8	(15)
Jonesboro	65.4	(11)
Russellville	70.8	(15)
Searcy	73.3	(16)

California

Arcata-Eureka	58.8	(7)
El Centro-Calexico-Brawley	57.6	(6)
Hanford-Lemoore	52.9	(3)
Hollister	61.1	(8)

Connecticut

Torrington	73.2	(16)

Florida

Key West	62.1	(9)
Vero Beach	75.0	(18)

Georgia

Brunswick	65.1	(11)
Dalton	66.9	(12)
Dublin	70.9	(15)
Gainesville	69.4	(14)
Hinesville	43.5	(0)
La Grange	64.1	(10)
Milledgeville	68.3	(13)
Rome	66.1	(12)
Statesboro	60.1	(8)
Thomasville	68.5	(13)
Valdosta	59.7	(7)
Waycross	72.5	(16)

Idaho

Coeur d'Alene	71.3	(15)
Idaho Falls	71.5	(15)
Pocatello	69.2	(14)
Twin Falls	67.8	(13)

Illinois

Carbondale	52.7	(3)
Danville	71.2	(15)
Freeport	71.2	(15)
Galesburg	69.1	(14)
Mattoon-Charleston	64.7	(11)
Ottawa	73.2	(16)
Quincy	71.1	(15)
Sterling	71.7	(15)

Indiana

Columbus	73.2	(16)
Marion	71.3	(15)
Michigan City-La Porte	73.1	(16)
New Castle	75.2	(18)
Richmond	67.6	(13)
Vincennes	70.6	(15)

Iowa

Ames	56.0	(5)
Burlington	72.8	(16)
Clinton	71.2	(15)

Mason City 68.8 (13)
Muscatine 72.0 (16)

Kansas
Hutchinson 69.9 (14)
Manhattan 51.4 (2)
Salina 66.7 (12)

Kentucky
Bowling Green 65.0 (11)
Frankfort 64.0 (10)
Madisonville 75.2 (18)
Paducah 68.2 (13)
Radcliff-Elizabethtown 63.5 (10)

Louisiana
Hammond 72.7 (16)
New Iberia 71.0 (15)
Ruston 62.1 (9)

Maine
Augusta-Waterville 70.9 (15)
Biddeford-Saco 71.6 (15)

Maryland
Salisbury 66.7 (12)

Michigan
Marquette 64.2 (10)
Mount Pleasant 65.0 (11)
Owosso 77.7 (19)
Traverse City 76.2 (18)

Minnesota
Faribault 75.5 (18)
Mankato 66.9 (12)
Red Wing 76.5 (19)
Willmar 72.9 (16)
Winona 72.1 (16)

Mississippi
Cleveland 59.4 (7)
Columbus 63.6 (10)
Greenville 59.6 (7)
Laurel 76.4 (18)
Meridian 66.4 (12)
Tupelo 69.0 (14)
Vicksburg 68.9 (13)

Missouri
Cape Girardeau-Sikeston 67.5 (13)
Jefferson City 70.7 (15)
Poplar Bluff 68.1 (13)
Warrensburg 58.6 (7)

Montana
Bozeman 58.5 (7)
Helena 68.5 (13)
Missoula 60.1 (8)

Nebraska
Grand Island 63.6 (10)

Nevada
Carson City 60.3 (8)
Elko 64.5 (11)

New Hampshire
Concord 69.7 (14)
Keene 70.4 (14)

New Mexico
Alamogordo 62.3 (9)
Carlsbad 72.9 (16)
Clovis 61.6 (9)
Farmington 72.0 (16)
Gallup 71.1 (15)
Hobbs 71.5 (15)
Roswell 69.9 (14)

New York
Cortland 64.4 (10)
Gloversville 71.4 (15)
Ithaca 55.3 (4)

Kingston	69.2	(14)
Olean	73.2	(16)
Plattsburgh	63.9	(10)
Watertown	59.3	(7)
North Carolina		
Albemarle	76.6	(19)
Eden	74.3	(17)
Havelock-New Bern	63.3	(10)
Henderson	65.3	(11)
Kinston	63.1	(10)
Lumberton	70.1	(14)
Roanoke Rapids	65.3	(11)
Sanford	72.6	(16)
Shelby	72.8	(16)
Statesville	75.1	(18)
Wilson	59.3	(7)
North Dakota		
Minot	59.7	(7)
Ohio		
Ashland	74.0	(17)
Athens	62.0	(9)
Chillicothe	70.5	(15)
Findlay-Fostoria-Tiffin	74.1	(17)
Fremont	74.5	(17)
Marion	70.9	(15)
Mount Vernon	72.2	(16)
New Philadelphia	75.0	(18)
Norwalk	71.6	(15)
Portsmouth	69.7	(14)
Sandusky	71.3	(15)
Sidney	74.3	(17)
Wooster	71.2	(15)
Zanesville	73.0	(16)
Oklahoma		
Ardmore	72.4	(16)
Chickasha	75.8	(18)
Duncan	74.7	(17)
McAlester	75.4	(18)
Muskogee	69.9	(14)
Stillwater	54.5	(4)
Oregon		
Albany-Corvallis	61.1	(8)
Bend	71.0	(15)
Coos Bay	66.5	(12)
Grants Pass	70.4	(14)
Klamath Falls	65.2	(11)
Pendleton	62.0	(9)
Roseburg	68.9	(13)
Pennsylvania		
Chambersburg	72.7	(16)
New Castle	76.1	(18)
Pottsville	78.1	(20)
Rhode Island		
Newport	59.4	(7)
South Carolina		
Greenwood	69.1	(14)
Hilton Head Island	64.9	(11)
Tennessee		
Cleveland	68.8	(13)
Columbia	69.0	(14)
Cookeville	66.8	(12)
Morristown	72.1	(16)
Tullahoma	73.5	(17)
Texas		
Corsicana	69.5	(14)
Del Rio	61.1	(8)
Eagle Pass	67.0	(12)
Huntsville	57.4	(6)
Lufkin	71.6	(15)
Nacogdoches	58.1	(6)
Palestine	72.8	(16)
Paris	68.9	(13)

Utah		
Logan	62.6	(9)
St. George	70.8	(15)
Vermont		
Rutland	68.5	(13)
Virginia		
Blacksburg-Radford-Christiansburg	57.8	(6)
Harrisonburg	66.2	(12)
Martinsville	73.8	(17)
Staunton-Waynesboro	71.8	(15)
Winchester	67.1	(12)
Washington		
Aberdeen	67.0	(12)
Longview	65.4	(11)
Mount Vernon	69.9	(14)
Port Angeles	70.2	(14)
Walla Walla	62.3	(9)
Wenatchee	61.9	(9)
West Virginia		
Beckley	75.5	(18)
Clarksburg	74.0	(17)
Fairmont	75.5	(18)
Morgantown	62.1	(9)
Wisconsin		
Fond du Lac	71.8	(15)
Manitowoc	73.9	(17)
Stevens Point	70.3	(14)
Watertown	71.9	(15)
Wyoming		
Rock Springs	70.2	(14)

Newspaper Strength

Thomas Jefferson believed newspapers were so essential to an enlightened society that he boldly wrote, "Were it left to me to decide whether we should have government without newspapers, or newspapers without a government, I should not hesitate a moment to prefer the latter."

The variety of news sources has greatly increased since Jefferson's day. Local and national news is available on radio, television, in magazines, and on the Internet. But the daily newspaper remains the major source of local news, with regular beats from city hall to the high school sports stadium. This category measures the penetration of local daily papers by dividing their daily circulation by the number of local residents.

Two Kansas micros hold the top places for newspaper circulation. The local Salina, Kansas, paper reaches nearly 64 percent of residents. In Hutchinson, Kansas, the local paper reaches 61 percent of local residents. Nationally, approximately one in four Americans subscribes to a daily paper.

Six micros do not have a local paper that is published every day. Albemarle, North Carolina; Albertville, Alabama; Blacksburg-Radford-Christiansburg, Virginia; Eagle Pass, Texas; Hinesville, Georgia; and Tullahoma, Tennessee, all lack local dailies.

Midwestern towns have the highest readership rates. The lowest rates are in the South.

Source: Circulation data derived from *Editor and Publisher Market Guide* (New York: Editor & Publisher Co., 1996). The data, published in 1996, are for 1994–95.

Scoring: Twenty points for penetration of 50 percent or more; no points for less than 2.5 percent. The spacing is every 2.5 percentage points.

Newspaper Strength: Highs and Lows

	Percent of Residents Subscribing to the Local Daily Newspaper
Highest	
1. Salina, Kans.	63.7
2. Hutchinson, Kans.	61.0
3. Tupelo, Miss.	55.9
4. Wenatchee, Wash.	50.3
5. Carbondale, Ill.	49.4
6. Grand Island, Nebr.	48.9
7. Paducah, Ky.	46.5
8. Minot, N.Dak.	44.9
9. Mason City, Iowa	42.7
10. Willmar, Minn.	41.6
Median	
96. Gallup, N.Mex.	23.0
97. Valdosta, Ga.	22.6
Lowest	
184. Biddeford-Saco, Maine	7.7
185. Eden, N.C.	7.5
186. Watertown, Wisc.	6.4
187. Jefferson City, Mo.	2.7
188. Albemarle, N.C.	0.0
Albertville, Ala.	0.0
Blacksburg-Radford-Christiansburg, Va.	0.0
Eagle Pass, Tex.	0.0
Hinesville, Ga.	0.0
Tullahoma, Tenn.	0.0

Note: The six cities tied for last place do not have a local daily newspaper.

Newspaper Strength Area by Area

(Percent of residents subscribing to the local daily paper and rating points)

Micro median	22.8	
Alabama		
Albertville	0.0	(0)
Auburn-Opelika	14.0	(5)
Cullman	14.0	(5)
Selma	18.6	(7)
Talladega	10.5	(4)
Alaska		
Fairbanks	20.8	(8)
Arizona		
Prescott	12.7	(5)
Sierra Vista	8.1	(3)
Arkansas		
Blytheville	9.4	(3)
El Dorado	24.1	(9)
Hot Springs	23.2	(9)
Jonesboro	36.6	(14)
Russellville	22.5	(9)
Searcy	12.6	(5)
California		
Arcata-Eureka	18.1	(7)
El Centro-Calexico-Brawley	12.5	(5)
Hanford-Lemoore	12.0	(4)
Hollister	9.7	(3)
Connecticut		
Torrington	8.3	(3)
Florida		
Key West	14.2	(5)
Vero Beach	37.2	(14)
Georgia		
Brunswick	24.8	(9)
Dalton	25.1	(10)
Dublin	29.2	(11)
Gainesville	22.3	(8)
Hinesville	0.0	(0)
La Grange	25.7	(10)
Milledgeville	20.4	(8)
Rome	24.5	(9)
Statesboro	14.7	(5)
Thomasville	24.9	(9)
Valdosta	22.6	(9)
Waycross	24.1	(9)
Idaho		
Coeur d'Alene	18.8	(7)
Idaho Falls	37.9	(15)
Pocatello	21.9	(8)
Twin Falls	38.1	(15)
Illinois		
Carbondale	49.4	(19)
Danville	23.4	(9)
Freeport	34.6	(13)
Galesburg	31.3	(12)
Mattoon-Charleston	37.5	(15)
Ottawa	11.7	(4)
Quincy	37.4	(14)
Sterling	25.2	(10)
Indiana		
Columbus	32.6	(13)
Marion	28.1	(11)
Michigan City-La Porte	24.9	(9)
New Castle	23.6	(9)
Richmond	26.8	(10)
Vincennes	33.8	(13)
Iowa		
Ames	12.3	(4)
Burlington	40.1	(16)
Clinton	32.7	(13)

Mason City 42.7 (17)
Muscatine 23.0 (9)

Kansas
Hutchinson 61.0 (20)
Manhattan 13.6 (5)
Salina 63.7 (20)

Kentucky
Bowling Green 26.9 (10)
Frankfort 22.6 (9)
Madisonville 23.8 (9)
Paducah 46.5 (18)
Radcliff-Elizabethtown 18.4 (7)

Louisiana
Hammond 12.7 (5)
New Iberia 20.2 (8)
Ruston 14.1 (5)

Maine
Augusta-Waterville 35.7 (14)
Biddeford-Saco 7.7 (3)

Maryland
Salisbury 35.5 (14)

Michigan
Marquette 27.3 (10)
Mount Pleasant 18.3 (7)
Owosso 16.5 (6)
Traverse City 27.3 (10)

Minnesota
Faribault 14.2 (5)
Mankato 31.1 (12)
Red Wing 19.1 (7)
Willmar 41.6 (16)
Winona 26.6 (10)

Mississippi
Cleveland 18.3 (7)
Columbus 23.2 (9)
Greenville 20.8 (8)
Laurel 14.8 (5)
Meridian 25.3 (10)
Tupelo 55.9 (20)
Vicksburg 30.0 (12)

Missouri
Cape Girardeau-Sikeston 10.2 (4)
Jefferson City 2.7 (1)
Poplar Bluff 33.6 (13)
Warrensburg 10.5 (4)

Montana
Bozeman 24.2 (9)
Helena 27.7 (11)
Missoula 35.5 (14)

Nebraska
Grand Island 48.9 (19)

Nevada
Carson City 26.2 (10)
Elko 17.1 (6)

New Hampshire
Concord 17.7 (7)
Keene 21.7 (8)

New Mexico
Alamogordo 15.1 (6)
Carlsbad 15.7 (6)
Clovis 20.3 (8)
Farmington 18.0 (7)
Gallup 23.0 (9)
Hobbs 20.4 (8)
Roswell 24.0 (9)

New York
Cortland 23.3 (9)
Gloversville 22.2 (8)
Ithaca 19.4 (7)

Kingston	13.3	(5)
Olean	24.7	(9)
Plattsburgh	26.6	(10)
Watertown	34.1	(13)
North Carolina		
Albemarle	0.0	(0)
Eden	7.5	(3)
Havelock-New Bern	19.7	(7)
Henderson	23.8	(9)
Kinston	22.5	(9)
Lumberton	12.9	(5)
Roanoke Rapids	21.1	(8)
Sanford	31.8	(12)
Shelby	19.9	(7)
Statesville	16.9	(6)
Wilson	25.3	(10)
North Dakota		
Minot	44.9	(17)
Ohio		
Ashland	24.2	(9)
Athens	21.4	(8)
Chillicothe	22.4	(8)
Findlay-Fostoria-Tiffin	34.4	(13)
Fremont	22.0	(8)
Marion	26.8	(10)
Mount Vernon	21.1	(8)
New Philadelphia	30.3	(12)
Norwalk	15.4	(6)
Portsmouth	21.3	(8)
Sandusky	31.5	(12)
Sidney	28.7	(11)
Wooster	23.6	(9)
Zanesville	27.6	(11)
Oklahoma		
Ardmore	27.6	(11)
Chickasha	11.6	(4)
Duncan	22.4	(8)
McAlester	28.7	(11)
Muskogee	27.8	(11)
Stillwater	15.8	(6)
Oregon		
Albany-Corvallis	20.6	(8)
Bend	28.2	(11)
Coos Bay	26.8	(10)
Grants Pass	26.7	(10)
Klamath Falls	29.0	(11)
Pendleton	20.3	(8)
Roseburg	19.9	(7)
Pennsylvania		
Chambersburg	17.3	(6)
New Castle	21.2	(8)
Pottsville	18.5	(7)
Rhode Island		
Newport	17.2	(6)
South Carolina		
Greenwood	25.6	(10)
Hilton Head Island	14.9	(5)
Tennessee		
Cleveland	21.0	(8)
Columbia	18.6	(7)
Cookeville	19.8	(7)
Morristown	36.7	(14)
Tullahoma	0.0	(0)
Texas		
Corsicana	17.3	(6)
Del Rio	14.7	(5)
Eagle Pass	0.0	(0)
Huntsville	11.5	(4)
Lufkin	19.5	(7)
Nacogdoches	15.0	(6)
Palestine	19.9	(7)
Paris	26.2	(10)

Utah		
Logan	19.3	(7)
St. George	30.5	(12)
Vermont		
Rutland	35.6	(14)
Virginia		
Blacksburg-Radford-Christiansburg	0.0	(0)
Harrisonburg	34.7	(13)
Martinsville	26.0	(10)
Staunton-Waynesboro	28.6	(11)
Winchester	29.9	(11)
Washington		
Aberdeen	25.8	(10)
Longview	28.9	(11)
Mount Vernon	22.6	(9)
Port Angeles	24.3	(9)
Walla Walla	27.6	(11)
Wenatchee	50.3	(20)
West Virginia		
Beckley	41.1	(16)
Clarksburg	27.8	(11)
Fairmont	26.0	(10)
Morgantown	25.6	(10)
Wisconsin		
Fond du Lac	21.8	(8)
Manitowoc	23.5	(9)
Stevens Point	22.0	(8)
Watertown	6.4	(2)
Wyoming		
Rock Springs	18.8	(7)

Broadcast Outlets

Arcata-Eureka, California, may never be mistaken for one of the nation's major broadcasting markets. But among the nation's small cities, it is the Los Angeles of the broadcast world. Arcata-Eureka has five television stations, one major cable company, and ten radio stations. If residents are clueless about local and national events, they can't blame it on empty airwaves.

This category measures the strength of local electronic media. An index has been created which assigns 3 points for each television station and 3 points for each cable service of 20,000 or more subscribers. Radio stations receive 1 point. Television and cable services receive more points because they have higher profiles and typically devote more resources than radio to local news.

Arcata-Eureka earns a broadcast index of 28. That's four times the micro median of 7 points. Four micros receive just 1 point for a single local radio station. Western micros dominate the top-ten list.

Source: Derived from *Broadcasting & Cable Yearbook* (New Providence, N.J.: R. R. Bowker, 1996). The data, published in 1996, are for 1996.

Scoring: Twenty points for an index of 20 or higher; no points for an index of 0. The spacing is every 1 index point.

Broadcast Outlets: Highs and Lows

Highest	Broadcast Index
1. Arcata-Eureka, Calif.	28
2. Bowling Green, Ky.	23
Fairbanks, Alaska	23
4. Meridian, Miss.	21
Minot, N.Dak.	21
Missoula, Mont.	21
7. Idaho Falls, Idaho	19
Quincy, Ill.	19
Roswell, N.Mex.	19
10. El Centro-Calexico-Brawley, Calif.	18
Jonesboro, Ark.	18
Salisbury, Md.	18

Median	Broadcast Index
96. Athens, Ohio	7
97. Findlay-Fostoria-Tiffin, Ohio	7

Lowest	Broadcast Index
171. Albertville, Ala.	2
190. Gloversville, N.Y.	1
Blytheville, Ark.	2
Muscatine, Iowa	1
Chickasha, Okla.	2
Newport, R.I.	1
Corsicana, Tex.	2
Torrington, Conn.	1
Duncan, Okla.	2
Faribault, Minn.	2
Fremont, Ohio	2
Hollister, Calif.	2
New Castle, Ind.	2
Norwalk, Ohio	2
Owosso, Mich.	2
Port Angeles, Wash.	2
Red Wing, Minn.	2
Searcy, Ark.	2
Sidney, Ohio	2
Sterling, Ill.	2
Tullahoma, Tenn.	2
Warrensburg, Mo.	2
Watertown, Wisc.	2

Broadcast Outlets Area by Area

(Number of local radio, television, and large cable systems,* and rating points)

Micro median (total) 7

	Radio	TV	Cable	Rating Points
Alabama				
Albertville	2			(2)
Auburn-Opelika	6	1		(9)
Cullman	4			(4)
Selma	5	1		(8)
Talladega	3			(3)
Alaska				
Fairbanks	11	4		(20)
Arizona				
Prescott	5	1		(8)
Sierra Vista	4		1	(7)
Arkansas				
Blytheville	2			(2)
El Dorado	7	1		(10)
Hot Springs	8	1	1	(14)
Jonesboro	6	3	1	(18)
Russellville	4			(4)
Searcy	2			(2)
California				
Arcata-Eureka	10	5	1	(20)
El Centro-Calexico-Brawley	9	2	1	(18)
Hanford-Lemoore	5	1		(8)
Hollister	2			(2)
Connecticut				
Torrington	1			(1)
Florida				
Key West	9	2		(15)
Vero Beach	7		1	(10)
Georgia				
Brunswick	9	1		(12)
Dalton	4	1		(7)
Dublin	4			(4)
Gainesville	7		1	(10)
Hinesville	3		1	(6)
La Grange	5			(5)
Milledgeville	5			(5)
Rome	6	1	1	(12)
Statesboro	5			(5)
Thomasville	3			(3)
Valdosta	11	1		(14)
Waycross	4	1		(7)
Idaho				
Coeur d'Alene	2	1		(5)
Idaho Falls	7	3	1	(19)
Pocatello	6	1		(9)
Twin Falls	8	3		(17)
Illinois				
Carbondale	4	1		(7)
Danville	5			(5)
Freeport	3			(3)
Galesburg	5			(5)
Mattoon-Charleston	8	1		(11)
Ottawa	3		1	(6)
Quincy	7	4		(19)
Sterling	2			(2)
Indiana				
Columbus	3		1	(6)
Marion	3	1		(6)
Michigan City-La Porte	4			(4)
New Castle	2			(2)
Richmond	7	1		(10)
Vincennes	5	1		(8)

*20,000 subscribers or more.

Broadcast Outlets Area by Area (continued)

Iowa				
Ames	6			(6)
Burlington	5	1		(8)
Clinton	4			(4)
Mason City	7	2		(13)
Muscatine	1			(1)
Kansas				
Hutchinson	4	1		(7)
Manhattan	5			(5)
Salina	8	1		(11)
Kentucky				
Bowling Green	8	4	1	(20)
Frankfort	4			(4)
Madisonville	5	2		(11)
Paducah	5	3	1	(17)
Radcliff-Elizabethtown	4	1	1	(10)
Louisiana				
Hammond	4			(4).
New Iberia	4			(4)
Ruston	3			(3)
Maine				
Augusta-Waterville	8	1		(11)
Biddeford-Saco	3	1		(6)
Maryland				
Salisbury	9	3		(18)
Michigan				
Marquette	6	2		(12)
Mount Pleasant	5	1		(8)
Owosso	2			(2)
Traverse City	7	2		(13)
Minnesota				
Faribault	2			(2)
Mankato	5	1		(8)
Red Wing	2			(2)
Willmar	4			(4)
Winona	6			(6)

Mississippi				
Cleveland	7			(7)
Columbus	7	1		(10)
Greenville	5	2		(11)
Laurel	4			(4)
Meridian	9	4		(20)
Tupelo	6	1		(9)
Vicksburg	4			(4)
Missouri				
Cape Girardeau-Sikeston	11	2		(17)
Jefferson City	5	2		(11)
Poplar Bluff	8	1		(11)
Warrensburg	2			(2)
Montana				
Bozeman	8	2		(14)
Helena	7	1		(10)
Missoula	9	4		(20)
Nebraska				
Grand Island	5	2		(11)
Nevada				
Carson City	4			(4)
Elko	4	1		(7)
New Hampshire				
Concord	7	1	1	(13)
Keene	6	1		(9)
New Mexico				
Alamogordo	5			(5)
Carlsbad	5	1		(8)
Clovis	7	1		(10)
Farmington	9	1		(12)
Gallup	7	1		(10)
Hobbs	6	1		(9)
Roswell	10	3		(19)
New York				
Cortland	3			(3)
Gloversville	1			(1)
Ithaca	7		1	(10)

Kingston	6	1		(9)
Olean	5			(5)
Plattsburgh	7	2		(13)
Watertown	7	3		(16)

North Carolina				
Albemarle	3			(3)
Eden	4			(4)
Havelock-New Bern	7			(7)
Henderson	3			(3)
Kinston	7			(7)
Lumberton	4			(4)
Roanoke Rapids	4	1		(7)
Sanford	4			(4)
Shelby	3			(3)
Statesville	4			(4)
Wilson	4	1		(7)

North Dakota				
Minot	9	4		(20)

Ohio				
Ashland	3			(3)
Athens	4	1		(7)
Chillicothe	7	1		(10)
Findlay-Fostoria-Tiffin	7			(7)
Fremont	2			(2)
Marion	3			(3)
Mount Vernon	3			(3)
New Philadelphia	3		1	(6)
Norwalk	2			(2)
Portsmouth	6	2		(12)
Sandusky	3	1	1	(9)
Sidney	2			(2)
Wooster	5			(5)
Zanesville	3	1		(6)

Oklahoma				
Ardmore	3			(3)
Chickasha	2			(2)
Duncan	2			(2)
McAlester	4			(4)
Muskogee	3			(3)
Stillwater	4			(4)

Oregon				
Albany-Corvallis	10	1	1	(16)
Bend	9	2		(15)
Coos Bay	6	2		(12)
Grants Pass	3			(3)
Klamath Falls	5	3		(14)
Pendleton	5			(5)
Roseburg	5	3		(14)

Pennsylvania				
Chambersburg	3			(3)
New Castle	3			(3)
Pottsville	3			(3)

Rhode Island				
Newport	1			(1)

South Carolina				
Greenwood	5	1		(8)
Hilton Head Island	4			(4)

Tennessee				
Cleveland	4	1		(7)
Columbia	5			(5)
Cookeville	6	2		(12)
Morristown	3		1	(6)
Tullahoma	2			(2)

Texas				
Corsicana	2			(2)
Del Rio	4	1		(7)
Eagle Pass	4	1		(7)
Huntsville	6			(6)
Lufkin	7	1		(10)
Nacogdoches	5	1		(8)
Palestine	3			(3)
Paris	5			(5)

Utah				
Logan	5			(5)
St. George	7	1		(10)

Vermont				
Rutland	6	1		(9)

Virginia				
Blacksburg-Radford-Christiansburg	9			(9)
Harrisonburg	9	1		(12)
Martinsville	4			(4)
Staunton-Waynesboro	8	1		(11)
Winchester	5			(5)
Washington				
Aberdeen	4			(4)
Longview	5		1	(8)
Mount Vernon	3			(3)
Port Angeles	2			(2)
Walla Walla	8			(8)
Wenatchee	6	1		(9)
West Virginia				
Beckley	6		1	(9)
Clarksburg	7	2		(13)
Fairmont	4		1	(7)
Morgantown	6	1	1	(12)
Wisconsin				
Fond du Lac	2	1		(5)
Manitowoc	4			(4)
Stevens Point	3			(3)
Watertown	2			(2)
Wyoming				
Rock Springs	5	1		(8)

Arts and Learning Institutions

Small cities may not offer the scope of art exhibits, libraries, or zoos that big cities do, but many foster an impressive array of libraries and museums and enjoy the cultural and educational resources of local colleges and universities. Small-city residents may also enjoy easier access to the arts than do residents of major metros.

This category measures each community's cultural and learning resources by calculating the number of libraries, museums, zoos and botanical gardens, and colleges and universities per 100,000 residents. Historical sites are not included.

Newport, Rhode Island, tops the list with an index of 26. The historical and long-established city boasts a college, a university, three libraries, and seventeen museums and arts centers. Other Northeastern small cities share the top-ten honors with Newport.

Longview, Washington, is home to the large and awe-inspiring Mount St. Helen's, but the city has little in the way of traditional art museums. The conquest of open spaces is much of the story of the West and the many historical sites and state parks reflect that history. Younger, Western, small cities are less likely to have fostered libraries, zoos, and art museums. So are rural small cities throughout the South. Longview, Washington, and Eden, North Carolina, have the fewest art and learning institutions on the micro list—an index of just 1.1 institutions per 100,000 residents.

Source: County Business Patterns, U.S. Bureau of the Census, Washington, D.C. Data, published in 1996, are for 1994.

Scoring: Twenty points for an index of 11 or higher; no points for an index less than 1.5. The space is every half index point.

Arts and Learning Institutions: Highs and Lows

	Institutions per 100,000 Residents
Highest	
1. Newport, R.I.	26.3
2. Rutland, Vt.	25.6
3. Cortland, N.Y.	20.3
4. Concord, N.H.	16.4
5. Biddeford-Saco, Maine	15.9
6. Watertown, N.Y.	15.6
7. Olean, N.Y.	14.0
8. Kingston, N.Y.	13.1
9. Torrington, Conn.	12.9
10. Coos Bay, Ore.	11.2
Median	
96. Greenwood, S.C.	4.9
97. Portsmouth, Ohio	4.9
Lowest	
184. Hanford-Lemoore, Calif.	1.8
185. Albany-Corvallis, Ore.	1.7
Kinston, N.C.	1.7
Twin Falls, Idaho	1.7
188. Pendleton, Ore.	1.6
189. Gallup, N.Mex.	1.5
Greenville, Miss.	1.5
191. Albertville, Ala.	1.3
192. Eden, N.C.	1.1
Longview, Wash.	1.1

Arts and Learning Institutions Area by Area

(Arts and learning institutions per 100,000 residents and rating points)

Area	Institutions	Points
Micro median	4.9	
Alabama		
Albertville	1.3	(0)
Auburn-Opelika	3.3	(4)
Cullman	2.8	(3)
Selma	10.4	(18)
Talladega	2.6	(3)
Alaska		
Fairbanks	4.7	(7)
Arizona		
Prescott	8.6	(15)
Sierra Vista	7.4	(12)
Arkansas		
Blytheville	2.0	(2)
El Dorado	6.5	(11)
Hot Springs	10.0	(18)
Jonesboro	4.1	(6)
Russellville	6.0	(10)
Searcy	6.7	(11)
California		
Arcata-Eureka	6.6	(11)
El Centro-Calexico-Brawley	2.2	(2)
Hanford-Lemoore	1.8	(1)
Hollister	2.4	(2)
Connecticut		
Torrington	12.9	(20)
Florida		
Key West	8.6	(15)
Vero Beach	2.1	(2)
Georgia		
Brunswick	4.6	(7)
Dalton	3.9	(5)
Dublin	2.4	(2)
Gainesville	2.9	(3)
Hinesville	3.4	(4)
La Grange	5.2	(8)
Milledgeville	4.8	(7)
Rome	4.8	(7)
Statesboro	4.2	(6)
Thomasville	9.9	(17)
Valdosta	3.6	(5)
Waycross	10.0	(18)
Idaho		
Coeur d'Alene	2.3	(2)
Idaho Falls	2.5	(3)
Pocatello	5.1	(8)
Twin Falls	1.7	(1)
Illinois		
Carbondale	4.9	(7)
Danville	2.3	(2)
Freeport	2.0	(2)
Galesburg	10.7	(19)
Mattoon-Charleston	3.8	(5)
Ottawa	2.7	(3)
Quincy	8.9	(15)
Sterling	3.3	(4)
Indiana		
Columbus	6.0	(10)
Marion	6.8	(11)
Michigan City-La Porte	1.8	(1)
New Castle	8.2	(14)
Richmond	11.0	(20)
Vincennes	7.5	(13)
Iowa		
Ames	5.4	(8)
Burlington	7.0	(12)
Clinton	5.9	(9)

Mason City	8.6	(15)
Muscatine	2.4	(2)
Kansas		
Hutchinson	6.4	(10)
Manhattan	8.1	(14)
Salina	6.1	(10)
Kentucky		
Bowling Green	3.6	(5)
Frankfort	11.0	(20)
Madisonville	2.2	(2)
Paducah	6.2	(10)
Radcliff-Elizabethtown	3.3	(4)
Louisiana		
Hammond	2.2	(2)
New Iberia	4.2	(6)
Ruston	7.0	(12)
Maine		
Augusta-Waterville	10.2	(18)
Biddeford-Saco	15.9	(20)
Maryland		
Salisbury	5.1	(8)
Michigan		
Marquette	8.6	(15)
Mount Pleasant	3.6	(5)
Owosso	2.8	(3)
Traverse City	3.4	(4)
Minnesota		
Faribault	7.8	(13)
Mankato	9.6	(17)
Red Wing	2.4	(2)
Willmar	4.9	(7)
Winona	10.3	(18)
Mississippi		
Cleveland	7.2	(12)
Columbus	4.9	(7)
Greenville	1.5	(1)
Laurel	4.8	(7)
Meridian	2.6	(3)
Tupelo	2.8	(3)
Vicksburg	4.1	(6)
Missouri		
Cape Girardeau-Sikeston	6.4	(10)
Jefferson City	9.9	(17)
Poplar Bluff	2.5	(3)
Warrensburg	6.5	(11)
Montana		
Bozeman	6.9	(11)
Helena	9.7	(17)
Missoula	3.5	(5)
Nebraska		
Grand Island	5.9	(9)
Nevada		
Carson City	6.6	(11)
Elko	2.5	(3)
New Hampshire		
Concord	16.4	(20)
Keene	9.9	(17)
New Mexico		
Alamogordo	5.5	(9)
Carlsbad	3.8	(5)
Clovis	4.2	(6)
Farmington	4.0	(6)
Gallup	1.5	(1)
Hobbs	5.3	(8)
Roswell	3.3	(4)
New York		
Cortland	20.3	(20)
Gloversville	3.7	(5)
Ithaca	10.4	(18)

Kingston	13.1	(20)
Olean	14.0	(20)
Plattsburgh	10.4	(18)
Watertown	15.6	(20)

North Carolina

Albemarle	3.7	(5)
Eden	1.1	(0)
Havelock-New Bern	3.6	(5)
Henderson	2.5	(3)
Kinston	1.7	(1)
Lumberton	2.7	(3)
Roanoke Rapids	3.5	(5)
Sanford	2.2	(2)
Shelby	5.7	(9)
Statesville	3.0	(4)
Wilson	4.5	(7)

North Dakota

Minot	8.6	(15)

Ohio

Ashland	4.0	(6)
Athens	5.0	(8)
Chillicothe	8.2	(14)
Findlay-Fostoria-Tiffin	5.5	(9)
Fremont	6.4	(10)
Marion	10.7	(19)
Mount Vernon	6.0	(10)
New Philadelphia	10.4	(18)
Norwalk	3.4	(4)
Portsmouth	4.9	(7)
Sandusky	9.0	(16)
Sidney	2.1	(2)
Wooster	2.8	(3)
Zanesville	8.4	(14)

Oklahoma

Ardmore	6.9	(11)
Chickasha	4.6	(7)
Duncan	4.6	(7)
McAlester	4.7	(7)
Muskogee	5.8	(9)
Stillwater	9.5	(17)

Oregon

Albany-Corvallis	1.7	(1)
Bend	6.6	(11)
Coos Bay	11.2	(20)
Grants Pass	8.6	(15)
Klamath Falls	5.0	(8)
Pendleton	1.6	(1)
Roseburg	3.1	(4)

Pennsylvania

Chambersburg	6.4	(10)
New Castle	4.1	(6)
Pottsville	8.4	(14)

Rhode Island

Newport	26.3	(20)

South Carolina

Greenwood	4.9	(7)
Hilton Head Island	3.1	(4)

Tennessee

Cleveland	2.6	(3)
Columbia	4.7	(7)
Cookeville	5.4	(8)
Morristown	3.8	(5)
Tullahoma	7.6	(13)

Texas

Corsicana	5.0	(8)
Del Rio	7.0	(12)
Eagle Pass	6.8	(11)
Huntsville	7.4	(12)
Lufkin	2.7	(3)
Nacogdoches	3.6	(5)
Palestine	4.0	(6)
Paris	2.2	(2)

Utah		
Logan	2.6	(3)
St. George	3.1	(4)
Vermont		
Rutland	25.6	(20)
Virginia		
Blacksburg-Radford-Christiansburg	4.0	(6)
Harrisonburg	7.4	(12)
Martinsville	4.1	(6)
Staunton-Waynesboro	6.8	(9)
Winchester	6.7	(11)
Washington		
Aberdeen	4.5	(7)
Longview	1.1	(0)
Mount Vernon	7.6	(13)
Port Angeles	3.2	(4)
Walla Walla	7.6	(13)
Wenatchee	3.6	(5)
West Virginia		
Beckley	5.1	(8)
Clarksburg	5.7	(9)
Fairmont	3.4	(4)
Morgantown	3.8	(5)
Wisconsin		
Fond du Lac	4.3	(6)
Manitowoc	6.1	(10)
Stevens Point	3.1	(4)
Watertown	4.0	(6)
Wyoming		
Rock Springs	2.5	(3)

Community Groups and Services

America's micropolitans can successfully balance the amenities of a small city with the closeness of community of a small town. Neighbors stopping to talk on a busy pedestrian shopping mall is one common example. A second example is a network of membership organizations that offer residents opportunities to pursue a range of business, volunteer, and personal interests in the community. Equally important is a network of social services that can help residents in need of assistance.

This category measures the number of membership organizations and social service organizations available per 100,000 residents. Such organizations include church groups, business and professional organizations, community service groups, and family services. The national average is 151 organizations per 100,000 residents; the median for micropolitans is 182.

Montana is a vast state with a rugged terrain and isolated communities. Maybe that's why the residents of Helena stick together. The city has more than 200 civic and social service organizations for its approximately 52,000 residents. That gives Helena a community organizations index of 389.5, the highest of all the micros.

Logan, Utah, has the lowest index. The city has just 61.9 organizations per 100,000 residents.

Midwestern and Eastern micros have the highest rate of membership and social service organizations. The lower rates are scattered throughout the nation, but include many Southwestern cities.

Source: County Business Patterns, U.S. Bureau of the Census, Washington, D.C. Data, published in 1996, are for 1994.

Scoring: Twenty points for an index of 300 or higher; no points for an index of below 72. The spacing is every 12 index points.

Community Groups and Services: Highs and Lows

	Social Service and Membership Organizations per 100,000 Residents
Highest	
1. Helena, Mont.	389.5
2. Red Wing, Minn.	306.9
3. Frankfort, Ky.	300.4
4. Burlington, Iowa	284.5
5. Jefferson City, Mo.	274.2
6. Concord, N.H.	271.4
7. Willmar, Minn.	263.8
8. Salina, Kans.	263.7
9. Mason City, Iowa	262.3
10. Augusta-Waterville, Maine	261.3
Median	
96. Kinston, N.C.	182.1
97. Pottsville, Pa.	182.1
Lowest	
184. Gallup, N.Mex.	102.3
185. Huntsville, Tex.	93.1
186. Hinesville, Ga.	91.7
187. Hanford-Lemoore, Calif.	90.2
188. Del Rio, Tex.	86.5
189. El Centro-Calexico-Brawley, Calif.	78.8
190. Eagle Pass, Tex.	74.5
191. Elko, Nev.	69.2
192. St. George, Utah	69.0
193. Logan, Utah	61.9

Community Groups and Services Area by Area

(Social service and membership organizations per 100,000 residents and rating points)

Micro median	182.1	
Alabama		
Albertville	136.7	(6)
Auburn-Opelika	144.8	(7)
Cullman	138.2	(6)
Selma	145.9	(7)
Talladega	142.0	(6)
Alaska		
Fairbanks	185.3	(10)
Arizona		
Prescott	155.5	(7)
Sierra Vista	135.0	(6)
Arkansas		
Blytheville	139.4	(6)
El Dorado	205.4	(12)
Hot Springs	198.0	(11)
Jonesboro	182.4	(10)
Russellville	173.3	(9)
Searcy	142.7	(6)
California		
Arcata-Eureka	248.9	(15)
El Centro-Calexico-Brawley	78.8	(1)
Hanford-Lemoore	90.2	(2)
Hollister	114.4	(4)
Connecticut		
Torrington	172.5	(9)
Florida		
Key West	168.7	(9)
Vero Beach	159.0	(8)
Georgia		
Brunswick	187.6	(10)
Dalton	135.3	(6)
Dublin	205.8	(12)
Gainesville	145.4	(7)
Hinesville	91.7	(2)
La Grange	178.9	(9)
Milledgeville	116.1	(4)
Rome	180.1	(10)
Statesboro	125.5	(5)
Thomasville	178.9	(9)
Valdosta	151.9	(7)
Waycross	155.9	(7)
Idaho		
Coeur d'Alene	170.6	(9)
Idaho Falls	127.6	(5)
Pocatello	146.6	(7)
Twin Falls	180.8	(10)
Illinois		
Carbondale	205.1	(12)
Danville	185.7	(10)
Freeport	185.7	(10)
Galesburg	190.1	(10)
Mattoon-Charleston	170.4	(9)
Ottawa	200.2	(11)
Quincy	212.5	(12)
Sterling	215.3	(12)
Indiana		
Columbus	201.4	(11)
Marion	220.7	(13)
Michigan City-La Porte	153.6	(7)
New Castle	204.0	(12)
Richmond	221.9	(13)
Vincennes	238.6	(14)
Iowa		
Ames	237.7	(14)
Burlington	284.5	(18)

Clinton	194.2	(11)
Mason City	262.3	(16)
Muscatine	193.7	(11)

Kansas

Hutchinson	239.4	(14)
Manhattan	170.5	(9)
Salina	263.7	(16)

Kentucky

Bowling Green	173.4	(9)
Frankfort	300.4	(20)
Madisonville	229.0	(14)
Paducah	214.8	(12)
Radcliff-Elizabethtown	153.8	(7)

Louisiana

Hammond	136.9	(6)
New Iberia	105.9	(3)
Ruston	162.4	(8)

Maine

Augusta-Waterville	261.3	(16)
Biddeford-Saco	168.2	(9)

Maryland

Salisbury	195.0	(11)

Michigan

Marquette	228.1	(14)
Mount Pleasant	210.6	(12)
Owosso	147.8	(7)
Traverse City	234.8	(14)

Minnesota

Faribault	176.6	(9)
Mankato	221.4	(13)
Red Wing	306.9	(20)
Willmar	263.8	(16)
Winona	206.8	(12)

Mississippi

Cleveland	137.0	(6)
Columbus	195.9	(11)
Greenville	157.2	(8)
Laurel	182.5	(10)
Meridian	213.4	(12)
Tupelo	197.9	(11)
Vicksburg	167.1	(8)

Missouri

Cape Girardeau-Sikeston	240.2	(15)
Jefferson City	274.2	(17)
Poplar Bluff	226.7	(13)
Warrensburg	128.2	(5)

Montana

Bozeman	240.4	(15)
Helena	389.5	(20)
Missoula	234.6	(14)

Nebraska

Grand Island	226.6	(13)

Nevada

Carson City	161.8	(8)
Elko	69.2	(0)

New Hampshire

Concord	271.4	(17)
Keene	196.3	(11)

New Mexico

Alamogordo	125.2	(5)
Carlsbad	170.5	(9)
Clovis	179.5	(9)
Farmington	102.7	(3)
Gallup	102.3	(3)
Hobbs	162.9	(8)
Roswell	173.8	(9)

New York

Cortland	174.5	(9)
Gloversville	148.8	(7)
Ithaca	199.4	(11)

Kingston	165.6	(8)
Olean	157.9	(8)
Plattsburgh	143.3	(6)
Watertown	151.7	(7)
North Carolina		
Albemarle	228.8	(14)
Eden	201.2	(11)
Havelock-New Bern	145.4	(7)
Henderson	227.4	(13)
Kinston	182.4	(10)
Lumberton	151.7	(7)
Roanoke Rapids	134.4	(6)
Sanford	204.9	(12)
Shelby	259.9	(16)
Statesville	173.8	(9)
Wilson	149.1	(7)
North Dakota		
Minot	212.4	(12)
Ohio		
Ashland	217.4	(13)
Athens	200.3	(11)
Chillicothe	157.0	(8)
Findlay-Fostoria-Tiffin	216.9	(13)
Fremont	194.5	(11)
Marion	186.9	(10)
Mount Vernon	189.6	(10)
New Philadelphia	227.5	(13)
Norwalk	181.0	(10)
Portsmouth	164.0	(8)
Sandusky	207.6	(12)
Sidney	154.3	(7)
Wooster	175.2	(9)
Zanesville	206.7	(12)
Oklahoma		
Ardmore	199.0	(11)
Chickasha	174.1	(9)
Duncan	187.5	(10)
McAlester	154.5	(7)
Muskogee	186.2	(10)
Stillwater	200.2	(11)
Oregon		
Albany-Corvallis	203.6	(11)
Bend	189.9	(10)
Coos Bay	199.3	(11)
Grants Pass	151.3	(7)
Klamath Falls	216.4	(13)
Pendleton	177.2	(9)
Roseburg	178.9	(9)
Pennsylvania		
Chambersburg	185.8	(10)
New Castle	176.9	(9)
Pottsville	181.7	(10)
Rhode Island		
Newport	180.4	(10)
South Carolina		
Greenwood	197.1	(11)
Hilton Head Island	144.0	(7)
Tennessee		
Cleveland	192.2	(11)
Columbia	167.4	(8)
Cookeville	175.4	(9)
Morristown	208.1	(12)
Tullahoma	204.2	(12)
Texas		
Corsicana	183.5	(10)
Del Rio	86.5	(2)
Eagle Pass	74.5	(1)
Huntsville	93.1	(2)
Lufkin	169.7	(9)
Nacogdoches	146.2	(7)
Palestine	166.5	(8)
Paris	215.9	(12)

Utah		
Logan	61.9	(0)
St. George	69.0	(0)
Vermont		
Rutland	233.6	(14)
Virginia		
Blacksburg-Radford-Christiansburg	144.0	(7)
Harrisonburg	211.9	(12)
Martinsville	179.4	(9)
Staunton-Waynesboro	201.0	(11)
Winchester	177.2	(9)
Washington		
Aberdeen	226.4	(13)
Longview	195.5	(11)
Mount Vernon	196.2	(11)
Port Angeles	216.9	(13)
Walla Walla	191.5	(10)
Wenatchee	250.6	(15)
West Virginia		
Beckley	153.6	(7)
Clarksburg	223.3	(13)
Fairmont	246.1	(15)
Morgantown	187.1	(10)
Wisconsin		
Fond du Lac	191.7	(10)
Manitowoc	179.1	(9)
Stevens Point	204.3	(12)
Watertown	179.6	(9)
Wyoming		
Rock Springs	149.5	(7)

The Results

Quincy, Illinois, stands on bluffs of the Mississippi River's east shore. Prior to the Civil War, homes throughout the town acted as the first "station" on the Underground Railroad for escaped slaves from Missouri. Quincy residents harbored the slaves until they could be moved onward to the next station north to freedom. The commitment of Quincy abolitionists was more than just a passing common kindness—several were tried and imprisoned in Missouri for their actions.

Quincy scores 75 points to rate first among small cities in this section. The city shows a stable and active community spirit. Seventy-one percent of residents own the home they live in and 1 in 3 residents subscribes to the local paper. Plenty of local radio and television stations keep the area informed (including a public television station). Local pride and a sense of history are reflected in restored historic homes that house local arts councils and community groups. An architectural museum features locally made ornamentations from Quincy homes and churches.

Quincy has also invested in a local civic center that features a five-hundred-seat theatre, exhibition hall, conference rooms, and a lobby that accommodates receptions of several hundred attendees. Together, the civic center and the convention and visitors bureau host a steady stream of both community and regional events.

The Midwest contains nine of the top twenty cities with the highest community scores. The balance of the cities are distributed through the country.

Hinesville, Georgia, scores lowest in this section. The same factors that put Hinesville at the bottom of the list for shopping, amusements, and restaurants are at work here, too. Many of the social services and organizations available to Hinesville's large military community are available on base at Fort Stewart. Much of the population is transient—a fact illustrated by Hinesville's low rate of homeownership: Fewer than half of residents own the homes they live in.

Transient populations such as Hinesville's are unlikely to sustain a local paper, and Hinesville indeed goes without one. Many residents, military and civilian alike, look to the media and cultural attractions of nearby Savannah.

Four Western states and five Southern states dominate the list of the ten lowest-scoring micros. Only one Midwestern city appears. The East has no representatives.

Community Assets Scores: Highs and Lows

	Total Rating Points
Highest	
1. Quincy, Ill.	75
2. Augusta-Waterville, Maine	74
Mason City, Iowa	74
4. Concord, N.H.	71
Helena, Mont.	71
Minot, N.Dak.	71
7. Burlington, Iowa	70
Paducah, Ky.	70
Rutland, Vt.	70
10. Salina, Kans.	69
11. Hot Springs, Ark.	67
New Philadelphia, Ohio	67
13. Richmond, Ind.	66
14. Coos Bay, Ore.	65
Hutchinson, Kans.	65
16. Sandusky, Ohio	64
17. Clarksburg, W.Va.	63
Frankfort, Ky.	63
Salisbury, Md.	63
Vincennes, Ind.	63
Watertown, N.Y.	63
Median	
96. Mount Vernon, Ohio	47
97. Muskogee, Okla.	47
Lowest	
184. Statesboro, Ga.	29
Warrensburg, Mo.	29
186. Blacksburg-Radford-Christiansburg, Va.	28
187. Elko, Nev.	27
188. Albertville, Ala.	25
189. Logan, Utah	24
190. Hollister, Calif.	19
191. Hanford-Lemoore, Calif.	18
192. Blytheville, Ark.	17
193. Hinesville, Ga.	12

Community Assets Performance Comparison

	Quincy, Illinois	Micro median	Hinesville, Georgia
Total Points in Section	75	47	12
Rank in Section	1		193
Homeownership			
Share of owner-occupied housing	71.1%	69.6%	43.5%
Homeownership points	(15)		(0)
Newspaper Strength			
Share of residents receiving local daily paper	37.4%	22.8%	0.0%
Newspaper points	(14)		(0)
Broadcast Outlets			
Number of radio, television, and cable outlets	11	7	4
Broadcast points	(19)		(6)
Arts and Learning Institutions			
Institutions per 100,000 residents	8.9	4.9	3.4
Institution points	(15)		(4)
Community Groups and Services			
Organizations per 100,000 residents	212.5	182.1	91.7
Groups and Services points	(12)		(2)

Community Assets Scores Area by Area

(Total community assets rating points)

Micro median 47

Alabama
Albertville 25
Auburn-Opelika 31
Cullman 37
Selma 49
Talladega 34

Alaska
Fairbanks 45

Arizona
Prescott 51
Sierra Vista 38

Arkansas
Blytheville 17
El Dorado 59
Hot Springs 67
Jonesboro 59
Russellville 47
Searcy 40

California
Arcata-Eureka 60
El Centro-Calexico-Brawley 32
Hanford-Lemoore 18
Hollister 19

Connecticut
Torrington 49

Florida
Key West 53
Vero Beach 52

Georgia
Brunswick 49
Dalton 40
Dublin 44
Gainesville 42
Hinesville 12
La Grange 42
Milledgeville 37
Rome 50
Statesboro 29
Thomasville 51
Valdosta 42
Waycross 57

Idaho
Coeur d'Alene 38
Idaho Falls 57
Pocatello 46
Twin Falls 56

Illinois
Carbondale 48
Danville 41
Freeport 43
Galesburg 60
Mattoon-Charleston 51
Ottawa 40
Quincy 75
Sterling 43

Indiana
Columbus 56
Marion 56
Michigan City-La Porte 37
New Castle 55
Richmond 66
Vincennes 63

Iowa
Ames 37
Burlington 70
Clinton 52
Mason City 74
Muscatine 39

Kansas
Hutchinson 65
Manhattan 35
Salina 69

Kentucky
Bowling Green 55
Frankfort 63
Madisonville 54
Paducah 70
Radcliff-Elizabethtown 38

Louisiana
Hammond 33
New Iberia 36
Ruston 37

Maine
Augusta-Waterville 74
Biddeford-Saco 53

Maryland
Salisbury 63

Michigan
Marquette 61
Mount Pleasant 43
Owosso 37
Traverse City 59

Minnesota
Faribault 47
Mankato 62
Red Wing 50
Willmar 59
Winona 62

Mississippi

Cleveland	39
Columbus	47
Greenville	35
Laurel	44
Meridian	57
Tupelo	57
Vicksburg	43

Missouri

Cape Girardeau-Sikeston	59
Jefferson City	61
Poplar Bluff	53
Warrensburg	29

Montana

Bozeman	56
Helena	71
Missoula	61

Nebraska

Grand Island	62

Nevada

Carson City	41
Elko	27

New Hampshire

Concord	71
Keene	59

New Mexico

Alamogordo	34
Carlsbad	44
Clovis	42
Farmington	44
Gallup	38
Hobbs	48
Roswell	55

New York

Cortland	51
Gloversville	36
Ithaca	50
Kingston	56
Olean	58
Plattsburgh	57
Watertown	63

North Carolina

Albemarle	41
Eden	35
Havelock-New Bern	36
Henderson	39
Kinston	37
Lumberton	33
Roanoke Rapids	37
Sanford	46
Shelby	51
Statesville	41
Wilson	38

North Dakota

Minot	71

Ohio

Ashland	48
Athens	43
Chillicothe	55
Findlay-Fostoria-Tiffin	59
Fremont	48
Marion	57
Mount Vernon	47
New Philadelphia	67
Norwalk	37
Portsmouth	49
Sandusky	64
Sidney	39
Wooster	41
Zanesville	59

Oklahoma

Ardmore	52
Chickasha	40
Duncan	44
McAlester	47
Muskogee	47
Stillwater	42

Oregon

Albany-Corvallis	44
Bend	62
Coos Bay	65
Grants Pass	49
Klamath Falls	57
Pendleton	32
Roseburg	47

Pennsylvania

Chambersburg	45
New Castle	44
Pottsville	54

Rhode Island

Newport	44

South Carolina

Greenwood	50
Hilton Head Island	31

Tennessee

Cleveland	42
Columbia	41
Cookeville	48
Morristown	53
Tullahoma	44

Texas

Corsicana	40
Del Rio	34
Eagle Pass	31
Huntsville	30
Lufkin	44

Nacogdoches	32
Palestine	40
Paris	42
Utah	
Logan	24
St. George	41
Vermont	
Rutland	70
Virginia	
Blacksburg-Radford-Christiansburg	28
Harrisonburg	61
Martinsville	46
Staunton-Waynesboro	57
Winchester	48
Washington	
Aberdeen	46
Longview	41
Mount Vernon	50
Port Angeles	42
Walla Walla	51
Wenatchee	49
West Virginia	
Beckley	58
Clarksburg	63
Fairmont	54
Morgantown	46
Wisconsin	
Fond du Lac	44
Manitowoc	46
Stevens Point	41
Watertown	34
Wyoming	
Rock Springs	39

6

Health Care

Wealth and health—the two vie for the American mind. The rapidly rising cost of medical insurance, doctor's visits, and hospital services makes the two preoccupations difficult to separate at times. Private, per capita spending on out-of-pocket payments and private health insurance, adjusted for inflation, rose 39 percent between 1985 and 1994. Out-of-pocket expenses totalled $1,805 per capita in 1994, according to U.S. Health Care Financing Administration.

Other changes in health care are also occurring. For example, an aging population will require an increasing amount of care. The share of adults aged sixty-five and older is projected to increase from 13 percent in 1994 to 17 percent in 2020. The elderly make twice the average annual visits to private physicians, just over five visits per year. They are also more likely to require treatment for serious and terminal illnesses. Seven in ten deaths among the elderly are attributable to heart disease, cancer, or stroke, according to the National Center for Health Statistics.

It is important that an area remain capable of maintaining a health-care system that meets the needs of its residents, from prenatal to assisted-living care. This section assesses each small city according to its supply of doctors and hospital beds, its financial commitment to local health care, and its rate of terminal cases.

The quality of an area's health care will increasingly depend on how well it can adapt to the changing health-care industry. More and more, this means adapting to Health Maintenance Organizations (HMOs). In 1988, 71 percent of employees who received health insurance through their employer were enrolled in traditional fee-for-service plans. That share has decreased to just 26 percent and now nearly three-quarters of insured workers are enrolled in HMOs.

"Consumers [in HMOs] now have access to a product that is more affordable, that has very low out-of-pocket costs, that has more comprehensive benefits, and that stresses prevention," says Karen Ignagni, president of the American Association of Health Plans, quoted in the *New York Times* in 1997.

But not everyone paints so simple a picture. Many HMO members complain that their choice of doctor has become limited to a list of physicians and practitioners provided by their insurance company. Others find their out-of-pocket expenses are rising rapidly. The Robert Wood Johnson Foundation reports that copayments (a per-use fee that replaces deductibles) for hospital stays rose from $4.50 per day in 1987 to $24.90 per day in 1993.

The addition of copayments can also discourage HMO members from seeking primary care, increasing their risk of developing an ailment that will require more intensive treatment. The addition of a $5 copayment reduced the number of visits to primary care physicians in Washington state by 11 percent, reports the Associated Press.

Supporters of HMOs argue that insurance companies are making the tough decisions that must be made to rein in a runaway health-care system, the cost of which has been mounting far faster than inflation. Others argue that insurance companies are now practicing medicine by telling doctors what tests and procedures are considered appropriate for specific complaints and will accordingly be reimbursed. According to the Associated Press, 3 out of 4 insurance companies use such practice guidelines. Currently, 700 hundred organizations have issued 1,800 sets of guidelines.

Members of HMOs are also finding that coverage of some traditional services has been eliminated. Hospital stays for mothers and their newborns is one such service. By 1997, the number of HMOs that had cancelled this coverage had increased so greatly that Congress stepped in. Legislation now requires health insurers to cover a forty-eight-hour hospital stay for mothers and newborns following delivery, if requested.

Recent changes in health care also extend beyond how we afford our health to where we receive that care. New technology that allows for outpatient surgery is reducing the number of overnight hospital stays. This advance, combined with heavy consolidation in the hospital industry, is leading to fewer hospitals. The number of hospitals declined nearly 7 percent between 1985 and 1994, according to the American Hospital Association. Government-run, nonprofit, and small hospitals closed at the fastest rate because the changing economics of the industry favor private, larger hospitals. While the overall number of hospitals declined between 1985 and 1994, the number of privately owned hospitals grew 24 percent.

New technology and new services are also reducing the share of elderly who reside in nursing homes. The number of nursing home residents increased just 4 percent between 1985 and 1994, despite an 18 percent increase in the oldest segment of the population. Many of the elderly now receive care in their own homes by home health-care agencies. There were 9,800 home health-care agencies in operation in 1994, according to the National Center for Health Statistics. Hospice programs, which care for the terminally ill in their own homes, are also increasingly popular alternatives to both nursing homes and hospitals.

The impact on small cities is still unclear. Small cities are more likely to have smaller hospitals and community hospitals, both of which are least favored by the changing industry. As states increasingly enroll Medicaid patients in HMOs, local community hospitals must adapt their practices and their budgets to meet the new insurance rules. To make the change, centers will require new information systems, staff training, and larger cash reserves, warns the Government Accounting Office in a 1997 report.

Little of this acts to ease the health worries of many Americans, but at the same time, Americans are a little healthier. We are eating more vegetables, exercising a little more, and smoking less, according to the National Center for Health Statistics.

Ranking micropolitan America. The ideal micropolitan community would have plenty of doctors, including specialists. The community would have adequate hospital space, a strong government commitment to health care, and have a low or average rate of terminal cases. Each small city is graded in five categories:

1. Doctor Availability: Is there a favorable ratio of doctors to residents, or is it hard to find a local general physician?
2. Specialist Availability: Does the area have a strong roster of doctors and surgeons who can handle specialized complaints?
3. Hospital Availability: Is there an adequate supply of hospital beds, or is a local room difficult to obtain?
4. Local Health Funding: Do area governments show a willingness to invest in hospitals and other health programs?
5. Death Rate: Does the local health-care system handle a low or average number of terminal patients, or does an above-average death rate place a greater strain on medical resources?

Doctor Availability

Nearly 600,000 nonfederal physicians were active nationwide in 1994, an increase of 21 percent since 1985. The number of active, private-practice doctors per 100,000 residents increased more than 10 percent over the period to reach 229. But small cities did not gain new doctors as quickly as did large cities. Many new doctors burdened with enormous tuition bills and start-up costs were drawn to the larger number of patients and higher fees available in big cities.

This category ranks each micropolitan area according to its total number of active, nongovernment doctors, projected to a rate per 100,000 residents. The most current data collected for small cities is for 1990. That year there were 130 doctors per 100,000 small-city residents, compared with a national rate of 216.

Morgantown, West Virginia, has by far the most favorable situation of any small city in terms of doctor availability. The medical center and medical school of West Virginia University account for a large share of Morgantown's five hundred practicing physicians. Morgantown has a rate of 671 doctors per 100,000 residents.

Hinesville, Georgia, on the other hand, has few doctors outside local Fort Stewart army base. There are just 44 nongovernment doctors per 100,000 residents in Hinesville.

Six of the ten micros with the highest rates are in the South. Cities with the lowest rates are distributed throughout the country.

Source: Derived from *County and City Data Book, 1994,* U.S. Bureau of the Census, Washington, D.C., and *Physician Characteristics and Distribution in the U.S., 1992* (Chicago: American Medical Association). Data are for 1990.

Scoring: Twenty points for 250 or more physicians per 100,000 residents; no points for fewer than 60. The spacing is every 10 physicians per 100,000 residents.

Doctor Availability: Highs and Lows

	Doctors per 100,000 Residents
Highest	
1. Morgantown, W.Va.	671
2. Milledgeville, Ga.	304
3. Winchester, Va.	291
4. Mason City, Iowa	259
5. Rome, Ga.	251
6. Wenatchee, Wash.	249
7. Missoula, Mont.	244
8. Staunton-Waynesboro, Va.	241
9. Thomasville, Ga.	239
10. Madisonville, Ky.	238
Median	
96. Roseburg, Ore.	130
97. Radcliff-Elizabethtown, Ky.	129
Lowest	
184. Del Rio, Tex.	65
Muscatine, Iowa	65
Talladega, Ala.	65
187. Cleveland, Miss.	64
188. Hollister, Calif.	63
189. Albertville, Ala.	62
190. Sidney, Ohio	58
191. Warrensburg, Mo.	56
192. Athens, Ohio	54
193. Hinesville, Ga.	44

Doctor Availability Area by Area

(Nonfederal, practicing physicians per 100,000 residents and rating points)

Micro median	130	
Alabama		
Albertville	62	(1)
Auburn-Opelika	117	(6)
Cullman	81	(3)
Selma	139	(8)
Talladega	65	(1)
Alaska		
Fairbanks	128	(7)
Arizona		
Prescott	106	(5)
Sierra Vista	69	(1)
Arkansas		
Blytheville	83	(3)
El Dorado	178	(12)
Hot Springs	178	(12)
Jonesboro	233	(18)
Russellville	148	(9)
Searcy	93	(4)
California		
Arcata-Eureka	174	(12)
El Centro-Calexico-Brawley	75	(2)
Hanford-Lemoore	81	(3)
Hollister	63	(1)
Connecticut		
Torrington	160	(11)
Florida		
Key West	131	(8)
Vero Beach	198	(14)
Georgia		
Brunswick	192	(14)
Dalton	141	(9)
Dublin	158	(10)
Gainesville	160	(11)
Hinesville	44	(0)
La Grange	137	(8)
Milledgeville	304	(20)
Rome	251	(20)
Statesboro	97	(4)
Thomasville	239	(18)
Valdosta	163	(11)
Waycross	121	(7)
Idaho		
Coeur d'Alene	145	(9)
Idaho Falls	174	(12)
Pocatello	133	(8)
Twin Falls	183	(13)
Illinois		
Carbondale	177	(12)
Danville	135	(8)
Freeport	139	(8)
Galesburg	153	(10)
Mattoon-Charleston	103	(5)
Ottawa	97	(4)
Quincy	185	(13)
Sterling	96	(4)
Indiana		
Columbus	160	(11)
Marion	127	(7)
Michigan City-La Porte	139	(8)
New Castle	75	(2)
Richmond	145	(9)
Vincennes	138	(8)
Iowa		
Ames	149	(9)
Burlington	162	(11)
Clinton	118	(6)

Mason City	259	(20)
Muscatine	65	(1)
Kansas		
Hutchinson	139	(8)
Manhattan	98	(4)
Salina	191	(14)
Kentucky		
Bowling Green	183	(13)
Frankfort	144	(9)
Madisonville	238	(18)
Paducah	231	(18)
Radcliff-Elizabethtown	129	(7)
Louisiana		
Hammond	102	(5)
New Iberia	104	(5)
Ruston	103	(5)
Maine		
Augusta-Waterville	208	(15)
Biddeford-Saco	105	(5)
Maryland		
Salisbury	238	(18)
Michigan		
Marquette	200	(15)
Mount Pleasant	75	(2)
Owosso	77	(2)
Traverse City	228	(17)
Minnesota		
Faribault	116	(6)
Mankato	112	(6)
Red Wing	120	(7)
Willmar	204	(15)
Winona	84	(3)
Mississippi		
Cleveland	64	(1)
Columbus	130	(8)
Greenville	112	(6)
Laurel	116	(6)
Meridian	209	(15)
Tupelo	213	(16)
Vicksburg	157	(10)
Missouri		
Cape Girardeau-Sikeston	148	(9)
Jefferson City	104	(5)
Poplar Bluff	199	(14)
Warrensburg	56	(0)
Montana		
Bozeman	166	(11)
Helena	204	(15)
Missoula	244	(19)
Nebraska		
Grand Island	133	(8)
Nevada		
Carson City	183	(13)
Elko	81	(3)
New Hampshire		
Concord	197	(14)
Keene	163	(11)
New Mexico		
Alamogordo	92	(4)
Carlsbad	111	(6)
Clovis	97	(4)
Farmington	102	(5)
Gallup	153	(10)
Hobbs	72	(2)
Roswell	116	(6)
New York		
Cortland	96	(4)
Gloversville	103	(5)
Ithaca	172	(12)

Kingston	156	(10)
Olean	126	(7)
Plattsburgh	138	(8)
Watertown	112	(6)
North Carolina		
Albemarle	77	(2)
Eden	81	(3)
Havelock-New Bern	173	(12)
Henderson	90	(4)
Kinston	126	(7)
Lumberton	79	(2)
Roanoke Rapids	97	(4)
Sanford	150	(10)
Shelby	116	(6)
Statesville	132	(8)
Wilson	126	(7)
North Dakota		
Minot	193	(14)
Ohio		
Ashland	78	(2)
Athens	54	(0)
Chillicothe	97	(4)
Findlay-Fostoria-Tiffin	113	(6)
Fremont	82	(3)
Marion	163	(11)
Mount Vernon	84	(3)
New Philadelphia	88	(3)
Norwalk	92	(4)
Portsmouth	90	(4)
Sandusky	139	(8)
Sidney	58	(0)
Wooster	83	(3)
Zanesville	146	(9)
Oklahoma		
Ardmore	128	(7)
Chickasha	103	(5)
Duncan	76	(2)
McAlester	118	(6)
Muskogee	135	(8)
Stillwater	112	(6)
Oregon		
Albany-Corvallis	136	(8)
Bend	204	(15)
Coos Bay	163	(11)
Grants Pass	125	(7)
Klamath Falls	121	(7)
Pendleton	133	(8)
Roseburg	130	(8)
Pennsylvania		
Chambersburg	112	(6)
New Castle	85	(3)
Pottsville	96	(4)
Rhode Island		
Newport	135	(8)
South Carolina		
Greenwood	210	(16)
Hilton Head Island	170	(12)
Tennessee		
Cleveland	128	(7)
Columbia	146	(9)
Cookeville	125	(7)
Morristown	107	(5)
Tullahoma	103	(5)
Texas		
Corsicana	133	(8)
Del Rio	65	(1)
Eagle Pass	66	(1)
Huntsville	96	(4)
Lufkin	112	(6)
Nacogdoches	159	(10)
Palestine	92	(4)
Paris	171	(12)

Utah		
Logan	123	(7)
St. George	105	(5)
Vermont		
Rutland	167	(11)
Virginia		
Blacksburg-Radford-Christiansburg	171	(12)
Harrisonburg	195	(14)
Martinsville	198	(14)
Staunton-Waynesboro	241	(19)
Winchester	291	(20)
Washington		
Aberdeen	84	(3)
Longview	149	(9)
Mount Vernon	200	(15)
Port Angeles	163	(11)
Walla Walla	206	(15)
Wenatchee	249	(19)
West Virginia		
Beckley	220	(17)
Clarksburg	186	(13)
Fairmont	107	(5)
Morgantown	671	(20)
Wisconsin		
Fond du Lac	121	(7)
Manitowoc	103	(5)
Stevens Point	117	(6)
Watertown	74	(2)
Wyoming		
Rock Springs	80	(3)

Specialist Availability

There are times when a general practitioner simply will not do. Many medical problems require the attention of specialists.

This category ranks each area according to its number of specialists in seven selected fields. The results are expressed as a rate per 100,000 residents. Included are allergists and immunologists, internists, obstetricians and gynecologists, ophthalmologists, urologists, pediatricians, and surgical specialists. Nationwide, more than 252,800 private-practice doctors are certified in these fields, equaling a rate of 99 specialists per 100,000 residents. Small cities have a lower median rate, at 52 specialists per 100,000 residents.

Missoula, Montana, has a wealth of specialists. More than 100 private-practice specialists are active in the above seven fields, giving the city a rate of 290 specialists per 100,000 residents.

Few specialists practice in the Albertville, Alabama, area. The city has just 4 specialists per 100,000 residents.

Source: Derived from *Directory of Board Certified Medical Specialists, 1992–93,* Research and Education Foundation, American Board of Medical Specialties, Evanston, Illinois. Data are for 1992.

Scoring: Twenty points for 140 or more specialists per 100,000 residents; no points for fewer than 7. The spacing is every 7 specialists per 100,000 residents.

Specialist Availability: Highs and Lows

	Medical and Surgical Specialists per 100,000 Residents
Highest	
1. Missoula, Mont.	290
2. Morgantown, W.Va.	277
3. Salisbury, Md.	138
4. Concord, N.H.	132
5. Traverse City, Mich.	129
6. Winchester, Va.	123
7. Walla Walla, Wash.	120
8. Paducah, Ky.	115
9. Wenatchee, Wash.	113
10. Mason City, Iowa	111
Median	
96. Chillicothe, Ohio	52
97. Harrisonburg, Va.	52
Lowest	
184. Athens, Ohio	15
185. Duncan, Okla.	14
Norwalk, Ohio	14
187. Cleveland, Miss.	12
Ottawa, Ill.	12
189. Warrensburg, Mo.	11
190. Eagle Pass, Tex.	10
191. Watertown, Wisc.	9
192. New Philadelphia, Ohio	5
193. Albertville, Ala.	4

Specialist Availability Area by Area

(Selected medical and surgical specialists in private practice per 100,000 residents and rating points)

Micro median	52	
Alabama		
Albertville	4	(0)
Auburn-Opelika	69	(9)
Cullman	24	(3)
Selma	58	(8)
Talladega	16	(2)
Alaska		
Fairbanks	55	(7)
Arizona		
Prescott	41	(5)
Sierra Vista	24	(3)
Arkansas		
Blytheville	27	(3)
El Dorado	56	(8)
Hot Springs	29	(4)
Jonesboro	103	(14)
Russellville	40	(5)
Searcy	44	(6)
California		
Arcata-Eureka	48	(6)
El Centro-Calexico-Brawley	30	(4)
Hanford-Lemoore	24	(3)
Hollister	29	(4)
Connecticut		
Torrington	24	(3)
Florida		
Key West	30	(4)
Vero Beach	107	(15)
Georgia		
Brunswick	66	(9)
Dalton	73	(10)
Dublin	83	(11)
Gainesville	89	(12)
Hinesville	23	(3)
La Grange	80	(11)
Milledgeville	54	(7)
Rome	99	(14)
Statesboro	48	(6)
Thomasville	106	(15)
Valdosta	56	(8)
Waycross	45	(6)
Idaho		
Coeur d'Alene	61	(8)
Idaho Falls	69	(9)
Pocatello	57	(8)
Twin Falls	89	(12)
Illinois		
Carbondale	70	(10)
Danville	47	(6)
Freeport	76	(10)
Galesburg	62	(8)
Mattoon-Charleston	44	(6)
Ottawa	12	(1)
Quincy	86	(12)
Sterling	50	(7)
Indiana		
Columbus	52	(7)
Marion	43	(6)
Michigan City-La Porte	52	(7)
New Castle	25	(3)
Richmond	69	(9)
Vincennes	57	(8)
Iowa		
Ames	75	(10)
Burlington	65	(9)

Clinton	51	(7)
Mason City	111	(15)
Muscatine	24	(3)
Kansas		
Hutchinson	71	(10)
Manhattan	49	(7)
Salina	79	(11)
Kentucky		
Bowling Green	91	(13)
Frankfort	58	(8)
Madisonville	95	(13)
Paducah	115	(16)
Radcliff-Elizabethtown	61	(8)
Louisiana		
Hammond	36	(5)
New Iberia	46	(6)
Ruston	57	(8)
Maine		
Augusta-Waterville	72	(10)
Biddeford-Saco	16	(2)
Maryland		
Salisbury	138	(19)
Michigan		
Marquette	79	(11)
Mount Pleasant	30	(4)
Owosso	28	(4)
Traverse City	129	(18)
Minnesota		
Faribault	16	(2)
Mankato	39	(5)
Red Wing	46	(6)
Willmar	68	(9)
Winona	40	(5)
Mississippi		
Cleveland	12	(1)
Columbus	53	(7)
Greenville	45	(6)
Laurel	50	(7)
Meridian	89	(12)
Tupelo	86	(12)
Vicksburg	71	(10)
Missouri		
Cape Girardeau-Sikeston	64	(9)
Jefferson City	41	(5)
Poplar Bluff	78	(11)
Warrensburg	11	(1)
Montana		
Bozeman	57	(8)
Helena	111	(15)
Missoula	290	(20)
Nebraska		
Grand Island	60	(8)
Nevada		
Carson City	70	(10)
Elko	32	(4)
New Hampshire		
Concord	132	(18)
Keene	32	(4)
New Mexico		
Alamogordo	33	(4)
Carlsbad	41	(5)
Clovis	50	(7)
Farmington	33	(4)
Gallup	55	(7)
Hobbs	21	(3)
Roswell	44	(6)
New York		
Cortland	51	(7)
Gloversville	29	(4)
Ithaca	74	(10)

Kingston	34	(4)
Olean	48	(6)
Plattsburgh	60	(8)
Watertown	52	(7)
North Carolina		
Albemarle	30	(4)
Eden	17	(2)
Havelock-New Bern	81	(11)
Henderson	45	(6)
Kinston	69	(9)
Lumberton	33	(4)
Roanoke Rapids	32	(4)
Sanford	61	(8)
Shelby	44	(6)
Statesville	57	(8)
Wilson	55	(7)
North Dakota		
Minot	66	(9)
Ohio		
Ashland	37	(5)
Athens	15	(2)
Chillicothe	52	(7)
Findlay-Fostoria-Tiffin	41	(5)
Fremont	30	(4)
Marion	73	(10)
Mount Vernon	29	(4)
New Philadelphia	5	(0)
Norwalk	14	(2)
Portsmouth	25	(3)
Sandusky	50	(7)
Sidney	20	(2)
Wooster	34	(4)
Zanesville	71	(10)
Oklahoma		
Ardmore	42	(6)
Chickasha	45	(6)
Duncan	14	(2)
McAlester	53	(7)
Muskogee	79	(11)
Stillwater	34	(4)
Oregon		
Albany-Corvallis	58	(8)
Bend	77	(11)
Coos Bay	58	(8)
Grants Pass	57	(8)
Klamath Falls	41	(5)
Pendleton	26	(3)
Roseburg	50	(7)
Pennsylvania		
Chambersburg	31	(4)
New Castle	25	(3)
Pottsville	29	(4)
Rhode Island		
Newport	60	(8)
South Carolina		
Greenwood	83	(11)
Hilton Head Island	75	(10)
Tennessee		
Cleveland	65	(9)
Columbia	72	(10)
Cookeville	47	(6)
Morristown	47	(6)
Tullahoma	21	(3)
Texas		
Corsicana	75	(10)
Del Rio	27	(3)
Eagle Pass	10	(1)
Huntsville	29	(4)
Lufkin	53	(7)
Nacogdoches	55	(7)
Palestine	46	(6)
Paris	97	(13)

Utah		
Logan	61	(8)
St. George	34	(4)
Vermont		
Rutland	56	(8)
Virginia		
Blacksburg-Radford-Christiansburg	51	(7)
Harrisonburg	52	(7)
Martinsville	52	(7)
Staunton-Waynesboro	62	(8)
Winchester	123	(17)
Washington		
Aberdeen	26	(3)
Longview	54	(7)
Mount Vernon	45	(6)
Port Angeles	35	(5)
Walla Walla	120	(17)
Wenatchee	113	(16)
West Virginia		
Beckley	97	(13)
Clarksburg	53	(7)
Fairmont	61	(8)
Morgantown	277	(20)
Wisconsin		
Fond du Lac	47	(6)
Manitowoc	48	(6)
Stevens Point	56	(8)
Watertown	9	(1)
Wyoming		
Rock Springs	30	(4)

Hospital Availability

The U.S. population is slowly but steadily increasing, and the number of elderly people has grown significantly. But just when you think that new hospitals would be springing up to accommodate these demographic trends, a strange thing happens. The number of hospitals has been decreasing for years. More than 500 hospitals dropped from the master files of the American Hospital Association between 1980 and 1993, a decrease of 7 percent.

But hospitals aren't closing as quickly as patients are disappearing. Hospitals in 1993 had 24 percent fewer residents than in 1980. One factor is increasingly sophisticated medical technology. Many procedures that previously required a stay in the hospital can now be performed on an outpatient basis. A second, and often related, factor is a declining propensity among health insurers to cover hospital stays.

The health-care field is changing rapidly and will continue to do so. But it remains important that your micropolis have sufficient room for overnight hospital visits when you need them. This category calculates the number of community hospital beds available per 100,000 residents. Federally sponsored hospitals and hospitals associated with institutions are not included in the data.

The Minot, North Dakota, area has two hospitals with a total of 764 beds. That equals a rate of 1,332 beds per 100,000 residents, far above the median 353 beds for small cities.

Hinesville, Georgia, has the fewest beds in community hospitals. Just 62 beds are available per 100,000 residents.

Cities with the highest rates of hospital beds are concentrated in the Midwest and South. The ten cities with the fewest beds are primarily in the West, including three in New Mexico.

Source: County and City Data Book, 1994, U.S. Bureau of the Census, Washington, D.C., and *Hospital Statistics, 1992–1993* (Chicago: American Hospital Association). Data are for 1991.

Scoring: Twenty points for 925 or more beds per 100,000 residents; no points for fewer than 70. The spacing is every 45 beds per 100,000 residents.

Hospital Availability: Highs and Lows

	Community Hospital Beds per 100,000 Residents
Highest	
1. Minot, N.Dak.	1,332
2. Paducah, Ky.	1,088
3. Meridian, Miss.	924
4. Burlington, Iowa	905
5. Tupelo, Miss.	892
6. Poplar Bluff, Mo.	891
7. Madisonville, Ky.	884
8. Vicksburg, Miss.	784
9. Paris, Tex.	769
10. Bowling Green, Ky.	723
Median	
96. Willmar, Minn.	356
97. Cleveland, Tenn.	350
Lowest	
184. Albany-Corvallis, Ore.	155
185. Eagle Pass, Tex.	151
Wooster, Ohio	151
187. Fairbanks, Alaska	150
188. Farmington, N.Mex.	144
189. Prescott, Ariz.	142
190. Elko, Nev.	141
191. Alamogordo, N.Mex.	128
192. Gallup, N.Mex.	112
193. Hinesville, Ga.	62

Hospital Availability Area by Area

(Community hospital beds per 100,000 residents and rating points)

Micro median	353	
Alabama		
Albertville	267	(5)
Auburn-Opelika	359	(7)
Cullman	290	(5)
Selma	606	(12)
Talladega	432	(9)
Alaska		
Fairbanks	150	(2)
Arizona		
Prescott	142	(2)
Sierra Vista	244	(4)
Arkansas		
Blytheville	411	(8)
El Dorado	648	(13)
Hot Springs	595	(12)
Jonesboro	681	(14)
Russellville	258	(5)
Searcy	395	(8)
California		
Arcata-Eureka	257	(5)
El Centro-Calexico-Brawley	190	(3)
Hanford-Lemoore	174	(3)
Hollister	241	(4)
Connecticut		
Torrington	234	(4)
Florida		
Key West	340	(7)
Vero Beach	563	(11)
Georgia		
Brunswick	532	(11)
Dalton	365	(7)
Dublin	469	(9)
Gainesville	470	(9)
Hinesville	62	(0)
La Grange	594	(12)
Milledgeville	362	(7)
Rome	617	(13)
Statesboro	269	(5)
Thomasville	627	(13)
Valdosta	467	(9)
Waycross	410	(8)
Idaho		
Coeur d'Alene	253	(5)
Idaho Falls	381	(7)
Pocatello	521	(11)
Twin Falls	316	(6)
Illinois		
Carbondale	346	(7)
Danville	476	(10)
Freeport	363	(7)
Galesburg	620	(13)
Mattoon-Charleston	321	(6)
Ottawa	468	(9)
Quincy	519	(10)
Sterling	360	(7)
Indiana		
Columbus	309	(6)
Marion	317	(6)
Michigan City-La Porte	480	(10)
New Castle	222	(4)
Richmond	462	(9)
Vincennes	695	(14)
Iowa		
Ames	498	(10)
Burlington	905	(19)
Clinton	661	(14)

Mason City	699	(14)
Muscatine	197	(3)
Kansas		
Hutchinson	275	(5)
Manhattan	287	(5)
Salina	707	(15)
Kentucky		
Bowling Green	723	(15)
Frankfort	349	(7)
Madisonville	884	(19)
Paducah	1,088	(20)
Radcliff-Elizabethtown	361	(6)
Louisiana		
Hammond	387	(8)
New Iberia	236	(4)
Ruston	503	(10)
Maine		
Augusta-Waterville	424	(8)
Biddeford-Saco	244	(4)
Maryland		
Salisbury	531	(11)
Michigan		
Marquette	526	(11)
Mount Pleasant	213	(4)
Owosso	220	(4)
Traverse City	622	(13)
Minnesota		
Faribault	266	(5)
Mankato	358	(7)
Red Wing	302	(6)
Willmar	356	(7)
Winona	424	(8)
Mississippi		
Cleveland	453	(9)
Columbus	544	(11)
Greenville	601	(12)
Laurel	443	(9)
Meridian	924	(19)
Tupelo	892	(19)
Vicksburg	784	(16)
Missouri		
Cape Girardeau-Sikeston	549	(11)
Jefferson City	469	(9)
Poplar Bluff	891	(19)
Warrensburg	176	(3)
Montana		
Bozeman	166	(3)
Helena	205	(4)
Missoula	417	(8)
Nebraska		
Grand Island	444	(9)
Nevada		
Carson City	260	(5)
Elko	141	(2)
New Hampshire		
Concord	306	(6)
Keene	252	(5)
New Mexico		
Alamogordo	128	(2)
Carlsbad	312	(6)
Clovis	238	(4)
Farmington	144	(2)
Gallup	112	(1)
Hobbs	500	(10)
Roswell	312	(6)
New York		
Cortland	360	(7)
Gloversville	384	(7)
Ithaca	200	(3)

Kingston	247	(4)
Olean	317	(6)
Plattsburgh	482	(10)
Watertown	300	(6)
North Carolina		
Albemarle	236	(4)
Eden	297	(6)
Havelock-New Bern	334	(6)
Henderson	209	(4)
Kinston	432	(9)
Lumberton	264	(5)
Roanoke Rapids	301	(6)
Sanford	325	(6)
Shelby	478	(10)
Statesville	453	(9)
Wilson	417	(8)
North Dakota		
Minot	1,332	(20)
Ohio		
Ashland	183	(3)
Athens	249	(4)
Chillicothe	244	(4)
Findlay-Fostoria-Tiffin	262	(5)
Fremont	299	(6)
Marion	390	(8)
Mount Vernon	244	(4)
New Philadelphia	272	(5)
Norwalk	378	(7)
Portsmouth	418	(8)
Sandusky	577	(12)
Sidney	222	(4)
Wooster	151	(2)
Zanesville	686	(14)
Oklahoma		
Ardmore	550	(11)
Chickasha	372	(7)
Duncan	232	(4)
McAlester	485	(10)
Muskogee	410	(8)
Stillwater	341	(7)
Oregon		
Albany-Corvallis	155	(2)
Bend	279	(5)
Coos Bay	291	(5)
Grants Pass	223	(4)
Klamath Falls	268	(5)
Pendleton	219	(4)
Roseburg	265	(5)
Pennsylvania		
Chambersburg	240	(4)
New Castle	527	(11)
Pottsville	415	(8)
Rhode Island		
Newport	162	(3)
South Carolina		
Greenwood	526	(11)
Hilton Head Island	178	(3)
Tennessee		
Cleveland	350	(7)
Columbia	472	(9)
Cookeville	319	(6)
Morristown	597	(12)
Tullahoma	403	(8)
Texas		
Corsicana	390	(8)
Del Rio	209	(4)
Eagle Pass	151	(2)
Huntsville	211	(4)
Lufkin	480	(10)
Nacogdoches	525	(11)
Palestine	329	(6)
Paris	769	(16)

Utah		
Logan	191	(3)
St. George	201	(3)
Vermont		
Rutland	301	(6)
Virginia		
Blacksburg-Radford-Christiansburg	522	(11)
Harrisonburg	284	(5)
Martinsville	253	(5)
Staunton-Waynesboro	257	(5)
Winchester	522	(11)
Washington		
Aberdeen	243	(4)
Longview	211	(4)
Mount Vernon	318	(6)
Port Angeles	206	(4)
Walla Walla	419	(8)
Wenatchee	395	(8)
West Virginia		
Beckley	667	(14)
Clarksburg	463	(9)
Fairmont	433	(9)
Morgantown	708	(15)
Wisconsin		
Fond du Lac	348	(7)
Manitowoc	436	(9)
Stevens Point	213	(4)
Watertown	269	(5)
Wyoming		
Rock Springs	248	(4)

Local Health Funding

A strong commitment by local government to medical care not only results in a healthier community, but also keeps medical costs down for the patient. Because they are subsidized and not-for-profit, public hospitals and clinics typically charge less than private institutions. They also guarantee medical care to residents who may not have health insurance or who rely on Medicare and Medicaid. Local governments are often in a position to effectively identify the educational and preventative care programs most beneficial to the community.

This category ranks each area according to the amount of money local governments allocate to hospitals, clinics, environmental health programs, and public health administration. The annual total is divided by the number of residents. The median amount for small cities is $77 per resident.

Columbus, Indiana, devotes an impressive 39 percent of its public dollars to health, equaling annual spending of $1,720 per resident. The area devotes nearly all of its health budget to the local community hospital.

Popular Bluff, Missouri, and Ruston, Louisiana, both spend less than $1 per person on health care. Their totals round to zero.

Southern cities make the greatest investment in public health, but there are exceptions: Four of the lowest-spending small cities are located in the South, three in Virginia.

Source: Census of Governments: Compendium of Government Finances, U.S. Bureau of the Census, Washington, D.C. Data, published in 1997, are for fiscal year 1991–92.

Scoring: Twenty points for spending of $390 or more per capita; no points for less than $10. The spacing is every $20 per capita.

Local Health Funding: Highs and Lows

	Annual Per Capita Health-Related Spending by Local Governments
Highest	**$**
1. Columbus, Ind.	1,720
2. Vincennes, Ind.	1,425
3. Rome, Ga.	1,365
4. Greenwood, S.C.	1,235
5. Havelock-New Bern, N.C.	1,135
6. Columbia, Tenn.	1,132
7. Dalton, Ga.	1,068
8. Brunswick, Ga.	1,027
9. Valdosta, Ga.	1,017
10. Mount Vernon, Wash.	890
Median	
96. Statesville, N.C.	77
97. Marion, Ohio	76
Lowest	
181. Farmington, N.Mex.	5
Harrisonburg, Va.	5
Martinsville, Va.	5
Michigan City-La Porte, Ind.	5
185. Augusta-Waterville, Maine	4
Newport, R.I.	4
Winchester, Va.	4
188. Minot, N.D.	3
Salisbury, Md.	3
190. Palestine, Tex.	2
191. Gallup, N.Mex.	1
192. Poplar Bluff, Mo.	0
193. Ruston, La.	0

Local Health Funding Area by Area

(Annual per capita health-related spending by local governments in dollars and rating points)

Area	Dollars	Points
Micro median	77	
Alabama		
Albertville	355	(18)
Auburn-Opelika	695	(20)
Cullman	332	(17)
Selma	44	(2)
Talladega	481	(20)
Alaska		
Fairbanks	22	(1)
Arizona		
Prescott	22	(1)
Sierra Vista	62	(3)
Arkansas		
Blytheville	31	(2)
El Dorado	30	(2)
Hot Springs	18	(1)
Jonesboro	12	(1)
Russellville	31	(2)
Searcy	296	(15)
California		
Arcata-Eureka	125	(6)
El Centro-Calexico-Brawley	593	(20)
Hanford-Lemoore	196	(10)
Hollister	596	(20)
Connecticut		
Torrington	15	(1)
Florida		
Key West	281	(14)
Vero Beach	84	(4)
Georgia		
Brunswick	1,027	(20)
Dalton	1,068	(20)
Dublin	178	(9)
Gainesville	83	(4)
Hinesville	124	(6)
La Grange	837	(20)
Milledgeville	798	(20)
Rome	1,365	(20)
Statesboro	720	(20)
Thomasville	129	(6)
Valdosta	1,017	(20)
Waycross	790	(20)
Idaho		
Coeur d'Alene	577	(20)
Idaho Falls	75	(4)
Pocatello	575	(20)
Twin Falls	656	(20)
Illinois		
Carbondale	23	(1)
Danville	17	(1)
Freeport	32	(2)
Galesburg	13	(1)
Mattoon-Charleston	8	(0)
Ottawa	18	(1)
Quincy	33	(2)
Sterling	620	(20)
Indiana		
Columbus	1,720	(20)
Marion	8	(0)
Michigan City-La Porte	5	(0)
New Castle	442	(20)
Richmond	12	(1)
Vincennes	1,425	(20)
Iowa		
Ames	734	(20)
Burlington	22	(1)

Clinton	57	(3)
Mason City	21	(1)
Muscatine	335	(17)
Kansas		
Hutchinson	34	(2)
Manhattan	58	(3)
Salina	31	(2)
Kentucky		
Bowling Green	91	(5)
Frankfort	751	(20)
Madisonville	63	(3)
Paducah	21	(1)
Radcliff-Elizabethtown	79	(4)
Louisiana		
Hammond	538	(20)
New Iberia	653	(20)
Ruston	0	(0)
Maine		
Augusta-Waterville	4	(0)
Biddeford-Saco	7	(0)
Maryland		
Salisbury	3	(0)
Michigan		
Marquette	167	(8)
Mount Pleasant	380	(19)
Owosso	91	(5)
Traverse City	177	(9)
Minnesota		
Faribault	500	(20)
Mankato	89	(4)
Red Wing	117	(6)
Willmar	877	(20)
Winona	38	(2)
Mississippi		
Cleveland	352	(18)
Columbus	641	(20)
Greenville	420	(20)
Laurel	713	(20)
Meridian	43	(2)
Tupelo	13	(1)
Vicksburg	14	(1)
Missouri		
Cape Girardeau-Sikeston	19	(1)
Jefferson City	22	(1)
Poplar Bluff	0	(0)
Warrensburg	281	(14)
Montana		
Bozeman	16	(1)
Helena	41	(2)
Missoula	36	(2)
Nebraska		
Grand Island	17	(1)
Nevada		
Carson City	819	(20)
Elko	498	(20)
New Hampshire		
Concord	7	(0)
Keene	16	(1)
New Mexico		
Alamogordo	7	(0)
Carlsbad	121	(6)
Clovis	28	(1)
Farmington	5	(0)
Gallup	1	(0)
Hobbs	68	(3)
Roswell	662	(20)
New York		
Cortland	94	(5)
Gloversville	46	(2)
Ithaca	95	(5)

Kingston	160	(8)
Olean	94	(5)
Plattsburgh	75	(4)
Watertown	99	(5)
North Carolina		
Albemarle	48	(2)
Eden	73	(4)
Havelock-New Bern	1,135	(20)
Henderson	267	(13)
Kinston	89	(4)
Lumberton	163	(8)
Roanoke Rapids	698	(20)
Sanford	34	(2)
Shelby	513	(20)
Statesville	77	(4)
Wilson	130	(7)
North Dakota		
Minot	3	(0)
Ohio		
Ashland	73	(4)
Athens	198	(10)
Chillicothe	44	(2)
Findlay-Fostoria-Tiffin	73	(4)
Fremont	23	(1)
Marion	76	(4)
Mount Vernon	50	(3)
New Philadelphia	47	(2)
Norwalk	56	(3)
Portsmouth	19	(1)
Sandusky	227	(11)
Sidney	38	(2)
Wooster	643	(20)
Zanesville	51	(3)
Oklahoma		
Ardmore	32	(2)
Chickasha	6	(0)
Duncan	8	(0)
McAlester	672	(20)
Muskogee	740	(20)
Stillwater	541	(20)
Oregon		
Albany-Corvallis	82	(4)
Bend	203	(10)
Coos Bay	812	(20)
Grants Pass	65	(3)
Klamath Falls	63	(3)
Pendleton	103	(5)
Roseburg	133	(7)
Pennsylvania		
Chambersburg	21	(1)
New Castle	69	(3)
Pottsville	65	(3)
Rhode Island		
Newport	4	(0)
South Carolina		
Greenwood	1,235	(20)
Hilton Head Island	357	(18)
Tennessee		
Cleveland	811	(20)
Columbia	1,132	(20)
Cookeville	603	(20)
Morristown	14	(1)
Tullahoma	83	(4)
Texas		
Corsicana	7	(0)
Del Rio	553	(20)
Eagle Pass	451	(20)
Huntsville	30	(2)
Lufkin	214	(11)
Nacogdoches	677	(20)
Palestine	2	(0)
Paris	46	(2)

Utah		
Logan	49	(2)
St. George	66	(3)
Vermont		
Rutland	6	(0)
Virginia		
Blacksburg-Radford-Christiansburg	7	(0)
Harrisonburg	5	(0)
Martinsville	5	(0)
Staunton-Waynesboro	6	(0)
Winchester	4	(0)
Washington		
Aberdeen	85	(4)
Longview	35	(2)
Mount Vernon	890	(20)
Port Angeles	655	(20)
Walla Walla	152	(8)
Wenatchee	44	(2)
West Virginia		
Beckley	7	(0)
Clarksburg	29	(1)
Fairmont	21	(1)
Morgantown	72	(4)
Wisconsin		
Fond du Lac	137	(7)
Manitowoc	58	(3)
Stevens Point	107	(5)
Watertown	83	(4)
Wyoming		
Rock Springs	637	(20)

Death Rate

Doctors and hospitals in areas with younger populations sew the most stitches and set the most broken bones. Besides treatment for playground falls and skiing accidents, younger populations also require more childbirth and pediatric services. Older populations require different services and more visits to the doctor. The incidence of the most serious illnesses such as cancer and heart disease increases with age.

The correlation between age and dying is a clear one. Seventy percent of deaths occur among the elderly (those aged sixty-five and older), according to the National Center for Health Statistics. The intent of this category is to measure the strain placed on each area's health care system by the number of terminal cases it handles. The number of deaths from thirty-four selected causes (including the most common causes of death such as cancer, heart disease, and infectious and parasitic diseases) is expressed as a rate per 1,000 residents. The numbers are *not* adjusted to compensate for the age of the population.

Alaska has the youngest population of any state. Seventy-two percent of Fairbanks's residents are under the age of forty, compared to the national average of 60 percent. Fairbanks's young population contributes to its very low death rate. The city has an annual rate of just 3.4 deaths per 1,000 residents. That is well below both the national rate of 8.6 and the small-city median of 9.3.

Hinesville, Georgia, ties with Fairbanks for first place. The local army base boosts the share of young adults in the population.

Hot Springs, Arkansas, has a much older population than the country as a whole. Twenty-two percent of Hot Springs's residents are aged sixty-five and older, compared with a national average of 13 percent. The annual death rate in Hot Springs is correspondingly higher than average also, at 14.6 deaths per 1,000 residents.

Cities with large shares of college students, military personnel, and immigrants have the youngest populations and the lowest death rates. Cities with older populations (often in the East and Midwest) have the highest rates.

Source: Vital Statistics of the United States, National Center for Health Statistics, Hyattsville, Maryland. Data are for 1991.

Scoring: Twenty points for 3.9 or fewer deaths per 1,000 residents; no points for 13.5 or above. The spacing is every 0.5 deaths per 1,000.

Death Rate: Highs and Lows

	Annual Deaths per 1,000 Residents
Lowest	
1. Fairbanks, Alaska	3.4
Hinesville, Ga.	3.4
3. Elko, Nev.	4.7
4. Eagle Pass, Tex.	4.8
5. Logan, Utah	5.0
6. Manhattan, Kans.	5.1
7. Rock Springs, Wyo.	5.3
8. Huntsville, Tex.	5.4
Idaho Falls, Idaho	5.4
10. Bozeman, Mont.	5.5
Median	
96. Kingston, N.Y.	9.2
97. Frankfort, Ky.	9.3
Highest	
184. Corsicana, Tex.	12.4
185. Poplar Bluff, Mo.	12.5
186. Ardmore, Okla.	12.7
McAlester, Okla.	12.7
188. Clarksburg, W.Va.	12.8
El Dorado, Ark.	12.8
190. Pottsville, Pa.	13.1
191. Fairmont, W.Va.	13.2
Sierra Vista, Ariz.	13.2
193. Hot Springs, Ark.	14.6

Death Rate Area by Area

(Deaths per 1,000 residents and rating points)

Area	Deaths	Points
Micro median	9.3	
Alabama		
Albertville	10.7	(6)
Auburn-Opelika	7.2	(13)
Cullman	9.6	(8)
Selma	11.3	(5)
Talladega	10.3	(7)
Alaska		
Fairbanks	3.4	(20)
Arizona		
Prescott	7.2	(13)
Sierra Vista	13.2	(1)
Arkansas		
Blytheville	9.5	(8)
El Dorado	12.8	(2)
Hot Springs	14.6	(0)
Jonesboro	9.4	(9)
Russellville	8.2	(11)
Searcy	9.3	(9)
California		
Arcata-Eureka	9.0	(9)
El Centro-Calexico-Brawley	6.8	(14)
Hanford-Lemoore	6.1	(15)
Hollister	5.9	(16)
Connecticut		
Torrington	8.3	(11)
Florida		
Key West	9.3	(9)
Vero Beach	11.8	(4)
Georgia		
Brunswick	9.6	(8)
Dalton	7.7	(12)
Dublin	10.2	(7)
Gainesville	7.7	(12)
Hinesville	3.4	(20)
La Grange	10.9	(6)
Milledgeville	8.0	(11)
Rome	10.2	(7)
Statesboro	7.3	(13)
Thomasville	10.9	(6)
Valdosta	7.9	(12)
Waycross	10.7	(6)
Idaho		
Coeur d'Alene	8.5	(10)
Idaho Falls	5.4	(17)
Pocatello	6.2	(15)
Twin Falls	5.6	(16)
Illinois		
Carbondale	7.9	(12)
Danville	11.1	(5)
Freeport	9.7	(8)
Galesburg	10.8	(6)
Mattoon-Charleston	10.4	(7)
Ottawa	10.7	(6)
Quincy	11.9	(4)
Sterling	10.0	(7)
Indiana		
Columbus	7.5	(12)
Marion	9.9	(8)
Michigan City-La Porte	9.5	(8)
New Castle	10.3	(7)
Richmond	10.5	(6)
Vincennes	12.1	(3)
Iowa		
Ames	6.1	(15)
Burlington	11.1	(5)
Clinton	10.6	(6)

Mason City	9.7	(8)
Muscatine	9.6	(8)
Kansas		
Hutchinson	10.3	(7)
Manhattan	5.1	(17)
Salina	9.2	(9)
Kentucky		
Bowling Green	9.0	(9)
Frankfort	9.3	(9)
Madisonville	11.5	(4)
Paducah	10.9	(6)
Radcliff-Elizabethtown	5.9	(16)
Louisiana		
Hammond	10.5	(6)
New Iberia	8.2	(11)
Ruston	7.9	(12)
Maine		
Augusta-Waterville	8.9	(10)
Biddeford-Saco	8.2	(11)
Maryland		
Salisbury	10.4	(7)
Michigan		
Marquette	7.6	(12)
Mount Pleasant	5.9	(16)
Owosso	8.0	(11)
Traverse City	8.2	(11)
Minnesota		
Faribault	7.9	(12)
Mankato	7.5	(12)
Red Wing	11.7	(4)
Willmar	9.1	(9)
Winona	8.7	(10)
Mississippi		
Cleveland	10.9	(6)
Columbus	7.6	(12)
Greenville	11.4	(5)
Laurel	11.4	(5)
Meridian	10.2	(7)
Tupelo	8.7	(10)
Vicksburg	11.1	(5)
Missouri		
Cape Girardeau-Sikeston	10.1	(7)
Jefferson City	8.2	(11)
Poplar Bluff	12.5	(2)
Warrensburg	6.5	(14)
Montana		
Bozeman	5.5	(16)
Helena	7.6	(12)
Missoula	6.3	(15)
Nebraska		
Grand Island	9.8	(8)
Nevada		
Carson City	10.9	(6)
Elko	4.7	(18)
New Hampshire		
Concord	8.2	(11)
Keene	8.6	(10)
New Mexico		
Alamogordo	6.8	(14)
Carlsbad	9.8	(8)
Clovis	7.4	(13)
Farmington	5.7	(16)
Gallup	6.8	(14)
Hobbs	8.1	(11)
Roswell	9.5	(8)
New York		
Cortland	8.9	(10)
Gloversville	10.7	(6)
Ithaca	5.9	(16)

Kingston	9.2	(9)
Olean	9.5	(8)
Plattsburgh	6.5	(14)
Watertown	7.9	(12)

North Carolina

Albemarle	10.1	(7)
Eden	9.9	(8)
Havelock-New Bern	8.1	(11)
Henderson	10.7	(6)
Kinston	11.0	(5)
Lumberton	9.1	(9)
Roanoke Rapids	12.2	(3)
Sanford	9.8	(8)
Shelby	10.1	(7)
Statesville	9.0	(9)
Wilson	10.6	(6)

North Dakota

Minot	7.1	(13)

Ohio

Ashland	9.1	(9)
Athens	7.8	(12)
Chillicothe	9.4	(9)
Findlay-Fostoria-Tiffin	8.6	(10)
Fremont	8.7	(10)
Marion	9.7	(8)
Mount Vernon	9.9	(8)
New Philadelphia	10.4	(7)
Norwalk	8.9	(10)
Portsmouth	12.1	(3)
Sandusky	10.1	(7)
Sidney	7.4	(13)
Wooster	7.8	(12)
Zanesville	10.2	(7)

Oklahoma

Ardmore	12.7	(2)
Chickasha	9.0	(9)
Duncan	10.1	(7)
McAlester	12.7	(2)
Muskogee	11.5	(4)
Stillwater	7.2	(13)

Oregon

Albany-Corvallis	7.1	(13)
Bend	8.2	(11)
Coos Bay	11.2	(5)
Grants Pass	11.3	(5)
Klamath Falls	8.7	(10)
Pendleton	9.1	(9)
Roseburg	10.3	(7)

Pennsylvania

Chambersburg	9.5	(8)
New Castle	12.0	(3)
Pottsville	13.1	(1)

Rhode Island

Newport	8.0	(11)

South Carolina

Greenwood	9.1	(9)
Hilton Head Island	7.5	(12)

Tennessee

Cleveland	8.7	(10)
Columbia	9.1	(9)
Cookeville	9.2	(9)
Morristown	10.7	(6)
Tullahoma	9.5	(8)

Texas

Corsicana	12.4	(3)
Del Rio	6.1	(15)
Eagle Pass	4.8	(18)
Huntsville	5.4	(17)
Lufkin	9.4	(9)
Nacogdoches	8.3	(11)
Palestine	9.6	(8)
Paris	12.2	(3)

Utah		
Logan	5.0	(17)
St. George	8.5	(10)
Vermont		
Rutland	9.3	(9)
Virginia		
Blacksburg-Radford-Christiansburg	7.3	(13)
Harrisonburg	8.3	(11)
Martinsville	10.0	(7)
Staunton-Waynesboro	9.1	(9)
Winchester	8.5	(10)
Washington		
Aberdeen	11.7	(4)
Longview	9.3	(9)
Mount Vernon	8.6	(10)
Port Angeles	10.9	(6)
Walla Walla	9.3	(9)
Wenatchee	10.0	(7)
West Virginia		
Beckley	11.9	(4)
Clarksburg	12.8	(2)
Fairmont	13.2	(1)
Morgantown	7.3	(13)
Wisconsin		
Fond du Lac	8.7	(10)
Manitowoc	9.8	(8)
Stevens Point	6.5	(14)
Watertown	9.4	(9)
Wyoming		
Rock Springs	5.3	(17)

The Results

There is likely to be a doctor in the house in Rome, Georgia, as well as an available specialist in town and beds in the community hospital. Rome scores first in the health-care section, with 74 out of a possible 100 points.

Rome's health-care system rivals many larger cities', and far exceeds that of the typical small city. The availability of doctors and specialists in Rome is nearly twice the median rate for small cities. Per capita spending on health care in Rome is the third highest of all micros, nearly eighteen times that of the typical small city.

Rome does receive a single-digit score in one category. The city has an above-average share of elderly residents and a high number of terminal cases reflect the resulting challenges to the local health system, but Rome's large supply of doctors and hospital beds, and its high investment in local health, offsets the additional demand.

Rome's commitment to health care is shared by other Georgia small cities. Six of the state's twelve micros are among the the top twenty cities in the health-care section. Eight more Southern cities join Georgia micros among the top twenty. Midwestern cities round out the list.

Sierra Vista, Arizona, scores just 12 points in the health-care section, placing it last. A full-service community hospital serves the area, but local government does not invest significantly in it and the rate of beds per residents is low. Outside of the hospital, the availability of doctors is far below that of other small cities.

Similarly, relatively few specialists are in private practice in Sierra Vista; the rate of available specialists is approximately half that of other small cities. Residents in need of specialized medical care that they cannot receive in town or in the hospital may have to drive to Tucson, seventy miles away. Sierra Vista also faces one of the highest death rates among small cities.

Low-scoring cities are distributed across the country, but three of the bottom ten are in Ohio.

Health Care Scores: Highs and Lows

	Total Rating Points
Highest	
1. Rome, Ga.	74
2. Morgantown, W.Va.	72
3. Traverse City, Mich.	68
4. Greenwood, S.C.	67
Twin Falls, Idaho	67
6. Milledgeville, Ga.	65
7. Ames, Iowa	64
Missoula, Mont.	64
9. Brunswick, Ga.	62
Pocatello, Idaho	62
11. Paducah, Ky.	61
12. Havelock-New Bern, N.C.	60
Valdosta, Ga.	60
Willmar, Minn.	60
15. Nacogdoches, Tex.	59
16. Columbus, Miss.	58
Dalton, Ga.	58
Mason City, Iowa	58
Thomasville, Ga.	58
Tupelo, Miss.	58
Winchester, Va.	58
Median	
96. Galesburg, Ill.	38
97. Statesville, N.C.	38
Lowest	
184. Ottawa, Ill.	21
Sidney, Ohio	21
Watertown, Wisc.	21
187. Pottsville, Pa.	20
188. Albemarle, N.C.	19
Portsmouth, Ohio	19
190. Aberdeen, Wash.	18
191. New Philadelphia, Ohio	17
192. Duncan, Okla.	15
193. Sierra Vista, Ariz.	12

Health Care Performance Comparison

	Rome, Georgia	Micro median	Sierra Vista, Arizona
Total Points in Section	74	38	12
Rank in Section	1		193
Doctor Availability			
Nonfederal physicians per 100,000 residents	251	130	69
Doctor Availability points	(20)		(1)
Specialist Availability			
Selected nonfederal medical specialists per 100,000 residents	99	52	24
Specialist Availability points	(14)		(3)
Hospital Availability			
Community hospital beds per 100,000 residents	617	353	244
Hospital Availability points	(13)		(4)
Local Health Funding			
Annual per capita spending by local governments	$1,365	$77	$62
Health Funding points	(20)		(3)
Death Rate			
Deaths per 1,000 residents	10.2	9.3	13.2
Death Rate points	(7)		(1)

Health Care Scores Area by Area

(Total health care rating points)

Micro median	38
Alabama	
Albertville	30
Auburn-Opelika	55
Cullman	36
Selma	35
Talladega	39
Alaska	
Fairbanks	37
Arizona	
Prescott	26
Sierra Vista	12
Arkansas	
Blytheville	24
El Dorado	37
Hot Springs	29
Jonesboro	56
Russellville	32
Searcy	42
California	
Arcata-Eureka	38
El Centro-Calexico-Brawley	43
Hanford-Lemoore	34
Hollister	45
Connecticut	
Torrington	30
Florida	
Key West	42
Vero Beach	48
Georgia	
Brunswick	62
Dalton	58
Dublin	46
Gainesville	48
Hinesville	29
La Grange	57
Milledgeville	65
Rome	74
Statesboro	48
Thomasville	58
Valdosta	60
Waycross	47
Idaho	
Coeur d'Alene	52
Idaho Falls	49
Pocatello	62
Twin Falls	67
Illinois	
Carbondale	42
Danville	30
Freeport	35
Galesburg	38
Mattoon-Charleston	24
Ottawa	21
Quincy	41
Sterling	45
Indiana	
Columbus	56
Marion	27
Michigan City-La Porte	33
New Castle	36
Richmond	34
Vincennes	53
Iowa	
Ames	64
Burlington	45
Clinton	36
Mason City	58
Muscatine	32
Kansas	
Hutchinson	32
Manhattan	36
Salina	51
Kentucky	
Bowling Green	55
Frankfort	53
Madisonville	57
Paducah	61
Radcliff-Elizabethtown	41
Louisiana	
Hammond	44
New Iberia	46
Ruston	35
Maine	
Augusta-Waterville	43
Biddeford-Saco	22
Maryland	
Salisbury	55
Michigan	
Marquette	57
Mount Pleasant	45
Owosso	26
Traverse City	68
Minnesota	
Faribault	45
Mankato	34
Red Wing	29
Willmar	60
Winona	28

Mississippi
Cleveland 35
Columbus 58
Greenville 49
Laurel 47
Meridian 55
Tupelo 58
Vicksburg 42

Missouri
Cape Girardeau-Sikeston 37
Jefferson City 31
Poplar Bluff 46
Warrensburg 32

Montana
Bozeman 39
Helena 48
Missoula 64

Nebraska
Grand Island 34

Nevada
Carson City 54
Elko 47

New Hampshire
Concord 49
Keene 31

New Mexico
Alamogordo 24
Carlsbad 31
Clovis 29
Farmington 27
Gallup 32
Hobbs 29
Roswell 46

New York
Cortland 33
Gloversville 24
Ithaca 46
Kingston 35
Olean 32
Plattsburgh 44
Watertown 36

North Carolina
Albemarle 19
Eden 23
Havelock-New Bern 60
Henderson 33
Kinston 34
Lumberton 28
Roanoke Rapids 37
Sanford 34
Shelby 49
Statesville 38
Wilson 35

North Dakota
Minot 56

Ohio
Ashland 23
Athens 28
Chillicothe 26
Findlay-Fostoria-Tiffin 30
Fremont 24
Marion 41
Mount Vernon 22
New Philadelphia 17
Norwalk 26
Portsmouth 19
Sandusky 45
Sidney 21
Wooster 41
Zanesville 43

Oklahoma
Ardmore 28
Chickasha 27
Duncan 15
McAlester 45
Muskogee 51
Stillwater 50

Oregon
Albany-Corvallis 35
Bend 52
Coos Bay 49
Grants Pass 27
Klamath Falls 30
Pendleton 29
Roseburg 34

Pennsylvania
Chambersburg 23
New Castle 23
Pottsville 20

Rhode Island
Newport 30

South Carolina
Greenwood 67
Hilton Head Island 55

Tennessee
Cleveland 53
Columbia 57
Cookeville 48
Morristown 30
Tullahoma 28

Texas
Corsicana 29
Del Rio 43
Eagle Pass 42
Huntsville 31
Lufkin 43
Nacogdoches 59
Palestine 24
Paris 46

Utah	
Logan	37
St. George	25
Vermont	
Rutland	34
Virginia	
Blacksburg-Radford-Christiansburg	43
Harrisonburg	37
Martinsville	33
Staunton-Waynesboro	41
Winchester	58
Washington	
Aberdeen	18
Longview	31
Mount Vernon	57
Port Angeles	46
Walla Walla	57
Wenatchee	52
West Virginia	
Beckley	48
Clarksburg	32
Fairmont	24
Morgantown	72
Wisconsin	
Fond du Lac	37
Manitowoc	31
Stevens Point	37
Watertown	21
Wyoming	
Rock Springs	48

7

Housing

Owning one's home is an essential part of the American dream, and it's a part of the dream that has come true for more people in recent years. Homeownership has increased after more than a decade of decline. In fact, sales to first-time buyers in 1995 represented the largest single-year increase in new homeowners in twenty years. Nearly 1.7 million new home-owners anted up for closing costs that year. An estimated 64.7 percent of the population now own the house they live in, according to the Joint Center for Housing Studies at Harvard University.

High prices and interest rates created barriers for many would-be home-buyers in the 1980s. For young adults aged twenty-five to thirty-four, the prime years of household formation, the barriers were especially high. Even for those who met the expenses, down payment and closing costs averaged a staggering 67 percent of their annual income. In 1970, that share was just 42 percent for young homebuyers.

Affordability barriers continued into the early 1990s and were compounded by falling wages. The two factors combined kept homeownership rates stagnant. The share of Americans who owned their home hovered between 63.8 and 64.1 in the ten-year period between 1985 and 1994, according to the Census Bureau. Homeownership rates slipped over the period for young adults. The share of adults aged twenty-five to thirty-four who owned their home declined steadily from 37.7 percent in 1985 to 34.4 percent in 1994. For adults aged thirty to thirty-four, the share declined from 54.0 percent to 50.6 percent.

By 1994, home prices and interest rates were attractive, but wages for many young adults were still too low. Down payment and closing costs took less of a bite out a young first-time buyer's income, but still averaged 58 percent of their annual income. But in recent years, lower interest rates, stable home prices, and, most importantly, gains in the economy have made homes more affordable. In fact, monthly mortgage checks in 1996 were easier to write than they had been for years. Mortgage payments as a percent of income dropped from 33.7 percent of a homeowner's income in the 1980s to 22.5 percent in 1996, according to the Joint Center for Housing Studies.

The benefits of homeownership extend beyond enjoyment and pride in the castle. They even extend beyond the excitement of fixing your own leaky faucets. Houses are one of the soundest investments most people ever make. Home equity represents about 44 percent of a household's total net worth, according to the Census Bureau. No other single investment or item claims as large a share of net worth and median home equity rose 8.4 percent during the recession of the early 1990s, even as the value of other household net worth such as savings and money market accounts declined. The Joint Center for Housing Studies describes home equity as "the nation's primary wealth-building vehicle."

This section rates each small city according to its housing market. It rates the age and size of local houses, their cost, local property tax levies, and heating and cooling needs.

Residents of crowded metropolitan areas are finding that owning a house in small-town America, whether a weekend retreat or a new residence, can carry a unique benefit. It affords peace of mind. "My daughters were growing up. I started noticing my gray hair, started worrying about mortality," corporate lawyer Stanley Gulking told the *New York Times*. "You ask yourself, 'What's it all for?' So instead of having a mid-life crisis, I bought a house in the country." He is not alone. The Joint Center for Housing Studies notes that nonmetro areas adjacent to metropolitan borders are seeing an increase in both home buying and housing construction. Remote areas related to recreational and retirement areas are also showing strong growth.

This trend will likely continue and even accelerate in the next fifteen years, says the Joint Center for Housing Studies. Many telecommuters, businesses, and aging baby boomers seeking to relocate will likely look past crowded cities and suburbs to small cities and rural locations. One attraction that will draw them will be lower home prices and lighter property taxes.

The lower cost of housing is one of the greatest savings small-city residents realize over their metropolitan neighbors. Homeowners in downtown metros paid monthly median housing expenses of $553 in 1993, according to the Census Bureau's American Housing Survey; suburban metro residents paid a median of $634. Monthly median costs outside of metro areas was significantly lower, just $319 per month.

Rome, Georgia, is a good example of small-city savings. Rome is located approximately sixty-five miles from metro hotspot Atlanta. Rome's overall housing costs are 16 percent lower than Atlanta's, according to the American Chamber of Commerce Researchers Association. Property taxes in Rome are 42 percent lower, according to the Census Bureau.

Ranking micropolitan America. The perfect small city would boast new, large, and reasonably-priced homes that can be inexpensively maintained. Each area is rated in five categories:

1. Housing Age: Does the community have a selection of modern homes, or are most of the units more than bit creaky?
2. Housing Size: Are there plenty of houses fit for growing families, or is space generally cramped?
3. Housing Costs: Could you afford to purchase a house in the area, or are prices too steep?
4. Property Taxes: Is the tax burden light, or will your annual bill be enormous?
5. Heating and Cooling: Will mild weather keep your utility bills down, or will you be running the furnace or air conditioner virtually all the time?

Housing Age

If a modern house is your dream, go West. Or go South. The micropolitans with the largest share of new homes are in fast-growing states such as Nevada and Georgia. The housing stock in the East is considerably older. Slow population growth for the region as a whole keeps new home construction down.

This category ranks each small city according to the share of housing that was constructed in the 1930s or earlier. The Census Bureau conducts the only comprehensive national survey of housing characteristics; the most recent survey was conducted as part of the 1990 census. That year, 18 percent of the nation's housing was built in 1939 or earlier.

Construction of the Trans-Alaska Pipeline in the late 1970s brought oil from Prudhoe Bay and brought construction workers, service workers, and their families to Alaska. In one three-year period, the population of Fairbanks leapt from 12,000 to 60,000. A construction boom ensued to meet the demand for housing. Just 2 percent of Fairbanks's homes were built prior to 1940.

Pennsylvania's population is older than the national average, and so is its housing stock. Pottsville, Pennsylvania, has the largest share of older homes among the nation's small cities: 57 percent of Pottsville's homes were built in 1939 or earlier. New homes are going up in the area, however. The share of older homes dropped from 70 percent just ten years earlier.

Source: Census of Housing, U.S. Bureau of the Census, Washington, D.C. Data are for 1990.

Scoring: Twenty points for 2.5 percent or less; no points for greater than 50 percent. The spacing is every 2.5 percent.

Housing Age: Highs and Lows

	Percent of Houses Built in 1939 or Earlier
Lowest	
1. Fairbanks, Alaska	1.9
2. Hinesville, Ga.	2.3
3. Carson City, Nev.	2.5
4. Hilton Head Island, S.C.	2.7
Vero Beach, Fla.	2.7
6. Farmington, N.Mex.	2.8
7. Hobbs, N.Mex.	4.0
8. Huntsville, Tex.	4.2
9. Gallup, N.Mex.	5.5
10. Dalton, Ga.	5.9
Median	
96. Missoula, Mont.	15.4
97. Pocatello, Idaho	15.7
Highest	
184. Burlington, Iowa	40.6
185. Rutland, Vt.	41.0
186. Clinton, Iowa	41.8
187. Freeport, Ill.	42.3
Winona, Minn.	42.3
189. Watertown, N.Y.	42.6
190. Olean, N.Y.	46.1
191. Cortland, N.Y.	46.4
192. Gloversville, N.Y.	50.8
193. Pottsville, Pa.	57.0

Housing Age Area by Area

(Percent of houses built in 1939 or earlier and rating points)

Area	Percent	Points
Micro median	15.5	
Alabama		
Albertville	7.6	(17)
Auburn-Opelika	6.8	(18)
Cullman	9.4	(17)
Selma	13.4	(15)
Talladega	10.1	(16)
Alaska		
Fairbanks	1.9	(20)
Arizona		
Prescott	7.2	(18)
Sierra Vista	13.1	(15)
Arkansas		
Blytheville	8.9	(17)
El Dorado	13.2	(15)
Hot Springs	10.4	(16)
Jonesboro	7.7	(17)
Russellville	7.3	(18)
Searcy	7.4	(18)
California		
Arcata-Eureka	19.9	(13)
El Centro-Calexico-Brawley	7.1	(18)
Hanford-Lemoore	8.5	(17)
Hollister	15.4	(14)
Connecticut		
Torrington	30.6	(8)
Florida		
Key West	9.0	(17)
Vero Beach	2.7	(19)
Georgia		
Brunswick	7.1	(18)
Dalton	5.9	(18)
Dublin	8.8	(17)
Gainesville	7.0	(18)
Hinesville	2.3	(20)
La Grange	15.8	(14)
Milledgeville	7.8	(17)
Rome	15.1	(14)
Statesboro	7.4	(18)
Thomasville	14.3	(15)
Valdosta	7.8	(17)
Waycross	11.8	(16)
Idaho		
Coeur d'Alene	10.7	(16)
Idaho Falls	12.1	(16)
Pocatello	15.7	(14)
Twin Falls	23.1	(11)
Illinois		
Carbondale	17.2	(14)
Danville	34.7	(7)
Freeport	42.3	(4)
Galesburg	40.5	(4)
Mattoon-Charleston	29.4	(9)
Ottawa	39.6	(5)
Quincy	39.7	(5)
Sterling	32.0	(8)
Indiana		
Columbus	18.0	(13)
Marion	28.5	(9)
Michigan City-La Porte	28.3	(9)
New Castle	32.2	(8)
Richmond	36.4	(6)
Vincennes	38.4	(5)
Iowa		
Ames	21.9	(12)
Burlington	40.6	(4)
Clinton	41.8	(4)

Mason City	33.4	(7)
Muscatine	36.6	(6)

Kansas

Hutchinson	32.1	(8)
Manhattan	17.0	(14)
Salina	24.5	(11)

Kentucky

Bowling Green	12.0	(16)
Frankfort	14.0	(15)
Madisonville	15.1	(14)
Paducah	15.4	(14)
Radcliff-Elizabethtown	7.5	(18)

Louisiana

Hammond	8.9	(17)
New Iberia	9.9	(17)
Ruston	7.8	(17)

Maine

Augusta-Waterville	32.1	(8)
Biddeford-Saco	30.4	(8)

Maryland

Salisbury	17.6	(13)

Michigan

Marquette	29.7	(9)
Mount Pleasant	18.7	(13)
Owosso	32.8	(7)
Traverse City	19.1	(13)

Minnesota

Faribault	30.8	(8)
Mankato	28.8	(9)
Red Wing	35.7	(6)
Willmar	22.3	(12)
Winona	42.3	(4)

Mississippi

Cleveland	10.0	(17)
Columbus	8.8	(17)
Greenville	8.9	(17)
Laurel	11.1	(16)
Meridian	10.2	(16)
Tupelo	7.1	(18)
Vicksburg	13.2	(15)

Missouri

Cape Girardeau-Sikeston	14.5	(15)
Jefferson City	16.4	(14)
Poplar Bluff	11.4	(16)
Warrensburg	15.9	(14)

Montana

Bozeman	17.5	(14)
Helena	22.1	(12)
Missoula	15.4	(14)

Nebraska

Grand Island	25.6	(10)

Nevada

Carson City	2.5	(20)
Elko	8.8	(17)

New Hampshire

Concord	29.2	(9)
Keene	36.3	(6)

New Mexico

Alamogordo	6.3	(18)
Carlsbad	8.1	(17)
Clovis	9.3	(17)
Farmington	2.8	(19)
Gallup	5.5	(18)
Hobbs	4.0	(19)
Roswell	9.0	(17)

New York

Cortland	46.4	(2)
Gloversville	50.8	(0)
Ithaca	35.1	(6)

Area	Value	Rank
Kingston	32.9	(7)
Olean	46.1	(2)
Plattsburgh	29.3	(9)
Watertown	42.6	(3)
North Carolina		
Albemarle	16.4	(14)
Eden	16.5	(14)
Havelock-New Bern	8.9	(17)
Henderson	11.8	(16)
Kinston	11.9	(16)
Lumberton	8.8	(17)
Roanoke Rapids	14.2	(15)
Sanford	6.6	(18)
Shelby	10.0	(17)
Statesville	11.9	(16)
Wilson	12.8	(15)
North Dakota		
Minot	16.8	(14)
Ohio		
Ashland	33.6	(7)
Athens	30.7	(8)
Chillicothe	28.3	(9)
Findlay-Fostoria-Tiffin	37.0	(6)
Fremont	38.1	(5)
Marion	36.5	(6)
Mount Vernon	35.0	(7)
New Philadelphia	36.0	(6)
Norwalk	35.1	(6)
Portsmouth	30.5	(8)
Sandusky	31.1	(8)
Sidney	29.4	(9)
Wooster	25.8	(10)
Zanesville	31.5	(8)
Oklahoma		
Ardmore	15.0	(15)
Chickasha	15.7	(14)
Duncan	12.2	(16)
McAlester	13.6	(15)
Muskogee	16.7	(14)
Stillwater	13.9	(15)
Oregon		
Albany-Corvallis	13.3	(15)
Bend	7.6	(17)
Coos Bay	18.2	(13)
Grants Pass	8.6	(17)
Klamath Falls	19.2	(13)
Pendleton	15.2	(14)
Roseburg	12.4	(16)
Pennsylvania		
Chambersburg	28.0	(9)
New Castle	39.4	(5)
Pottsville	57.0	(0)
Rhode Island		
Newport	33.1	(7)
South Carolina		
Greenwood	12.7	(15)
Hilton Head Island	2.7	(19)
Tennessee		
Cleveland	7.3	(18)
Columbia	13.6	(15)
Cookeville	6.1	(18)
Morristown	7.0	(18)
Tullahoma	9.4	(17)
Texas		
Corsicana	16.7	(14)
Del Rio	8.5	(17)
Eagle Pass	6.0	(18)
Huntsville	4.2	(19)
Lufkin	7.5	(18)
Nacogdoches	10.0	(17)
Palestine	10.8	(16)
Paris	12.2	(16)

Utah		
Logan	23.7	(11)
St. George	6.0	(18)
Vermont		
Rutland	41.0	(4)
Virginia		
Blacksburg-Radford-Christiansburg	12.2	(16)
Harrisonburg	17.7	(13)
Martinsville	9.3	(17)
Staunton-Waynesboro	19.2	(13)
Winchester	14.6	(15)
Washington		
Aberdeen	30.3	(8)
Longview	18.4	(13)
Mount Vernon	19.2	(13)
Port Angeles	13.7	(15)
Walla Walla	26.6	(10)
Wenatchee	23.1	(11)
West Virginia		
Beckley	18.7	(13)
Clarksburg	36.2	(6)
Fairmont	35.6	(6)
Morgantown	22.0	(12)
Wisconsin		
Fond du Lac	36.0	(6)
Manitowoc	37.8	(5)
Stevens Point	24.3	(11)
Watertown	38.6	(5)
Wyoming		
Rock Springs	16.3	(14)

Housing Size

Most homebuyers don't shop for a palatial estate, but for a home with enough room to house the family comfortably. This category ranks each micro on the share of its housing containing three or more bedrooms.

Ohio micros offer the largest houses. Six of the ten small cities with the largest share of roomy houses reside in that state and Sidney, Ohio, tops the list. Seventy percent of houses in Sidney have three or more bedrooms, far above the national average of 53 percent.

Homes in Key West, Florida, are known for their historic gingerbread architecture, but not for their abundance of living space. Fewer than one-third of Key West houses boast three or more bedrooms.

Midwestern cities typically offer the largest houses. Western and southern cities offer smaller houses.

Source: Census of Housing, U.S. Bureau of the Census, Washington, D.C. Data are for 1990.

Scoring: Twenty points for 67 percent or higher; no points for less than 39 percent. The spacing is every 1.5 percent.

Housing Size: Highs and Lows

	Percent of Homes with 3 or More Bedrooms
Highest	
1. Sidney, Ohio	69.9
2. Pottsville, Pa.	69.2
3. Fremont, Ohio	67.0
4. Owosso, Mich.	66.5
5. Marion, Ohio	66.2
6. Findlay-Fostoria-Tiffin, Ohio	65.9
7. Norwalk, Ohio	65.5
8. Manitowoc, Wisc.	65.2
9. Fond du Lac, Wisc.	64.9
Mount Vernon, Ohio	64.9
Median	
96. Chickasha, Okla.	56.6
97. Duncan, Okla.	56.5
Lowest	
184. Hot Springs, Ark.	45.3
185. Eagle Pass, Tex.	45.2
186. Arcata-Eureka, Calif.	44.8
187. Fairbanks, Alaska	43.5
188. Carbondale, Ill.	43.2
189. El Centro-Calexico-Brawley, Calif.	42.9
190. Prescott, Ariz.	42.2
191. Gallup, N.Mex.	40.4
192. Vero Beach, Fla.	39.2
193. Key West, Fla.	29.8

Housing Size Area by Area

(Percent of homes with three or more bedrooms and rating points)

Area	Percent	Points
Micro median	56.6	
Alabama		
Albertville	61.6	(16)
Auburn-Opelika	50.0	(8)
Cullman	60.9	(15)
Selma	58.5	(14)
Talladega	61.4	(16)
Alaska		
Fairbanks	43.5	(4)
Arizona		
Prescott	42.2	(3)
Sierra Vista	51.0	(9)
Arkansas		
Blytheville	52.6	(10)
El Dorado	55.1	(12)
Hot Springs	45.3	(5)
Jonesboro	55.5	(12)
Russellville	59.3	(14)
Searcy	57.2	(13)
California		
Arcata-Eureka	44.8	(5)
El Centro-Calexico-Brawley	42.9	(3)
Hanford-Lemoore	53.4	(10)
Hollister	59.3	(14)
Connecticut		
Torrington	60.7	(15)
Florida		
Key West	29.8	(0)
Vero Beach	39.2	(1)
Georgia		
Brunswick	58.8	(14)
Dalton	53.7	(11)
Dublin	60.9	(15)
Gainesville	59.7	(15)
Hinesville	53.2	(10)
La Grange	56.3	(12)
Milledgeville	58.5	(14)
Rome	53.7	(11)
Statesboro	54.0	(11)
Thomasville	61.2	(16)
Valdosta	59.6	(15)
Waycross	62.6	(17)
Idaho		
Coeur d'Alene	55.1	(12)
Idaho Falls	62.4	(16)
Pocatello	58.1	(14)
Twin Falls	55.9	(12)
Illinois		
Carbondale	43.2	(4)
Danville	52.7	(10)
Freeport	62.3	(16)
Galesburg	56.0	(12)
Mattoon-Charleston	49.7	(8)
Ottawa	57.3	(13)
Quincy	53.6	(11)
Sterling	61.7	(16)
Indiana		
Columbus	60.3	(15)
Marion	57.3	(13)
Michigan City-La Porte	59.1	(14)
New Castle	57.7	(13)
Richmond	57.6	(13)
Vincennes	47.4	(6)
Iowa		
Ames	52.0	(10)
Burlington	54.8	(11)
Clinton	58.9	(14)

Mason City	55.1	(12)
Muscatine	58.0	(14)
Kansas		
Hutchinson	51.7	(9)
Manhattan	51.9	(9)
Salina	55.1	(12)
Kentucky		
Bowling Green	57.4	(13)
Frankfort	54.5	(11)
Madisonville	54.3	(11)
Paducah	53.1	(10)
Radcliff-Elizabethtown	59.4	(14)
Louisiana		
Hammond	55.4	(12)
New Iberia	52.6	(10)
Ruston	55.0	(12)
Maine		
Augusta-Waterville	53.4	(10)
Biddeford-Saco	56.1	(12)
Maryland		
Salisbury	64.1	(18)
Michigan		
Marquette	54.9	(11)
Mount Pleasant	57.4	(13)
Owosso	66.5	(19)
Traverse City	58.8	(14)
Minnesota		
Faribault	61.0	(16)
Mankato	59.4	(14)
Red Wing	62.4	(16)
Willmar	57.6	(13)
Winona	57.0	(13)
Mississippi		
Cleveland	57.0	(13)
Columbus	62.7	(17)
Greenville	55.0	(12)
Laurel	62.4	(16)
Meridian	57.6	(13)
Tupelo	58.5	(14)
Vicksburg	59.7	(15)
Missouri		
Cape Girardeau-Sikeston	55.1	(12)
Jefferson City	59.4	(14)
Poplar Bluff	52.0	(10)
Warrensburg	52.8	(10)
Montana		
Bozeman	52.4	(10)
Helena	54.8	(11)
Missoula	50.4	(8)
Nebraska		
Grand Island	53.5	(11)
Nevada		
Carson City	52.2	(10)
Elko	50.4	(8)
New Hampshire		
Concord	54.2	(11)
Keene	55.8	(12)
New Mexico		
Alamogordo	58.2	(14)
Carlsbad	54.4	(11)
Clovis	59.7	(15)
Farmington	50.6	(9)
Gallup	40.4	(2)
Hobbs	56.9	(13)
Roswell	56.4	(12)
New York		
Cortland	60.0	(15)
Gloversville	55.8	(12)
Ithaca	54.5	(11)

Kingston	57.5	(13)
Olean	61.5	(16)
Plattsburgh	59.7	(15)
Watertown	56.9	(13)
North Carolina		
Albemarle	56.5	(13)
Eden	53.1	(10)
Havelock-New Bern	60.5	(15)
Henderson	57.5	(13)
Kinston	57.2	(13)
Lumberton	61.7	(16)
Roanoke Rapids	60.2	(15)
Sanford	61.5	(16)
Shelby	58.6	(14)
Statesville	58.3	(14)
Wilson	56.7	(13)
North Dakota		
Minot	57.7	(13)
Ohio		
Ashland	63.9	(17)
Athens	53.6	(11)
Chillicothe	56.5	(13)
Findlay-Fostoria-Tiffin	65.9	(19)
Fremont	67.0	(20)
Marion	66.2	(19)
Mount Vernon	64.9	(18)
New Philadelphia	60.9	(15)
Norwalk	65.5	(19)
Portsmouth	55.4	(12)
Sandusky	62.3	(16)
Sidney	69.9	(20)
Wooster	64.7	(18)
Zanesville	56.9	(13)
Oklahoma		
Ardmore	55.0	(12)
Chickasha	56.6	(13)
Duncan	56.5	(13)
McAlester	53.2	(10)
Muskogee	53.3	(10)
Stillwater	45.5	(5)
Oregon		
Albany-Corvallis	55.3	(12)
Bend	56.0	(12)
Coos Bay	49.2	(8)
Grants Pass	47.6	(7)
Klamath Falls	49.1	(8)
Pendleton	52.7	(10)
Roseburg	52.4	(10)
Pennsylvania		
Chambersburg	63.8	(17)
New Castle	61.4	(16)
Pottsville	69.2	(20)
Rhode Island		
Newport	55.4	(12)
South Carolina		
Greenwood	54.6	(11)
Hilton Head Island	53.9	(11)
Tennessee		
Cleveland	58.4	(14)
Columbia	58.8	(14)
Cookeville	59.9	(15)
Morristown	60.5	(15)
Tullahoma	64.2	(18)
Texas		
Corsicana	52.2	(10)
Del Rio	50.9	(9)
Eagle Pass	45.2	(5)
Huntsville	45.3	(5)
Lufkin	54.5	(11)
Nacogdoches	48.3	(7)
Palestine	56.1	(12)
Paris	55.3	(12)

Utah	
Logan	60.5 (15)
St. George	55.7 (12)
Vermont	
Rutland	57.3 (13)
Virginia	
Blacksburg-Radford-Christiansburg	56.2 (12)
Harrisonburg	63.0 (17)
Martinsville	57.0 (13)
Staunton-Waynesboro	64.4 (18)
Winchester	64.0 (18)
Washington	
Aberdeen	51.3 (9)
Longview	54.4 (11)
Mount Vernon	53.2 (10)
Port Angeles	50.6 (9)
Walla Walla	52.0 (10)
Wenatchee	48.0 (7)
West Virginia	
Beckley	57.6 (13)
Clarksburg	57.1 (13)
Fairmont	54.5 (11)
Morgantown	51.3 (9)
Wisconsin	
Fond du Lac	64.9 (18)
Manitowoc	65.2 (18)
Stevens Point	63.4 (17)
Watertown	64.7 (18)
Wyoming	
Rock Springs	60.0 (15)

Housing Costs

Tim Ewing recalls stopping by an open house in his northwest Washington, D.C., neighborhood early one Saturday morning. Local home prices were through the roof at the time, and competition among buyers was fierce. The small 1930s bungalow was auctioned off in the driveway within fifteen minutes.

Stories such as Ewing's cause dismay among homebuyers, especially young and first-time buyers. More and more homebuyers are moving farther from central cities and suburbs in an attempt to find affordable housing.

Micropolitans offer an attractive alternative to the acres of townhouses that fringe many suburbs. The median price of a home in micropolitan America was $53,100 at the time these data were collected. That was $25,000 below the national median.

This category measures the median value of owner-occupied housing in each micropolitan. Note that the values are for 1990, which is the latest available data for nationwide home costs at such a detailed geographic level. Overall, the seller's market of the late 1980s that is reflected in these numbers changed to a buyer's market in the early- to mid-1990s. And, of course, housing markets are greatly affected by very local trends, so use these numbers to compare the micropolitans to each other, and contact a local realtor for up-to-the-date market values.

Micropolitans in the Midwest and South offer some of the most affordable housing. McAlester, Oklahoma, leads the group, with a median value of $34,300. The price of a home in McAlester might cover just the downpayment on a house in Hollister, California. Hollister, located in the foothills of the Diablo Range, less than an hour's drive from Monterey Bay, has the highest home value—$205,100.

Source: Census of Housing, U.S. Bureau of the Census, Washington, D.C. Data are for 1990.

Scoring: Twenty points for a median value of less than $37,000; no points for $151,000 or more. The spacing is every $6,000.

Housing Costs: Highs and Lows

	Median Value of Owner-Occupied Homes
Lowest	**$**
1. McAlester, Okla.	34,300
2. Poplar Bluff, Mo.	35,600
3. New Castle, Ind.	36,100
4. Galesburg, Ill.	36,800
5. Portsmouth, Ohio	37,000
6. Eagle Pass, Tex.	37,300
7. Pottsville, Pa.	37,900
8. Ardmore, Okla.	38,000
9. Paris, Tex.	38,200
10. Cleveland, Miss.	38,400
Median	
96. Hot Springs, Ark.	53,000
97. Mount Pleasant, Mich.	53,200
Highest	
184. Carson City, Nev.	98,900
185. Keene, N.H.	111,000
186. Hilton Head Island, S.C.	112,000
187. Kingston, N.Y.	114,700
188. Biddeford-Saco, Maine	115,000
189. Concord, N.H.	117,500
190. Key West, Fla.	147,800
191. Newport, R.I.	160,100
192. Torrington, Conn.	165,800
193. Hollister, Calif.	205,100

Housing Costs Area by Area

(Median value of owner-occupied housing in dollars and rating points)

Micro median	53,100	
Alabama		
Albertville	48,200	(18)
Auburn-Opelika	63,600	(15)
Cullman	47,200	(18)
Selma	43,100	(18)
Talladega	44,100	(18)
Alaska		
Fairbanks	87,200	(11)
Arizona		
Prescott	85,300	(11)
Sierra Vista	59,700	(16)
Arkansas		
Blytheville	41,300	(19)
El Dorado	40,000	(19)
Hot Springs	53,000	(17)
Jonesboro	50,400	(17)
Russellville	47,300	(18)
Searcy	43,200	(18)
California		
Arcata-Eureka	88,500	(11)
El Centro-Calexico-Brawley	72,100	(14)
Hanford-Lemoore	70,400	(14)
Hollister	205,100	(0)
Connecticut		
Torrington	165,800	(0)
Florida		
Key West	147,800	(1)
Vero Beach	77,900	(13)
Georgia		
Brunswick	65,800	(15)
Dalton	60,800	(16)
Dublin	46,900	(18)
Gainesville	76,300	(13)
Hinesville	60,100	(16)
La Grange	55,000	(16)
Milledgeville	55,100	(16)
Rome	49,000	(17)
Statesboro	58,800	(16)
Thomasville	46,400	(18)
Valdosta	60,400	(16)
Waycross	40,753	(19)
Idaho		
Coeur d'Alene	64,300	(15)
Idaho Falls	63,400	(15)
Pocatello	52,929	(17)
Twin Falls	50,900	(17)
Illinois		
Carbondale	46,700	(18)
Danville	38,500	(19)
Freeport	50,500	(17)
Galesburg	36,800	(20)
Mattoon-Charleston	44,400	(18)
Ottawa	49,700	(17)
Quincy	43,500	(18)
Sterling	44,300	(18)
Indiana		
Columbus	57,200	(16)
Marion	39,900	(19)
Michigan City-La Porte	52,600	(17)
New Castle	36,100	(20)
Richmond	42,200	(19)
Vincennes	39,600	(19)
Iowa		
Ames	63,700	(15)
Burlington	41,500	(19)
Clinton	39,000	(19)

Mason City	45,300	(18)
Muscatine	50,500	(17)
Kansas		
Hutchinson	40,000	(19)
Manhattan	59,327	(16)
Salina	45,000	(18)
Kentucky		
Bowling Green	57,300	(16)
Frankfort	59,500	(16)
Madisonville	39,600	(19)
Paducah	47,400	(18)
Radcliff-Elizabethtown	57,700	(16)
Louisiana		
Hammond	51,400	(17)
New Iberia	49,400	(17)
Ruston	55,700	(16)
Maine		
Augusta-Waterville	79,500	(12)
Biddeford-Saco	115,000	(6)
Maryland		
Salisbury	70,500	(14)
Michigan		
Marquette	44,400	(18)
Mount Pleasant	53,200	(17)
Owosso	46,800	(18)
Traverse City	68,491	(14)
Minnesota		
Faribault	68,000	(14)
Mankato	61,373	(15)
Red Wing	63,700	(15)
Willmar	56,800	(16)
Winona	54,600	(17)
Mississippi		
Cleveland	38,400	(19)
Columbus	48,300	(18)
Greenville	41,100	(19)
Laurel	41,800	(19)
Meridian	47,500	(18)
Tupelo	53,700	(17)
Vicksburg	50,400	(17)
Missouri		
Cape Girardeau-Sikeston	47,479	(18)
Jefferson City	56,567	(16)
Poplar Bluff	35,600	(20)
Warrensburg	54,900	(17)
Montana		
Bozeman	69,900	(14)
Helena	61,900	(15)
Missoula	65,500	(15)
Nebraska		
Grand Island	47,700	(18)
Nevada		
Carson City	98,900	(9)
Elko	81,300	(12)
New Hampshire		
Concord	117,500	(6)
Keene	111,000	(7)
New Mexico		
Alamogordo	57,500	(16)
Carlsbad	44,700	(18)
Clovis	51,600	(17)
Farmington	58,600	(16)
Gallup	40,700	(19)
Hobbs	39,300	(19)
Roswell	43,500	(18)
New York		
Cortland	66,000	(15)
Gloversville	55,900	(16)

Ithaca	94,700	(10)
Kingston	114,700	(7)
Olean	42,000	(19)
Plattsburgh	65,200	(15)
Watertown	59,600	(16)
North Carolina		
Albemarle	52,500	(17)
Eden	48,200	(18)
Havelock-New Bern	65,800	(15)
Henderson	53,000	(17)
Kinston	52,300	(17)
Lumberton	44,100	(18)
Roanoke Rapids	44,500	(18)
Sanford	60,800	(16)
Shelby	52,900	(17)
Statesville	62,600	(15)
Wilson	58,400	(16)
North Dakota		
Minot	53,600	(17)
Ohio		
Ashland	52,500	(17)
Athens	46,900	(18)
Chillicothe	49,600	(17)
Findlay-Fostoria-Tiffin	55,845	(16)
Fremont	57,300	(16)
Marion	42,100	(19)
Mount Vernon	48,900	(18)
New Philadelphia	49,700	(17)
Norwalk	56,800	(16)
Portsmouth	37,000	(19)
Sandusky	64,400	(15)
Sidney	59,900	(16)
Wooster	65,600	(15)
Zanesville	46,600	(18)
Oklahoma		
Ardmore	38,000	(19)
Chickasha	42,200	(19)
Duncan	38,600	(19)
McAlester	34,300	(20)
Muskogee	40,100	(19)
Stillwater	50,000	(17)
Oregon		
Albany-Corvallis	60,377	(16)
Bend	75,000	(13)
Coos Bay	49,900	(17)
Grants Pass	74,400	(13)
Klamath Falls	52,700	(17)
Pendleton	48,000	(18)
Roseburg	56,000	(16)
Pennsylvania		
Chambersburg	70,400	(14)
New Castle	41,300	(19)
Pottsville	37,900	(19)
Rhode Island		
Newport	160,100	(0)
South Carolina		
Greenwood	50,000	(17)
Hilton Head Island	112,000	(7)
Tennessee		
Cleveland	55,000	(16)
Columbia	60,400	(16)
Cookeville	55,000	(16)
Morristown	51,000	(17)
Tullahoma	50,211	(17)
Texas		
Corsicana	39,900	(19)
Del Rio	45,400	(18)
Eagle Pass	37,300	(19)
Huntsville	59,200	(16)
Lufkin	43,300	(18)
Nacogdoches	54,000	(17)
Palestine	42,400	(19)
Paris	38,200	(19)

Utah		
Logan	66,800	(15)
St. George	78,300	(13)
Vermont		
Rutland	94,000	(10)
Virginia		
Blacksburg-Radford-Christiansburg	64,472	(15)
Harrisonburg	76,964	(13)
Martinsville	51,552	(17)
Staunton-Waynesboro	67,406	(14)
Winchester	89,133	(11)
Washington		
Aberdeen	48,600	(18)
Longview	61,400	(15)
Mount Vernon	80,800	(12)
Port Angeles	78,700	(13)
Walla Walla	56,200	(16)
Wenatchee	71,800	(14)
West Virginia		
Beckley	43,600	(18)
Clarksburg	44,100	(18)
Fairmont	42,000	(19)
Morgantown	64,600	(15)
Wisconsin		
Fond du Lac	55,700	(16)
Manitowoc	49,200	(17)
Stevens Point	58,600	(16)
Watertown	56,973	(16)
Wyoming		
Rock Springs	70,500	(14)

Property Taxes

The arrival of the property tax bill is never one of the highlights of homeownership. This is particularly true in the East, where levies run the highest. But homeowners everywhere are seeing their property taxes rise, often in lock-step with federal cutbacks in moneys to states and localities.

This category weighs each area's property tax burden, dividing the total levy by the number of residents. The national average is $695. Small cities have considerably lighter burdens, with a median of $415.

Cullman, Alabama, has the lightest burden of all: Property taxes equal just $79 per resident. Taxes are low partly because government expenditures are low. Cullman spends just $507 per resident on local schools, far below the micropolitan median of $859. In other areas, the city is not required to spend heavily. A relatively low crime rate and mild winters do not require big budgets for police protection and road maintenance.

Rock Springs, Wyoming, has property taxes far on the other end of the scale. The annual property tax bill comes to $1,568 per person. But that's little surprise, because Rock Springs invests heavily in its civic life. Spending on parks and recreation, education, police protection, and local roads total $2,323 per resident, more than twice the micropolitan median.

Cities with the lowest property taxes are predominately in the South. Small cities in the East, particularly the most affluent ones, claim the majority of the bottom-ten list.

Source: Census of Governments: Compendium of Government Finances, U.S. Bureau of the Census, Washington, D.C. Data, published in 1997, are for fiscal year 1991–92.

Source: Twenty points for property taxes of less than $125 per resident; no points for $1,075 or more. The spacing is every $50 per resident.

Property Taxes: Highs and Lows

	Property Taxes Per Capita
Lowest	**$**
1. Cullman, Ala.	79
2. Talladega, Ala.	111
3. Hammond, La.	114
4. Albertville, Ala.	121
5. Clovis, N.Mex.	124
Poplar Bluff, Mo.	124
7. Roswell, N.Mex.	137
8. Auburn-Opelika, Ala.	139
9. Selma, Ala.	140
10. Alamogordo, N.Mex.	142
Median	
96. Pocatello, Idaho	415
Arcata-Eureka, Calif.	415
Highest	
184. Red Wing, Minn.	993
185. Vero Beach, Fla.	1,015
186. Traverse City, Mich.	1,024
187. Newport, R.I.	1,047
188. Torrington, Conn.	1,128
189. Key West, Fla.	1,138
190. Kingston, N.Y.	1,219
191. Concord, N.H.	1,308
192. Keene, N.H.	1,382
193. Rock Springs, Wyo.	1,568

Property Taxes Area by Area

(Property taxes per capita in dollars and rating points)

Micro median	415	
Alabama		
Albertville	121	(20)
Auburn-Opelika	139	(19)
Cullman	79	(20)
Selma	140	(19)
Talladega	111	(20)
Alaska		
Fairbanks	584	(10)
Arizona		
Prescott	643	(9)
Sierra Vista	475	(12)
Arkansas		
Blytheville	154	(19)
El Dorado	258	(17)
Hot Springs	257	(17)
Jonesboro	219	(18)
Russellville	289	(16)
Searcy	169	(19)
California		
Arcata-Eureka	415	(14)
El Centro-Calexico-Brawley	459	(13)
Hanford-Lemoore	330	(15)
Hollister	515	(12)
Connecticut		
Torrington	1,128	(0)
Florida		
Key West	1,138	(0)
Vero Beach	1,015	(2)
Georgia		
Brunswick	638	(9)
Dalton	589	(10)
Dublin	312	(16)
Gainesville	499	(12)
Hinesville	194	(18)
La Grange	404	(14)
Milledgeville	285	(16)
Rome	462	(13)
Statesboro	236	(17)
Thomasville	345	(15)
Valdosta	274	(17)
Waycross	309	(16)
Idaho		
Coeur d'Alene	613	(10)
Idaho Falls	480	(12)
Pocatello	415	(14)
Twin Falls	459	(13)
Illinois		
Carbondale	322	(16)
Danville	500	(12)
Freeport	383	(14)
Galesburg	514	(12)
Mattoon-Charleston	455	(13)
Ottawa	569	(11)
Quincy	356	(15)
Sterling	443	(13)
Indiana		
Columbus	644	(9)
Marion	602	(10)
Michigan City-La Porte	495	(12)
New Castle	463	(13)
Richmond	568	(11)
Vincennes	419	(14)
Iowa		
Ames	564	(11)
Burlington	681	(8)
Clinton	667	(9)

Mason City	749	(7)
Muscatine	703	(8)
Kansas		
Hutchinson	737	(7)
Manhattan	511	(12)
Salina	562	(11)
Kentucky		
Bowling Green	201	(18)
Frankfort	185	(18)
Madisonville	227	(17)
Paducah	197	(18)
Radcliff-Elizabethtown	246	(17)
Louisiana		
Hammond	114	(20)
New Iberia	200	(18)
Ruston	213	(18)
Maine		
Augusta-Waterville	619	(10)
Biddeford-Saco	942	(3)
Maryland		
Salisbury	466	(13)
Michigan		
Marquette	571	(11)
Mount Pleasant	482	(12)
Owosso	600	(10)
Traverse City	1,024	(2)
Minnesota		
Faribault	499	(12)
Mankato	554	(11)
Red Wing	993	(2)
Willmar	518	(12)
Winona	419	(14)
Mississippi		
Cleveland	331	(15)
Columbus	342	(15)
Greenville	374	(15)
Laurel	302	(16)
Meridian	374	(15)
Tupelo	403	(14)
Vicksburg	534	(11)
Missouri		
Cape Girardeau-Sikeston	246	(17)
Jefferson City	338	(15)
Poplar Bluff	124	(20)
Warrensburg	197	(18)
Montana		
Bozeman	525	(11)
Helena	770	(7)
Missoula	689	(8)
Nebraska		
Grand Island	606	(10)
Nevada		
Carson City	358	(15)
Elko	432	(13)
New Hampshire		
Concord	1,308	(0)
Keene	1,382	(0)
New Mexico		
Alamogordo	142	(19)
Carlsbad	162	(19)
Clovis	124	(20)
Farmington	343	(15)
Gallup	172	(19)
Hobbs	187	(18)
Roswell	137	(19)
New York		
Cortland	730	(7)
Gloversville	869	(5)
Ithaca	807	(6)

Kingston	1,219	(0)
Olean	725	(7)
Plattsburgh	557	(11)
Watertown	686	(8)
North Carolina		
Albemarle	281	(16)
Eden	305	(16)
Havelock-New Bern	277	(16)
Henderson	261	(17)
Kinston	347	(15)
Lumberton	259	(17)
Roanoke Rapids	291	(16)
Sanford	435	(13)
Shelby	281	(16)
Statesville	298	(16)
Wilson	346	(15)
North Dakota		
Minot	405	(14)
Ohio		
Ashland	461	(13)
Athens	431	(13)
Chillicothe	420	(14)
Findlay-Fostoria-Tiffin	535	(11)
Fremont	513	(12)
Marion	461	(13)
Mount Vernon	470	(13)
New Philadelphia	420	(14)
Norwalk	455	(13)
Portsmouth	299	(16)
Sandusky	714	(8)
Sidney	473	(13)
Wooster	527	(11)
Zanesville	388	(14)
Oklahoma		
Ardmore	219	(18)
Chickasha	177	(18)
Duncan	180	(18)
McAlester	144	(19)
Muskogee	270	(17)
Stillwater	202	(18)
Oregon		
Albany-Corvallis	787	(6)
Bend	931	(3)
Coos Bay	839	(5)
Grants Pass	513	(12)
Klamath Falls	691	(8)
Pendleton	667	(9)
Roseburg	736	(7)
Pennsylvania		
Chambersburg	357	(15)
New Castle	404	(14)
Pottsville	338	(15)
Rhode Island		
Newport	1,047	(1)
South Carolina		
Greenwood	171	(19)
Hilton Head Island	818	(6)
Tennessee		
Cleveland	308	(16)
Columbia	291	(16)
Cookeville	228	(17)
Morristown	290	(16)
Tullahoma	270	(17)
Texas		
Corsicana	530	(11)
Del Rio	537	(11)
Eagle Pass	243	(17)
Huntsville	348	(15)
Lufkin	426	(13)
Nacogdoches	398	(14)
Palestine	402	(14)
Paris	476	(12)

Utah		
Logan	297	(16)
St. George	467	(13)
Vermont		
Rutland	937	(3)
Virginia		
Blacksburg-Radford-Christiansburg	317	(16)
Harrisonburg	397	(14)
Martinsville	289	(16)
Staunton-Waynesboro	365	(15)
Winchester	481	(12)
Washington		
Aberdeen	302	(16)
Longview	385	(14)
Mount Vernon	381	(14)
Port Angeles	325	(15)
Walla Walla	472	(13)
Wenatchee	309	(16)
West Virginia		
Beckley	253	(17)
Clarksburg	287	(16)
Fairmont	332	(15)
Morgantown	298	(16)
Wisconsin		
Fond du Lac	749	(7)
Manitowoc	556	(11)
Stevens Point	625	(9)
Watertown	612	(10)
Wyoming		
Rock Springs	1,568	(0)

Heating and Cooling

Homeowners in the Midwest may brave the cold winter weather without a shiver, but many flinch when they open the heating bill. Likewise, they may have trouble keeping their cool when the electric bill arrives in August.

This category compares the heating and cooling needs of each area using a measure known as the degree day. Degree days are calculated by determining the difference between each day's average temperature and 65 degrees. Every degree below 65 degrees yields one heating degree day; every degree above 65 degrees yields one cooling degree day. For example, a temperature of 58 results in seven heating degree days. The higher the number of degree days, the greater the need for energy to keep the house comfortable.

Air conditioners and furnaces receive the least workout in Hollister, California. Mild weather year round results in just 3,396 degree days over the course of the year—3,353 for heating, and 43 for cooling.

Fairbanks, Alaska, is a nightmare for anyone hoping to hold down the utility bills. The temperature drops below zero 222 days out of an average year, the major reason for Fairbanks's astronomical total of 14,024 degree days.

Southern cities dominate the list of towns with the lowest heating and cooling needs. The Midwest generally requires the most energy.

Source: Climatography of the United States, no. 81, National Oceanic and Atmospheric Administration, Silver Spring, Maryland. Data are daily averages for the years 1950 through 1980.

Scoring: Twenty points for fewer than 4,000 degree days per year; no points for 9,400 or more. The spacing is every 300 degree days.

Heating and Cooling: Highs and Lows

	Total Annual Degree Days
Lowest	
1. Hollister, Calif.	3,396
2. Vero Beach, Fla.	3,779
3. Hinesville, Ga.	4,046
4. Brunswick, Ga.	4,058
5. Thomasville, Ga.	4,102
6. Hilton Head Island, S.C.	4,128
7. Hammond, La.	4,157
8. New Iberia, La.	4,204
9. Waycross, Ga.	4,210
10. Valdosta, Ga.	4,249
Median	
96. Cape Girardeau-Sikeston, Mo.	5,780
97. Winchester, Va.	5,808
Highest	
184. Winona, Minn.	8,472
185. Stevens Point, Wisc.	8,533
186. Faribault, Minn.	8,616
187. Mankato, Minn.	8,621
188. Red Wing, Minn.	8,631
189. Willmar, Minn.	8,912
190. Bozeman, Mont.	9,063
191. Marquette, Mich.	9,668
192. Minot, N.Dak.	9,838
193. Fairbanks, Alaska	14,024

Heating and Cooling Area by Area

(Total annual heating and cooling degree days and rating points)

Area	Degree days	Points
Micro median	5,794	
Alabama		
Albertville	4,831	(16)
Auburn-Opelika	4,477	(17)
Cullman	4,987	(15)
Selma	4,473	(17)
Talladega	4,581	(17)
Alaska		
Fairbanks	14,024	(0)
Arizona		
Prescott	5,626	(13)
Sierra Vista	4,369	(17)
Arkansas		
Blytheville	5,435	(14)
El Dorado	4,864	(16)
Hot Springs	5,139	(15)
Jonesboro	5,444	(14)
Russellville	5,260	(14)
Searcy	5,183	(15)
California		
Arcata-Eureka	4,727	(16)
El Centro-Calexico-Brawley	4,930	(15)
Hanford-Lemoore	4,268	(19)
Hollister	3,396	(20)
Connecticut		
Torrington	6,756	(9)
Florida		
Key West	4,870	(16)
Vero Beach	3,779	(20)
Georgia		
Brunswick	4,058	(19)
Dalton	5,000	(15)
Dublin	4,509	(17)
Gainesville	4,808	(16)
Hinesville	4,046	(19)
La Grange	4,413	(17)
Milledgeville	4,568	(17)
Rome	4,723	(16)
Statesboro	4,276	(19)
Thomasville	4,102	(19)
Valdosta	4,249	(19)
Waycross	4,210	(19)
Idaho		
Coeur d'Alene	6,856	(9)
Idaho Falls	8,283	(4)
Pocatello	7,568	(7)
Twin Falls	6,892	(9)
Illinois		
Carbondale	5,958	(12)
Danville	6,608	(10)
Freeport	7,666	(6)
Galesburg	7,219	(8)
Mattoon-Charleston	6,691	(10)
Ottawa	6,959	(9)
Quincy	6,909	(9)
Sterling	7,397	(7)
Indiana		
Columbus	6,473	(10)
Marion	7,052	(8)
Michigan City-La Porte	7,082	(8)
New Castle	6,919	(9)
Richmond	6,701	(9)
Vincennes	6,383	(11)
Iowa		
Ames	7,666	(6)
Burlington	7,173	(8)
Clinton	7,354	(7)

Mason City	8,321	(4)
Muscatine	7,181	(8)
Kansas		
Hutchinson	6,549	(10)
Manhattan	6,644	(10)
Salina	6,753	(9)
Kentucky		
Bowling Green	5,738	(13)
Frankfort	5,068	(15)
Madisonville	5,561	(13)
Paducah	5,703	(13)
Radcliff-Elizabethtown	5,496	(14)
Louisiana		
Hammond	4,157	(19)
New Iberia	4,204	(19)
Ruston	4,677	(16)
Maine		
Augusta-Waterville	7,951	(5)
Biddeford-Saco	7,755	(6)
Maryland		
Salisbury	5,485	(14)
Michigan		
Marquette	9,668	(0)
Mount Pleasant	7,477	(7)
Owosso	7,402	(7)
Traverse City	8,175	(5)
Minnesota		
Faribault	8,616	(3)
Mankato	8,621	(3)
Red Wing	8,631	(3)
Willmar	8,912	(2)
Winona	8,472	(4)
Mississippi		
Cleveland	5,064	(15)
Columbus	4,863	(16)
Greenville	4,881	(16)
Laurel	4,576	(17)
Meridian	4,637	(16)
Tupelo	5,049	(15)
Vicksburg	4,507	(17)
Missouri		
Cape Girardeau-Sikeston	5,780	(13)
Jefferson City	6,227	(11)
Poplar Bluff	5,678	(13)
Warrensburg	6,386	(11)
Montana		
Bozeman	9,063	(2)
Helena	8,470	(4)
Missoula	8,055	(5)
Nebraska		
Grand Island	7,510	(7)
Nevada		
Carson City	6,139	(11)
Elko	7,654	(6)
New Hampshire		
Concord	7,835	(6)
Keene	7,441	(7)
New Mexico		
Alamogordo	4,815	(16)
Carlsbad	4,988	(15)
Clovis	5,263	(14)
Farmington	6,312	(11)
Gallup	6,577	(10)
Hobbs	5,162	(15)
Roswell	4,989	(15)
New York		
Cortland	7,697	(6)
Gloversville	7,673	(6)
Ithaca	7,505	(7)

Kingston	6,957	(9)
Olean	7,170	(8)
Plattsburgh	8,332	(4)
Watertown	7,722	(6)
North Carolina		
Albemarle	4,710	(16)
Eden	5,141	(15)
Havelock-New Bern	4,516	(17)
Henderson	4,840	(16)
Kinston	4,735	(16)
Lumberton	4,724	(16)
Roanoke Rapids	4,820	(16)
Sanford	4,716	(16)
Shelby	4,999	(15)
Statesville	5,057	(15)
Wilson	4,848	(16)
North Dakota		
Minot	9,838	(0)
Ohio		
Ashland	6,923	(9)
Athens	6,213	(11)
Chillicothe	6,123	(11)
Findlay-Fostoria-Tiffin	7,017	(8)
Fremont	6,696	(10)
Marion	7,018	(8)
Mount Vernon	6,845	(9)
New Philadelphia	6,578	(10)
Norwalk	6,887	(9)
Portsmouth	5,839	(12)
Sandusky	6,837	(9)
Sidney	6,714	(9)
Wooster	6,919	(9)
Zanesville	6,493	(10)
Oklahoma		
Ardmore	5,144	(15)
Chickasha	5,465	(14)
Duncan	5,344	(14)
McAlester	5,431	(14)
Muskogee	5,447	(14)
Stillwater	5,713	(13)
Oregon		
Albany-Corvallis	5,189	(15)
Bend	7,184	(8)
Coos Bay	4,667	(16)
Grants Pass	4,918	(15)
Klamath Falls	6,894	(9)
Pendleton	5,989	(12)
Roseburg	4,823	(16)
Pennsylvania		
Chambersburg	6,335	(11)
New Castle	6,527	(10)
Pottsville	6,566	(10)
Rhode Island		
Newport	6,503	(10)
South Carolina		
Greenwood	4,822	(16)
Hilton Head Island	4,128	(19)
Tennessee		
Cleveland	5,161	(15)
Columbia	5,258	(14)
Cookeville	5,694	(13)
Morristown	5,230	(14)
Tullahoma	5,007	(15)
Texas		
Corsicana	4,992	(15)
Del Rio	4,782	(16)
Eagle Pass	4,932	(15)
Huntsville	4,556	(17)
Lufkin	4,581	(17)
Nacogdoches	4,631	(16)
Palestine	4,728	(16)
Paris	5,231	(14)

Utah		
Logan	7,344	(7)
St. George	5,372	(14)
Vermont		
Rutland	7,532	(7)
Virginia		
Blacksburg-Radford-Christiansburg	6,092	(12)
Harrisonburg	5,813	(12)
Martinsville	5,338	(14)
Staunton-Waynesboro	5,878	(12)
Winchester	5,808	(12)
Washington		
Aberdeen	5,346	(14)
Longview	5,198	(15)
Mount Vernon	5,480	(14)
Port Angeles	5,729	(13)
Walla Walla	5,892	(12)
Wenatchee	6,440	(10)
West Virginia		
Beckley	6,043	(12)
Clarksburg	6,217	(11)
Fairmont	6,115	(11)
Morgantown	6,274	(11)
Wisconsin		
Fond du Lac	8,089	(5)
Manitowoc	7,905	(5)
Stevens Point	8,533	(3)
Watertown	7,782	(6)
Wyoming		
Rock Springs	8,158	(5)

The Results

What's the small city with a high share of new, large, and affordable houses, low property taxes, and moderate utility bills? It's hard to name one, but easy to name three. Albertville, Alabama; Talladega, Alabama; and Waycross, Georgia, each score 87 points in the housing section, tying for first place.

Modern and roomy houses are the norm in these micros. In Albertville, fewer than 8 houses in 100 were constructed prior to 1940. Twenty-eight percent had been constructed between 1980 and 1989, according to the 1990 Census of Housing. The national average that year was 21 percent. More than 60 percent of houses in each of the three cities contain three or more bedrooms.

Affordable prices and reasonable property taxes result in homeownership rates in Alabama that are well above national averages. Seventy percent of Alabama residents owned their home in 1995, compared with a national average of 64.7 percent, according to the Census Bureau.

Median cost of a home in the three cities ranges from $40,753 in Waycross to $48,200 in Albertville, well below the typical small city. Property taxes in Albertville and Talladega are one-quarter of the already reasonable median for small cities. The levy in Talladega comes to just $111 per resident. Property taxes in Waycross are higher, at $309 per resident, but remain reasonable by any standard, especially compared to Atlanta, Georgia's, levy of $790. Mild winters and reasonable summers relieve Alabama and Georgia residents of costly utility bills. Waycross is among the ten small cities with the fewest degree days and Albertville and Talladega follow close behind.

Newport, Rhode Island, is a community with a lot to boast about, but affordable housing isn't one of them. The city's many beautiful old homes hark back to an era when East Coast elite summered in Newport. Median home value in Newport is a lofty $160,100—three times the small city median. The high home values and wealth of community services boost Newport's property taxes skyward also. Property taxes equal $1,047 per resident. That is more than twice the levy of the typical micro and far more comparable to property taxes in metropolitan Providence, Rhode Island.

Housing Scores: Highs and Lows

	Total Rating Points
Highest	
1. Albertville, Ala.	87
Talladega, Ala.	87
Waycross, Ga.	87
4. Cullman, Ala.	85
Hammond, La.	85
6. Hobbs, N.Mex.	84
Laurel, Miss.	84
Lumberton, N.C.	84
Tullahoma, Tenn.	84
Valdosta, Ga.	84
11. Alamogordo, N.Mex.	83
Clovis, N.Mex.	83
Columbus, Miss.	83
Dublin, Ga.	83
Hinesville, Ga.	83
Searcy, Ark.	83
Selma, Ala.	83
Thomasville, Ga.	83
19. New Iberia, La.	81
Roswell, N.Mex.	81
Statesboro, Ga.	81
Median	
96. Aberdeen, Wash.	65
97. Carson City, Nev.	65
Lowest	
184. Ithaca, N.Y.	40
185. Gloversville, N.Y.	39
186. Rutland, Vt.	37
187. Kingston, N.Y.	36
188. Biddeford-Saco, Maine	35
189. Key West, Fla.	34
190. Concord, N.H.	32
Keene, N.H.	32
Torrington, Conn.	32
193. Newport, R.I.	30

Housing Performance Comparison

	Albertville, Alabama	Talladega, Alabama	Waycross, Georgia	Micro median	Newport, Rhode Island
Total Points in Section	87	87	87	65	30
Rank in Section	1 (tie)	1 (tie)	1 (tie)		193
Housing Age					
Percent of housing built before 1940	7.6	10.1	11.8	15.5	33.1
Housing Age points	(17)	(16)	(16)		(7)
Housing Size					
Percent of houses with three or more bedrooms	61.6	61.4	62.6	56.6	55.4
Housing Size points	(16)	(16)	(17)		(12)
Housing Costs					
Median value of owner-occupied houses	$48,200	$44,100	$40,753	$53,100	$160,100
Housing Cost points	(18)	(18)	(19)		(0)
Property Taxes					
Property taxes per capita	$121	$111	$309	$415	$1,047
Property Tax points	(20)	(20)	(16)		(1)
Heating and Cooling					
Annual heating and cooling degree days	4,831	4,581	4,210	5,794	6,503
Heating and Cooling points	(16)	(17)	(19)		(10)

Housing Scores Area by Area

(Total housing rating points)

Micro median	65
Alabama	
Albertville	87
Auburn-Opelika	77
Cullman	85
Selma	83
Talladega	87
Alaska	
Fairbanks	45
Arizona	
Prescott	54
Sierra Vista	69
Arkansas	
Blytheville	79
El Dorado	79
Hot Springs	70
Jonesboro	78
Russellville	80
Searcy	83
California	
Arcata-Eureka	59
El Centro-Calexico-Brawley	63
Hanford-Lemoore	75
Hollister	60
Connecticut	
Torrington	32
Florida	
Key West	34
Vero Beach	55
Georgia	
Brunswick	75
Dalton	70
Dublin	83
Gainesville	74
Hinesville	83
La Grange	73
Milledgeville	80
Rome	71
Statesboro	81
Thomasville	83
Valdosta	84
Waycross	87
Idaho	
Coeur d'Alene	62
Idaho Falls	63
Pocatello	66
Twin Falls	62
Illinois	
Carbondale	64
Danville	58
Freeport	57
Galesburg	56
Mattoon-Charleston	58
Ottawa	55
Quincy	58
Sterling	62
Indiana	
Columbus	63
Marion	59
Michigan City-La Porte	60
New Castle	63
Richmond	58
Vincennes	55
Iowa	
Ames	54
Burlington	50
Clinton	53
Mason City	48
Muscatine	53
Kansas	
Hutchinson	53
Manhattan	61
Salina	61
Kentucky	
Bowling Green	76
Frankfort	75
Madisonville	74
Paducah	73
Radcliff-Elizabethtown	79
Louisiana	
Hammond	85
New Iberia	81
Ruston	79
Maine	
Augusta-Waterville	45
Biddeford-Saco	35
Maryland	
Salisbury	72
Michigan	
Marquette	49
Mount Pleasant	62
Owosso	61
Traverse City	48
Minnesota	
Faribault	53
Mankato	52
Red Wing	42
Willmar	55
Winona	52

Mississippi

Cleveland	79
Columbus	83
Greenville	79
Laurel	84
Meridian	78
Tupelo	78
Vicksburg	75

Missouri

Cape Girardeau-Sikeston	75
Jefferson City	70
Poplar Bluff	79
Warrensburg	70

Montana

Bozeman	51
Helena	49
Missoula	50

Nebraska

Grand Island	56

Nevada

Carson City	65
Elko	56

New Hampshire

Concord	32
Keene	32

New Mexico

Alamogordo	83
Carlsbad	80
Clovis	83
Farmington	70
Gallup	68
Hobbs	84
Roswell	81

New York

Cortland	45
Gloversville	39
Ithaca	40
Kingston	36
Olean	52
Plattsburgh	54
Watertown	46

North Carolina

Albemarle	76
Eden	73
Havelock-New Bern	80
Henderson	79
Kinston	77
Lumberton	84
Roanoke Rapids	80
Sanford	79
Shelby	79
Statesville	76
Wilson	75

North Dakota

Minot	58

Ohio

Ashland	63
Athens	61
Chillicothe	64
Findlay-Fostoria-Tiffin	60
Fremont	63
Marion	65
Mount Vernon	65
New Philadelphia	62
Norwalk	63
Portsmouth	67
Sandusky	56
Sidney	67
Wooster	63
Zanesville	63

Oklahoma

Ardmore	79
Chickasha	78
Duncan	80
McAlester	78
Muskogee	74
Stillwater	68

Oregon

Albany-Corvallis	64
Bend	53
Coos Bay	59
Grants Pass	64
Klamath Falls	55
Pendleton	63
Roseburg	65

Pennsylvania

Chambersburg	66
New Castle	64
Pottsville	64

Rhode Island

Newport	30

South Carolina

Greenwood	78
Hilton Head Island	62

Tennessee

Cleveland	79
Columbia	75
Cookeville	79
Morristown	80
Tullahoma	84

Texas

Corsicana	69
Del Rio	71
Eagle Pass	74
Huntsville	72
Lufkin	77

Nacogdoches	71
Palestine	77
Paris	73

Utah

Logan	64
St. George	70

Vermont

Rutland	37

Virginia

Blacksburg-Radford-Christiansburg	71
Harrisonburg	69
Martinsville	77
Staunton-Waynesboro	72
Winchester	68

Washington

Aberdeen	65
Longview	68
Mount Vernon	63
Port Angeles	65
Walla Walla	61
Wenatchee	58

West Virginia

Beckley	73
Clarksburg	64
Fairmont	62
Morgantown	63

Wisconsin

Fond du Lac	52
Manitowoc	56
Stevens Point	56
Watertown	55

Wyoming

Rock Springs	48

8

Public Safety

There is a crime story that has run on the front page of newspapers nationwide every year this decade. It's not a murder. It's the absence of a murder. The crime rate has fallen each year since 1991.

The number of crimes in 1995 was still staggering—13.9 million serious offenses were reported to local police, according to the Federal Bureau of Investigation. But nonetheless, 7 percent fewer crimes were reported that year than in 1991. The rate of crime per 100,000 population is currently at its lowest point since 1985. In 1995, the rate stood at 5,278 crimes per 100,000 U.S. residents. That is 11 percent lower than in 1991 and 4 percent below 1986.

The decline appears to have continued through 1996, also. Preliminary data indicate that the homicide rate has now reached a thirty-year low.

No one is sure exactly why crime is decreasing, although plenty of lawmakers have stepped forward to accept the honor. The so-called War on Drugs coincides with the decline, but there is little data that proves more police, more jails, and mandatory imprisonment are behind the decrease. In Los Angeles, for instance, murder fell 37 percent even as arrests declined and the L.A. police force suffered through low morale and a crisis in leadership. It's more likely that crime is reacting to a combination of small efforts, from neighborhood organizations to the mandatory five-day waiting period for handgun purchases.

Criminologists also suggest that crime may behave much like an epidemic, reports the *New York Times*. "Acts of violence lead to further acts of violence, creating a contagion effect and a sudden jump in crime rates that is hard to explain," says John Laub, a professor of criminology at Northeastern University. Epidemic outbreaks will decline just as rapidly as they grew, even without the discovery of a vaccine. Often they do so in response to a combination of small measures that have a large overall effect. In a similar way, it's possible that a flare-up in crime can turn a corner and begin cooling off without any one, central cause. Recent declines are likely the result of "the whole being far greater than the sum of its parts," says Jeffrey Fagan, the director of the Center for Violence Research and Prevention at Columbia University.

Unfortunately, the news is not all good. Even though overall crime rates have been declining, the rate of crimes committed by teens has been steadily rising. Violent crime arrests of youths aged eighteen and younger stand 67 percent above levels of a decade ago, according to the FBI. In 1995, teenagers comprised 22 percent of serious crime convictions, 14 percent of violent crime convictions, and 25 percent of convictions for property crimes.

Crack cocaine brought many youths into the drug trade in the late 1980s, says James Q. Wilson of the University of California at Los Angeles. The crack trade put an increasing number of automatic handguns in the palms of teenagers. Adult homicide rates fell through this period, but the overall homicide rate remained high due to increasing teen homicides, he points out. "When you had fifteen-year-olds selling crack, they were wild cowboys who shot off their guns if somebody dissed them," says Geoffrey Canada, president of the Rheedlen Centers for Children and Families in Harlem.

The victims of teens are almost always other teens. The homicide rate of youths aged fourteen to seventeen increased 120 percent between 1985 and 1995, according to the Bureau of Justice Statistics. In comparison, the rate for young adults aged eighteen to twenty-four increased 61 percent over this period and the rate for adults aged twenty-five and older declined 13 percent. Youths aged fourteen to seventeen now have a higher death rate from homicide than do adults, at 10.8 per 100,000 compared with 8.0.

The toll has been enormous and Canada says he is seeing young teens turning away from the violence. The death toll in their families, combined with increased efforts by police and neighborhood groups, is reducing teen involvement in the drug trade, he says.

Small cities have not been immune to these trends, but on the whole they have remained safer. Many are far safer from violent crime than are larger cities. Overall crime rates in small cities were approximately 10 percent lower than the national average in 1995, and nearly 50 percent below those of mid-sized metropolitan areas, where the highest total crime rates occur. Small-city residents are half as likely as the nation as a whole to be a victim of violent crime. And compared with the nation's eight largest metros, small cities experience 69 to 74 percent less violent crime.

This section evaluates each small city according to its level of public safety.

It measures the rates of violent, property, and teen crime, as well as investment in police and fire departments.

The majority of the nation's crime statistics are derived from the FBI's Uniform Crime Reporting Program. Each year, local police departments voluntarily submit data on the crimes they investigated during the previous year. The FBI compiles these records in the *Uniform Crime Report.* Because local police involvement in the report varies slightly from year to year, the total number of crimes reported reflects how many, and which, police departments take part. Approximately 16,000 law enforcement agencies usually report, representing 95 percent of the nation's population. Estimates are made for those areas that do not report.

It's important to keep in mind that the data used in the following categories reflect only those crimes that are reported to police. They do not, of course, reflect crimes that go unreported, and they do not reflect the share of incidents that end in criminal convictions. It's also important to remember that the data represent only those areas where police filed reports in a given year. Some years, few police departments may report for a given area, resulting in low "coverage" and potentially less reliable data for that area. Such occurrences are marked in the tables that follow.

Ranking micropolitan America. The ideal small city would have a low crime rate, especially when it comes to violent offenses and teenage crime. It would also have a well-funded police force and a professional fire department. Each area is graded in five categories:

1. Total Crime Rate: Can you live free from the worry of any sort of crime, including the smallest, or is there a high rate of reported offenses?
2. Violent Crime Rate: Can you walk the street without physical fear, or are violent incidences a daily occurrence?
3. Juvenile Crime Rate: Is crime a problem among the teenage population, or is the area relatively free from that trend?
4. Local Police Funding: Does the local government show a willingness to adequately fund the police department?
5. Local Fire Funding: Are local officials likewise forthcoming with their financial support for the fire department?

Total Crime Rate

Just over 5 percent of the population was a victim to a crime in 1994, or approximately 1 person in 19. At that rate, a crime was committed every two seconds throughout the year. For residents in small cities, the rate was 25 percent lower.

This category rates each area according to the number of major crimes reported per 100,000 residents. Crimes in this category include murder, rape, robbery, aggravated assault, burglary, larceny, and motor vehicle theft. The national average, including metros, is 5,374 offenses per 100,000 residents.

Cleveland, Mississippi, offers a safe haven for those weary of big-city crime. Only 156 crimes were reported over the year, for a rate of 365 per 100,000.

The majority of the highest rates belong to southern towns. Hammond, Louisiana, has the highest, with 17,698 crimes per 100,000. An average of fifteen burglaries, larcenies, and car thefts occurred every day in Hammond.

Midwestern towns have the lowest crime rates. Six Ohio micropolitans rank among the ten safest. Nine of the ten small cities with the highest rates are in the South.

Source: Derived from the Federal Bureau of Investigation's Uniform Crime Reporting Program. County-level calculations are made by the Inter-University Consortium for Political and Social Research (ICPSR) at the University of Michigan, Ann Arbor. Data are for 1994.

Scoring: Twenty points for 999 or fewer crimes reported per 100,000 residents; no points for 10,500 or more. The spacing is every 500 crimes per 100,000 residents.

Total Crime Rate: Highs and Lows

	Reported Crimes per 100,000 Residents
Lowest	
1. Cleveland, Miss.††	365
2. Clinton, Iowa	595
3. Sidney, Ohio	610
4. Wooster, Ohio	1,227
5. Elko, Nev.	1,402
6. Ashland, Ohio	1,466
7. New Philadelphia, Ohio	1,487
8. Statesville, N.C.	1,616
9. Athens, Ohio	1,663
10. Findlay-Fostoria-Tiffin, Ohio††	1,678
Median	
96. Marion, Ohio	4,056
Highest	
183. Henderson, N.C.	7,582
184. Salina, Kans.**	7,788
185. Hilton Head Island, S.C.	7,922
186. Wilson, N.C.	8,067
187. Paris, Tex.	8,120
188. Selma, Ala.	8,814
189. Key West, Fla.	8,834
190. Greenville, Miss.	9,309
191. Tullahoma, Tenn.††	14,632
192. Hammond, La.	17,698

Notes: No data are available for Mt. Vernon, Ohio.
†† 51 to 75 percent of local law enforcement agencies reporting.
** 1992 data

Total Crime Rate Area by Area

(Reported crimes per 100,000 residents and rating points)

Area	Rate	Points
Micro median	4,056	
Alabama		
Albertville	2,770	(16)
Auburn-Opelika	5,818	(10)
Cullman	2,312	(17)
Selma	8,814	(4)
Talladega	3,761	(14)
Alaska		
Fairbanks	6,578	(8)
Arizona		
Prescott	5,604	(10)
Sierra Vista	3,364	(15)
Arkansas		
Blytheville	6,858	(8)
El Dorado	4,521	(12)
Hot Springs	4,994	(12)
Jonesboro	5,352	(11)
Russellville	3,846	(14)
Searcy	2,853	(16)
California		
Arcata-Eureka	7,451	(7)
El Centro-Calexico-Brawley	6,370	(9)
Hanford-Lemoore	4,189	(13)
Hollister	3,881	(14)
Connecticut		
Torrington	1,759	(18)
Florida		
Key West	8,834	(4)
Vero Beach	5,734	(10)
Georgia		
Brunswick	7,423	(7)
Dalton	4,074	(13)
Dublin	4,738	(12)
Gainesville	4,806	(12)
Hinesville	4,766	(12)
La Grange	5,394	(11)
Milledgeville*††	2,590	(16)
Rome	5,253	(11)
Statesboro	4,086	(13)
Thomasville	5,642	(10)
Valdosta	6,189	(9)
Waycross	4,940	(12)
Idaho		
Coeur d'Alene	5,441	(11)
Idaho Falls	4,697	(12)
Pocatello	4,053	(13)
Twin Falls	4,819	(12)
Illinois**		
Carbondale	6,847	(8)
Danville	4,965	(12)
Freeport	3,876	(14)
Galesburg	4,002	(13)
Mattoon-Charleston	2,393	(17)
Ottawa	2,625	(16)
Quincy	3,562	(14)
Sterling	3,347	(15)
Indiana		
Columbus	4,381	(13)
Marion	4,491	(13)
Michigan City-La Porte	7,371	(7)
New Castle	2,390	(17)
Richmond	3,699	(14)
Vincennes	2,383	(17)
Iowa		
Ames	3,726	(14)
Burlington*	3,337	(15)
Clinton	595	(20)

Mason City	6,043	(9)
Muscatine	3,574	(14)
Kansas**		
Hutchinson	5,414	(11)
Manhattan	3,580	(14)
Salina	7,788	(6)
Kentucky		
Bowling Green	4,913	(12)
Frankfort	4,704	(12)
Madisonville	3,894	(14)
Paducah	6,061	(9)
Radcliff-Elizabethtown	2,823	(16)
Louisiana		
Hammond	17,698	(0)
New Iberia	3,680	(14)
Ruston	6,148	(9)
Maine		
Augusta-Waterville	3,210	(15)
Biddeford-Saco	3,402	(15)
Maryland		
Salisbury	6,815	(8)
Michigan		
Marquette	3,777	(14)
Mount Pleasant†	3,256	(15)
Owosso†	2,605	(16)
Traverse City	2,876	(16)
Minnesota		
Faribault	3,834	(14)
Mankato	3,632	(14)
Red Wing	3,795	(14)
Willmar	4,243	(13)
Winona	3,658	(14)
Mississippi		
Cleveland††	365	(20)
Columbus	2,588	(16)
Greenville	9,309	(3)
Laurel	4,977	(12)
Meridian	2,827	(16)
Tupelo	4,196	(13)
Vicksburg	6,431	(9)
Missouri		
Cape Girardeau-Sikeston*	3,901	(14)
Jefferson City	2,848	(16)
Poplar Bluff	3,643	(14)
Warrensburg*	4,950	(12)
Montana		
Bozeman*†	2,488	(17)
Helena**	4,239	(13)
Missoula*	5,653	(10)
Nebraska		
Grand Island	6,405	(9)
Nevada		
Carson City	4,707	(12)
Elko	1,402	(19)
New Hampshire		
Concord	2,157	(17)
Keene	1,753	(18)
New Mexico		
Alamogordo	2,768	(16)
Carlsbad	1,750	(18)
Clovis	4,688	(12)
Farmington	3,945	(14)
Gallup	4,890	(12)
Hobbs	5,585	(10)
Roswell	6,567	(8)
New York		
Cortland	4,112	(13)
Gloversville†	4,063	(13)

Ithaca	4,671	(12)
Kingston	2,963	(16)
Olean	3,056	(15)
Plattsburgh	2,238	(17)
Watertown	2,474	(17)

North Carolina

Albemarle	4,788	(12)
Eden	4,724	(12)
Havelock-New Bern	5,376	(11)
Henderson	7,582	(6)
Kinston	6,273	(9)
Lumberton	4,769	(12)
Roanoke Rapids	4,940	(12)
Sanford	7,040	(7)
Shelby	5,301	(11)
Statesville	1,616	(18)
Wilson	8,067	(5)

North Dakota

Minot	2,781	(16)

Ohio

Ashland	1,466	(19)
Athens	1,663	(18)
Chillicothe	4,132	(13)
Findlay-Fostoria-Tiffin††	1,678	(18)
Fremont	2,721	(16)
Marion	4,056	(13)
Mount Vernon	n/a	
New Philadelphia	1,487	(19)
Norwalk	2,153	(17)
Portsmouth††	4,059	(13)
Sandusky	5,149	(11)
Sidney	610	(20)
Wooster	1,227	(19)
Zanesville	3,297	(15)

Oklahoma

Ardmore	7,216	(7)
Chickasha	3,553	(14)
Duncan	3,506	(14)
McAlester	3,063	(15)
Muskogee	5,571	(10)
Stillwater	4,312	(13)

Oregon

Albany-Corvallis	6,281	(9)
Bend	5,577	(10)
Coos Bay	5,286	(11)
Grants Pass	5,113	(11)
Klamath Falls	3,931	(14)
Pendleton	3,128	(15)
Roseburg	4,594	(12)

Pennsylvania

Chambersburg	2,533	(16)
New Castle	2,254	(17)
Pottsville	3,570	(14)

Rhode Island

Newport	3,716	(14)

South Carolina

Greenwood	6,119	(9)
Hilton Head Island	7,922	(6)

Tennessee

Cleveland	3,122	(15)
Columbia	4,571	(12)
Cookeville	2,539	(16)
Morristown	3,444	(15)
Tullahoma††	14,632	(0)

Texas

Corsicana	5,426	(11)
Del Rio	5,199	(11)
Eagle Pass	6,550	(8)
Huntsville	3,362	(15)
Lufkin	3,950	(14)
Nacogdoches	4,559	(12)
Palestine	3,929	(14)
Paris	8,120	(5)

Utah

Logan	2,579	(16)
St. George†	4,285	(13)

Vermont

Rutland	4,998	(12)

Virginia

Blacksburg-Radford-Christiansburg	2,925	(16)
Harrisonburg	2,397	(17)
Martinsville	3,936	(14)
Staunton-Waynesboro	2,511	(16)
Winchester	3,936	(14)

Washington

Aberdeen	5,805	(10)
Longview	5,242	(11)
Mount Vernon	5,498	(11)
Port Angeles	3,898	(14)
Walla Walla	7,050	(7)
Wenatchee	6,522	(8)

West Virginia

Beckley	4,017	(13)
Clarksburg	1,860	(18)
Fairmont	2,127	(17)
Morgantown	3,681	(14)

Wisconsin

Fond du Lac	3,401	(15)
Manitowoc	2,898	(16)
Stevens Point	3,428	(15)
Watertown	2,602	(16)

Wyoming

Rock Springs	4,979	(12)

Notes:
† 76 to 95 percent of police departments reporting.
†† 51 to 75 percent of police departments reporting.
n/a data not available, or less than 30 percent of local law enforcement agencies reporting.
* 1993 data
** 1992 data

Violent Crime Rate

A safe neighborhood where we can walk without fear and our children can play in safety is one of our primary desires. In recent years that desire has led many people out of metropolitan areas and into smaller communities.

Smaller is safer when it comes to cities. An estimated 716 people in 100,000 were victims of violent crime nationwide in 1994. The rate for small cities that year was less than half that—316 per 100,000. This category calculates the violent-crime rate for each area, projecting its annual totals as a rate per 100,000 residents. Violent crimes include homicide, rape, robbery, and aggravated assault.

Clinton, Iowa, is virtually free of violence. Just nine violent crimes were reported in 1994—one robbery and eight aggravated assaults—equalling a rate of 15 crimes per 100,000 residents.

It was a different story in Hammond, Louisiana, in 1994. Police responded to 1,688 reports of violent crime, including eleven homicides and 1,469 aggravated assaults. The violent crime rate in Hammond that year topped 1,900 per 100,000 residents.

Midwestern micros have the lowest rates of violent crimes. Southern cities have the highest.

Source: Derived from the Federal Bureau of Investigation's Uniform Crime Reporting Program. County-level calculations are made by the Inter-University Consortium for Political and Social Research (ICPSR) at the University of Michigan, Ann Arbor. Data are for 1994.

Scoring: Twenty points for fewer than 50 violent crimes reported per 100,000 residents; no points for 1,475 or more. The spacing is every 75 crimes per 100,000 residents.

Violent Crime Rate: Highs and Lows

	Reported Violent Crimes per 100,000 Residents
Lowest	
1. Clinton, Iowa	15
2. New Castle, Ind.	32
3. Ashland, Ohio	41
4. Winona, Minn.	57
5. Wooster, Ohio	61
6. Sidney, Ohio	63
7. Norwalk, Ohio	72
8. Searcy, Ark.	74
9. Watertown, Wisc.	80
10. Athens, Ohio	83
Median	
96. Grand Island, Nebr.	316
Highest	
183. Brunswick, Ga.	966
184. Wilson, N.C.	986
185. Hilton Head Island, S.C.	1,032
186. Salisbury, Md.	1,065
187. Blytheville, Ark.	1,191
188. Greenwood, S.C.	1,460
189. Paris, Tex.	1,633
190. Selma, Ala.	1,650
191. Paducah, Ky.	1,657
192. Hammond, La.	1,903

Note: No data are available for Mt. Vernon, Ohio.

Violent Crime Rate Area by Area

(Reported violent crimes per 100,000 residents and rating points)

Area	Rate	Points
Micro median	316	
Alabama		
Albertville	304	(16)
Auburn-Opelika	720	(11)
Cullman	242	(17)
Selma	1,650	(0)
Talladega	342	(16)
Alaska		
Fairbanks	739	(10)
Arizona		
Prescott	468	(14)
Sierra Vista	251	(17)
Arkansas		
Blytheville	1,191	(5)
El Dorado	399	(15)
Hot Springs	346	(16)
Jonesboro	495	(14)
Russellville	236	(17)
Searcy	74	(19)
California		
Arcata-Eureka	544	(13)
El Centro-Calexico-Brawley	734	(10)
Hanford-Lemoore	607	(12)
Hollister	740	(10)
Connecticut		
Torrington	132	(18)
Florida		
Key West	950	(7)
Vero Beach	563	(13)
Georgia		
Brunswick	966	(7)
Dalton	317	(16)
Dublin	679	(11)
Gainesville	373	(15)
Hinesville	263	(17)
La Grange	606	(12)
Milledgeville*††	325	(16)
Rome	622	(12)
Statesboro	305	(16)
Thomasville	570	(13)
Valdosta	658	(11)
Waycross	288	(16)
Idaho		
Coeur d'Alene	470	(14)
Idaho Falls	306	(16)
Pocatello	291	(16)
Twin Falls	307	(16)
Illinois**		
Carbondale	528	(13)
Danville	466	(14)
Freeport	221	(17)
Galesburg	171	(18)
Mattoon-Charleston	85	(19)
Ottawa	93	(19)
Quincy	186	(18)
Sterling	90	(19)
Indiana		
Columbus	274	(17)
Marion	947	(8)
Michigan City-La Porte	578	(12)
New Castle	32	(20)
Richmond	117	(19)
Vincennes	106	(19)
Iowa		
Ames	121	(19)
Burlington*	114	(19)
Clinton	15	(20)

Mason City	660	(11)
Muscatine	335	(16)
Kansas**		
Hutchinson	442	(14)
Manhattan	305	(16)
Salina	406	(15)
Kentucky		
Bowling Green	696	(11)
Frankfort	706	(11)
Madisonville	776	(10)
Paducah	1,657	(0)
Radcliff-Elizabethtown	444	(14)
Louisiana		
Hammond	1,903	(0)
New Iberia	387	(15)
Ruston	714	(11)
Maine		
Augusta-Waterville	97	(19)
Biddeford-Saco	98	(19)
Maryland		
Salisbury	1,065	(6)
Michigan		
Marquette	192	(18)
Mount Pleasant†	265	(17)
Owosso†	241	(17)
Traverse City	211	(17)
Minnesota		
Faribault	169	(18)
Mankato	133	(18)
Red Wing	137	(18)
Willmar	266	(17)
Winona	57	(19)
Mississippi		
Cleveland††	143	(18)
Columbus	230	(17)
Greenville	746	(10)
Laurel	622	(12)
Meridian	328	(16)
Tupelo	330	(16)
Vicksburg	535	(13)
Missouri		
Cape Girardeau-Sikeston*	264	(17)
Jefferson City	171	(18)
Poplar Bluff	209	(17)
Warrensburg*	226	(17)
Montana		
Bozeman*†	111	(19)
Helena**	369	(15)
Missoula*	197	(18)
Nebraska		
Grand Island	316	(16)
Nevada		
Carson City	514	(13)
Elko	400	(15)
New Hampshire		
Concord	101	(19)
Keene	186	(18)
New Mexico		
Alamogordo	231	(17)
Carlsbad	135	(18)
Clovis	516	(13)
Farmington	713	(11)
Gallup	543	(13)
Hobbs	881	(8)
Roswell	668	(11)
New York		
Cortland	200	(17)
Gloversville†	230	(17)
Ithaca	140	(18)

Kingston	349	(16)
Olean	348	(16)
Plattsburgh	261	(17)
Watertown	157	(18)
North Carolina		
Albemarle	355	(15)
Eden	607	(12)
Havelock-New Bern	652	(11)
Henderson	770	(10)
Kinston	963	(7)
Lumberton	529	(13)
Roanoke Rapids	551	(13)
Sanford	558	(13)
Shelby	622	(12)
Statesville	166	(18)
Wilson	986	(7)
North Dakota		
Minot	85	(19)
Ohio		
Ashland	41	(20)
Athens	83	(19)
Chillicothe	215	(17)
Findlay-Fostoria-Tiffin††	101	(19)
Fremont	141	(18)
Marion	134	(18)
Mount Vernon	n/a	
New Philadelphia	111	(19)
Norwalk	72	(19)
Portsmouth††	316	(16)
Sandusky	437	(14)
Sidney	63	(19)
Wooster	61	(19)
Zanesville	470	(14)
Oklahoma		
Ardmore	562	(13)
Chickasha	526	(13)
Duncan	341	(16)
McAlester	322	(16)
Muskogee	746	(10)
Stillwater	346	(16)
Oregon		
Albany-Corvallis	281	(16)
Bend	222	(17)
Coos Bay	162	(18)
Grants Pass	242	(17)
Klamath Falls	421	(15)
Pendleton	154	(18)
Roseburg	275	(16)
Pennsylvania		
Chambersburg	379	(15)
New Castle	269	(17)
Pottsville	141	(18)
Rhode Island		
Newport	389	(15)
South Carolina		
Greenwood	1,460	(1)
Hilton Head Island	1,032	(6)
Tennessee		
Cleveland	350	(15)
Columbia	509	(13)
Cookeville	125	(18)
Morristown	199	(18)
Tullahoma††	133	(18)
Texas		
Corsicana	625	(12)
Del Rio	338	(16)
Eagle Pass	779	(10)
Huntsville	428	(14)
Lufkin	441	(14)
Nacogdoches	647	(12)
Palestine	586	(12)
Paris	1,633	(0)

Utah

Logan	83	(19)
St. George†	232	(17)

Vermont

Rutland	188	(18)

Virginia

Blacksburg-Radford-Christiansburg	166	(18)
Harrisonburg	99	(19)
Martinsville	425	(14)
Staunton-Waynesboro	165	(18)
Winchester	273	(17)

Washington

Aberdeen	294	(16)
Longview	295	(16)
Mount Vernon	188	(18)
Port Angeles	208	(17)
Walla Walla	814	(9)
Wenatchee	351	(15)

West Virginia

Beckley	606	(12)
Clarksburg	129	(18)
Fairmont	169	(18)
Morgantown	177	(18)

Wisconsin

Fond du Lac	200	(17)
Manitowoc	107	(19)
Stevens Point	123	(19)
Watertown	80	(19)

Wyoming

Rock Springs	366	(15)

Notes:
† 76 to 95 percent of police departments reporting.
†† 51 to 75 percent of police departments reporting.
n/a data not available, or fewer than 30 percent of local law enforcement agencies reporting.
* 1993 data.
** 1992 data.

Juvenile Crime Rate

Perhaps the most disturbing crime trend of the past two decades is the increase in teenage crime, especially violent crime. The share of teen arrests has risen 22 percent since 1986, compared with an increase in the teen population of just 2.7 percent. Youths aged seventeen and younger constituted 18.7 percent of all violent crime arrests in 1995.

With the rise has come a dizzying increase in the number of young homicide victims. As was mentioned, youths aged fourteen to seventeen now have a higher rate of death by homicide than do adults aged twenty-five and older, at 10.8 deaths per 100,000 young teens, compared with 8.0 for the adults.

This category measures the teen crime rate in each area for all crimes by calculating the number of teens arrested per 1,000 teenagers. Arrests are for all crimes, from curfew infringements to homicide. Keep in mind that the data represent arrests, not convictions. Records of convictions by age are not available for small areas such as counties. See the section introduction for complete information regarding inconsistencies in reporting data.

Fairmont, West Virginia, is seeing little of the teenage crime prevalent in some parts of the country. Fewer than 8 teens in 1,000 were arrested in 1994.

Manitowoc, Wisconsin, lies at the other end of the spectrum, however. Local police made 2,819 arrests of teens in 1994, nearly 233 out of every 1,000 teens. Just 2 percent of arrests were for violent crimes; 23 percent were for property crimes, larceny being the most common. Arrests for vandalism, liquor law violations, curfew violations, disorderly conduct, and loitering accounted for 42 percent of all arrests.

Midwestern and Southern cities have the lowest teen-arrest rates. Cities with the highest rates are distributed throughout the country.

Source: Derived from the Federal Bureau of Investigation's Uniform Crime Reporting Program. County-level calculations are made by the Inter-University Consortium for Political and Social Research (ICPSR) at the University of Michigan, Ann Arbor. Data are for 1994.

Scoring: Twenty points for 9 or fewer arrests per 1,000 teens; no points for 200 or more. The spacing is every 10 arrests per 1,000 teens.

Juvenile Crime Rate: Highs and Lows

Lowest	Arrests per 1,000 Juveniles
1. Fairmont, W.Va.	7.6
2. Rutland, Vt.	8.3
3. Morristown, Tenn.†††	11.0
4. Albertville, Ala.	13.5
5. Talladega, Ala.	13.6
6. Cullman, Ala.	13.9
7. Tullahoma, Tenn.†††	14.9
8. Clinton, Iowa††	17.4
9. Jefferson City, Mo.†††	19.9
10. Mattoon-Charleston, Ill.	20.2
11. Harrisonburg, Va.	21.1
12. Bozeman, Mont.††	21.6
13. McAlester, Okla.	21.7
14. Owosso, Mich.	22.5
15. Blacksburg-Radford Christiansburg, Va.	23.6
Median	
94. Plattsburgh, N.Y.	65.4
95. New Castle, Pa.	65.6

Highest	Arrests per 1,000 Juveniles
180. Hanford-Lemoore, Calif.	165.1
181. Grand Island, Nebr.	165.7
182. Fond du Lac, Wisc.	166.4
183. Watertown, Wisc.	173.8
184. Clovis, N.Mex.†	176.9
185. Carson City, Nev.	185.6
186. Wenatchee, Wash.	191.0
187. Salina, Kans.**	209.7
188. Pocatello, Idaho	212.4
189. Manitowoc, Wisc.	232.8

Notes: † 76 to 95 percent of police departments reporting.
†† 51 to 75 percent of police departments reporting.
††† 31 to 50 percent of police departments reporting.
** 1992 data

No data are available for Cleveland, Mississippi; Tupelo, Mississippi; Findlay-Fostoria-Tiffin, Ohio; and Mount Vernon, Ohio.

The list of lowest arrest rates has been extended to include the top ten cities with 100 percent of their police departments reporting.

Juvenile Crime Rate Area by Area

(Arrest per 1,000 juveniles and rating points)

Micro median	65.5	
Alabama		
Albertville	13.5	(19)
Auburn-Opelika	38.5	(17)
Cullman	13.9	(19)
Selma	55.0	(15)
Talladega	13.6	(19)
Alaska		
Fairbanks	46.3	(16)
Arizona		
Prescott	140.3	(6)
Sierra Vista†	118.4	(9)
Arkansas		
Blytheville	130.6	(7)
El Dorado	60.9	(14)
Hot Springs	79.6	(13)
Jonesboro	48.6	(16)
Russellville	30.9	(17)
Searcy	24.6	(18)
California		
Arcata-Eureka	80.0	(12)
El Centro-Calexico-Brawley	63.3	(14)
Hanford-Lemoore	165.1	(4)
Hollister	77.3	(13)
Connecticut		
Torrington††	39.4	(17)
Florida		
Key West	65.6	(14)
Vero Beach	91.2	(11)
Georgia		
Brunswick	62.3	(14)
Dalton	31.8	(17)
Dublin†	72.2	(13)
Gainesville†	38.4	(17)
Hinesville	79.9	(13)
La Grange††	27.2	(18)
Milledgeville	52.8	(15)
Rome*	52.1	(15)
Statesboro†	34.6	(17)
Thomasville†	50.9	(15)
Valdosta	26.1	(18)
Waycross	77.9	(13)
Idaho		
Coeur d'Alene	92.6	(11)
Idaho Falls	163.1	(4)
Pocatello	212.4	(0)
Twin Falls	93.3	(11)
Illinois**		
Carbondale	35.9	(17)
Danville	68.3	(14)
Freeport	74.4	(13)
Galesburg	73.9	(13)
Mattoon-Charleston	20.2	(18)
Ottawa†	40.5	(16)
Quincy	83.8	(12)
Sterling	68.1	(14)
Indiana		
Columbus **	61.6	(14)
Marion**	114.3	(9)
Michigan City-La Porte†	150.6	(5)
New Castle†††	53.1	(15)
Richmond†	113.1	(9)
Vincennes††	34.3	(17)
Iowa		
Ames	27.5	(18)
Burlington*	58.6	(15)
Clinton††	17.4	(19)

Mason City 127.3 (8)
Muscatine 110.1 (9)

Kansas**
Hutchinson 137.7 (7)
Manhattan 59.8 (15)
Salina 209.7 (0)

Kentucky
Bowling Green** 83.7 (12)
Frankfort† 37.2 (17)
Madisonville† 66.2 (14)
Paducah† 60.0 (14)
Radcliff-Elizabethtown** 45.4 (16)

Louisiana
Hammond ††† 60.9 (14)
New Iberia† 93.9 (11)
Ruston*† 23.7 (18)

Maine
Augusta-Waterville 50.7 (15)
Biddeford-Saco 86.1 (12)

Maryland
Salisbury 112.3 (9)

Michigan
Marquette† 73.5 (13)
Mount Pleasant† 28.5 (18)
Owosso† 22.5 (18)
Traverse City 53.7 (15)

Minnesota
Faribault 77.4 (13)
Mankato 76.9 (13)
Red Wing 101.8 (10)
Willmar 133.8 (7)
Winona 131.2 (7)

Mississippi
Cleveland n/a
Columbus*††† 35.5 (17)
Greenville*† 88.2 (12)
Laurel††† 67.9 (14)
Meridian†† 105.3 (10)
Tupelo n/a
Vicksburg 71.8 (13)

Missouri
Cape Girardeau-Sikeston**† 71.0 (13)
Jefferson City*††† 19.9 (19)
Poplar Bluff** 107.4 (10)
Warrensburg††† 27.5 (18)

Montana
Bozeman*†† 21.6 (18)
Helena** 64.5 (14)
Missoula** 112.6 (9)

Nebraska
Grand Island 165.7 (4)

Nevada
Carson City 185.6 (2)
Elko†† 123.7 (8)

New Hampshire†
Concord 34.4 (17)
Keene 52.2 (15)

New Mexico
Alamogordo*†† 92.4 (11)
Carlsbad††† 101.6 (10)
Clovis† 176.9 (3)
Farmington** 93.7 (11)
Gallup† 102.2 (10)
Hobbs† 115.0 (9)
Roswell† 119.3 (9)

New York
Cortland 51.5 (15)
Gloversville† 129.3 (8)

Area	Rate	(Rank)
Ithaca	50.6	(15)
Kingston†	95.0	(11)
Olean	65.2	(14)
Plattsburgh	65.4	(14)
Watertown	55.0	(15)
North Carolina		
Albemarle	47.5	(16)
Eden	60.7	(14)
Havelock-New Bern	60.4	(14)
Henderson	59.9	(15)
Kinston	67.8	(14)
Lumberton	95.9	(11)
Roanoke Rapids	66.1	(14)
Sanford	120.1	(8)
Shelby	31.7	(17)
Statesville†	50.0	(15)
Wilson	42.2	(16)
North Dakota		
Minot	118.0	(9)
Ohio		
Ashland†	28.0	(18)
Athens	42.0	(16)
Chillicothe†	73.4	(13)
Findlay-Fostoria-Tiffin	n/a	
Fremont††	48.5	(16)
Marion††	38.9	(17)
Mount Vernon	n/a	
New Philadelphia†††	38.2	(17)
Norwalk	60.7	(14)
Portsmouth†††	46.0	(16)
Sandusky††	90.1	(11)
Sidney††	39.1	(17)
Wooster*†	33.9	(17)
Zanesville†††	44.5	(16)
Oklahoma		
Ardmore	50.0	(15)
Chickasha	39.8	(17)
Duncan	45.4	(16)
McAlester	21.7	(18)
Muskogee	99.9	(11)
Stillwater	52.2	(15)
Oregon		
Albany-Corvallis	111.5	(9)
Bend	129.4	(8)
Coos Bay	140.1	(6)
Grants Pass	107.6	(10)
Klamath Falls	60.5	(14)
Pendleton††	125.8	(8)
Roseburg	145.9	(6)
Pennsylvania		
Chambersburg	87.1	(12)
New Castle	65.6	(14)
Pottsville†	61.3	(14)
Rhode Island		
Newport	135.7	(7)
South Carolina		
Greenwood	89.1	(12)
Hilton Head Island	133.4	(7)
Tennessee*		
Cleveland	85.6	(12)
Columbia††	32.5	(17)
Cookeville†	32.3	(17)
Morristown†††	11.0	(19)
Tullahoma†††	14.9	(19)
Texas		
Corsicana	54.3	(15)
Del Rio	141.8	(6)
Eagle Pass	82.4	(12)
Huntsville	31.8	(17)
Lufkin	101.6	(10)
Nacogdoches	44.7	(16)
Palestine	47.2	(16)
Paris	63.1	(14)

Utah		
Logan	60.9	(14)
St. George†	131.8	(7)
Vermont**		
Rutland†	8.3	(20)
Virginia		
Blacksburg-Radford-Christiansburg	23.6	(18)
Harrisonburg	21.1	(18)
Martinsville	52.7	(15)
Staunton-Waynesboro	71.1	(13)
Winchester	69.3	(14)
Washington		
Aberdeen	90.1	(11)
Longview**	81.2	(12)
Mount Vernon	108.1	(10)
Port Angeles	89.6	(12)
Walla Walla	83.4	(12)
Wenatchee	191.0	(1)
West Virginia		
Beckley	44.6	(16)
Clarksburg	27.1	(18)
Fairmont	7.6	(20)
Morgantown	39.0	(17)
Wisconsin		
Fond du Lac	166.4	(4)
Manitowoc	232.8	(0)
Stevens Point	135.7	(7)
Watertown	173.8	(3)
Wyoming		
Rock Springs	68.0	(14)

Notes:
- † 76 to 95 percent of police departments reporting.
- †† 51 to 75 percent of police departments reporting.
- ††† 31 to 50 percent of police departments reporting.
- n/a data not available, or fewer than 30 percent of police departments reporting.
- * 1993 data.
- ** 1992 data.

Local Police Funding

Keeping the law and order can be an expensive task. Spending on law enforcement, correctional facilities, and criminal courts rose 63 percent in constant dollars for county and city governments between 1982 and 1992, according to the Bureau of Justice Statistics.

This category evaluates the financial commitment of each area to its police. The amount of money allocated to law enforcement by both county and city governments is divided by the number of residents. Included are all expenditures for police patrols, equipment, custody of those awaiting trial, and traffic-safety operations. The national average is $123 for every man, woman, and child.

Some cities, of course, may spend relatively little money on law enforcement because they have relatively little enforcing to do. Others may spend impressive amounts of money, and still have high crime rates to show for it. Because it would be unreasonable to "penalize" the former with a low score while "rewarding" the latter with a high score, the scoring in this category takes total crime rate into account.

Scores are adjusted for any city whose unadjusted funding score differs by eight points or more from its total crime score. (The difference in scores is divided in half and added to the funding score). For example, Mount Pleasant, Michigan, spends just $39 per resident on police protection, earning it an unadjusted score of 2. But Mount Pleasant has a relatively low total crime rate, with a score of 15. Using the above formula, Mount Pleasant's police funding score is adjusted to 9.

Key West, Florida, spends the most per capita on law enforcement. The amount comes to $256 per resident. This figure is somewhat skewed because Key West provides police protection for the many tourists who are not counted in the per capita figure, but above-average spending in Key West parallels an above-average crime rate. Key West's score in this section is adjusted downward as a result.

Manhattan, Kansas, spends the least of any micropolitan on law enforcement; just $24 per resident. Manhattan's crime rate is slightly below the median for all micros.

Western cities are more likely to spend the most on police protection. Eastern and southern cities are more likely to spend the least.

Source: Census of Governments: Compendium of Government Finances, U.S. Bureau of the Census, Washington, D.C. Data, published in 1997, are for fiscal year 1991–92.

Scoring: Twenty points for spending of $125 or more per capita; no points for less than $30. The spacing is every $5 per capita.

Local Police Funding: Highs and Lows

	Annual Per Capita Police-Related Spending by Local Governments
Highest	$
1. Key West, Fla.	256
2. Vero Beach, Fla.	187
3. Elko, Nev.	172
4. New Iberia, La.	167
5. Rock Springs, Wyo.	165
6. Pocatello, Idaho	158
7. El Centro-Calexico-Brawley, Calif.	153
8. Brunswick, Ga.	139
9. Carlsbad, N.Mex.	136
10. Aberdeen, Wash.	134
Manitowoc, Wisc.	134
Roswell, N.Mex.	134
Median	
96. Salina, Kans.	73
97. Talladega, Ala.	73
Lowest	
183. Searcy, Ark.	37
Vincennes, Ind.	37
185. Warrensburg, Mo.	36
186. Palestine, Tex.	33
187. Lufkin, Tex.	32
Pottsville, Pa.	32
189. Plattsburgh, N.Y.	31
190. New Castle, Ind.	30
191. New Castle, Pa.	29
192. Chambersburg, Pa.	25
193. Manhattan, Kans.	24

Local Police Funding Area by Area

(Annual per capita police-related spending by local governments in dollars and rating points*)

Micro median	73	
Alabama		
Albertville	76	(10)
Auburn-Opelika	87	(12)
Cullman	66	(13)
Selma	59	(6)
Talladega	73	(9)
Alaska		
Fairbanks	57	(6)
Arizona		
Prescott	99	(14)
Sierra Vista	105	(16)
Arkansas		
Blytheville	63	(7)
El Dorado	55	(6)
Hot Springs	72	(9)
Jonesboro	43	(7)
Russellville	38	(8)
Searcy	37	(9)
California		
Arcata-Eureka	109	(12)
El Centro-Calexico-Brawley	153	(15)
Hanford-Lemoore	108	(16)
Hollister	105	(16)
Connecticut		
Torrington	105	(16)
Florida		
Key West	256	(12)
Vero Beach	187	(15)
Georgia		
Brunswick	139	(14)
Dalton	73	(9)
Dublin	67	(8)
Gainesville	95	(14)
Hinesville	50	(5)
La Grange	102	(15)
Milledgeville	68	(12)
Rome	72	(9)
Statesboro	65	(8)
Thomasville	77	(10)
Valdosta	86	(12)
Waycross	69	(8)
Idaho		
Coeur d'Alene	96	(14)
Idaho Falls	122	(19)
Pocatello	158	(20)
Twin Falls	72	(9)
Illinois		
Carbondale	100	(15)
Danville	85	(12)
Freeport	87	(12)
Galesburg	66	(8)
Mattoon-Charleston	74	(13)
Ottawa	67	(12)
Quincy	64	(7)
Sterling	82	(11)
Indiana		
Columbus	68	(8)
Marion	60	(7)
Michigan City-La Porte	80	(11)
New Castle	30	(9)
Richmond	71	(9)
Vincennes	37	(10)
Iowa		
Ames	66	(8)
Burlington	83	(11)

Clinton	84	(16)
Mason City	88	(12)
Muscatine	75	(10)
Kansas		
Hutchinson	119	(18)
Manhattan	24	(7)
Salina	73	(9)
Kentucky		
Bowling Green	57	(6)
Frankfort	48	(8)
Madisonville	64	(7)
Paducah	54	(5)
Radcliff-Elizabethtown	60	(12)
Louisiana		
Hammond	98	(7)
New Iberia	167	(20)
Ruston	97	(14)
Maine		
Augusta-Waterville	56	(11)
Biddeford-Saco	82	(11)
Maryland		
Salisbury	77	(10)
Michigan		
Marquette	54	(10)
Mount Pleasant	39	(9)
Owosso	75	(10)
Traverse City	77	(10)
Minnesota		
Faribault	79	(10)
Mankato	114	(17)
Red Wing	118	(18)
Willmar	83	(11)
Winona	115	(18)
Mississippi		
Cleveland	81	(16)
Columbus	55	(11)
Greenville	100	(9)
Laurel	64	(7)
Meridian	66	(8)
Tupelo	73	(9)
Vicksburg	71	(9)
Missouri		
Cape Girardeau-Sikeston	67	(8)
Jefferson City	56	(11)
Poplar Bluff	54	(5)
Warrensburg	36	(7)
Montana		
Bozeman	59	(12)
Helena	69	(8)
Missoula	88	(12)
Nebraska		
Grand Island	58	(6)
Nevada		
Carson City	129	(16)
Elko	172	(20)
New Hampshire		
Concord	82	(11)
Keene	65	(13)
New Mexico		
Alamogordo	82	(11)
Carlsbad	136	(20)
Clovis	86	(12)
Farmington	96	(14)
Gallup	81	(11)
Hobbs	124	(15)
Roswell	134	(14)
New York		
Cortland	65	(8)
Gloversville	60	(7)
Ithaca	70	(9)

Kingston	77	(10)
Olean	79	(10)
Plattsburgh	31	(9)
Watertown	100	(15)

North Carolina

Albemarle	59	(6)
Eden	82	(11)
Havelock-New Bern	80	(11)
Henderson	68	(8)
Kinston	85	(12)
Lumberton	66	(8)
Roanoke Rapids	72	(9)
Sanford	99	(14)
Shelby	71	(9)
Statesville	70	(14)
Wilson	102	(10)

North Dakota

Minot	73	(9)

Ohio

Ashland	71	(14)
Athens	64	(7)
Chillicothe	61	(7)
Findlay-Fostoria-Tiffin	81	(11)
Fremont	82	(11)
Marion	72	(9)
Mount Vernon	70	(9)
New Philadelphia	57	(13)
Norwalk	85	(12)
Portsmouth	44	(8)
Sandusky	99	(14)
Sidney	63	(7)
Wooster	75	(10)
Zanesville	68	(8)

Oklahoma

Ardmore	63	(7)
Chickasha	47	(9)
Duncan	71	(9)
McAlester	54	(10)
Muskogee	59	(6)
Stillwater	70	(9)

Oregon

Albany-Corvallis	86	(12)
Bend	85	(12)
Coos Bay	83	(11)
Grants Pass	70	(9)
Klamath Falls	61	(7)
Pendleton	67	(8)
Roseburg	77	(10)

Pennsylvania

Chambersburg	25	(8)
New Castle	29	(9)
Pottsville	32	(8)

Rhode Island

Newport	128	(20)

South Carolina

Greenwood	64	(7)
Hilton Head Island	87	(12)

Tennessee

Cleveland	57	(11)
Columbia	92	(13)
Cookeville	79	(10)
Morristown	66	(8)
Tullahoma	76	(5)

Texas

Corsicana	81	(11)
Del Rio	85	(12)
Eagle Pass	49	(4)
Huntsville	65	(8)
Lufkin	32	(8)
Nacogdoches	66	(8)
Palestine	33	(8)
Paris	97	(10)

Utah		
Logan	50	(11)
St. George	69	(8)
Vermont		
Rutland	41	(8)
Virginia		
Blacksburg-Radford-Christiansburg	99	(14)
Harrisonburg	44	(10)
Martinsville	60	(7)
Staunton-Waynesboro	65	(12)
Winchester	70	(9)
Washington		
Aberdeen	134	(15)
Longview	128	(16)
Mount Vernon	94	(13)
Port Angeles	97	(14)
Walla Walla	128	(14)
Wenatchee	99	(14)
West Virginia		
Beckley	46	(9)
Clarksburg	59	(12)
Fairmont	41	(10)
Morgantown	48	(9)
Wisconsin		
Fond du Lac	92	(13)
Manitowoc	134	(20)
Stevens Point	101	(15)
Watertown	117	(18)
Wyoming		
Rock Springs	165	(16)

*See text for notes on adjustment of some scores.

Local Fire Funding

In the 1936 movie *Mr. Deeds Goes to Town,* Gary Cooper plays a likeable small-town resident who moves to Manhattan somewhat against his will to inherit a fortune. In one scene, hearing sirens, he jumps up from an opera fundraising meeting and hops onto a passing firetruck. He is volunteer firefighter back home.

Most small cities have full-time firefighters these days. But the image of volunteer firefighters, including neighbors in a "bucket brigade," is an enduring image of small-city spirit.

A less romantic measure, but as important, is a city's financial commitment to fire protection. This category measures that commitment by dividing the money spent annually by county and city governments on fire protection by the number of residents. The national average is $59.

Three cities tie for first place. Marion, Ohio; Newport, Rhode Island; and Roswell, New Mexico, each allocate $102 per resident for fire protection.

Lufkin, Texas, spends the least. Local government budgets contribute just $3 per resident for fire protection.

Western and Midwestern cities spend the most on their fire departments. Southern cities spend the least.

Source: Census of Governments: Compendium of Government Finances, U.S. Bureau of the Census, Washington, D.C. Data, published in 1997, are for fiscal year 1991–92.

Scoring: Twenty points for spending of $100 or more per capita; no points for less than $5. The spacing is every $5 per capita.

Local Fire Funding: Highs and Lows

	Annual Per Capita Spending on Fire Protection by Local Governments
Highest	**$**
1. Marion, Ohio	102
Newport, R.I.	102
Roswell, N.Mex.	102
4. Bend, Ore.	97
5. Winona, Minn.	94
6. Sandusky, Ohio	87
7. Idaho Falls, Idaho	83
8. Prescott, Ariz.	80
9. Manitowoc, Wisc.	79
10. Red Wing, Minn.	78
Walla Walla, Wash.	78
Median	
96. Milledgeville, Ga.	40
97. Ashland, Ohio	40
Lowest	
183. Beckley, W.Va.	18
St. George, Utah	18
185. Russellville, Ark.	16
186. Huntsville, Tex.	15
187. Helena, Mont.	14
188. Chambersburg, Pa.	12
189. Cleveland, Miss.	11
Searcy, Ark.	11
191. Hinesville, Ga.	9
Pottsville, Pa.	9
193. Lufkin, Tex.	3

Local Fire Funding Area by Area

(Annual per capita spending by local governments on fire protection in dollars and rating points)

Micro median	40	
Alabama		
Albertville	38	(7)
Auburn-Opelika	51	(10)
Cullman	19	(3)
Selma	35	(7)
Talladega	22	(4)
Alaska		
Fairbanks	76	(15)
Arizona		
Prescott	80	(16)
Sierra Vista	36	(7)
Arkansas		
Blytheville	29	(5)
El Dorado	28	(5)
Hot Springs	38	(7)
Jonesboro	38	(7)
Russellville	16	(3)
Searcy	11	(2)
California		
Arcata-Eureka	51	(10)
El Centro-Calexico-Brawley	69	(13)
Hanford-Lemoore	48	(9)
Hollister	43	(8)
Connecticut		
Torrington	46	(9)
Florida		
Key West	59	(11)
Vero Beach	71	(14)
Georgia		
Brunswick	63	(12)
Dalton	45	(9)
Dublin	36	(7)
Gainesville	56	(11)
Hinesville	9	(1)
La Grange	69	(13)
Milledgeville	40	(8)
Rome	67	(13)
Statesboro	22	(4)
Thomasville	47	(9)
Valdosta	42	(8)
Waycross	31	(6)
Idaho		
Coeur d'Alene	40	(8)
Idaho Falls	83	(16)
Pocatello	55	(11)
Twin Falls	42	(8)
Illinois		
Carbondale	27	(5)
Danville	62	(12)
Freeport	53	(10)
Galesburg	48	(9)
Mattoon-Charleston	52	(10)
Ottawa	28	(5)
Quincy	51	(10)
Sterling	34	(6)
Indiana		
Columbus	65	(13)
Marion	44	(8)
Michigan City-La Porte	48	(9)
New Castle	21	(4)
Richmond	54	(10)
Vincennes	36	(7)
Iowa		
Ames	34	(6)
Burlington	47	(9)

Clinton	52	(10)
Mason City	31	(6)
Muscatine	38	(7)
Kansas		
Hutchinson	58	(11)
Manhattan	22	(4)
Salina	58	(11)
Kentucky		
Bowling Green	45	(9)
Frankfort	19	(3)
Madisonville	76	(15)
Paducah	63	(12)
Radcliff-Elizabethtown	49	(9)
Louisiana		
Hammond	36	(7)
New Iberia	42	(8)
Ruston	47	(9)
Maine		
Augusta-Waterville	41	(8)
Biddeford-Saco	55	(11)
Maryland		
Salisbury	45	(9)
Michigan		
Marquette	26	(5)
Mount Pleasant	20	(4)
Owosso	24	(4)
Traverse City	36	(7)
Minnesota		
Faribault	23	(4)
Mankato	37	(7)
Red Wing	78	(15)
Willmar	29	(5)
Winona	94	(18)
Mississippi		
Cleveland	11	(2)
Columbus	43	(8)
Greenville	58	(11)
Laurel	39	(7)
Meridian	42	(8)
Tupelo	60	(12)
Vicksburg	62	(12)
Missouri		
Cape Girardeau-Sikeston	30	(6)
Jefferson City	34	(6)
Poplar Bluff	38	(7)
Warrensburg	21	(4)
Montana		
Bozeman	34	(6)
Helena	14	(2)
Missoula	36	(7)
Nebraska		
Grand Island	31	(6)
Nevada		
Carson City	63	(12)
Elko	54	(10)
New Hampshire		
Concord	56	(11)
Keene	34	(6)
New Mexico		
Alamogordo	27	(5)
Carlsbad	66	(13)
Clovis	37	(7)
Farmington	59	(11)
Gallup	42	(8)
Hobbs	66	(13)
Roswell	102	(20)
New York		
Cortland	60	(12)
Gloversville	49	(9)
Ithaca	77	(15)

Kingston	72	(14)
Olean	51	(10)
Plattsburgh	50	(10)
Watertown	70	(14)

North Carolina

Albemarle	37	(7)
Eden	30	(6)
Havelock-New Bern	28	(5)
Henderson	50	(10)
Kinston	39	(7)
Lumberton	29	(5)
Roanoke Rapids	28	(5)
Sanford	57	(11)
Shelby	33	(6)
Statesville	40	(8)
Wilson	61	(12)

North Dakota

Minot	43	(8)

Ohio

Ashland	40	(8)
Athens	31	(6)
Chillicothe	39	(7)
Findlay-Fostoria-Tiffin	45	(9)
Fremont	30	(6)
Marion	102	(20)
Mount Vernon	34	(6)
New Philadelphia	33	(6)
Norwalk	30	(6)
Portsmouth	35	(7)
Sandusky	87	(17)
Sidney	33	(6)
Wooster	32	(6)
Zanesville	39	(7)

Oklahoma

Ardmore	28	(5)
Chickasha	30	(6)
Duncan	36	(7)
McAlester	32	(6)
Muskogee	62	(12)
Stillwater	50	(10)

Oregon

Albany-Corvallis	71	(14)
Bend	97	(19)
Coos Bay	48	(9)
Grants Pass	26	(5)
Klamath Falls	72	(14)
Pendleton	53	(10)
Roseburg	68	(13)

Pennsylvania

Chambersburg	12	(2)
New Castle	19	(3)
Pottsville	9	(1)

Rhode Island

Newport	102	(20)

South Carolina

Greenwood	25	(5)
Hilton Head Island	66	(13)

Tennessee

Cleveland	30	(6)
Columbia	57	(11)
Cookeville	35	(7)
Morristown	40	(8)
Tullahoma	45	(9)

Texas

Corsicana	40	(8)
Del Rio	38	(7)
Eagle Pass	30	(6)
Huntsville	15	(3)
Lufkin	3	(0)
Nacogdoches	40	(8)
Palestine	31	(6)
Paris	56	(11)

Utah		
Logan	34	(6)
St. George	18	(3)
Vermont		
Rutland	39	(7)
Virginia		
Blacksburg-Radford-Christiansburg	21	(4)
Harrisonburg	27	(5)
Martinsville	23	(4)
Staunton-Waynesboro	35	(7)
Winchester	23	(4)
Washington		
Aberdeen	64	(12)
Longview	48	(9)
Mount Vernon	46	(9)
Port Angeles	49	(9)
Walla Walla	78	(15)
Wenatchee	53	(10)
West Virginia		
Beckley	18	(3)
Clarksburg	31	(6)
Fairmont	31	(6)
Morgantown	23	(4)
Wisconsin		
Fond du Lac	52	(10)
Manitowoc	79	(15)
Stevens Point	52	(10)
Watertown	42	(8)
Wyoming		
Rock Springs	72	(14)

The Results

It's safest in the Midwest. And in the very middle of the Midwest, Clinton, Iowa, is the safest small city of all. Clinton boasts the second lowest total crime rate among small cities and just 11 percent of the national average, according to the FBI. Few crimes in Clinton are violent. The reported violent offenses in 1994 totaled just one robbery and seven aggravated assaults. One murder was reported in the Clinton area in the five years between 1990 and 1994. The resulting violent crime rate in Clinton is just 15 per 100,000 residents, the lowest of any small city and only 2 percent of the rate for all U.S. cities, large and small.

Clinton also has little trouble with juvenile crime. Seventeen teens in 1,000 were arrested in Clinton in 1994, compared with the median small-city rate of sixty-six. It should be noted, however, that police records on juvenile arrests in 1994 covered just 57 percent of the population in the Clinton area. Estimates were made for the missing data.

Keeping the peace does not require large amounts of money in Clinton. Government spending on law enforcement equals $84 per resident, which, although above the micropolitan median, does not rate Clinton among top-spending small towns. The same applies to local spending on fire protection. Clinton spends above the median, but below many other small cities.

One thousand miles due south, Hammond, Louisiana, has a serious crime problem. Approximately 17,700 major crimes were reported in Hammond per 100,000 residents in 1994, more than four times the median for small cities. Hammond's violent crime rate was 1,903 that year, higher than New Orleans (1,335), New York City (1,393), and Los Angeles (1,423).

Unlike Clinton, Iowa, a significant share of crimes in Hammond are violent. Eleven murders occurred in Hammond in 1994, a rate of more than 12 murders per 100,000 population. Nearly 1 in 3 major crimes involved an aggravated assault, and the equivalent of 1 in 20 residents was the victim of a larceny.

Hammond's crime statistics are complicated by inconsistencies in the number of agencies that submit data to the FBI from one year to the next. Data used in these ratings cover 95 percent of the local population, but considerably lower coverage in the recent past makes it difficult to compare Hammond's extraordinarily high 1994 rates to previous years.

Six other southern micros join Hammond on the bottom-ten list. Not all small cities in the south score poorly; several have some of the highest scores. The majority of top-scoring micros, however, are in the Midwest and Northeast.

Public Safety Scores: Highs and Lows

		Total Rating Points
Highest		
1.	Clinton, Iowa	85
2.	Ashland, Ohio	79
	Carlsbad, N.Mex.	79
	Watertown, N.Y.	79
5.	Torrington, Conn.	78
6.	Marion, Ohio	77
	Mattoon-Charleston, Ill.	77
8.	Newport, R.I.	76
	Winona, Minn.	76
10.	Concord, N.H.	75
	Red Wing, Minn.	75
12.	New Philadelphia, Ohio	74
13.	Findlay-Fostoria-Tiffin, Ohio	73
	Statesville, N.C.	73
15.	Clarksburg, W.Va.	72
	Elko, Nev.	72
	Bozeman, Mont.	72
18.	Fairmont, W.Va.	71
	Rock Springs, Wyo.	71
	Wooster, Ohio	71
Median		
96.	Alamogordo, N.Mex.	60
97.	Albany-Corvallis, Ore.	60
Lowest		
184.	Salisbury, Md.	42
185.	Grand Island, Nebr.	41
	Salina, Kans.	41
187.	Eagle Pass, Tex.	40
	Paducah, Ky.	40
	Paris, Tex.	40
190.	Greenwood, S.C.	34
191.	Blytheville, Ark.	32
	Selma, Ala.	32
193.	Hammond, La.	28

Public Safety Performance Comparison

	Clinton, Iowa	Micro median	Hammond, Louisiana
Total Points in Section	85	60	28
Rank in Section	1		193
Total Crime Rate			
Reported crimes per 100,000 residents	595	4,056	17,698
Total Crime points	(20)		(0)
Violent Crime Rate			
Reported violent crimes per 100,000 residents	15	316	1,903
Violent Crime points	(20)		(0)
Juvenile Crime Rate			
Arrest per 1,000 juveniles	17.4	65.5	60.9
Juvenile Crime Rate points	(19)		(14)
Local Police Funding*			
Annual per capita spending by local governments	$84	$73	$98
Police Funding points	(16)		(7)
Local Fire Funding			
Annual per capita spending by local governments	$52	$40	$36
Fire Funding points	(10)		(7)

*Note: See text for notes on adjustment of some scores in this category.

Public Safety Scores Area by Area

(Total public safety rating points)

Micro median	60
Alabama	
Albertville	68
Auburn-Opelika	60
Cullman	69
Selma	32
Talladega	62
Alaska	
Fairbanks	55
Arizona	
Prescott	60
Sierra Vista	64
Arkansas	
Blytheville	32
El Dorado	52
Hot Springs	57
Jonesboro	55
Russellville	59
Searcy	64
California	
Arcata-Eureka	54
El Centro-Calexico-Brawley	61
Hanford-Lemoore	54
Hollister	61
Connecticut	
Torrington	78
Florida	
Key West	48
Vero Beach	63
Georgia	
Brunswick	54
Dalton	64
Dublin	51
Gainesville	69
Hinesville	48
La Grange	69
Milledgeville	67
Rome	60
Statesboro	58
Thomasville	57
Valdosta	58
Waycross	55
Idaho	
Coeur d'Alene	58
Idaho Falls	67
Pocatello	60
Twin Falls	56
Illinois	
Carbondale	58
Danville	64
Freeport	66
Galesburg	61
Mattoon-Charleston	77
Ottawa	68
Quincy	61
Sterling	65
Indiana	
Columbus	65
Marion	45
Michigan City-La Porte	44
New Castle	65
Richmond	61
Vincennes	70
Iowa	
Ames	65
Burlington	69
Clinton	85
Mason City	46
Muscatine	56
Kansas	
Hutchinson	61
Manhattan	56
Salina	41
Kentucky	
Bowling Green	50
Frankfort	51
Madisonville	60
Paducah	40
Radcliff-Elizabethtown	67
Louisiana	
Hammond	28
New Iberia	68
Ruston	61
Maine	
Augusta-Waterville	68
Biddeford-Saco	68
Maryland	
Salisbury	42
Michigan	
Marquette	60
Mount Pleasant	63
Owosso	65
Traverse City	65
Minnesota	
Faribault	59
Mankato	69
Red Wing	75
Willmar	53
Winona	76

Mississippi

Cleveland	69
Columbus	69
Greenville	45
Laurel	52
Meridian	58
Tupelo	63
Vicksburg	56

Missouri

Cape Girardeau-Sikeston	58
Jefferson City	70
Poplar Bluff	53
Warrensburg	58

Montana

Bozeman	72
Helena	52
Missoula	56

Nebraska

Grand Island	41

Nevada

Carson City	55
Elko	72

New Hampshire

Concord	75
Keene	70

New Mexico

Alamogordo	60
Carlsbad	79
Clovis	47
Farmington	61
Gallup	54
Hobbs	55
Roswell	62

New York

Cortland	65
Gloversville	54
Ithaca	69
Kingston	67
Olean	65
Plattsburgh	67
Watertown	79

North Carolina

Albemarle	56
Eden	55
Havelock-New Bern	52
Henderson	49
Kinston	49
Lumberton	49
Roanoke Rapids	53
Sanford	53
Shelby	55
Statesville	73
Wilson	50

North Dakota

Minot	61

Ohio

Ashland	79
Athens	66
Chillicothe	57
Findlay-Fostoria-Tiffin	73
Fremont	67
Marion	77
Mount Vernon	65
New Philadelphia	74
Norwalk	68
Portsmouth	60
Sandusky	67
Sidney	69
Wooster	71
Zanesville	60

Oklahoma

Ardmore	47
Chickasha	59
Duncan	62
McAlester	65
Muskogee	49
Stillwater	63

Oregon

Albany-Corvallis	60
Bend	66
Coos Bay	55
Grants Pass	52
Klamath Falls	64
Pendleton	59
Roseburg	57

Pennsylvania

Chambersburg	53
New Castle	60
Pottsville	55

Rhode Island

Newport	76

South Carolina

Greenwood	34
Hilton Head Island	44

Tennessee

Cleveland	59
Columbia	66
Cookeville	68
Morristown	68
Tullahoma	51

Texas

Corsicana	57
Del Rio	52
Eagle Pass	40
Huntsville	57
Lufkin	46

Nacogdoches	56
Palestine	56
Paris	40
Utah	
Logan	66
St. George	48
Vermont	
Rutland	65
Virginia	
Blacksburg-Radford-Christiansburg	70
Harrisonburg	69
Martinsville	54
Staunton-Waynesboro	66
Winchester	58
Washington	
Aberdeen	64
Longview	64
Mount Vernon	61
Port Angeles	66
Walla Walla	57
Wenatchee	48
West Virginia	
Beckley	53
Clarksburg	72
Fairmont	71
Morgantown	62
Wisconsin	
Fond du Lac	59
Manitowoc	70
Stevens Point	66
Watertown	64
Wyoming	
Rock Springs	71

Note: Cleveland, Mississippi; Tupelo, Mississippi; Findlay-Fostoria-Tiffin, Ohio; and Marion, Ohio, lack data in one or more crime categories. For the purpose of this total scoring category, these micros are assigned interpolated scores based on comparable cities in their state.

9

Transportation

Sitting on his porch, contemplating the dirt road running past it, Anse Bundren reasons that if God had intended people to move around He would have made them long-ways like a snake. Instead He made them up-and-down, like a tree.

The fictional character in William Faulkner's 1930 novel *As I Lay Dying* is soon forced to set out on an epic journey that takes him a shorter distance than many of us now commute each day to work. Times have changed. The average American traveled 17,200 miles in 1995. Most of that mileage was racked up going to and from work.

Travel is such an integral part of our lives that the average household spent $1,600 more traveling than eating in 1994. If you had set the steering wheel straight on an average car or light truck in 1995, it would have gone nearly halfway around the world. The 4 million miles of U.S. roads are capable of circling the globe 157 times, or reaching to the moon and back 8 times. On these roads, 136 million cars drove 1.5 trillion miles in 1995.

Transportation statistics make great factoids, but more than that, they speak volumes about major changes in the way we live and work. The population grew 28 percent in the quarter century between 1970 and 1995, but travel grew 95 percent over the same period. Changes in the labor force, the job market, and our cities greatly affect the reasons we spend so much time on the road.

One reason in the increased mileage is an increased number of commuters. The labor force grew by 59 percent between 1970 and 1995, largely due to the increase in working women. Employed persons with a driver's license drove 15,280 miles in 1990, compared with 8,048 miles for those outside the work force.

The jobs we commute to are no longer as close to where we live as they once were. Nor are they concentrated in city centers as they once were. Forty-four percent of metro-area commutes led from one suburb to another in 1990. Suburb-to-downtown commutes totaled only 20 percent that year. The sprawl of suburbs has far outpaced investment in public transportation, resulting in enormous increases in the number of cars on the road. Nearly 87 percent of commuters drove to work in 1990. Few of these cars hold more than the driver; more than 73 percent of people drive alone. Suburbs, once bedroom havens where even the car had its own room, are experiencing the same traffic congestion that plagues central cities.

All this driving takes its toll on more than our free time. The cost in time and fuel spent in traffic delays averaged $880 million nationwide in 1991, according to Texas Transportation Institute. The New York metro area racked up expenses of $6.6 billion that year; Los Angeles's tab totaled $7.8 billion. Those expenses aren't nebulous costs that disappear into the federal budget. Traffic jams cost the average driver $340 in 1991. That's a paycheck for many employees. Delays cost drivers $740 apiece in the Washington, D.C., metro area in 1991, and in San Bernadino-Riverside, California, $870.

One of the greatest attractions a small cities can offer weary metro residents is an escape from these urban traffic woes. This section rates each area according to the ease of local travel, including the availability of public transit. It also measures the degree of ease in heading out of town, whether by car or plane.

Travel time to work for small city residents averaged 17.5 minutes in 1990. Metropolitan workers required 23.2 minutes on average to make it to work. The difference amounts to an hour per week. Some micropolitan commutes are the dreams of suburban residents. Each morning Winchester, Virginia, resident Lorne Bair walks three blocks to the pedestrian mall to open his bookstore for business. His wife, Lee Ann Dransfield, walks to the nearby community arts school to teach her piano students. But all of their neighbors aren't so lucky. Some drive up to thirty and seventy-five miles each morning to jobs in the Washington, D.C., metro area. For many of them, however, the drive is preferable to living in the suburbs.

Fortunately, not all of our travel takes us to work. That's why it's important to have access to highways and airports when we want to get away on pleasure trips. Overall, small cities do not offer the same access to highways and air service as do metropolitan centers. But many small cities are located close to interstates and more than one-third offer at least commuter air service to regional hub airports.

Rating micropolitan America. The ideal small city would allow its residents a quick commute to work, and the option of public transportation. It would offer easy access to interstate highways and major airlines. Each area is tested in five categories:

1. Commuting Ease: Can you get where you are going without hassle, or is rush hour a smaller version of big-city traffic?
2. Public Transit Usage: Is there a bus system that local residents find useful?
3. Highway Availability: Is the area served by an interstate highway and other major roads, or do small roads make for a slow drive to a neighboring city?
4. Local Highway Funding: Does the local government spend what it takes to maintain and expand the area's roads and bridges?
5. Aviation Availability: Can you easily get a flight to another town, or will you be grounded?

Commuting Ease

One of the joys of small-city life is the lack of traffic congestion. It is entirely possible to drive home after an exhausting day at work without enduring a mile-long backup on the expressway.

This category measures the ease with which one can commute in each micro, based on the average time it takes residents to get from home to work. The national average is 22.4 minutes.

The commute is no sweat in Minot, North Dakota. The average travel time to work is just 12.5 minutes. Forty-one percent of commuters are at work in less than ten minutes in Minot. Another 40 percent need between ten and twenty minutes.

Commuters in Hammond, Louisiana, have the longest commute of micropolitan residents. Their average travel time to work is 25.8 minutes. Eighteen percent of commuters in Hammond require between thirty and sixty minutes to get to work. Fifteen percent must drive more than an hour. The reason isn't traffic jams; one in four Hammond residents work outside of the county.

The shortest commutes are in the Midwest, but the cities with the longest drives are scattered throughout the country.

Source: Census of the Population, U.S. Bureau of the Census, Washington, D.C. Data are for 1990.

Scoring: Twenty points for a commute of 13 minutes or less; no points for 22.5 minutes or longer. The spacing is every half minute.

Commuting Ease: Highs and Lows

	Average Travel Time to Work in Minutes
Shortest Time	
1. Minot, N.Dak.	12.5
2. Mason City, Iowa	12.7
3. Grand Island, Nebr.	13.5
Salina, Kans.	13.5
5. Walla Walla, Wash.	13.6
6. Mattoon-Charleston, Ill.	14.0
7. Clovis, N.Mex.	14.1
8. Bozeman, Mont.	14.2
Twin Falls, Idaho	14.2
10. Manhattan, Kans.	14.3
Mankato, Minn.	14.3
Median	
96. Hanford-Lemoore, Calif.	17.5
97. Norwalk, Ohio	17.5
Longest Time	
184. Gainesville, Ga.	22.1
185. Torrington, Conn.	22.2
186. Chickasha, Okla.	22.6
New Castle, Ind.	22.6
188. Idaho Falls, Idaho	22.9
189. Hollister, Calif.	23.3
190. Owosso, Mich.	24.1
191. Cullman, Ala.	25.0
192. Elko, Nev.	25.7
193. Hammond, La.	25.8

Commuting Ease Area by Area

(Average travel time to work in minutes and rating points)

Area	Minutes	Points
Micro median	17.5	
Alabama		
Albertville	22.0	(1)
Auburn-Opelika	17.6	(10)
Cullman	25.0	(0)
Selma	17.7	(10)
Talladega	20.8	(4)
Alaska		
Fairbanks	15.5	(14)
Arizona		
Prescott	18.4	(9)
Sierra Vista	15.4	(15)
Arkansas		
Blytheville	14.9	(16)
El Dorado	16.7	(12)
Hot Springs	20.1	(5)
Jonesboro	16.0	(13)
Russellville	17.9	(10)
Searcy	20.1	(5)
California		
Arcata-Eureka	16.1	(13)
El Centro-Calexico-Brawley	16.5	(12)
Hanford-Lemoore	17.5	(10)
Hollister	23.3	(0)
Connecticut		
Torrington	22.2	(1)
Florida		
Key West	14.8	(16)
Vero Beach	17.4	(11)
Georgia		
Brunswick	16.7	(12)
Dalton	17.4	(11)
Dublin	18.8	(8)
Gainesville	22.1	(1)
Hinesville	15.0	(15)
La Grange	17.9	(10)
Milledgeville	17.4	(11)
Rome	19.3	(7)
Statesboro	17.6	(10)
Thomasville	17.5	(10)
Valdosta	15.6	(14)
Waycross	17.8	(10)
Idaho		
Coeur d'Alene	19.1	(7)
Idaho Falls	22.9	(0)
Pocatello	16.6	(12)
Twin Falls	14.2	(17)
Illinois		
Carbondale	15.6	(14)
Danville	17.5	(10)
Freeport	17.3	(11)
Galesburg	16.3	(13)
Mattoon-Charleston	14.0	(17)
Ottawa	18.6	(8)
Quincy	15.3	(15)
Sterling	16.7	(12)
Indiana		
Columbus	17.3	(11)
Marion	17.1	(11)
Michigan City-La Porte	19.5	(6)
New Castle	22.6	(0)
Richmond	16.1	(13)
Vincennes	16.4	(13)
Iowa		
Ames	15.1	(15)
Burlington	15.1	(15)
Clinton	16.6	(12)

Mason City	12.7	(20)
Muscatine	15.9	(14)
Kansas		
Hutchinson	15.1	(15)
Manhattan	14.3	(17)
Salina	13.5	(18)
Kentucky		
Bowling Green	17.0	(11)
Frankfort	16.7	(12)
Madisonville	18.5	(8)
Paducah	17.0	(11)
Radcliff-Elizabethtown	17.0	(11)
Louisiana		
Hammond	25.8	(0)
New Iberia	20.5	(4)
Ruston	15.9	(14)
Maine		
Augusta-Waterville	19.3	(7)
Biddeford-Saco	21.8	(2)
Maryland		
Salisbury	17.3	(11)
Michigan		
Marquette	15.0	(15)
Mount Pleasant	15.6	(14)
Owosso	24.1	(0)
Traverse City	17.3	(11)
Minnesota		
Faribault	16.8	(12)
Mankato	14.3	(17)
Red Wing	18.3	(9)
Willmar	14.7	(16)
Winona	14.4	(17)
Mississippi		
Cleveland	15.2	(15)
Columbus	18.2	(9)
Greenville	15.4	(15)
Laurel	20.0	(5)
Meridian	18.0	(9)
Tupelo	16.9	(12)
Vicksburg	18.7	(8)
Missouri		
Cape Girardeau-Sikeston	16.5	(12)
Jefferson City	18.3	(9)
Poplar Bluff	17.8	(10)
Warrensburg	18.7	(8)
Montana		
Bozeman	14.2	(17)
Helena	14.4	(17)
Missoula	15.3	(15)
Nebraska		
Grand Island	13.5	(18)
Nevada		
Carson City	16.0	(13)
Elko	25.7	(0)
New Hampshire		
Concord	21.5	(2)
Keene	18.1	(9)
New Mexico		
Alamogordo	18.1	(9)
Carlsbad	19.1	(7)
Clovis	14.1	(17)
Farmington	20.6	(4)
Gallup	19.1	(7)
Hobbs	15.8	(14)
Roswell	14.5	(16)
New York		
Cortland	17.7	(10)
Gloversville	19.2	(7)
Ithaca	16.4	(13)

Kingston	21.6	(2)
Olean	17.9	(10)
Plattsburgh	16.3	(13)
Watertown	16.3	(13)

North Carolina

Albemarle	20.8	(4)
Eden	20.6	(4)
Havelock-New Bern	17.7	(10)
Henderson	16.9	(12)
Kinston	18.5	(8)
Lumberton	19.8	(6)
Roanoke Rapids	19.3	(7)
Sanford	19.7	(6)
Shelby	19.0	(7)
Statesville	19.8	(6)
Wilson	17.0	(11)

North Dakota

Minot	12.5	(20)

Ohio

Ashland	17.9	(10)
Athens	18.3	(9)
Chillicothe	22.0	(1)
Findlay-Fostoria-Tiffin	16.8	(12)
Fremont	17.6	(10)
Marion	19.3	(7)
Mount Vernon	21.2	(3)
New Philadelphia	17.6	(10)
Norwalk	17.5	(10)
Portsmouth	21.3	(3)
Sandusky	17.2	(11)
Sidney	16.1	(13)
Wooster	17.3	(11)
Zanesville	19.9	(6)

Oklahoma

Ardmore	16.0	(13)
Chickasha	22.6	(0)
Duncan	16.9	(12)
McAlester	18.6	(8)
Muskogee	19.7	(6)
Stillwater	14.7	(16)

Oregon

Albany-Corvallis	18.5	(8)
Bend	16.3	(13)
Coos Bay	17.3	(11)
Grants Pass	18.4	(9)
Klamath Falls	15.6	(14)
Pendleton	15.4	(15)
Roseburg	18.7	(8)

Pennsylvania

Chambersburg	18.6	(8)
New Castle	18.4	(9)
Pottsville	20.4	(5)

Rhode Island

Newport	17.6	(10)

South Carolina

Greenwood	17.4	(11)
Hilton Head Island	17.9	(10)

Tennessee

Cleveland	18.6	(8)
Columbia	21.0	(3)
Cookeville	16.8	(12)
Morristown	18.0	(9)
Tullahoma	20.0	(5)

Texas

Corsicana	21.5	(2)
Del Rio	14.7	(16)
Eagle Pass	14.5	(16)
Huntsville	19.3	(7)
Lufkin	16.8	(12)
Nacogdoches	17.1	(11)
Palestine	18.8	(8)
Paris	16.7	(12)

Utah		
Logan	16.4	(13)
St. George	15.5	(14)
Vermont		
Rutland	17.2	(11)
Virginia		
Blacksburg-Radford-Christiansburg	17.0	(11)
Harrisonburg	17.7	(10)
Martinsville	17.9	(10)
Staunton-Waynesboro	19.1	(7)
Winchester	21.8	(2)
Washington		
Aberdeen	19.3	(7)
Longview	17.9	(10)
Mount Vernon	19.7	(6)
Port Angeles	16.2	(13)
Walla Walla	13.6	(18)
Wenatchee	15.0	(15)
West Virginia		
Beckley	20.9	(4)
Clarksburg	18.6	(8)
Fairmont	20.4	(5)
Morgantown	17.1	(11)
Wisconsin		
Fond du Lac	16.7	(12)
Manitowoc	16.2	(13)
Stevens Point	15.4	(15)
Watertown	17.8	(10)
Wyoming		
Rock Springs	21.4	(3)

Public Transit Usage

Mass transit is essential to the nation's metropolitan centers, but it is not as crucial to smaller cities. Bus service is nonetheless important for residents who do not have or do not want to use their car, or for those who cannot drive for one reason or another.

This category ranks each area according to the number of people who rely on public transit to get them to and from their jobs, expressed as a rate per 1,000 commuters. Commuters, many with rigid work schedules and a keen eye for the easiest route, can be considered the ultimate test of a city's bus system.

Nearly 6,700 people take the bus to work each weekday in Idaho Falls, Idaho. That equals 1 in 7 employed residents, or a rate of 144 out of every 1,000 people traveling to work. That is a much higher rate than the national average of 53 commuters per 1,000, and it even surpasses the metropolitan rate of 65 commuters per 1,000.

Fewer than 1 commuter in 1,000 takes the bus to work in ten of the nation's small cities. Commuters in Chickasha, Oklahoma, must propel themselves to work, having no bus service at all.

Source: Census of the Population, U.S. Bureau of the Census, Washington, D.C. Data are for 1990.

Scoring: Twenty points for a rate of 21 commuters per 1,000; no points for fewer than 2. The spacing is every 1 commuter per 1,000.

Public Transit Usage: Highs and Lows

	Number of Commuters Who Use Public Transit per 1,000 Commuters
Highest	
1. Idaho Falls, Idaho	144
2. Elko, Nev.	126
3. Rock Springs, Wyo.	78
4. Ames, Iowa	50
5. Carlsbad, N.Mex.	42
6. Ithaca, N.Y.	30
7. Pocatello, Idaho	23
8. Aberdeen, Wash.	20
Vicksburg, Miss.	20
10. Hilton Head Island, S.C.	19
Median	
96. Columbus, Miss.	5
97. Laurel, Miss.	5
Lowest	
183. Albemarle, N.C.	1
Cleveland, Tenn.	1
Farmington, N.Mex.	1
Grants Pass, Ore.	1
Hutchinson, Kans.	1
Madisonville, Ky.	1
Owosso, Mich.	1
Prescott, Ariz.	1
Vero Beach, Fla.	1
Wenatchee, Wash.	1
193. Chickasha, Okla.	0

Public Transit Usage Area by Area

(Number of commuters who use public transit per 1,000 commuters and rating points)

Area	Commuters	Points
Micro median	5	
Alabama		
Albertville	2	(1)
Auburn-Opelika	3	(2)
Cullman	2	(1)
Selma	15	(14)
Talladega	8	(7)
Alaska		
Fairbanks	13	(12)
Arizona		
Prescott	1	(0)
Sierra Vista	17	(16)
Arkansas		
Blytheville	4	(3)
El Dorado	2	(1)
Hot Springs	8	(7)
Jonesboro	3	(2)
Russellville	3	(2)
Searcy	3	(2)
California		
Arcata-Eureka	8	(7)
El Centro-Calexico-Brawley	8	(7)
Hanford-Lemoore	15	(14)
Hollister	4	(3)
Connecticut		
Torrington	10	(9)
Florida		
Key West	11	(10)
Vero Beach	1	(0)
Georgia		
Brunswick	5	(4)
Dalton	3	(2)
Dublin	14	(13)
Gainesville	3	(2)
Hinesville	8	(7)
La Grange	18	(17)
Milledgeville	18	(17)
Rome	11	(10)
Statesboro	3	(2)
Thomasville	3	(2)
Valdosta	3	(2)
Waycross	6	(5)
Idaho		
Coeur d'Alene	3	(2)
Idaho Falls	144	(20)
Pocatello	23	(20)
Twin Falls	5	(4)
Illinois		
Carbondale	6	(5)
Danville	7	(6)
Freeport	11	(10)
Galesburg	9	(8)
Mattoon-Charleston	3	(2)
Ottawa	6	(5)
Quincy	8	(7)
Sterling	7	(6)
Indiana		
Columbus	5	(4)
Marion	4	(3)
Michigan City-La Porte	11	(10)
New Castle	3	(2)
Richmond	9	(8)
Vincennes	4	(3)
Iowa		
Ames	50	(20)
Burlington	6	(5)

Clinton 9 (8)
Mason City 8 (7)
Muscatine 9 (8)

Kansas
Hutchinson 1 (0)
Manhattan 7 (6)
Salina 4 (3)

Kentucky
Bowling Green 5 (4)
Frankfort 6 (5)
Madisonville 1 (0)
Paducah 7 (6)
Radcliff-Elizabethtown 5 (4)

Louisiana
Hammond 2 (1)
New Iberia 6 (5)
Ruston 4 (3)

Maine
Augusta-Waterville 7 (6)
Biddeford-Saco 8 (7)

Maryland
Salisbury 15 (14)

Michigan
Marquette 9 (8)
Mount Pleasant 7 (6)
Owosso 1 (0)
Traverse City 6 (5)

Minnesota
Faribault 7 (6)
Mankato 13 (12)
Red Wing 5 (4)
Willmar 8 (7)
Winona 10 (9)

Mississippi
Cleveland 6 (5)
Columbus 5 (4)
Greenville 9 (8)
Laurel 5 (4)
Meridian 10 (9)
Tupelo 4 (3)
Vicksburg 20 (19)

Missouri
Cape Girardeau-Sikeston 4 (3)
Jefferson City 9 (8)
Poplar Bluff 10 (9)
Warrensburg 2 (1)

Montana
Bozeman 4 (3)
Helena 3 (2)
Missoula 11 (10)

Nebraska
Grand Island 2 (1)

Nevada
Carson City 4 (3)
Elko 126 (20)

New Hampshire
Concord 6 (5)
Keene 3 (2)

New Mexico
Alamogordo 5 (4)
Carlsbad 42 (20)
Clovis 4 (3)
Farmington 1 (0)
Gallup 7 (6)
Hobbs 2 (1)
Roswell 2 (1)

New York
Cortland 9 (8)
Gloversville 18 (17)
Ithaca 30 (20)

Kingston	17	(16)
Olean	10	(9)
Plattsburgh	8	(7)
Watertown	13	(12)
North Carolina		
Albemarle	1	(0)
Eden	4	(3)
Havelock-New Bern	6	(5)
Henderson	2	(1)
Kinston	7	(6)
Lumberton	3	(2)
Roanoke Rapids	8	(7)
Sanford	3	(2)
Shelby	3	(2)
Statesville	3	(2)
Wilson	8	(7)
North Dakota		
Minot	5	(4)
Ohio		
Ashland	2	(1)
Athens	7	(6)
Chillicothe	4	(3)
Findlay-Fostoria-Tiffin	2	(1)
Fremont	3	(2)
Marion	8	(7)
Mount Vernon	5	(4)
New Philadelphia	4	(3)
Norwalk	3	(2)
Portsmouth	4	(3)
Sandusky	3	(2)
Sidney	3	(2)
Wooster	5	(4)
Zanesville	6	(5)
Oklahoma		
Ardmore	2	(1)
Chickasha	0	(0)
Duncan	2	(1)
McAlester	2	(1)
Muskogee	2	(1)
Stillwater	2	(1)
Oregon		
Albany-Corvallis	6	(5)
Bend	3	(2)
Coos Bay	4	(3)
Grants Pass	1	(0)
Klamath Falls	7	(6)
Pendleton	2	(1)
Roseburg	4	(3)
Pennsylvania		
Chambersburg	2	(1)
New Castle	9	(8)
Pottsville	4	(3)
Rhode Island		
Newport	12	(11)
South Carolina		
Greenwood	2	(1)
Hilton Head Island	19	(18)
Tennessee		
Cleveland	1	(0)
Columbia	3	(2)
Cookeville	2	(1)
Morristown	2	(1)
Tullahoma	3	(2)
Texas		
Corsicana	2	(1)
Del Rio	5	(4)
Eagle Pass	10	(9)
Huntsville	4	(3)
Lufkin	3	(2)
Nacogdoches	3	(2)
Palestine	3	(2)
Paris	4	(3)

Utah		
Logan	6	(5)
St. George	2	(1)
Vermont		
Rutland	4	(3)
Virginia		
Blacksburg-Radford-Christiansburg	18	(17)
Harrisonburg	10	(9)
Martinsville	4	(3)
Staunton-Waynesboro	5	(4)
Winchester	9	(8)
Washington		
Aberdeen	20	(19)
Longview	2	(1)
Mount Vernon	4	(3)
Port Angeles	17	(16)
Walla Walla	12	(11)
Wenatchee	1	(0)
West Virginia		
Beckley	4	(3)
Clarksburg	11	(10)
Fairmont	5	(4)
Morgantown	15	(14)
Wisconsin		
Fond du Lac	6	(5)
Manitowoc	9	(8)
Stevens Point	3	(2)
Watertown	4	(3)
Wyoming		
Rock Springs	78	(20)

Highway Availability

It's wonderful if your small city is just one hundred miles from the bright lights of a metropolitan downtown or the haunting silence of a vast national forest. But such proximity means little if your only access is by way of a two-lane county road rife with stop signs and no-passing zones.

This category evaluates the quality of each area's highway system by means of a highway index. It awards points on the following scale: 10 points for a main (two-digit) interstate highway, 5 for a spur (three-digit) interstate highway or a four-lane U.S. road, 2 for a state principal highway, and 1 for any other state road. To qualify for points, these roads need only to pass through any part of the micropolitan area.

Michigan City-La Porte, Indiana, leads the way with an index of 48. The area is well-served by interstates, four-lane divided highways, and principal highways.

Located on the very southern tip of the United States, Key West, Florida, has the least access to highways. U.S. 1 connects the Key to the mainland, earning Key West just 3 points. But maybe the residents of the casual "Conch Republic" wouldn't want it any other way.

Source: Derived from *Rand McNally Road Atlas,* Rand McNally & Company, Skokie, Illinois. Data are for 1997.

Scoring: Twenty points for an index of 43 or higher; no points for an index below 5. The spacing is every 2 index points.

Highway Availability: Highs and Lows

		Highway Index
Highest		
1.	Michigan City-La Porte, Ind.	48
2.	Concord, N.H.	44
3.	Cape Girardeau-Sikeston, Mo.	42
	Findlay-Fostoria-Tiffin, Ohio	42
5.	Watertown, Wisc.	39
6.	Muskogee, Okla.	38
7.	Meridian, Miss.	37
	Radcliff-Elizabethtown, Ky.	37
	Torrington, Conn.	37
10.	New Castle, Pa.	35
Median		
96.	Corsicana, Tex.	19
97.	McAlester, Okla.	19
Lowest		
181.	Burlington, Iowa	7
	Cleveland, Miss.	7
	Eagle Pass, Tex.	7
	Fairbanks, Alaska	7
	Freeport, Ill.	7
	Hollister, Calif.	7
	Hutchinson, Kans.	7
	Marquette, Mich.	7
	Walla Walla, Wash.	7
190.	Wenatchee, Wash.	6
191.	Coos Bay, Ore.	5
	Port Angeles, Wash.	5
193.	Key West, Fla.	3

Highway Availability Area by Area

(Highway index and rating points)

Micro median	19	
Alabama		
Albertville	8	(2)
Auburn-Opelika	29	(13)
Cullman	20	(8)
Selma	10	(3)
Talladega	21	(9)
Alaska		
Fairbanks	7	(2)
Arizona		
Prescott	30	(13)
Sierra Vista	19	(8)
Arkansas		
Blytheville	15	(6)
El Dorado	10	(3)
Hot Springs	8	(2)
Jonesboro	11	(4)
Russellville	14	(5)
Searcy	17	(7)
California		
Arcata-Eureka	12	(4)
El Centro-Calexico-Brawley	20	(8)
Hanford-Lemoore	17	(7)
Hollister	7	(2)
Connecticut		
Torrington	37	(17)
Florida		
Key West	3	(0)
Vero Beach	25	(11)
Georgia		
Brunswick	24	(10)
Dalton	23	(10)
Dublin	27	(12)
Gainesville	19	(8)
Hinesville	19	(8)
La Grange	22	(9)
Milledgeville	13	(5)
Rome	22	(9)
Statesboro	26	(11)
Thomasville	13	(5)
Valdosta	23	(10)
Waycross	19	(8)
Idaho		
Coeur d'Alene	17	(7)
Idaho Falls	18	(7)
Pocatello	27	(12)
Twin Falls	8	(2)
Illinois		
Carbondale	11	(4)
Danville	20	(8)
Freeport	7	(2)
Galesburg	21	(9)
Mattoon-Charleston	17	(7)
Ottawa	28	(12)
Quincy	14	(5)
Sterling	17	(7)
Indiana		
Columbus	24	(10)
Marion	24	(10)
Michigan City-La Porte	48	(20)
New Castle	28	(12)
Richmond	25	(11)
Vincennes	13	(5)
Iowa		
Ames	21	(9)
Burlington	7	(2)
Clinton	12	(4)

Mason City	17	(7)
Muscatine	9	(3)
Kansas		
Hutchinson	7	(2)
Manhattan	26	(11)
Salina	18	(7)
Kentucky		
Bowling Green	23	(10)
Frankfort	29	(13)
Madisonville	31	(14)
Paducah	29	(13)
Radcliff-Elizabethtown	37	(17)
Louisiana		
Hammond	30	(13)
New Iberia	11	(4)
Ruston	18	(7)
Maine		
Augusta-Waterville	31	(14)
Biddeford-Saco	26	(11)
Maryland		
Salisbury	20	(8)
Michigan		
Marquette	7	(2)
Mount Pleasant	21	(9)
Owosso	15	(6)
Traverse City	14	(5)
Minnesota		
Faribault	16	(6)
Mankato	18	(7)
Red Wing	13	(5)
Willmar	13	(5)
Winona	20	(8)
Mississippi		
Cleveland	7	(2)
Columbus	18	(7)
Greenville	10	(3)
Laurel	18	(7)
Meridian	37	(17)
Tupelo	18	(7)
Vicksburg	17	(7)
Missouri		
Cape Girardeau-Sikeston	42	(19)
Jefferson City	27	(12)
Poplar Bluff	13	(5)
Warrensburg	10	(3)
Montana		
Bozeman	21	(9)
Helena	19	(8)
Missoula	18	(7)
Nebraska		
Grand Island	24	(10)
Nevada		
Carson City	11	(4)
Elko	20	(8)
New Hampshire		
Concord	44	(20)
Keene	13	(5)
New Mexico		
Alamogordo	11	(4)
Carlsbad	11	(4)
Clovis	12	(4)
Farmington	13	(5)
Gallup	17	(7)
Hobbs	18	(7)
Roswell	16	(6)
New York		
Cortland	19	(8)
Gloversville	9	(3)
Ithaca	10	(3)

Kingston 27 (12)
Olean 30 (13)
Plattsburgh 23 (10)
Watertown 30 (13)

North Carolina
Albemarle 8 (2)
Eden 18 (7)
Havelock-New Bern 17 (7)
Henderson 19 (8)
Kinston 15 (6)
Lumberton 26 (11)
Roanoke Rapids 22 (9)
Sanford 13 (5)
Shelby 19 (8)
Statesville 33 (15)
Wilson 28 (12)

North Dakota
Minot 19 (8)

Ohio
Ashland 32 (14)
Athens 17 (7)
Chillicothe 23 (10)
Findlay-Fostoria-Tiffin 42 (19)
Fremont 24 (10)
Marion 19 (8)
Mount Vernon 14 (5)
New Philadelphia 25 (11)
Norwalk 22 (9)
Portsmouth 11 (4)
Sandusky 25 (11)
Sidney 15 (6)
Wooster 30 (13)
Zanesville 27 (12)

Oklahoma
Ardmore 26 (11)
Chickasha 27 (12)
Duncan 13 (5)
McAlester 19 (8)
Muskogee 38 (17)
Stillwater 17 (7)

Oregon
Albany-Corvallis 25 (11)
Bend 11 (4)
Coos Bay 5 (1)
Grants Pass 16 (6)
Klamath Falls 17 (7)
Pendleton 33 (15)
Roseburg 20 (8)

Pennsylvania
Chambersburg 21 (9)
New Castle 35 (16)
Pottsville 32 (14)

Rhode Island
Newport 10 (3)

South Carolina
Greenwood 15 (6)
Hilton Head Island 15 (6)

Tennessee
Cleveland 22 (9)
Columbia 24 (10)
Cookeville 21 (9)
Morristown 17 (7)
Tullahoma 29 (13)

Texas
Corsicana 19 (8)
Del Rio 11 (4)
Eagle Pass 7 (2)
Huntsville 16 (6)
Lufkin 11 (4)
Nacogdoches 12 (4)
Palestine 17 (7)
Paris 11 (4)

Highway Availability Area by Area (continued)

Utah		
Logan	12	(4)
St. George	15	(6)
Vermont		
Rutland	27	(12)
Virginia		
Blacksburg-Radford-Christiansburg	24	(10)
Harrisonburg	31	(14)
Martinsville	13	(5)
Staunton-Waynesboro	32	(14)
Winchester	25	(11)
Washington		
Aberdeen	15	(6)
Longview	19	(8)
Mount Vernon	17	(7)
Port Angeles	5	(1)
Walla Walla	7	(2)
Wenatchee	6	(1)
West Virginia		
Beckley	22	(9)
Clarksburg	21	(9)
Fairmont	16	(6)
Morgantown	27	(12)
Wisconsin		
Fond du Lac	17	(7)
Manitowoc	22	(9)
Stevens Point	17	(7)
Watertown	39	(18)
Wyoming		
Rock Springs	21	(9)

Local Highway Funding

Americans drive hard, and U.S. roads often deteriorate faster than they are repaired. The U.S. Federal Highways Administration judged fewer than half of the nation's roads to be in good or very good shape in 1993. Only 35 percent of urban interstates were reported to be in good condition, while 40 percent were reported to be in "mediocre" or "poor" repair. Rural interstates fared better, perhaps because of lighter traffic. Forty-four percent were judged to be in good or very good condition.

This category ranks each area according to its financial commitment to its roadway network. Total annual expenditures by county and city governments are divided by the number of residents. Included are all allocations for construction, maintenance, and operations of roads and bridges, as well as funding for street lighting and snow removal.

Cold-weather cities face the greatest expenses with their highways and generally spend the most on them. Eight of the top-ten-spending micros are located in Minnesota, Wisconsin, and New York. Willmar, Minnesota, dedicates $427 per person on its roads, four times the national average. But not all of the big spenders are northern cities. Laurel, Mississippi, spends a healthy $227 per resident. The micropolitan median is $98 per capita.

Southern cities spend the least per capita on their roads and Albemarle, North Carolina, spends the very least—just $15 per resident.

Source: Census of Governments: Compendium of Government Finances, U.S. Bureau of the Census. Data, published in 1997, are for fiscal year 1991–92.

Scoring: Twenty points for $210 or more per capita; no points for less than $20. The spacing is every $10 per capita.

Local Highway Funding: Highs and Lows

	Annual Per Capita Highway-Related Spending by Local Governments
Highest	**$**
1. Willmar, Minn.	427
2. Mankato, Minn.	368
3. Watertown, N.Y.	304
4. Red Wing, Minn.	303
5. Olean, N.Y.	291
6. Stevens Point, Wisc.	284
7. Manitowoc, Wisc.	262
8. Cortland, N.Y.	252
9. Wenatchee, Wash.	236
10. Laurel, Miss.	227
Median	
96. Bend, Ore.	98
97. Key West, Fla.	98
Lowest	
184. Havelock-New Bern, N.C.	27
185. Beckley, W.Va.	26
Hilton Head Island, S.C.	26
187. Henderson, N.C.	25
Kinston, N.C.	25
189. Winchester, Va.	24
190. Hinesville, Ga.	22
191. Shelby, N.C.	21
192. Fairmont, W.Va.	17
193. Albemarle, N.C.	15

Local Highway Funding Area by Area

(Annual per capita highway-related spending by local governments in dollars and rating points)

Micro median	98	
Alabama		
Albertville	80	(7)
Auburn-Opelika	62	(5)
Cullman	105	(9)
Selma	48	(3)
Talladega	74	(6)
Alaska		
Fairbanks	97	(8)
Arizona		
Prescott	179	(16)
Sierra Vista	96	(8)
Arkansas		
Blytheville	68	(5)
El Dorado	90	(8)
Hot Springs	57	(4)
Jonesboro	77	(6)
Russellville	64	(5)
Searcy	58	(4)
California		
Arcata-Eureka	108	(9)
El Centro-Calexico-Brawley	111	(10)
Hanford-Lemoore	96	(8)
Hollister	84	(7)
Connecticut		
Torrington	141	(13)
Florida		
Key West	98	(8)
Vero Beach	148	(13)
Georgia		
Brunswick	82	(7)
Dalton	176	(16)
Dublin	85	(7)
Gainesville	35	(2)
Hinesville	22	(1)
La Grange	78	(6)
Milledgeville	50	(4)
Rome	99	(8)
Statesboro	74	(6)
Thomasville	67	(5)
Valdosta	105	(9)
Waycross	121	(11)
Idaho		
Coeur d'Alene	126	(11)
Idaho Falls	79	(6)
Pocatello	138	(12)
Twin Falls	160	(15)
Illinois		
Carbondale	89	(7)
Danville	111	(10)
Freeport	98	(8)
Galesburg	128	(11)
Mattoon-Charleston	104	(9)
Ottawa	133	(12)
Quincy	123	(11)
Sterling	129	(11)
Indiana		
Columbus	150	(14)
Marion	63	(5)
Michigan City-La Porte	82	(7)
New Castle	88	(7)
Richmond	87	(7)
Vincennes	76	(6)
Iowa		
Ames	141	(13)
Burlington	151	(14)

Clinton	193	(18)
Mason City	121	(11)
Muscatine	136	(12)
Kansas		
Hutchinson	123	(11)
Manhattan	104	(9)
Salina	124	(11)
Kentucky		
Bowling Green	50	(4)
Frankfort	42	(3)
Madisonville	39	(2)
Paducah	85	(7)
Radcliff-Elizabethtown	60	(5)
Louisiana		
Hammond	78	(6)
New Iberia	112	(10)
Ruston	130	(12)
Maine		
Augusta-Waterville	96	(8)
Biddeford-Saco	87	(7)
Maryland		
Salisbury	79	(6)
Michigan		
Marquette	199	(18)
Mount Pleasant	138	(12)
Owosso	130	(12)
Traverse City	150	(14)
Minnesota		
Faribault	179	(16)
Mankato	368	(20)
Red Wing	303	(20)
Willmar	427	(20)
Winona	198	(18)
Mississippi		
Cleveland	82	(7)
Columbus	81	(7)
Greenville	123	(11)
Laurel	227	(20)
Meridian	102	(9)
Tupelo	165	(15)
Vicksburg	93	(8)
Missouri		
Cape Girardeau-Sikeston	90	(8)
Jefferson City	108	(9)
Poplar Bluff	60	(5)
Warrensburg	75	(6)
Montana		
Bozeman	107	(9)
Helena	77	(6)
Missoula	84	(7)
Nebraska		
Grand Island	103	(9)
Nevada		
Carson City	105	(9)
Elko	142	(13)
New Hampshire		
Concord	107	(9)
Keene	97	(8)
New Mexico		
Alamogordo	61	(5)
Carlsbad	160	(15)
Clovis	93	(8)
Farmington	112	(10)
Gallup	92	(8)
Hobbs	106	(9)
Roswell	180	(17)
New York		
Cortland	252	(20)
Gloversville	179	(16)
Ithaca	167	(15)

Kingston	187	(17)
Olean	291	(20)
Plattsburgh	161	(15)
Watertown	304	(20)
North Carolina		
Albemarle	15	(0)
Eden	28	(1)
Havelock-New Bern	27	(1)
Henderson	25	(1)
Kinston	25	(1)
Lumberton	30	(2)
Roanoke Rapids	31	(2)
Sanford	29	(1)
Shelby	21	(1)
Statesville	33	(2)
Wilson	33	(2)
North Dakota		
Minot	126	(11)
Ohio		
Ashland	112	(10)
Athens	90	(8)
Chillicothe	110	(10)
Findlay-Fostoria-Tiffin	101	(9)
Fremont	101	(9)
Marion	86	(7)
Mount Vernon	125	(11)
New Philadelphia	87	(7)
Norwalk	129	(11)
Portsmouth	77	(6)
Sandusky	112	(10)
Sidney	140	(13)
Wooster	130	(12)
Zanesville	88	(7)
Oklahoma		
Ardmore	151	(14)
Chickasha	128	(11)
Duncan	118	(10)
McAlester	101	(9)
Muskogee	40	(3)
Stillwater	73	(6)
Oregon		
Albany-Corvallis	131	(12)
Bend	98	(8)
Coos Bay	87	(7)
Grants Pass	101	(9)
Klamath Falls	178	(16)
Pendleton	90	(8)
Roseburg	173	(16)
Pennsylvania		
Chambersburg	56	(4)
New Castle	68	(5)
Pottsville	69	(5)
Rhode Island		
Newport	32	(2)
South Carolina		
Greenwood	31	(2)
Hilton Head Island	26	(1)
Tennessee		
Cleveland	78	(6)
Columbia	87	(7)
Cookeville	129	(11)
Morristown	73	(6)
Tullahoma	94	(8)
Texas		
Corsicana	137	(12)
Del Rio	62	(5)
Eagle Pass	46	(3)
Huntsville	64	(5)
Lufkin	72	(6)
Nacogdoches	96	(8)
Palestine	55	(4)
Paris	114	(10)

Utah		
Logan	68	(5)
St. George	108	(9)
Vermont		
Rutland	142	(13)
Virginia		
Blacksburg-Radford-Christiansburg	70	(6)
Harrisonburg	61	(5)
Martinsville	35	(2)
Staunton-Waynesboro	47	(3)
Winchester	24	(1)
Washington		
Aberdeen	163	(15)
Longview	149	(13)
Mount Vernon	165	(15)
Port Angeles	127	(11)
Walla Walla	129	(11)
Wenatchee	236	(20)
West Virginia		
Beckley	26	(1)
Clarksburg	32	(2)
Fairmont	17	(0)
Morgantown	34	(2)
Wisconsin		
Fond du Lac	170	(16)
Manitowoc	262	(20)
Stevens Point	284	(20)
Watertown	225	(20)
Wyoming		
Rock Springs	180	(17)

Aviation Availability

Travelers without much time or those with a long distance to go usually prefer to fly. It's often the the quickest and most convenient way to cover long distances. Catching a plane is typically easiest in and around the country's largest cities, where the major airlines concentrate their services. But many small cities have large airports and many others are connected to metro hubs via feeder lines. Other small cities are within a reasonable drive of regularly scheduled air service.

This category rates each micropolis according to its accessibility to regularly scheduled passenger air service by using three criteria. The first is the volume of passenger traffic on aircraft with sixty or more seats. Thirty-one micropolitans have regularly scheduled traffic of these larger planes. The second criterion measures the availability of regular air transportation on planes with fewer than sixty seats. This would include many of the feeder lines carrying passengers to hub airports. The Federal Aviation Administration (FAA) does not measure traffic of commuter airplanes, therefore small plane traffic in this category is measured by identifying those airports with scheduled passenger traffic that do not provide large-craft flights. Residents in forty micropolitans have local airports offering smaller aircraft service. The third criterion measures the road mileage to the nearest airport providing regular passenger service. Thirty-six micros are within thirty miles of an airport.

Fairbanks, Alaska, is a micropolis with metropolitan air service. The more than 250,000 passengers annually boarding large aircraft in Fairbanks qualify that city as a small hub in the eyes of the FAA. At the other extreme, two Texas micros on the Mexican border are a long haul from routine air service. Residents of Del Rio and Eagle Pass, Texas, must drive approximately 150 miles to reach the San Antonio Airport.

Small cities in the vast expanses of the West and Midwest have the best access to air service. Small cities in the South have the least convenient access to air service.

Source: Data on passenger traffic aboard regularly scheduled planes of sixty or more seats are from *Airport Activity Statistics of Certified Route Air Carriers,* Bureau of Transportation Statistics, Federal Aviation Administration, Washington, D.C. The data are for 1994. Data on airports that offer regularly scheduled passenger service, as well as road mileage, are from *The Rand McNally Commercial Atlas and Marketing Guide, 1996,* Rand McNally & Company, Skokie, Illinois.

Scoring: Twenty points for airports with annual traffic exceeding 100,000 passengers on planes of 60 or more seats; 18 points for those with passenger traffic of 25,000 to 99,999; 16 points for those with passenger traffic less than 25,000. Micros with local airports providing regularly scheduled flights on planes with fewer than 60 seats receive 15 points. Ten points are awarded to micros within 10 to 30 miles of a passenger airport; 6 points for those within 31 to 69 miles; 3 points for those within 70 to 100 miles. No points for micros located more than 100 miles from a passenger airport.

Aviation Availability: Highs and Lows

		Aviation Availability Index
Highest		
1.	Fairbanks, Alaska	20
	Bozeman, Mont.	20
	Missoula, Mont.	20
	Traverse City, Mich.	20
5.	Columbus, Miss.	18
	Elko, Nev.	18
	Helena, Mont.	18
	Idaho Falls, Idaho	18
	Ithaca, N.Y.	18
	Minot, N.Dak.	18
	Port Angeles, Wash.	18
	Wenatchee, Wash.	18
Median		
96.	New Castle, Pa.	10
97.	Pottsville, Pa.	10
Lowest		
182.	Ardmore, Okla.	3
	Cookeville, Tenn.	3
	Lufkin, Tex.	3
	McAlester, Okla.	3
	Paris, Tex.	3
	Roseburg, Ore.	3
	Russellville, Ark.	3
	Sidney, Ohio	3
	Tullahoma, Tenn.	3
191.	Del Rio, Tex.	0
	Eagle Pass, Tex.	0
	Vicksburg, Miss.	0

Aviation Availability Area by Area

(Number of passengers boarding planes of 60 or more seats, aviation index, and rating points)

Area	Passengers	Index	Points
Micro median		10	
Alabama			
Albertville	0	6	(6)
Auburn-Opelika	0	6	(6)
Cullman	0	6	(6)
Selma	0	6	(6)
Talladega	0	6	(6)
Alaska			
Fairbanks	293,590	20	(20)
Arizona			
Prescott	0	15	(15)
Sierra Vista	0	15	(15)
Arkansas			
Blytheville	0	6	(6)
El Dorado	0	15	(15)
Hot Springs	0	15	(15)
Jonesboro	0	15	(15)
Russellville	0	3	(3)
Searcy	0	6	(6)
California			
Arcata-Eureka	5,788	16	(16)
El Centro-Calexico-Brawley	0	15	(15)
Hanford-Lemoore	0	10	(10)
Hollister	0	6	(6)
Connecticut			
Torrington	0	6	(6)
Florida			
Key West	0	15	(15)
Vero Beach	0	6	(6)
Georgia			
Brunswick	21,369	16	(16)
Dalton	0	10	(10)
Dublin	0	6	(6)
Gainesville	0	6	(6)
Hinesville	0	6	(6)
La Grange	0	6	(6)
Milledgeville	0	10	(10)
Rome	0	6	(6)
Statesboro	0	6	(6)
Thomasville	0	6	(6)
Valdosta	18,744	16	(16)
Waycross	0	6	(6)
Idaho			
Coeur d'Alene	4,307	16	(16)
Idaho Falls	97,326	18	(18)
Pocatello	14,795	16	(16)
Twin Falls	12,421	16	(16)
Illinois			
Carbondale	0	15	(15)
Danville	0	15	(15)
Freeport	0	10	(10)
Galesburg	0	15	(15)
Mattoon-Charleston	0	15	(15)
Ottawa	0	6	(6)
Quincy	12,714	16	(16)
Sterling	0	15	(15)
Indiana			
Columbus	0	6	(6)
Marion	0	10	(10)
Michigan City-La Porte	0	10	(10)
New Castle	0	10	(10)
Richmond	0	10	(10)
Vincennes	0	6	(6)
Iowa			
Ames	0	10	(10)
Burlington	21,240	16	(16)

Area			
Clinton	0	6	(6)
Mason City	90	16	(16)
Muscatine	0	6	(6)
Kansas			
Hutchinson	0	6	(6)
Manhattan	0	15	(15)
Salina	0	15	(15)
Kentucky			
Bowling Green	0	6	(6)
Frankfort	0	15	(15)
Madisonville	0	6	(6)
Paducah	10,722	16	(16)
Radcliff-Elizabethtown	0	6	(6)
Louisiana			
Hammond	0	6	(6)
New Iberia	0	10	(10)
Ruston	0	6	(6)
Maine			
Augusta-Waterville	0	15	(15)
Biddeford-Saco	0	10	(10)
Maryland			
Salisbury	0	15	(15)
Michigan			
Marquette	20,592	16	(16)
Mount Pleasant	0	10	(10)
Owosso	0	10	(10)
Traverse City	120,356	20	(20)
Minnesota			
Faribault	0	6	(6)
Mankato	0	15	(15)
Red Wing	0	6	(6)
Willmar	0	6	(6)
Winona	0	6	(6)

Area			
Mississippi			
Cleveland	0	10	(10)
Columbus	25,582	18	(18)
Greenville	0	15	(15)
Laurel	0	15	(15)
Meridian	16,859	16	(16)
Tupelo	0	15	(15)
Vicksburg	0	0	(0)
Missouri			
Cape Girardeau-Sikeston	6,166	16	(16)
Jefferson City	0	10	(10)
Poplar Bluff	0	6	(6)
Warrensburg	0	6	(6)
Montana			
Bozeman	164,700	20	(20)
Helena	58,857	18	(18)
Missoula	162,965	20	(20)
Nebraska			
Grand Island	974	16	(16)
Nevada			
Carson City	0	10	(10)
Elko	93,248	18	(18)
New Hampshire			
Concord	0	10	(10)
Keene	0	15	(15)
New Mexico			
Alamogordo	0	15	(15)
Carlsbad	0	15	(15)
Clovis	0	15	(15)
Farmington	50	16	(16)
Gallup	0	15	(15)
Hobbs	0	15	(15)
Roswell	0	15	(15)

New York

Cortland	0	10	(10)
Gloversville	0	6	(6)
Ithaca	44,949	18	(18)
Kingston	0	10	(10)
Olean	0	6	(6)
Plattsburgh	0	15	(15)
Watertown	0	15	(15)

North Carolina

Albemarle	0	6	(6)
Eden	0	6	(6)
Havelock-New Bern	0	15	(15)
Henderson	0	6	(6)
Kinston	0	15	(15)
Lumberton	0	10	(10)
Roanoke Rapids	0	6	(6)
Sanford	0	6	(6)
Shelby	0	10	(10)
Statesville	0	6	(6)
Wilson	0	10	(10)

North Dakota

Minot	72,548	18	(18)

Ohio

Ashland	0	6	(6)
Athens	0	6	(6)
Chillicothe	0	6	(6)
Findlay-Fostoria-Tiffin	0	6	(6)
Fremont	0	6	(6)
Marion	0	6	(6)
Mount Vernon	0	6	(6)
New Philadelphia	0	6	(6)
Norwalk	0	6	(6)
Portsmouth	0	6	(6)
Sandusky	0	6	(6)
Sidney	0	3	(3)
Wooster	0	6	(6)
Zanesville	0	6	(6)

Oklahoma

Ardmore	0	3	(3)
Chickasha	0	6	(6)
Duncan	0	6	(6)
McAlester	0	3	(3)
Muskogee	0	6	(6)
Stillwater	0	6	(6)

Oregon

Albany-Corvallis	0	6	(6)
Bend	0	10	(10)
Coos Bay	19,346	16	(16)
Grants Pass	0	10	(10)
Klamath Falls	14,037	16	(16)
Pendleton	11,265	16	(16)
Roseburg	0	3	(3)

Pennsylvania

Chambersburg	0	6	(6)
New Castle	0	10	(10)
Pottsville	0	10	(10)

Rhode Island

Newport	0	10	(10)

South Carolina

Greenwood	0	6	(6)
Hilton Head Island	0	15	(15)

Tennessee

Cleveland	0	10	(10)
Columbia	0	6	(6)
Cookeville	0	3	(3)
Morristown	0	6	(6)
Tullahoma	0	3	(3)

Texas

Corsicana	0	6	(6)
Del Rio	0	0	(0)
Eagle Pass	0	0	(0)
Huntsville	0	6	(6)
Lufkin	0	3	(3)

Nacogdoches	0	6	(6)
Palestine	0	6	(6)
Paris	0	3	(3)
Utah			
Logan	0	10	(10)
St. George	0	15	(15)
Vermont			
Rutland	0	15	(15)
Virginia			
Blacksburg-Radford-Christiansburg	0	6	(6)
Harrisonburg	0	10	(10)
Martinsville	0	10	(10)
Staunton-Waynesboro	0	15	(15)
Winchester	0	6	(6)
Washington			
Aberdeen	0	6	(6)
Longview	0	6	(6)
Mount Vernon	0	10	(10)
Port Angeles	27,654	18	(18)
Walla Walla	23,068	16	(16)
Wenatchee	41,314	18	(18)
West Virginia			
Beckley	0	15	(15)
Clarksburg	0	15	(15)
Fairmont	0	10	(10)
Morgantown	0	15	(15)
Wisconsin			
Fond du Lac	0	10	(10)
Manitowoc	0	10	(10)
Stevens Point	0	10	(10)
Watertown	0	6	(6)
Wyoming			
Rock Springs	0	15	(15)

The Results

Watertown, New York, ranks first for overall transportation convenience. The city may be tucked upstate along the shore of Lake Ontario, but residents have easy access to major highways and local air service. Watertown scores 73 of a possible 100 points in the section.

Watertown residents have a sixteen-minute commute to work on average, a minute below the micro median and a full six minutes shorter than the national average. The bus service carries 13 in 1,000 commuters daily, a rate far above the median of 5 in 1,000 for all small cities. Interstate 81, which runs from Ontario, Canada, all the way south to Tennessee, passes through the center of the Watertown area. Local Watertown governments invest significantly in the local roads. However, a considerable share of this funding is essential maintenance in winter, when the area receives an average 9.5 feet of snow. The Watertown airport provides commuter service to national hubs. In addition, the Syracuse International Airport is an hour's drive to the south.

Midwestern and Western small cities have the best transportation networks. Together they capture eight of the top ten slots.

Albemarle, North Carolina, lies in the south-central part of the state, between Charlotte and the Uwharrie National Forest. Residents of Albemarle have relatively convenient access to both attractions, but their options for major roads or local airports to other destinations are more limited. Albemarle scores just 12 points, the lowest in the transportation section.

The average travel time to work in Albemarle is twenty-one minutes, several minutes above the median of other small cities. There is little public transit to meet the needs of commuters, many of whom work in factories and plants located outside of town. Just 1 resident in 1,000 takes the bus to work in Albemarle.

Several primary roads crisscross the Albemarle area, but residents may drive thirty miles or more to reach an interstate or four-lane divided highway. The temperate North Carolina climate relieves Albemarle of many of the road maintenance expenses incurred by snow and ice, but at just $15 per capita, Albemarle spends less on its roads than other North Carolina micros. The nearest airport is in Charlotte, approximately forty-five miles away. The Charlotte airport, however, is a hub airport, offering flights throughout the country and the world.

Six other southern small cities join Albemarle among the ten micros with lowest scores in transportation. Three of North Carolina's eleven micros are on the list.

Transportation Scores: Highs and Lows

Highest

		Total Rating Points
1.	Watertown, N.Y.	73
2.	Pocatello, Idaho	72
3.	Mankato, Minn.	71
4.	Ithaca, N.Y.	69
5.	Ames, Iowa	67
6.	Rock Springs, Wyo.	64
7.	Sierra Vista, Ariz.	62
8.	Carlsbad, N.Mex.	61
	Mason City, Iowa	61
	Minot, N.Dak.	61
11.	Manitowoc, Wisc.	60
	Meridian, Miss.	60
	Plattsburgh, N.Y.	60
14.	Elko, Nev.	59
	Klamath Falls, Ore.	59
	Marquette, Mich.	59
	Missoula, Mont.	59
	Port Angeles, Wash.	59
19.	Bozeman, Mont.	58
	Cape Girardeau-Sikeston, Mo.	58
	Manhattan, Kans	58
	Olean, N.Y.	58
	Walla Walla, Wash.	58
	Winona, Minn.	58

Median

		Total Rating Points
96.	Staunton-Waynesboro, Va.	43
97.	Albany-Corvallis, Ore.	42

Lowest

		Total Rating Points
184.	Cullman, Ala.	24
	Searcy, Ark.	24
	Warrensburg, Mo.	24
187.	Portsmouth, Ohio	22
188.	Eden, N.C.	21
189.	Sanford, N.C.	20
190.	Gainesville, Ga.	19
191.	Hollister, Calif.	18
192.	Albertville, Ala.	17
193.	Albemarle, N.C.	12

Transportation Performance Comparison

	Watertown, New York	Micro median	Albemarle, North Carolina
Total Points in Section	73	44	12
Rank in Section	1		193
Commuting Ease			
Average travel time to work in minutes	16.3	17.5	20.8
Commuting Ease points	(13)		(4)
Public Transit Usage			
Users of public transit per 1,000 commuters	13	5	1
Public Transit points	(12)		(0)
Highway Availability			
Highway index	30	19	8
Highway points	(13)		(2)
Local Highway Funding			
Annual per capita spending by local governments	$304	$98	$15
Highway Funding points	(20)		(0)
Aviation Availability			
Aviation index	15	10	6
Aviation points	(15)		(6)

Transportation Scores Area by Area

(Total transportation rating points)

Area	Points
Micro median	44
Alabama	
Albertville	17
Auburn-Opelika	36
Cullman	24
Selma	36
Talladega	32
Alaska	
Fairbanks	56
Arizona	
Prescott	53
Sierra Vista	62
Arkansas	
Blytheville	36
El Dorado	39
Hot Springs	33
Jonesboro	40
Russellville	25
Searcy	24
California	
Arcata-Eureka	49
El Centro-Calexico-Brawley	52
Hanford-Lemoore	49
Hollister	18
Connecticut	
Torrington	46
Florida	
Key West	49
Vero Beach	41
Georgia	
Brunswick	49
Dalton	49
Dublin	46
Gainesville	19
Hinesville	37
La Grange	48
Milledgeville	47
Rome	40
Statesboro	35
Thomasville	28
Valdosta	51
Waycross	40
Idaho	
Coeur d'Alene	43
Idaho Falls	51
Pocatello	72
Twin Falls	54
Illinois	
Carbondale	45
Danville	49
Freeport	41
Galesburg	56
Mattoon-Charleston	50
Ottawa	43
Quincy	54
Sterling	51
Indiana	
Columbus	45
Marion	39
Michigan City-La Porte	53
New Castle	31
Richmond	49
Vincennes	33
Iowa	
Ames	67
Burlington	52
Clinton	48
Mason City	61
Muscatine	43
Kansas	
Hutchinson	34
Manhattan	58
Salina	54
Kentucky	
Bowling Green	35
Frankfort	48
Madisonville	30
Paducah	53
Radcliff-Elizabethtown	43
Louisiana	
Hammond	26
New Iberia	33
Ruston	42
Maine	
Augusta-Waterville	50
Biddeford-Saco	37
Maryland	
Salisbury	54
Michigan	
Marquette	59
Mount Pleasant	51
Owosso	28
Traverse City	55
Minnesota	
Faribault	46
Mankato	71
Red Wing	44
Willmar	54
Winona	58

Mississippi

Cleveland	39
Columbus	45
Greenville	52
Laurel	51
Meridian	60
Tupelo	52
Vicksburg	42

Missouri

Cape Girardeau-Sikeston	58
Jefferson City	48
Poplar Bluff	35
Warrensburg	24

Montana

Bozeman	58
Helena	51
Missoula	59

Nebraska

Grand Island	54

Nevada

Carson City	39
Elko	59

New Hampshire

Concord	46
Keene	39

New Mexico

Alamogordo	37
Carlsbad	61
Clovis	47
Farmington	35
Gallup	43
Hobbs	46
Roswell	55

New York

Cortland	56
Gloversville	49
Ithaca	69
Kingston	57
Olean	58
Plattsburgh	60
Watertown	73

North Carolina

Albemarle	12
Eden	21
Havelock-New Bern	38
Henderson	28
Kinston	36
Lumberton	31
Roanoke Rapids	31
Sanford	20
Shelby	28
Statesville	31
Wilson	42

North Dakota

Minot	61

Ohio

Ashland	41
Athens	36
Chillicothe	30
Findlay-Fostoria-Tiffin	47
Fremont	37
Marion	35
Mount Vernon	29
New Philadelphia	37
Norwalk	38
Portsmouth	22
Sandusky	40
Sidney	37
Wooster	46
Zanesville	36

Oklahoma

Ardmore	42
Chickasha	29
Duncan	34
McAlester	29
Muskogee	33
Stillwater	36

Oregon

Albany-Corvallis	42
Bend	37
Coos Bay	38
Grants Pass	34
Klamath Falls	59
Pendleton	55
Roseburg	38

Pennsylvania

Chambersburg	28
New Castle	48
Pottsville	37

Rhode Island

Newport	36

South Carolina

Greenwood	26
Hilton Head Island	50

Tennessee

Cleveland	33
Columbia	28
Cookeville	36
Morristown	29
Tullahoma	31

Texas

Corsicana	29
Del Rio	29
Eagle Pass	30
Huntsville	27
Lufkin	27

Nacogdoches	31
Palestine	27
Paris	32
Utah	
Logan	37
St. George	45
Vermont	
Rutland	54
Virginia	
Blacksburg-Radford-Christiansburg	50
Harrisonburg	48
Martinsville	30
Staunton-Waynesboro	43
Winchester	28
Washington	
Aberdeen	53
Longview	38
Mount Vernon	41
Port Angeles	59
Walla Walla	58
Wenatchee	54
West Virginia	
Beckley	32
Clarksburg	44
Fairmont	25
Morgantown	54
Wisconsin	
Fond du Lac	50
Manitowoc	60
Stevens Point	54
Watertown	57
Wyoming	
Rock Springs	64

10

Urban Proximity

Big cities can be a lot of fun to visit, even if you wouldn't want to live there. Metropolitan regions have the enormous resources needed to support cultural attractions and sports franchises that could not survive financially in small cities. They are magnets for national and international retailers, either in downtown shopping districts or in suburban malls. Big cities have the large numbers of viewers and advertisers required to sustain major television stations.

Small-city residents, anxious to lose the congestion and stress of urban life, do not have to abandon all of the above urban attractions; many micropolitans benefit considerably from being close to a metropolitan center. Residents of Mount Vernon, Port Angeles, and Aberdeen, Washington, can all make day or weekend trips to enjoy Seattle's museums, aquarium, zoo, and symphony. They can shop in Seattle's major retail stores, and watch its professional sports teams. At the end of the day, they can return home to smaller communities where the parking is easier, the housing is less expensive, and the violent crime rate is lower.

This section measures the ease in which residents of each micropolitan area can access metropolitan attractions. Each micro is rated on the road mileage to the nearest urban centers that provide cultural activities, shopping, and big-league sporting events.

The majority of Americans will increasingly view central cities as resources for occasional use, rather than as full-time homes. Trends in migration, housing, and employment all point toward a continued shift in daily activity from the centers of urban areas to the fringes. In the 1950s and 1960s, even as more and more central-city residents moved out to the suburbs, central cities still held the jobs and so retained a place in new suburban dwellers' lives. By the 1980s, however, employment was rapidly sprawling out from center cities, and trips to major urban centers became occasional weekend events. "For many, in fact, a trip in Washington (D.C.) has become a special occasion—a time to take a visiting relative to see the monuments," wrote John Milliken, vice chairman of the Arlington (Virginia) County Board, in a 1987 *Washington Post* column.

The travel section of the Sunday newspaper confirms Milliken's observation and shows how the relationship between the center city and the fringe communities has become even more distant. Downtown hotels now advertise special weekend packages luring nearby residents to getaway weekends in the city.

Central cities are stepping up their efforts to provide cultural events and sports for out-of-town visitors from both near and far. Many major urban renewal projects focus on creating shopping areas and visitor attractions. For example, the Inner Harbor area of Baltimore, Maryland, had once been a neighborhood so rough that visiting Navy ships were advised to grant sailors shore leave only in groups of four or more. Now the Inner Harbor is an open-air visitor's attraction, with sightseeing, shopping, and restaurants. Many of the families and couples who watch the street performers, tour the historic USS *Constellation,* or window shop have come from towns just outside city limits. The Inner Harbor features plenty of parking and is minutes from the interstate. The new stadium for the city's popular Orioles baseball team was built nearby, making it more convenient to out-of-towners and further concentrating visitor activities at the harbor.

Furthermore, the migration out of central cities to the suburbs does not show signs of reversing. New housing construction in inner cities is practically at a standstill nationwide, according to the Joint Center for Housing Studies. Even in fast-growing metro areas such as Atlanta, housing on the suburban fringes absorbs the newcomers. The Joint Center for Housing Studies expects the trend to increase, because housing and jobs will likely continue to grow quickly outside of center cities. Advances in telecommunications will allow many business to relocate to cheaper, less densely populated suburbs. First-time home buyers will purchase the more-affordable housing on the outskirts of suburbs. And many baby boomers seeking vacation or retirement homes will look outside urban centers where they can get more space and better value for their housing dollar.

Only one worry nags many of those considering a move: Can they survive being away from the city's attractions? Stuart Hollander, a tax lawyer who left San Francisco, contends that most people overstate their need for such immediate access. "A lot of people say they miss the opera," he suggests. "I can't say that. We didn't go to the opera."

Ranking micropolitan America. The ideal small city would be reasonably close to regional centers for cultural activities, shopping, and professional sports. It would also receive television programming from a large city. Each area is evaluated in five categories:

1. Metro Center Proximity: Is the micropolis near the center city or a dominant city of an officially designated metropolitan area?
2. Arts Center Proximity: Can you easily reach a city with museums, art galleries, orchestras, and live theater?
3. Retail Center Proximity: When you desire a change of pace, can you easily drive to a large city with a good variety of shops?
4. Sports Center Proximity: Can you quickly get to a professional sporting event?
5. Television Market: Does your town have access to a large choice of TV stations from a big market?

Metro Center Proximity

America's small cities are not lonely outposts in the Great American Backwater, despite the stereotypes maintained by urbanites. More than half of all micropolitan areas—107 of 193—are within fifty miles of a metropolitan downtown. Another fifty-six are within fifty-one to one hundred miles.

This category ranks each area according to the road mileage between it and the closest metro center. A dominant city in any of the nation's 328 Metropolitan Statistical Areas qualifies as a metro center.

Ashland, Ohio, is the small city with the quickest access to a large neighbor. Ashland is only a fourteen-mile drive to Mansfield.

Fairbanks, Alaska, the northernmost micro in the nation, is also the most isolated. A resident heading for a metro center must drive 361 miles south to Anchorage.

The compact East has the largest number of small cities that are close to metropolitan areas. The vast West, unsurprisingly, has a virtual monopoly on cities that are distant from metro centers.

Source: Derived from *Rand McNally Road Atlas,* Rand McNally & Company, Skokie, Illinois. Data are for 1997.

Scoring: Twenty points for road mileage of less than 20 miles; no points for 210 miles or more. The spacing is every ten miles.

Metro Center Proximity: Highs and Lows

		Road Mileage to Nearest Metro Center
Lowest		
1.	Ashland, Ohio	14
2.	Biddeford-Saco, Maine	16
	New Castle, Pa.	16
	Vero Beach, Fla.	16
5.	Wilson, N.C.	18
6.	Kingston, N.Y.	19
7.	Concord, N.H.	20
	Hanford-Lemoore, Calif.	20
	New Castle, Ind.	20
	New Iberia, La.	20
	Torrington, Conn.	20
Median		
96.	Corsicana, Tex.	46
97.	Aberdeen, Wash.	47
Highest		
184.	Pocatello, Idaho	160
185.	Key West, Fla.	161
186.	Missoula, Mont.	166
187.	Rock Springs, Wyo.	172
188.	Roswell, N.Mex.	173
189.	Marquette, Mich.	175
190.	Farmington, N.Mex.	182
191.	Idaho Falls, Idaho	203
192.	Elko, Nev.	226
193.	Fairbanks, Alaska	361

Metro Center Proximity Area by Area

(Miles from nearest officially designated metropolitan area and rating points)

Micro median	47	
Alabama		
Albertville	22	(19)
Auburn-Opelika	32	(18)
Cullman	32	(18)
Selma	49	(17)
Talladega	23	(19)
Alaska		
Fairbanks	361	(0)
Arizona		
Prescott	89	(13)
Sierra Vista	70	(14)
Arkansas		
Blytheville	68	(15)
El Dorado	85	(13)
Hot Springs	55	(16)
Jonesboro	66	(15)
Russellville	76	(14)
Searcy	44	(17)
California		
Arcata-Eureka	155	(6)
El Centro-Calexico-Brawley	117	(10)
Hanford-Lemoore	20	(19)
Hollister	28	(19)
Connecticut		
Torrington	20	(19)
Florida		
Key West	161	(5)
Vero Beach	16	(20)
Georgia		
Brunswick	71	(14)
Dalton	28	(19)
Dublin	56	(16)
Gainesville	39	(18)
Hinesville	41	(17)
La Grange	45	(17)
Milledgeville	29	(19)
Rome	54	(16)
Statesboro	54	(16)
Thomasville	37	(18)
Valdosta	78	(14)
Waycross	76	(14)
Idaho		
Coeur d'Alene	33	(18)
Idaho Falls	203	(1)
Pocatello	160	(5)
Twin Falls	129	(9)
Illinois		
Carbondale	96	(12)
Danville	35	(18)
Freeport	29	(19)
Galesburg	48	(17)
Mattoon-Charleston	44	(17)
Ottawa	45	(17)
Quincy	102	(11)
Sterling	57	(16)
Indiana		
Columbus	39	(18)
Marion	32	(18)
Michigan City-La Porte	25	(19)
New Castle	20	(19)
Richmond	41	(17)
Vincennes	54	(16)
Iowa		
Ames	28	(19)
Burlington	78	(14)
Clinton	37	(18)

Mason City	82	(13)
Muscatine	30	(18)
Kansas		
Hutchinson	52	(16)
Manhattan	54	(16)
Salina	90	(12)
Kentucky		
Bowling Green	61	(15)
Frankfort	23	(19)
Madisonville	48	(17)
Paducah	96	(12)
Radcliff-Elizabethtown	36	(18)
Louisiana		
Hammond	41	(17)
New Iberia	20	(19)
Ruston	31	(18)
Maine		
Augusta-Waterville	30	(18)
Biddeford-Saco	16	(20)
Maryland		
Salisbury	102	(11)
Michigan		
Marquette	175	(4)
Mount Pleasant	53	(16)
Owosso	25	(19)
Traverse City	134	(8)
Minnesota		
Faribault	48	(17)
Mankato	75	(14)
Red Wing	50	(16)
Willmar	63	(15)
Winona	29	(19)
Mississippi		
Cleveland	98	(12)
Columbus	61	(15)
Greenville	102	(11)
Laurel	33	(18)
Meridian	88	(13)
Tupelo	78	(14)
Vicksburg	44	(17)
Missouri		
Cape Girardeau-Sikeston	126	(9)
Jefferson City	33	(18)
Poplar Bluff	151	(6)
Warrensburg	36	(18)
Montana		
Bozeman	140	(7)
Helena	91	(12)
Missoula	166	(5)
Nebraska		
Grand Island	98	(12)
Nevada		
Carson City	32	(18)
Elko	226	(0)
New Hampshire		
Concord	20	(19)
Keene	37	(18)
New Mexico		
Alamogordo	69	(15)
Carlsbad	142	(7)
Clovis	102	(11)
Farmington	182	(3)
Gallup	138	(8)
Hobbs	86	(13)
Roswell	173	(4)
New York		
Cortland	34	(18)
Gloversville	50	(16)
Ithaca	28	(19)

Kingston 19 (20)
Olean 73 (14)
Plattsburgh 32 (18)
Watertown 74 (14)

North Carolina
Albemarle 35 (18)
Eden 26 (19)
Havelock-New Bern 50 (16)
Henderson 36 (18)
Kinston 27 (19)
Lumberton 34 (18)
Roanoke Rapids 44 (17)
Sanford 36 (18)
Shelby 40 (17)
Statesville 27 (19)
Wilson 18 (20)

North Dakota
Minot 111 (10)

Ohio
Ashland 14 (20)
Athens 39 (18)
Chillicothe 46 (17)
Findlay-Fostoria-Tiffin 38 (18)
Fremont 32 (18)
Marion 39 (18)
Mount Vernon 25 (19)
New Philadelphia 26 (19)
Norwalk 36 (18)
Portsmouth 49 (17)
Sandusky 33 (18)
Sidney 34 (18)
Wooster 32 (18)
Zanesville 56 (16)

Oklahoma
Ardmore 72 (14)
Chickasha 42 (17)
Duncan 33 (18)
McAlester 91 (12)
Muskogee 50 (16)
Stillwater 64 (15)

Oregon
Albany-Corvallis 29 (19)
Bend 127 (9)
Coos Bay 115 (10)
Grants Pass 28 (19)
Klamath Falls 76 (14)
Pendleton 58 (16)
Roseburg 71 (14)

Pennsylvania
Chambersburg 21 (19)
New Castle 16 (20)
Pottsville 35 (18)

Rhode Island
Newport 22 (19)

South Carolina
Greenwood 41 (17)
Hilton Head Island 31 (18)

Tennessee
Cleveland 31 (18)
Columbia 44 (17)
Cookeville 76 (14)
Morristown 41 (17)
Tullahoma 58 (16)

Texas
Corsicana 46 (17)
Del Rio 150 (6)
Eagle Pass 154 (6)
Huntsville 56 (16)
Lufkin 83 (13)
Nacogdoches 70 (14)
Palestine 48 (17)
Paris 64 (15)

Utah		
Logan	79	(14)
St. George	117	(10)
Vermont		
Rutland	45	(17)
Virginia		
Blacksburg-Radford-Christiansburg	30	(18)
Harrisonburg	59	(16)
Martinsville	28	(19)
Staunton-Waynesboro	38	(18)
Winchester	41	(17)
Washington		
Aberdeen	47	(17)
Longview	44	(17)
Mount Vernon	27	(19)
Port Angeles	79	(14)
Walla Walla	45	(17)
Wenatchee	105	(11)
West Virginia		
Beckley	59	(16)
Clarksburg	74	(14)
Fairmont	70	(14)
Morgantown	72	(14)
Wisconsin		
Fond du Lac	38	(18)
Manitowoc	27	(19)
Stevens Point	34	(18)
Watertown	34	(18)
Wyoming		
Rock Springs	172	(4)

Arts Center Proximity

Residents of Torrington, Connecticut, find small-city life no barrier to metropolitan fine arts. Torrington lies just thirty-six miles west of Hartford, making a weekend concert or play an easy drive.

This category evaluates each small city's proximity to the cultural wealth of a metropolitan area. It does so by measuring the road mileage to the nearest major arts center. Thirty-two large U.S. cities are classified as regional arts centers, based in part on their scores in the *Places Rated Almanac.* Three Canadian centers have also been placed on the list.

Torrington finishes first, as Torrington residents have easy access to Hartford's theaters, symphony, art museums, opera, ballet, and summer arts festivals.

Anyone in Fairbanks, Alaska, seeking a major cultural fix by car would be forced to drive 2,121 miles through the Yukon and British Columbia to reach Vancouver, Canada, and even then he risks missing the first act.

Midwestern and Southern cities generally have the best access to arts centers. Small towns in the West have the worst.

Source: Derived from *Rand McNally Road Atlas,* Rand McNally & Company, Skokie, Illinois; and *Places Rated Almanac,* Richard Boyer and David Savageau, Prentice Hall, New York. Data are for 1997.

Scoring: Twenty points for road mileage of 40 miles or less; no points for 383 miles or more. The spacing is every eight miles.

Regional Arts Centers and Their Codes

Atlanta, Ga.	(ATL)
Baltimore, Md.	(BAL)
Boston, Mass.	(BOS)
Buffalo, N.Y.	(BUF)
Charlotte, N.C.	(CHA)
Chicago, Ill.	(CHI)
Cincinnati, Ohio	(CIN)
Cleveland, Ohio	(CLE)
Columbus, Ohio	(COL)
Dallas, Tex.	(DAL)
Dayton, Ohio	(DAY)
Denver, Colo.	(DEN)
Detroit, Mich.	(DET)
Hartford, Conn.	(HAR)
Honolulu, Hawaii	(HON)
Houston, Tex.	(HOU)
Indianapolis, Ind.	(IND)
Los Angeles, Calif.	(LA)
Milwaukee, Wisc.	(MIL)
Minneapolis, Minn.	(MIN)
Montreal, Canada	(MON)
New Haven, Conn.	(NH)
New Orleans, La.	(NO)
New York, N.Y.	(N.Y.)
Norfolk, Va.	(NOR)
Philadelphia, Pa.	(PHI)
Pittsburgh, Pa.	(PIT)
Rochester, N.Y.	(ROC)
Saint Louis, Mo.	(STL)
San Diego, Calif.	(SD)
San Francisco, Calif.	(SF)
Seattle, Wash.	(SEA)
Toronto, Canada	(TOR)
Vancouver, Canada	(VAN)
Washington, D.C.	(WAS)

Arts Center Proximity: Highs and Lows

	Road Mileage to Nearest Arts Center
Lowest	
1. Torrington, Conn.	36
2. Statesville, N.C.	38
3. Sidney, Ohio	39
4. Albemarle, N.C.	41
Richmond, Ind.	41
Shelby, N.C.	41
7. Mount Vernon, Ohio	42
8. Chillicothe, Ohio	46
Columbus, Ind.	46
Corsicana, Tex.	46
Median	
96. Nacogdoches, Tex.	139
97. Greenwood, S.C.	146
Highest	
184. Alamogordo, N.Mex.	546
185. Elko, Nev.	553
186. Logan, Utah	561
187. Helena, Mont.	593
188. Pocatello, Idaho	609
189. Twin Falls, Idaho	646
190. Idaho Falls, Idaho	658
191. Bozeman, Mont.	682
192. Key West, Fla.	821
193. Fairbanks, Alaska	2,121

Arts Center Proximity Area by Area

(Nearest regional arts center, road mileage to arts center, and rating points)

Micro median	143	
Alabama		
Albertville (ATL)	133	(14)
Auburn-Opelika (ATL)	105	(16)
Cullman (ATL)	137	(14)
Selma (ATL)	217	(10)
Talladega (ATL)	108	(16)
Alaska		
Fairbanks (VAN)	2,121	(0)
Arizona		
Prescott (LA)	385	(0)
Sierra Vista (SD)	488	(0)
Arkansas		
Blytheville (STL)	216	(10)
El Dorado (DAL)	268	(7)
Hot Springs (DAL)	287	(6)
Jonesboro (STL)	265	(7)
Russellville (DAL)	364	(2)
Searcy (DAL)	366	(2)
California		
Arcata-Eureka (SF)	282	(6)
El Centro-Calexico-Brawley (SD)	117	(15)
Hanford-Lemoore (LA)	182	(12)
Hollister (SF)	85	(17)
Connecticut		
Torrington (HAR)	36	(20)
Florida		
Key West (ATL)	821	(0)
Vero Beach (ATL)	531	(0)
Georgia		
Brunswick (ATL)	281	(6)
Dalton (ATL)	85	(17)
Dublin (ATL)	132	(14)
Gainesville (ATL)	50	(19)
Hinesville (ATL)	243	(8)
La Grange (ATL)	64	(18)
Milledgeville (ATL)	110	(16)
Rome (ATL)	65	(18)
Statesboro (ATL)	178	(12)
Thomasville (ATL)	270	(7)
Valdosta (ATL)	225	(9)
Waycross (ATL)	254	(8)
Idaho		
Coeur d'Alene (SEA)	313	(4)
Idaho Falls (DEN)	658	(0)
Pocatello (DEN)	609	(0)
Twin Falls (SEA)	646	(0)
Illinois		
Carbondale (STL)	99	(16)
Danville (IND)	91	(17)
Freeport (CHI)	115	(15)
Galesburg (CHI)	184	(12)
Mattoon-Charleston (STL)	123	(15)
Ottawa (CHI)	90	(17)
Quincy (STL)	159	(13)
Sterling (CHI)	122	(15)
Indiana		
Columbus (IND)	46	(19)
Marion (IND)	67	(18)
Michigan City-La Porte (CHI)	56	(19)
New Castle (IND)	48	(19)
Richmond (DAY)	41	(19)
Vincennes (IND)	121	(15)
Iowa		
Ames (MIN)	217	(10)
Burlington (CHI)	230	(9)
Clinton (CHI)	150	(13)

Mason City (MIN) 136 (14)
Muscatine (CHI) 202 (11)

Kansas
Hutchinson (DAL) 417 (0)
Manhattan (STL) 371 (1)
Salina (DEN) 404 (0)

Kentucky
Bowling Green (CIN) 213 (10)
Frankfort (CIN) 81 (17)
Madisonville (STL) 215 (10)
Paducah (STL) 170 (12)
Radcliff-Elizabethtown (CIN) 137 (14)

Louisiana
Hammond (NO) 48 (19)
New Iberia (NO) 131 (14)
Ruston (DAL) 256 (8)

Maine
Augusta-Waterville (BOS) 163 (13)
Biddeford-Saco (BOS) 88 (17)

Maryland
Salisbury (BAL) 106 (16)

Michigan
Marquette (MIL) 290 (6)
Mount Pleasant (DET) 149 (13)
Owosso (DET) 82 (17)
Traverse City (DET) 246 (8)

Minnesota
Faribault (MIN) 48 (19)
Mankato (MIN) 75 (18)
Red Wing (MIN) 60 (18)
Willmar (MIN) 96 (16)
Winona (MIN) 116 (15)

Mississippi
Cleveland (NO) 302 (5)
Columbus (ATL) 270 (7)
Greenville (NO) 290 (6)
Laurel (NO) 135 (14)
Meridian (NO) 184 (12)
Tupelo (ATL) 292 (6)
Vicksburg (NO) 207 (10)

Missouri
Cape Girardeau-Sikeston (STL) 123 (15)
Jefferson City (STL) 126 (15)
Poplar Bluff (STL) 138 (14)
Warrensburg (STL) 220 (10)

Montana
Bozeman (SEA) 682 (0)
Helena (SEA) 593 (0)
Missoula (SEA) 481 (0)

Nebraska
Grand Island (DEN) 407 (0)

Nevada
Carson City (SF) 234 (9)
Elko (SF) 553 (0)

New Hampshire
Concord (BOS) 78 (17)
Keene (BOS) 83 (17)

New Mexico
Alamogordo (DEN) 546 (0)
Carlsbad (DAL) 460 (0)
Clovis (DAL) 418 (0)
Farmington (DEN) 399 (0)
Gallup (DEN) 515 (0)
Hobbs (DAL) 391 (0)
Roswell (DAL) 487 (0)

New York

Cortland (ROC)	118	(15)
Gloversville (NH)	182	(12)
Ithaca (ROC)	92	(17)
Kingston (NY)	104	(16)
Olean (BUF)	73	(18)
Plattsburgh (MON)	67	(18)
Watertown (ROC)	153	(13)

North Carolina

Albemarle (CHA)	41	(19)
Eden (CHA)	138	(14)
Havelock-New Bern (NOR)	172	(12)
Henderson (NOR)	139	(14)
Kinston (NOR)	158	(13)
Lumberton (CHA)	125	(15)
Roanoke Rapids (NOR)	90	(17)
Sanford (CHA)	131	(14)
Shelby (CHA)	41	(19)
Statesville (CHA)	38	(20)
Wilson (NOR)	131	(14)

North Dakota

Minot (MIN)	495	(0)

Ohio

Ashland (CLE)	65	(18)
Athens (COL)	74	(18)
Chillicothe (COL)	46	(19)
Findlay-Fostoria-Tiffin (COL)	108	(16)
Fremont (CLE)	85	(17)
Marion (COL)	47	(19)
Mount Vernon (COL)	42	(19)
New Philadelphia (CLE)	78	(17)
Norwalk (CLE)	48	(19)
Portsmouth (COL)	99	(16)
Sandusky (CLE)	60	(18)
Sidney (DAY)	39	(20)
Wooster (CLE)	62	(18)
Zanesville (COL)	56	(19)

Oklahoma

Ardmore (DAL)	110	(16)
Chickasha (DAL)	202	(11)
Duncan (DAL)	162	(13)
McAlester (DAL)	175	(12)
Muskogee (DAL)	239	(8)
Stillwater (DAL)	258	(7)

Oregon

Albany-Corvallis (SEA)	247	(8)
Bend (SEA)	332	(3)
Coos Bay (SEA)	391	(0)
Grants Pass (SF)	396	(0)
Klamath Falls (SF)	362	(2)
Pendleton (SEA)	382	(1)
Roseburg (SEA)	350	(2)

Pennsylvania

Chambersburg (BAL)	76	(18)
New Castle (PIT)	56	(19)
Pottsville (PHI)	97	(16)

Rhode Island

Newport (BOS)	74	(18)

South Carolina

Greenwood (ATL)	146	(14)
Hilton Head Island (ATL)	285	(6)

Tennessee

Cleveland (ATL)	112	(16)
Columbia (ATL)	252	(8)
Cookeville (ATL)	206	(10)
Morristown (ATL)	265	(7)
Tullahoma (ATL)	193	(11)

Texas

Corsicana (DAL)	46	(19)
Del Rio (HOU)	347	(2)
Eagle Pass (HOU)	402	(0)
Huntsville (HOU)	72	(18)
Lufkin (HOU)	120	(15)

Nacogdoches (HOU)	139	(14)
Palestine (DAL)	112	(16)
Paris (DAL)	106	(16)

Utah

Logan (DEN)	561	(0)
St. George (LA)	365	(1)

Vermont

Rutland (BOS)	171	(12)

Virginia

Blacksburg-Radford-Christiansburg (WAS)	257	(7)
Harrisonburg (WAS)	126	(15)
Martinsville (NOR)	221	(9)
Staunton-Waynesboro (WAS)	152	(13)
Winchester (WAS)	71	(18)

Washington

Aberdeen (SEA)	108	(16)
Longview (SEA)	125	(15)
Mount Vernon (SEA)	63	(18)
Port Angeles (SEA)	87	(17)
Walla Walla (SEA)	274	(7)
Wenatchee (SEA)	147	(14)

West Virginia

Beckley (COL)	243	(8)
Clarksburg (PIT)	111	(16)
Fairmont (PIT)	92	(17)
Morgantown (PIT)	77	(17)

Wisconsin

Fond du Lac (MIL)	63	(18)
Manitowoc (MIL)	82	(17)
Stevens Point (MIL)	154	(13)
Watertown (MIL)	57	(19)

Wyoming

Rock Springs (DEN)	360	(2)

Retail Center Proximity

Okay, admit it. Sometimes you just have to shop *big*. To do that, you may have to go beyond your small city and hit a major retail hub.

This category rates each area on its proximity to a large city that provides truly major shopping. The *Rand McNally Commercial Atlas* divides the country into forty-seven major trading areas, and the key cities of these regions are listed here as retail centers.

Ames, Iowa, is the micro closest to a retail hub: Des Moines is just twenty-eight miles south of Ames on Interstate 35. If you're skeptical about Des Moines being a shopping paradise, consider just a sample of what it has to offer: 26 department stores, 244 clothing and accessory stores, 40 jewelry stores, 69 home electronics and computer stores, and 23 book stores. In all, Des Moines has a total of 2,479 retail establishments.

Fairbanks, Alaska, doesn't do so well in this section. Fairbanks is in Seattle's retail region. The road distance between the two cities is 2,265 miles.

Southern cities generally provide the best access to metropolitan shopping. The longest drives to retail hubs are in the West.

Source: Derived from *Rand McNally Commercial Atlas* and *Rand McNally Road Atlas,* Rand McNally & Company, Skokie, Illinois. Data are for 1997.

Scoring: Twenty points for road mileage of 35 miles or less; no points for 264 miles or more. The spacing is every 12 miles.

Regional Retail Centers and Their Codes

Atlanta, Ga.	(ATL)
Birmingham, Ala.	(BIR)
Boston, Mass.	(BOS)
Buffalo, N.Y.	(BUF)
Charlotte, N.C.	(CHA)
Chicago, Ill.	(CHI)
Cincinnati, Ohio	(CIN)
Cleveland, Ohio	(CLE)
Columbus, Ohio	(COL)
Dallas, Tex.	(DAL)
Denver, Colo.	(DEN)
Des Moines, Iowa	(DM)
Detroit, Mich.	(DET)
El Paso, Tex.	(ELP)
Honolulu, Hawaii	(HON)
Houston, Tex.	(HOU)
Indianapolis, Ind.	(IND)
Jacksonville, Fla.	(JAC)
Kansas City, Mo.	(KC)
Knoxville, Tenn.	(KNO)
Little Rock, Ark.	(LR)
Los Angeles, Calif.	(LA)
Louisville, Ky.	(LOU)
Memphis, Tenn.	(MEM)
Miami, Fla.	(MIA)
Milwaukee, Wisc.	(MIL)
Minneapolis, Minn.	(MIN)
Nashville, Tenn.	(NAS)
New Orleans, La.	(NO)
New York, N.Y.	(NY)
Oklahoma City, Okla.	(OKC)
Omaha, Nebr.	(OMA)
Philadelphia, Pa.	(PHI)
Phoenix, Ariz.	(PHO)
Pittsburgh, Pa.	(PIT)
Portland, Ore.	(POR)
Richmond, Va.	(RIC)
Saint Louis, Mo.	(STL)
Salt Lake City, Utah	(SLC)
San Antonio, Tex.	(SA)
San Francisco, Calif.	(SF)
Seattle, Wash.	(SEA)
Spokane, Wash.	(SPO)
Tampa, Fla.	(TAM)
Tulsa, Okla.	(TUL)
Washington, D.C.	(WAS)
Wichita, Kans.	(WIC)

Retail Center Proximity: Highs and Lows

	Road Mileage to Nearest Retail Center
Lowest	
1. Ames, Iowa	28
2. Coeur d'Alene, Idaho	33
3. Radcliff-Elizabethtown, Ky.	36
4. Statesville, N.C.	38
5. Shelby, N.C.	40
6. Morristown, Tenn.	41
7. Albemarle, N.C.	42
Chickasha, Okla.	42
9. Columbia, Tenn.	44
10. Columbus, Ind.	46
Median	
96. Palestine, Tex.	112
97. Manhattan, Kans.	114
Highest	
184. Helena, Mont.	313
185. Plattsburgh, N.Y.	319
186. Rock Springs, Wyo.	360
187. Gallup, N.Mex.	380
188. Hobbs, N.Mex.	391
189. Bozeman, Mont.	402
190. Clovis, N.Mex.	418
191. Farmington, N.Mex.	444
192. Minot, N.Dak.	495
193. Fairbanks, Alaska	2,265

Retail Center Proximity Area by Area

(Nearest regional retail center, road mileage to retail center, and rating points)

Micro median	113	
Alabama		
Albertville (BIR)	65	(17)
Auburn-Opelika (ATL)	105	(14)
Cullman (BIR)	51	(18)
Selma (BIR)	86	(15)
Talladega (BIR)	55	(18)
Alaska		
Fairbanks (SEA)	2,265	(0)
Arizona		
Prescott (PHO)	96	(14)
Sierra Vista (PHO)	188	(7)
Arkansas		
Blytheville (MEM)	68	(17)
El Dorado (LR)	116	(13)
Hot Springs (LR)	55	(18)
Jonesboro (LR)	126	(12)
Russellville (LR)	76	(16)
Searcy (LR)	48	(18)
California		
Arcata-Eureka (SF)	282	(0)
El Centro-Calexico-Brawley (LA)	227	(4)
Hanford-Lemoore (SF)	212	(5)
Hollister (SF)	88	(15)
Connecticut		
Torrington (NY)	103	(14)
Florida		
Key West (MIA)	161	(9)
Vero Beach (MIA)	138	(11)
Georgia		
Brunswick (JAC)	71	(17)
Dalton (ATL)	85	(15)
Dublin (ATL)	137	(11)
Gainesville (ATL)	50	(18)
Hinesville (ATL)	243	(2)
La Grange (ATL)	64	(17)
Milledgeville (ATL)	110	(13)
Rome (ATL)	65	(17)
Statesboro (ATL)	198	(6)
Thomasville (ATL)	162	(9)
Valdosta (JAC)	121	(12)
Waycross (JAC)	79	(16)
Idaho		
Coeur d'Alene (SPO)	33	(20)
Idaho Falls (SLC)	211	(5)
Pocatello (SLC)	162	(9)
Twin Falls (SLC)	209	(5)
Illinois		
Carbondale (STL)	99	(14)
Danville (CHI)	137	(11)
Freeport (CHI)	115	(13)
Galesburg (CHI)	184	(7)
Mattoon-Charleston (CHI)	184	(7)
Ottawa (CHI)	90	(15)
Quincy (STL)	159	(9)
Sterling (DM)	223	(4)
Indiana		
Columbus (IND)	46	(19)
Marion (IND)	67	(17)
Michigan City-La Porte (CHI)	56	(18)
New Castle (IND)	48	(18)
Richmond (IND)	73	(16)
Vincennes (IND)	121	(12)
Iowa		
Ames (DM)	28	(20)
Burlington (DM)	162	(9)

Clinton (DM)	199	(6)
Mason City (DM)	120	(12)
Muscatine (DM)	148	(10)

Kansas

Hutchinson (WIC)	52	(18)
Manhattan (KC)	114	(13)
Salina (WIC)	90	(15)

Kentucky

Bowling Green (LOU)	112	(13)
Frankfort (LOU)	52	(18)
Madisonville (LOU)	158	(9)
Paducah (LOU)	220	(4)
Radcliff-Elizabethtown (LOU)	36	(19)

Louisiana

Hammond (NO)	48	(18)
New Iberia (NO)	131	(12)
Ruston (NO)	289	(0)

Maine

Augusta-Waterville (BOS)	163	(9)
Biddeford-Saco (BOS)	88	(15)

Maryland

Salisbury (WAS)	115	(13)

Michigan

Marquette (MIL)	290	(0)
Mount Pleasant (DET)	149	(10)
Owosso (DET)	82	(16)
Traverse City (DET)	246	(2)

Minnesota

Faribault (MIN)	48	(18)
Mankato (MIN)	75	(16)
Red Wing (MIN)	60	(17)
Willmar (MIN)	96	(14)
Winona (MIL)	225	(4)

Mississippi

Cleveland (MEM)	110	(13)
Columbus (MEM)	168	(8)
Greenville (MEM)	147	(10)
Laurel (NO)	135	(11)
Meridian (MEM)	230	(3)
Tupelo (MEM)	107	(14)
Vicksburg (MEM)	254	(1)

Missouri

Cape Girardeau-Sikeston (STL)	129	(12)
Jefferson City (STL)	133	(11)
Poplar Bluff (STL)	151	(10)
Warrensburg (KC)	55	(18)

Montana

Bozeman (SPO)	402	(0)
Helena (SPO)	313	(0)
Missoula (SPO)	201	(6)

Nebraska

Grand Island (OMA)	136	(11)

Nevada

Carson City (SF)	234	(3)
Elko (SLC)	236	(3)

New Hampshire

Concord (BOS)	78	(16)
Keene (BOS)	83	(16)

New Mexico

Alamogordo (ELP)	112	(13)
Carlsbad (ELP)	163	(9)
Clovis (DAL)	418	(0)
Farmington (ELP)	444	(0)
Gallup (ELP)	380	(0)
Hobbs (DAL)	391	(0)
Roswell (ELP)	232	(3)

New York

Cortland (BUF)	185	(7)
Gloversville (NY)	206	(5)
Ithaca (BUF)	142	(11)
Kingston (NY)	107	(14)
Olean (BUF)	79	(16)
Plattsburgh (NY)	319	(0)
Watertown (BUF)	226	(4)

North Carolina

Albemarle (CHA)	42	(19)
Eden (CHA)	124	(12)
Havelock-New Bern (CHA)	265	(0)
Henderson (CHA)	178	(8)
Kinston (CHA)	214	(5)
Lumberton (CHA)	126	(12)
Roanoke Rapids (CHA)	228	(3)
Sanford (CHA)	114	(13)
Shelby (CHA)	40	(19)
Statesville (CHA)	38	(19)
Wilson (CHA)	184	(7)

North Dakota

Minot (MIN)	495	(0)

Ohio

Ashland (CLE)	65	(17)
Athens (COL)	74	(16)
Chillicothe (COL)	46	(19)
Findlay-Fostoria-Tiffin (DET)	112	(13)
Fremont (DET)	98	(14)
Marion (COL)	47	(19)
Mount Vernon (COL)	67	(17)
New Philadelphia (CLE)	83	(16)
Norwalk (CLE)	52	(18)
Portsmouth (CIN)	119	(13)
Sandusky (CLE)	60	(17)
Sidney (CIN)	92	(15)
Wooster (CLE)	62	(17)
Zanesville (COL)	56	(18)

Oklahoma

Ardmore (OKC)	97	(14)
Chickasha (OKC)	42	(19)
Duncan (OKC)	86	(15)
McAlester (OKC)	128	(12)
Muskogee (TUL)	50	(18)
Stillwater (OKC)	64	(17)

Oregon

Albany-Corvallis (POR)	75	(16)
Bend (POR)	160	(9)
Coos Bay (POR)	217	(4)
Grants Pass (POR)	246	(2)
Klamath Falls (POR)	280	(0)
Pendleton (POR)	208	(5)
Roseburg (POR)	178	(8)

Pennsylvania

Chambersburg (WAS)	93	(15)
New Castle (PIT)	56	(18)
Pottsville (PHI)	97	(14)

Rhode Island

Newport (BOS)	74	(16)

South Carolina

Greenwood (CHA)	116	(13)
Hilton Head Island (ATL)	285	(0)

Tennessee

Cleveland (ATL)	112	(13)
Columbia (NAS)	44	(19)
Cookeville (NAS)	76	(16)
Morristown (KNO)	41	(19)
Tullahoma (NAS)	72	(16)

Texas

Corsicana (DAL)	54	(18)
Del Rio (SA)	150	(10)
Eagle Pass (SA)	205	(5)
Huntsville (HOU)	72	(16)
Lufkin (HOU)	120	(12)

Nacogdoches (HOU)	139	(11)
Palestine (DAL)	112	(13)
Paris (DAL)	106	(14)

Utah

Logan (SLC)	79	(16)
St. George (SLC)	296	(0)

Vermont

Rutland (NY)	257	(1)

Virginia

Blacksburg-Radford-Christiansburg (RIC)	200	(6)
Harrisonburg (WAS)	128	(12)
Martinsville (RIC)	173	(8)
Staunton-Waynesboro (RIC)	103	(14)
Winchester (WAS)	76	(16)

Washington

Aberdeen (SEA)	108	(13)
Longview (POR)	52	(18)
Mount Vernon (SEA)	63	(17)
Port Angeles (SEA)	87	(15)
Walla Walla (SPO)	160	(9)
Wenatchee (SEA)	147	(10)

West Virginia

Beckley (CIN)	272	(0)
Clarksburg (PIT)	111	(13)
Fairmont (PIT)	92	(15)
Morgantown (PIT)	77	(16)

Wisconsin

Fond du Lac (MIL)	63	(17)
Manitowoc (MIL)	82	(16)
Stevens Point (MIL)	154	(10)
Watertown (MIL)	54	(18)

Wyoming

Rock Springs (DEN)	360	(0)

Sports Center Proximity

Green Bay, Wisconsin, is often cited as proof that a small city can support a major-league sports team. Green Bay's football team, the Packers, are wildly popular—just witness a stadium full of fans wearing large wedges of fake cheese on their heads. But Green Bay is a "small city" only relative to the large metros that host other major-league sports teams. More than 210,000 people live in Green Bay, designating the city as an official metropolitan area. No micropolitan area has a big-league professional franchise.

This category measures the distance from each micropolitan to the closest of thirty-three regional sports centers. Sports centers are here considered to be cities with teams in at least two of the following leagues: Major League Baseball (National and American Leagues), the National Football League, the National Basketball Association, the National Hockey League, and Major League Soccer.

Statesville, North Carolina, is just thirty-seven miles from Charlotte, home to both major-league basketball and football. Shelby and Albemarle, North Carolina, also share Charlotte as their sports center, being just several miles farther away than Statesville. Fairbanks, Alaska, on the other hand, is a 2,265 mile drive from Seattle, its closest sports center.

Southern and Midwestern small cities are generally the closest to a sports center. Western small cities are the farthest.

Source: Derived from *Rand McNally Road Atlas,* Rand McNally & Company, Skokie, Illinois. Data are for 1997.

Scoring: Twenty points for road mileage of 38 miles or less; no points for more than 380 miles. The spacing is every 18 miles.

Regional Sports Centers and Their Codes

Atlanta, Ga.	(ATL)
Baltimore, Md.	(BAL)
Boston, Mass.	(BOS)
Buffalo, N.Y.	(BUF)
Charlotte, N.C.	(CHA)
Chicago, Ill.	(CHI)
Cincinnati, Ohio	(CIN)
Cleveland, Ohio	(CLE)
Dallas, Tex.	(DAL)
Denver, Colo.	(DEN)
Detroit, Mich.	(DET)
Houston, Tex.	(HOU)
Indianapolis, Ind.	(IND)
Kansas City, Mo.	(KC)
Los Angeles, Calif.	(LA)
Miami, Fla.	(MIA)
Milwaukee, Wisc.	(MIL)
Minneapolis, Minn.	(MIN)
Montreal, Canada	(MON)
East Rutherford, N.J.	(NJ)
New York, N.Y.	(NY)
Philadelphia, Pa.	(PHI)
Phoenix, Ariz.	(PHO)
Pittsburgh, Pa.	(PIT)
Saint Louis, Mo.	(STL)
San Diego, Calif.	(SD)
San Francisco-Oakland, Calif.	(SF)
San Jose, Calif.	(SJ)
Seattle, Wash.	(SEA)
Tampa Bay, Fla.	(TAM)
Toronto, Canada	(TOR)
Vancouver, Canada	(VAN)
Washington, D.C.	(WAS)

Sports Center Proximity: Highs and Lows

	Road Mileage to Nearest Sports Center
Lowest	
1. Statesville, N.C.	38
2. Shelby, N.C.	40
3. Albemarle, N.C.	41
4. Hollister, Calif.	44
5. Columbus, Ind.	46
Corsicana, Tex.	46
7. Warrensburg, Mo.	47
8. Faribault, Minn.	48
New Castle, Ind.	48
Norwalk, Ohio	48
Median	
96. Cullman, Ala.	151
97. Athens, Ohio	152
Highest	
184. Roswell, N.Mex.	487
185. Minot, N.Dak.	495
186. Logan, Utah	561
187. Elko, Nev.	582
188. Helena, Mont.	593
189. Pocatello, Idaho	609
190. Twin Falls, Idaho	646
191. Idaho Falls, Idaho	658
192. Bozeman, Mont.	682
193. Fairbanks, Alaska	2,265

Sports Center Proximity Area by Area

(Nearest regional sports center, road mileage to sports center, and rating points)

Micro median	152	
Alabama		
Albertville (ATL)	141	(14)
Auburn-Opelika (ATL)	105	(16)
Cullman (ATL)	151	(13)
Selma (ATL)	217	(10)
Talladega (ATL)	108	(16)
Alaska		
Fairbanks (SEA)	2,265	(0)
Arizona		
Prescott (PHO)	96	(16)
Sierra Vista (PHO)	188	(11)
Arkansas		
Blytheville (STL)	216	(10)
El Dorado (DAL)	268	(7)
Hot Springs (DAL)	287	(6)
Jonesboro (STL)	265	(7)
Russellville (KC)	347	(2)
Searcy (STL)	355	(2)
California		
Arcata-Eureka (SF)	282	(6)
El Centro-Calexico-Brawley (SD)	117	(15)
Hanford-Lemoore (LA)	182	(12)
Hollister (SJ)	44	(19)
Connecticut		
Torrington (NY)	103	(16)
Florida		
Key West (MIA)	161	(13)
Vero Beach (MIA)	138	(14)
Georgia		
Brunswick (ATL)	281	(6)
Dalton (ATL)	49	(19)
Dublin (ATL)	137	(14)
Gainesville (ATL)	51	(19)
Hinesville (ATL)	243	(8)
La Grange (ATL)	64	(18)
Milledgeville (ATL)	110	(16)
Rome (ATL)	65	(18)
Statesboro (ATL)	209	(10)
Thomasville (ATL)	266	(7)
Valdosta (ATL)	225	(9)
Waycross (ATL)	253	(8)
Idaho		
Coeur d'Alene (SEA)	313	(4)
Idaho Falls (DEN)	658	(0)
Pocatello (DEN)	609	(0)
Twin Falls (SEA)	646	(0)
Illinois		
Carbondale (STL)	99	(16)
Danville (IND)	91	(17)
Freeport (CHI)	68	(18)
Galesburg (CHI)	184	(11)
Mattoon-Charleston (STL)	123	(15)
Ottawa (CHI)	90	(17)
Quincy (STL)	159	(13)
Sterling (CHI)	122	(15)
Indiana		
Columbus (IND)	46	(19)
Marion (IND)	67	(18)
Michigan City-La Porte (CHI)	56	(19)
New Castle (IND)	48	(19)
Richmond (CIN)	62	(18)
Vincennes (IND)	121	(15)
Iowa		
Ames (MIN)	217	(10)
Burlington (CHI)	230	(9)

Clinton (CHI)	150	(13)
Mason City (MIN)	136	(14)
Muscatine (CHI)	202	(10)

Kansas

Hutchinson (KC)	208	(10)
Manhattan (KC)	114	(15)
Salina (KC)	171	(12)

Kentucky

Bowling Green (CIN)	213	(10)
Frankfort (CIN)	81	(17)
Madisonville (STL)	215	(10)
Paducah (STL)	170	(12)
Radcliff-Elizabethtown (CIN)	137	(14)

Louisiana

Hammond (HOU)	294	(5)
New Iberia (HOU)	223	(9)
Ruston (DAL)	256	(7)

Maine

Augusta-Waterville (BOS)	163	(13)
Biddeford-Saco (BOS)	88	(17)

Maryland

Salisbury (BAL)	110	

Michigan

Marquette (MIL)	290	(6)
Mount Pleasant (DET)	149	(13)
Owosso (DET)	82	(17)
Traverse City (DET)	246	(8)

Minnesota

Faribault (MIN)	48	(19)
Mankato (MIN)	75	(16)
Red Wing (MIN)	60	(18)
Willmar (MIN)	91	(17)
Winona (MIN)	116	(15)

Mississippi

Cleveland (DAL)	417	(0)
Columbus (ATL)	270	(7)
Greenville (DAL)	380	(0)
Laurel (ATL)	363	(1)
Meridian (ATL)	302	(5)
Tupelo (ATL)	292	(5)
Vicksburg (DAL)	363	(1)

Missouri

Cape Girardeau-Sikeston (STL)	128	(15)
Jefferson City (STL)	126	(15)
Poplar Bluff (STL)	195	(11)
Warrensburg (KC)	47	(19)

Montana

Bozeman (SEA)	682	(0)
Helena (SEA)	593	(0)
Missoula (SEA)	481	(0)

Nebraska

Grand Island (KC)	335	(3)

Nevada

Carson City (SF)	234	(9)
Elko (SF)	582	(0)

New Hampshire

Concord (BOS)	78	(17)
Keene (BOS)	83	(17)

New Mexico

Alamogordo (PHO)	444	(0)
Carlsbad (DAL)	460	(0)
Clovis (DAL)	418	(0)
Farmington (DEN)	399	(0)
Gallup (PHO)	325	(4)
Hobbs (DAL)	391	(0)
Roswell (DAL)	487	(0)

New York

Cortland (BUF)	185	(11)
Gloversville (NY)	206	(10)
Ithaca (BUF)	142	(14)
Kingston (NY)	107	(16)
Olean (BUF)	79	(17)
Plattsburgh (MON)	68	(18)
Watertown (MON)	177	(12)

North Carolina

Albemarle (CHA)	41	(19)
Eden (CHA)	137	(14)
Havelock-New Bern (CHA)	265	(7)
Henderson (CHA)	178	(12)
Kinston (CHA)	223	(9)
Lumberton (CHA)	122	(15)
Roanoke Rapids (WAS)	184	(11)
Sanford (CHA)	133	(14)
Shelby (CHA)	40	(19)
Statesville (CHA)	38	(20)
Wilson (CHA)	210	(10)

North Dakota

Minot (MIN)	495	(0)

Ohio

Ashland (CLE)	65	(18)
Athens (CIN)	152	(13)
Chillicothe (CIN)	94	(16)
Findlay-Fostoria-Tiffin (DET)	114	(15)
Fremont (CLE)	85	(17)
Marion (CLE)	115	(15)
Mount Vernon (CLE)	184	(11)
New Philadelphia (CLE)	83	(17)
Norwalk (CLE)	48	(19)
Portsmouth (CIN)	119	(15)
Sandusky (CLE)	65	(18)
Sidney (CIN)	92	(17)
Wooster (CLE)	62	(18)
Zanesville (PIT)	130	(14)

Oklahoma

Ardmore (DAL)	110	(16)
Chickasha (DAL)	202	(10)
Duncan (DAL)	162	(13)
McAlester (DAL)	175	(12)
Muskogee (DAL)	239	(8)
Stillwater (DAL)	258	(7)

Oregon

Albany-Corvallis (POR)	87	(17)
Bend (POR)	162	(13)
Coos Bay (POR)	117	(15)
Grants Pass (POR)	246	(8)
Klamath Falls (POR)	280	(6)
Pendleton (POR)	208	(10)
Roseburg (POR)	176	(12)

Pennsylvania

Chambersburg (BAL)	69	(18)
New Castle (PIT)	56	(19)
Pottsville (PHI)	97	(16)

Rhode Island

Newport (BOS)	74	(18)

South Carolina

Greenwood (CHA)	120	(15)
Hilton Head Island (CHA)	253	(8)

Tennessee

Cleveland (ATL)	112	(15)
Columbia (ATL)	252	(8)
Cookeville (ATL)	206	(10)
Morristown (ATL)	265	(7)
Tullahoma (ATL)	193	(11)

Texas

Corsicana (DAL)	46	(19)
Del Rio (HOU)	347	(2)
Eagle Pass (HOU)	402	(0)
Huntsville (HOU)	72	(18)
Lufkin (HOU)	120	(15)

Nacogdoches (HOU)	139	(14)
Palestine (DAL)	112	(15)
Paris (DAL)	106	(16)

Utah

Logan (DEN)	561	(0)
St. George (LA)	365	(1)

Vermont

Rutland (BOS)	171	(12)

Virginia

Blacksburg-Radford-Christiansburg (WAS)	257	(7)
Harrisonburg (WAS)	128	(15)
Martinsville (CHA)	167	(12)
Staunton-Waynesboro (WAS)	152	(13)
Winchester (WAS)	76	(17)

Washington

Aberdeen (SEA)	106	(16)
Longview (POR)	49	(19)
Mount Vernon (SEA)	63	(19)
Port Angeles (SEA)	87	(17)
Walla Walla (SEA)	274	(6)
Wenatchee (SEA)	147	(13)

West Virginia

Beckley (PIT)	247	(8)
Clarksburg (PIT)	111	(15)
Fairmont (PIT)	92	(17)
Morgantown (PIT)	77	(17)

Wisconsin

Fond du Lac (MIL)	63	(18)
Manitowoc (MIL)	82	(17)
Stevens Point (MIL)	154	(13)
Watertown (MIL)	57	(18)

Wyoming

Rock Springs (DEN)	360	(2)

Television Market

Perhaps nothing ties a small city more tightly to a large community than television. Signals from distant stations expose small-town residents to a daily dose of big-city news, commercials, and sporting events. An avid television viewer may know more about happenings in a far-off metropolis than in his or her own town.

This category ranks each area according to the relative size of the larger regional television market of which it is a part. Nielsen Media Research divides the country into 211 designated market areas (DMAs), and lists them according to the number of television households in each. New York, New York, is the number one DMA, with nearly 6.7 million viewing households. It is generally true that the higher the rank, the greater the choice of stations and the better the quality of local programming.

Kingston, New York, is on the northern edge of the New York City DMA, and thus ranks first in the category. Kingston does not receive all the television channels out of New York, but chooses from many of the stations available to metro residents.

Contrary to what many might expect, Fairbanks, Alaska, does not finish last in this category. It finishes second-to-last. Helena, Montana, has the lowest rating among small cities. Helena is considered to be its own DMA, ranked 208th nationwide.

Source: Broadcasting and Cable Yearbook (New Providence, N.J.: R. R. Bowker, 1996). Data are for 1996.

Scoring: Twenty points for a ranking of one through ten; no points for 201 or higher. The spacing is every ten ranking places.

Television Market: Highs and Lows

		Market Rank
Highest		
1.	Kingston, N.Y.	1
2.	Michigan City-La Porte, Ind.	3
	Ottawa, Ill.	3
4.	Concord, N.H.	6
	Keene, N.H.	6
6.	Winchester, Va.	7
7.	Corsicana, Tex.	8
	Palestine, Tex.	8
	Paris, Tex.	8
10.	Gainesville, Ga.	10
	La Grange, Ga.	10
	Rome, Ga.	10
Median		
96.	Blacksburg-Radford-Christiansburg, Va.	67
97.	Martinsville, Va.	67
Lowest		
184.	Meridian, Miss.	182
185.	Mankato, Minn.	186
186.	Arcata-Eureka, Calif.	188
187.	Bozeman, Mont.	191
188.	Twin Falls, Idaho	195
189.	Harrisonburg, Va.	201
190.	Bend, Ore.	203
191.	Zanesville, Ohio	204
192.	Fairbanks, Alaska	205
193.	Helena, Mont.	208

Television Market Area by Area

(National television market rank and rating points)

Area	Rank	(Points)
Micro median	67	
Alabama		
Albertville	86	(12)
Auburn-Opelika	125	(8)
Cullman	51	(15)
Selma	113	(9)
Talladega	51	(15)
Alaska		
Fairbanks	205	(0)
Arizona		
Prescott	17	(19)
Sierra Vista	80	(13)
Arkansas		
Blytheville	42	(16)
El Dorado	133	(7)
Hot Springs	58	(15)
Jonesboro	180	(3)
Russellville	58	(15)
Searcy	58	(15)
California		
Arcata-Eureka	188	(2)
El Centro-Calexico-Brawley	176	(3)
Hanford-Lemoore	56	(15)
Hollister	122	(8)
Connecticut		
Torrington	26	(18)
Florida		
Key West	16	(19)
Vero Beach	45	(16)
Georgia		
Brunswick	55	(15)
Dalton	82	(12)
Dublin	123	(8)
Gainesville	10	(20)
Hinesville	100	(11)
La Grange	10	(20)
Milledgeville	123	(8)
Rome	10	(20)
Statesboro	100	(11)
Thomasville	116	(9)
Valdosta	116	(9)
Waycross	111	(9)
Idaho		
Coeur d'Alene	74	(13)
Idaho Falls	168	(4)
Pocatello	168	(4)
Twin Falls	195	(1)
Illinois		
Carbondale	78	(13)
Danville	81	(12)
Freeport	136	(7)
Galesburg	88	(12)
Mattoon-Charleston	81	(12)
Ottawa	3	(20)
Quincy	158	(5)
Sterling	88	(12)
Indiana		
Columbus	25	(18)
Marion	25	(18)
Michigan City-La Porte	3	(20)
New Castle	25	(18)
Richmond	53	(15)
Vincennes	142	(6)
Iowa		
Ames	72	(13)
Burlington	88	(12)
Clinton	88	(12)

Mason City	147	(6)
Muscatine	88	(12)
Kansas		
Hutchinson	63	(14)
Manhattan	140	(7)
Salina	63	(14)
Kentucky		
Bowling Green	181	(2)
Frankfort	68	(14)
Madisonville	94	(11)
Paducah	78	(13)
Radcliff-Elizabethtown	50	(16)
Louisiana		
Hammond	41	(16)
New Iberia	121	(8)
Ruston	133	(7)
Maine		
Augusta-Waterville	79	(13)
Biddeford-Saco	79	(13)
Maryland		
Salisbury	163	(4)
Michigan		
Marquette	175	(3)
Mount Pleasant	60	(15)
Owosso	60	(15)
Traverse City	117	(9)
Minnesota		
Faribault	14	(19)
Mankato	186	(2)
Red Wing	14	(19)
Willmar	14	(19)
Winona	135	(7)
Mississippi		
Cleveland	178	(3)
Columbus	129	(8)
Greenville	178	(3)
Laurel	165	(4)
Meridian	182	(2)
Tupelo	129	(8)
Vicksburg	91	(11)
Missouri		
Cape Girardeau-Sikeston	78	(13)
Jefferson City	146	(6)
Poplar Bluff	78	(13)
Warrensburg	32	(17)
Montana		
Bozeman	191	(1)
Helena	208	(0)
Missoula	174	(3)
Nebraska		
Grand Island	101	(10)
Nevada		
Carson City	120	(9)
Elko	36	(17)
New Hampshire		
Concord	6	(20)
Keene	6	(20)
New Mexico		
Alamogordo	48	(16)
Carlsbad	48	(16)
Clovis	126	(8)
Farmington	48	(16)
Gallup	48	(16)
Hobbs	48	(16)
Roswell	48	(16)
New York		
Cortland	69	(14)
Gloversville	52	(15)
Ithaca	69	(14)

Kingston	1	(20)
Olean	39	(17)
Plattsburgh	92	(13)
Watertown	171	(3)

North Carolina

Albemarle	28	(18)
Eden	47	(16)
Havelock-New Bern	104	(10)
Henderson	30	(18)
Kinston	104	(10)
Lumberton	114	(9)
Roanoke Rapids	30	(18)
Sanford	30	(18)
Shelby	28	(18)
Statesville	28	(18)
Wilson	30	(18)

North Dakota

Minot	153	(5)

Ohio

Ashland	13	(19)
Athens	57	(15)
Chillicothe	34	(17)
Findlay-Fostoria-Tiffin	65	(14)
Fremont	65	(14)
Marion	34	(17)
Mount Vernon	34	(17)
New Philadelphia	13	(19)
Norwalk	13	(19)
Portsmouth	57	(15)
Sandusky	13	(19)
Sidney	53	(15)
Wooster	13	(19)
Zanesville	204	(0)

Oklahoma

Ardmore	160	(5)
Chickasha	43	(16)
Duncan	139	(7)
McAlester	59	(15)
Muskogee	59	(15)
Stillwater	43	(16)

Oregon

Albany-Corvallis	119	(9)
Bend	203	(0)
Coos Bay	119	(9)
Grants Pass	144	(6)
Klamath Falls	144	(6)
Pendleton	124	(8)
Roseburg	119	(9)

Pennsylvania

Chambersburg	44	(16)
New Castle	19	(19)
Pottsville	49	(16)

Rhode Island

Newport	46	(16)

South Carolina

Greenwood	35	(17)
Hilton Head Island	100	(11)

Tennessee

Cleveland	82	(12)
Columbia	33	(17)
Cookeville	33	(17)
Morristown	62	(14)
Tullahoma	33	(17)

Texas

Corsicana	8	(20)
Del Rio	37	(17)
Eagle Pass	37	(17)
Huntsville	11	(19)
Lufkin	110	(10)
Nacogdoches	110	(10)
Palestine	8	(20)
Paris	8	(20)

Utah		
Logan	36	(17)
St. George	36	(17)
Vermont		
Rutland	92	(11)
Virginia		
Blacksburg-Radford-Christiansburg	67	(14)
Harrisonburg	201	(0)
Martinsville	67	(14)
Staunton-Waynesboro	54	(15)
Winchester	7	(20)
Washington		
Aberdeen	12	(19)
Longview	24	(18)
Mount Vernon	12	(19)
Port Angeles	12	(19)
Walla Walla	124	(8)
Wenatchee	12	(19)
West Virginia		
Beckley	148	(6)
Clarksburg	162	(4)
Fairmont	162	(4)
Morgantown	19	(19)
Wisconsin		
Fond du Lac	71	(13)
Manitowoc	71	(13)
Stevens Point	131	(7)
Watertown	31	(17)
Wyoming		
Rock Springs	36	(17)

The Results

Well, it was close, but Statesville, North Carolina, beat out Fairbanks, Alaska, in overall urban proximity. Statesville finished with 96 points, Fairbanks with 0.

Statesville is well situated to enjoy the metropolitan benefits of Charlotte, thirty-eight miles to the southeast, and of Winston-Salem, forty-one miles to the northeast. The small city lies several miles from the intersection of Interstate 77 and Interstate 40, providing easy access to a total of four cities in the two metro areas.

Ten years ago Statesville would not have rated so highly in its easy access to urban riches, but the small city has benefited from the rapid growth of nearby metros. Charlotte's population grew at twice the national rate in the first half of the 1990s and the economic boom has attracted more metropolitan features to the area. Prior to Charlotte's expansion, the nearest arts and sports center to Statesville was 281 miles away in Atlanta. That distance fell to just thirty-eight miles when Charlotte acquired a professional basketball and football team and became considered a regional arts center. Charlotte's population growth moved its television market rating up from thirty-first in the nation to twenty-eighth.

But the roads from Statesville to Charlotte and Winston-Salem are two-way streets. As the metros expand outward, Statesville will surely be absorbed into one or both of them, likely sooner than later.

In contrast, Fairbanks is well assured of never being swallowed by a major metropolitan neighbor anytime soon. Fairbanks rates last in urban proximity, without having scored a point. But no one moves to Fairbanks because of its easy access to Seattle, Vancouver, or even Anchorage. They go there for the gold, the high-paying jobs of the Trans-Alaska pipeline, and for the frontier. The local chamber of commerce describes the city's attraction in the simple phrase, "Fairbanks: Extremely Alaska."

Urban Proximity Scores: Highs and Lows

	Total Rating Points
Highest	
1. Statesville, N.C.	96
2. Michigan City-La Porte, Ind.	95
New Castle, Pa.	95
4. Gainesville, Ga.	94
5. Albemarle, N.C.	93
Columbus, Ind.	93
Corsicana, Tex.	93
New Castle, Ind.	93
Norwalk, Ohio	93
10. Ashland, Ohio	92
Faribault, Minn.	92
Mount Vernon, Wash.	92
Shelby, N.C.	92
14. La Grange, Ga.	90
Sandusky, Ohio	90
Watertown, Wisc.	90
Wooster, Ohio	90
18. Concord, N.H.	89
Marion, Ind.	89
Rome, Ga.	89
Median	
96. Lufkin, Tex.	65
97. Muskogee, Okla.	65
Lowest	
183. Clovis, N.Mex.	19
Farmington, N.Mex.	19
Marquette, Mich.	19
186. Pocatello, Idaho	18
187. Minot, N.Dak.	15
Twin Falls, Idaho	15
189. Missoula, Mont.	14
190. Helena, Mont.	12
191. Idaho Falls, Idaho	10
192. Bozeman, Mont.	8
193. Fairbanks, Alaska	0

Urban Proximity Performance Comparison

	Statesville, North Carolina	Micro median	Fairbanks, Alaska
Total Points in Section	96	65	0
Rank in Section	1		193
Metro Center Proximity			
Miles to nearest official metro center	27	47	361
Metro Center points	(19)		(0)
Arts Center Proximity			
Miles to nearest arts center	38	143	2,121
Arts Center points	(20)		(0)
Retail Center Proximity			
Miles to nearest retail center	38	113	2,265
Retail Center points	(19)		(0)
Sports Center Proximity			
Miles to nearest sports center	38	152	2,265
Sports Center points	(20)		(0)
Television Market			
National television market rank	28	67	205
Television Market points	(18)		(0)

Urban Proximity Scores Area by Area

(Total urban proximity rating points)

Micro median 65

Alabama
Albertville 76
Auburn-Opelika 72
Cullman 78
Selma 61
Talladega 84

Alaska
Fairbanks 0

Arizona
Prescott 62
Sierra Vista 45

Arkansas
Blytheville 68
El Dorado 47
Hot Springs 61
Jonesboro 44
Russellville 49
Searcy 54

California
Arcata-Eureka 20
El Centro-Calexico-Brawley 47
Hanford-Lemoore 63
Hollister 78

Connecticut
Torrington 87

Florida
Key West 46
Vero Beach 61

Georgia
Brunswick 58
Dalton 82
Dublin 63
Gainesville 94
Hinesville 46
La Grange 90
Milledgeville 72
Rome 89
Statesboro 55
Thomasville 50
Valdosta 53
Waycross 55

Idaho
Coeur d'Alene 59
Idaho Falls 10
Pocatello 18
Twin Falls 15

Illinois
Carbondale 71
Danville 75
Freeport 72
Galesburg 59
Mattoon-Charleston 66
Ottawa 86
Quincy 51
Sterling 62

Indiana
Columbus 93
Marion 89
Michigan City-La Porte 95
New Castle 93
Richmond 85
Vincennes 64

Iowa
Ames 72
Burlington 53
Clinton 62
Mason City 59
Muscatine 61

Kansas
Hutchinson 58
Manhattan 52
Salina 53

Kentucky
Bowling Green 50
Frankfort 85
Madisonville 57
Paducah 53
Radcliff-Elizabethtown 81

Louisiana
Hammond 75
New Iberia 62
Ruston 40

Maine
Augusta-Waterville 66
Biddeford-Saco 82

Maryland
Salisbury 44

Michigan
Marquette 19
Mount Pleasant 67
Owosso 84
Traverse City 35

Minnesota
Faribault 92
Mankato 66
Red Wing 88
Willmar 81
Winona 60

Mississippi

Cleveland	33
Columbus	45
Greenville	30
Laurel	48
Meridian	35
Tupelo	47
Vicksburg	40

Missouri

Cape Girardeau-Sikeston	64
Jefferson City	65
Poplar Bluff	54
Warrensburg	82

Montana

Bozeman	8
Helena	12
Missoula	14

Nebraska

Grand Island	36

Nevada

Carson City	48
Elko	20

New Hampshire

Concord	89
Keene	88

New Mexico

Alamogordo	44
Carlsbad	32
Clovis	19
Farmington	19
Gallup	28
Hobbs	29
Roswell	23

New York

Cortland	65
Gloversville	58
Ithaca	75
Kingston	86
Olean	82
Plattsburgh	67
Watertown	46

North Carolina

Albemarle	93
Eden	75
Havelock-New Bern	45
Henderson	70
Kinston	56
Lumberton	69
Roanoke Rapids	66
Sanford	77
Shelby	92
Statesville	96
Wilson	69

North Dakota

Minot	15

Ohio

Ashland	92
Athens	80
Chillicothe	88
Findlay-Fostoria-Tiffin	76
Fremont	80
Marion	88
Mount Vernon	83
New Philadelphia	88
Norwalk	93
Portsmouth	76
Sandusky	90
Sidney	85
Wooster	90
Zanesville	67

Oklahoma

Ardmore	65
Chickasha	73
Duncan	66
McAlester	63
Muskogee	65
Stillwater	62

Oregon

Albany-Corvallis	69
Bend	34
Coos Bay	38
Grants Pass	35
Klamath Falls	28
Pendleton	40
Roseburg	45

Pennsylvania

Chambersburg	86
New Castle	95
Pottsville	80

Rhode Island

Newport	87

South Carolina

Greenwood	76
Hilton Head Island	43

Tennessee

Cleveland	74
Columbia	69
Cookeville	67
Morristown	64
Tullahoma	71

Texas

Corsicana	93
Del Rio	37
Eagle Pass	28
Huntsville	87
Lufkin	65

Nacogdoches	63
Palestine	81
Paris	81
Utah	
Logan	47
St. George	29
Vermont	
Rutland	53
Virginia	
Blacksburg-Radford-Christiansburg	52
Harrisonburg	58
Martinsville	62
Staunton-Waynesboro	73
Winchester	88
Washington	
Aberdeen	81
Longview	87
Mount Vernon	92
Port Angeles	82
Walla Walla	47
Wenatchee	67
West Virginia	
Beckley	38
Clarksburg	62
Fairmont	67
Morgantown	83
Wisconsin	
Fond du Lac	84
Manitowoc	82
Stevens Point	61
Watertown	90
Wyoming	
Rock Springs	25

Conclusion

The Report Cards

The dire problems of central cities—failing finances, overcrowded and underfunded schools, high costs—appear no closer to solution. The excessive strain continues to drive out the residents who can leave. And the strain of life in crowded suburbs has become an accepted feature of many metro areas: numbing sprawl, stressful traffic jams, and rising prices. It seems that the lines at the suburban grocery store can only grow longer, the nightly traffic jam linger longer toward sunset.

Thinking "big" can't solve these problems. Bigger roads, bigger grocery stores? Bigger traffic lights?

This book is inspired by the belief that the buck can stop, that in small cities there is an alternative to a chaotic metropolitan existence. A similar thought has already motivated many Americans, including some who had once fervently embraced an urban way of life. "A lot of yuppies have realized a very fast-paced life can't be kept up for a long time," says Douglas McCabe, a professor of industrial and labor relations at Georgetown University. "They're leaving high-pressure corporations, high-pressure consulting firms, and establishing small family firms, moving to smaller cities and rural communities."

Yuppies or young families or retired couples can all find happier, more relaxed existence in the smaller cities of America. But which of the country's 193 micropolitan areas should they choose to be their new home?

The previous ten sections have given partial answers. Each section has graded all communities according to their performances in five relevant categories. The maximum possible score in any category is 20 points. The five category totals for each city are then combined for a section score, which represents the community's relative strength in a broad field, such as economics, health care, or transportation. The highest total in any section is 100 points.

The overall desirability of any small city depends on a combination of factors. Adding each community's ten section totals yields a final score, which provides a measure of that town's quality of life.

Mount Vernon, Washington, leads the nation's micropolitan areas with 605 points. Eagle Pass, Texas, is in last place with 371.

Total Scores

	Micropolitan Area	Rating Points
1.	Mount Vernon, Wash.	605
2.	Ames, Iowa	602
3.	Morgantown, W.Va.	592
4.	Ithaca, N.Y.	584
5.	Traverse City, Mich.	582
6.	Port Angeles, Wash.	570
7.	Sandusky, Ohio	568
8.	Columbus, Ind.	565
9.	Concord, N.H.	563
10.	Mason City, Iowa	558
11.	Wenatchee, Wash.	557
12.	Rome, Ga.	556
13.	Bozeman, Mont.	555
14.	Mankato, Minn.	553
15.	Bend, Ore.	551
	Longview, Wash.	551
17.	Frankfort, Ky.	547
	Plattsburgh, N.Y.	547
19.	Willmar, Minn.	546
20.	Burlington, Iowa	544
21.	Tupelo, Miss.	542
22.	Winchester, Va.	541
23.	Albany-Corvallis, Ore.	540
	Carbondale, Ill.	540
25.	Coeur d'Alene, Idaho	539
	Rutland, Vt.	539
27.	Mattoon-Charleston, Ill.	536
28.	Harrisonburg, Va.	535
	La Grange, Ga.	535
30.	Marion, Ohio	534
	Salina, Kans.	534
	Valdosta, Ga.	534
33.	Cookeville, Tenn.	533
	Kingston, N.Y.	533
	Olean, N.Y.	533
36.	Findlay-Fostoria-Tiffin, Ohio	531
	Milledgeville, Ga.	531
	Missoula, Mont.	531
	Stillwater, Okla.	531
40.	Clinton, Iowa	529
	Dalton, Ga.	529
	Paducah, Ky.	529
	Red Wing, Minn.	529
44.	Ashland, Ohio	528
45.	Augusta-Waterville, Maine	527
	Brunswick, Ga.	527
47.	Mount Pleasant, Mich.	526
48.	Minot, N.Dak.	525
	Quincy, Ill.	525
	Rock Springs, Wyo.	525
51.	Cape Girardeau-Sikeston, Mo.	524
	Walla Walla, Wash.	524
	Watertown, N.Y.	524
54.	Bowling Green, Ky.	523
	Jefferson City, Mo.	523
	Winona, Minn.	523
57.	Cortland, N.Y.	521
	Keene, N.H.	521
59.	Aberdeen, Wash.	520
	Jonesboro, Ark.	520
	Richmond, Ind.	520
	Salisbury, Md.	520
	Torrington, Conn.	520
64.	Staunton-Waynesboro, Va.	519
	Statesville, N.C.	519
66.	Meridian, Miss.	518
	Sanford, N.C.	518
	Wooster, Ohio	518
69.	Key West, Fla.	517
	Stevens Point, Wisc.	517
71.	Galesburg, Ill.	516
72.	Carson City, Nev.	515
	Clarksburg, W.Va.	515
	Newport, R.I.	515
75.	New Philadelphia, Ohio	514
76.	Columbia, Tenn.	513

	Micropolitan Area	Rating Points
77.	Faribault, Minn.	512
78.	Greenwood, S.C.	511
	Vero Beach, Fla.	511
80.	Athens, Ohio	510
	Columbus, Miss.	510
	Gainesville, Ga.	510
	Vincennes, Ind.	510
84.	Auburn-Opelika, Ala.	509
	Fond du Lac, Wisc.	509
	New Castle, Ind.	509
	Zanesville, Ohio	509
88.	Blacksburg-Radford-Christiansburg, Va.	507
89.	Manitowoc, Wisc.	506
	Statesboro, Ga.	506
91.	Prescott, Ariz.	505
92.	Arcata-Eureka, Calif.	504
	Thomasville, Ga.	504
94.	Hilton Head Island, S.C.	503
95.	Dublin, Ga.	502
	Marquette, Mich.	502
97.	Hot Springs, Ark.	501
	Pocatello, Idaho	501
99.	Radcliff-Elizabethtown, Ky.	500
100.	Paris, Tex.	498
	Watertown, Wisc.	498
102.	Coos Bay, Ore.	497
	Shelby, N.C.	497
104.	Manhattan, Kans.	496
	Wilson, N.C.	496
106.	Cleveland, Tenn.	494
107.	Fremont, Ohio	493
	Nacogdoches, Tex.	493
	Waycross, Ga.	493
110.	New Castle, Penn.	491
	Sterling, Ill.	491
112.	Freeport, Ill.	489
	Norwalk, Ohio	489
114.	Ardmore, Okla.	487
	Chillicothe, Ohio	487
	Corsicana, Tex.	487
	Ottawa, Ill.	487
118.	Mount Vernon, Ohio	486
	Twin Falls, Idaho	486
120.	Danville, Ill.	485
	Idaho Falls, Idaho	485
122.	Helena, Mont.	484
	Muskogee, Okla.	484
124.	Havelock-New Bern, N.C.	483
125.	Laurel, Miss.	482
	Morristown, Tenn.	482
	Ruston, La.	482
	Vicksburg, Miss.	482
129.	Roswell, N.Mex.	481
130.	Muscatine, Iowa	480
131.	Poplar Bluff, Mo.	479
	Sidney, Ohio	479
133.	Biddeford-Saco, Maine	478
	Carlsbad, N.Mex.	478
	Hutchinson, Kans.	478
	Madisonville, Ky.	478
137.	Marion, Ind.	477
	McAlester, Okla.	477
139.	St. George, Utah	476
140.	El Dorado, Ark.	475
141.	Tullahoma, Tenn.	472
142.	Michigan City-La Porte, Ind.	471
	Beckley, W.Va.	471
144.	Albertville, Ala.	470
	Roseburg, Ore.	470
146.	Cullman, Ala.	469
147.	Klamath Falls, Ore.	468
	New Iberia, La.	468
149.	Grand Island, Nebr.	467
	Kinston, N.C.	467

Total Scores (continued)

Micropolitan Area	Rating Points
Searcy, Ark.	467
Warrensburg, Mo.	467
153. Elko, Nev.	466
Huntsville, Tex.	466
Logan, Utah	466
156. Russellville, Ark.	465
157. Sierra Vista, Ariz.	462
158. Duncan, Okla.	461
Lufkin, Tex.	461
Talladega, Ala.	461
161. Fairmont, W.Va.	459
162. Henderson, N.C.	458
163. Owosso, Mich.	457
Roanoke Rapids, N.C.	457
165. Chickasha, Okla.	454
166. Lumberton, N.C.	453
167. Hollister, Calif.	452
Pendleton, Ore.	452
169. Portsmouth, Ohio	450
170. Hobbs, N.Mex.	448
171. Albemarle, N.C.	446
172. Grants Pass, Ore.	443
Palestine, Tex.	443
174. Fairbanks, Alaska	442
Selma, Ala.	442
176. Chambersburg, Penn.	441
177. Pottsville, Penn.	440
178. Cleveland, Miss.	439
Greenville, Miss.	439
180. Eden, N.C.	437
181. El Centro-Calexico-Brawley, Calif.	434
Hammond, La.	434
183. Alamogordo, N.Mex.	433
Clovis, N.Mex.	433
185. Martinsville, Va.	430
186. Gallup, N.Mex.	426
187. Gloversville, N.Y.	420
188. Farmington, N.Mex.	416
189. Blytheville, Ark.	410
190. Hanford-Lemoore, Calif.	405
191. Del Rio, Tex.	403
192. Hinesville, Ga.	400
193. Eagle Pass, Tex.	371

The Top Ten

1. Mount Vernon, Washington

Tucked into the very northwest corner of the continental United States, Mount Vernon lies in the heart of the Pacific Northwest fishing region. The micro's boundaries run from Skagit Bay back to the northern heights of the Cascade Mountains, but come spring, eyes are drawn inland as the daffodil, iris, and tulip fields of the Mount Vernon area burst into color. Much of the country's commercial bulb flowers are grown in this region. The flowers thrive in the moderate Mount Vernon climate. Just 43 degrees separate the average July high of 75 from the average January low of 32.

Local government invests highly in the community. School funding is 26 percent above the national average. Local funding for health and hospitals is the tenth highest among small cities and five times the national average. Despite the high levels of spending, property taxes remain well below the median for small cities. The yearly tax bill for Mount Vernon homeowners is just 55 percent of the national average.

Personal incomes in Mount Vernon are significantly above those of the typical small city, matching more closely the higher average income of the country as a whole. The Mount Vernon area has very low incidence of violent crime, with a rate considerably below the median for all micropolitans and just 26 percent of the national rate. The area's low population density reflects the nearby wealth of state parks and national forests. But metropolitan attractions are not far away, either. Bellingham is just twenty-seven miles to the north via Interstate 5. The arts, shopping, and sports teams of Seattle are an hour's drive to the south. Mount Vernon residents looking to go beyond Bellingham or Seattle have easy access to nearby air service.

It's not all daffodils and tulips in Mount Vernon. Although violent crime rates are low, the rate of total crime is nearly one-third higher in Mount Vernon than in the typical small city. The rate of juvenile arrests is also above the median rate for small cities.

Mount Vernon's prime location and many attractions have not gone unnoticed by the housing market. Home prices in Mount Vernon are the highest among Washington's small cities. Price tags are 52 percent above the median costs of a home in micropolitan America. And although personal income is high, it barely budged through the first half of the decade, increasing less than 1 percent.

2. Ames, Iowa

First came the college: Iowa State University, founded in 1869. Next came the city: Ames, incorporated in 1870. This wooded town on the rolling prairie of central Iowa has always followed the lead of its university. The result has been a healthy and stable economy and a flourishing cultural environment.

Personal incomes in Ames are significantly higher than those of the typical small city, and they grew at four times the national average between 1990 and 1994. Ames's manufacturing workers claim the sixth highest value added by manufacture figure among small cities. The university offers an array of cultural attractions at its modern Iowa State Center, which contains an auditorium, a gallery, a theater, and an indoor sports coliseum. Some aspects of Ames's community life are less developed apart from the university. Homeownership, newspaper readership, and local broadcast outlets are below those of the typical small city. Rates of arts and learning institutions are above the median, however, and membership and social service organizations are particularly strong.

Ames shines the brightest when it comes to educational attainment. The area boasts the second highest overall education score among U.S. micros. Educational levels in Ames dramatically surpass national averages. Ames has the highest share of high school graduates of any small city, and the second highest share of college graduates. Fewer than 2 percent of young adults drop out of high school, the lowest rate in micropolitan America, and far below national rates.

Total crime rates in Ames are nearly one-third below the national average. Violent crime is far rarer. The rate of reported violent crimes is just 17 percent of the national average. The rate of juvenile arrest is one of the lowest in micropolitan America.

Ames also has the fourth highest transportation score among small cities. Short commutes, popular public transit, and above-median spending on roads characterize travel around the Ames area. Residents seeking a temporary change from life in a college town have easy access to a metropolitan venue. Des Moines is just a twenty-eight-mile drive south on Interstate 35.

3. Morgantown, West Virginia

Colonel Zackquill Morgan, son of frontiersman Morgan Morgan, founded Morgan's Town in 1766. In 1867, four years after the western counties of Virginia became the state of West Virginia amid the Civil War, West Virginia University was founded in Morgantown. The school now offers 164 bachelor's, master's, doctoral, and professional degree programs to nearly 22,000 students.

The Appalachian plateau makes for steep terrain and dramatic scenery in Morgantown. Nearby Cooper's Rock State Forest features an overlook 1,300 feet above Cheat River Gorge. The area is popular for hiking, biking, camping, skiing, and white-water rafting.

West Virginia University's medical center and school of medicine draw a high number of doctors and health-care professionals to Morgantown. More than 500 physicians are in private practice in the area, giving the micro an extraordinary rate of 671 physicians per 100,000 residents. Specialists are prevalent in

Morgantown, also. The ratio of medical specialists is more than five times the micro median, and nearly three times the national average.

All those doctors do their part in boosting Morgantown's median income. Median personal income in the area is 10 percent above that of typical micro. Incomes have been busy, rising 15.1 percent between 1990 and 1994, a rate more than five times that of income growth for the country as a whole. Above-median incomes do not quite outpace above-median home prices, however. The cost of a house in Morgantown runs about 20 percent above the micropolitan median, but the prices are attractive when viewed from a national perspective, with prices approximately 20 percent below the national average. Property taxes are light by either measure, at 43 percent below the micro median and 72 percent below the national average.

Morgantown residents enjoy a high level of public safety. The rate of violent crime is just 25 percent the national rate and 56 percent of the micro median; the total crime rate is 68 percent the national average and 9 percent below the micro median. Getting to and from Morgantown is not a problem, either. Morgantown is among the fewer than 10 percent of small cities served by two interstates. The local airport provides commuter service to major hubs, including Pittsburgh, just seventy-seven miles away. That same proximity to Pittsburgh provides Morgantown residents with a nearby big-city dose of arts, retail, and sports.

4. Ithaca, New York

Much of the land surrounding New York's Finger Lakes was awarded to Revolutionary War veterans as payment for their military service. The area bore the names of the native American tribes who had inhabited the region, but the newly surveyed counties and towns were named on a classical Roman and Greek motif: Homer, Ovid, Virgil, Rome, Ulysses, and Marathon. At the southern end of Cayuga Lake, set among creeks and gorges, Ithaca was named in honor of Ulysses' home, of which in all his travels, he said he knew of no more beautiful place.

Ithaca boasts brains as well as beauty. The presence of both Cornell University and Ithaca College—their students, faculty, families, and community programs—creates a strong educational environment in Ithaca. An outstanding 7 in 10 Ithaca residents are either college graduates or college students. Fewer than 3 young adults in 100 drop out of high school. That's the fourth lowest rate among small cities and a small fraction of the national average.

The Finger Lakes, mountains, and state parks and forests lure the bookish out-of-doors for hiking, camping, and skiing. Spending on local parks and recreation is double that of the typical micro.

Ithaca can be a transient town, however. Approximately half the residents are renters, a very high rate for a small city but not an uncommon one for college or military towns. Community life is active despite the transient overtones. The university and college contribute a variety of theater, music, and membership groups.

The ratios of doctors and medical specialists are significantly above the micro median. The ratio of community hospital beds is low, but the predominantly young Ithaca population as a whole has less need of hospital stays. The total crime rate exceeds the micro median, but the incidence of violent crime is very low. The violent crime rate is just 20 percent of the national average and 44 percent of the micro median.

Ithaca earns the fifth highest overall transportation score among small cities. Area commuters have a relatively short trip to work and the local bus system is popular (especially among students who face a long, steep climb up East Hill to Cornell University). Spending on roads is above that of the typical micro, and the local airport handles large-jet service. The drive out of town is beautiful, but long. Ithaca has one of the lowest highway availability indexes among small cities.

5. Traverse City, Michigan

Up in the northwest corner of Michigan's Lower Peninsula, Traverse City looks out to Lake Michigan from Traverse Bay. More than 250 miles of shoreline border the area. The city is flanked by the Old Mission Peninsula to the west and state forests to the southeast and southwest. More than three hundred inland lakes, rivers, and streams dot the interior. The area is rich in outdoor activities: boating, hiking, riding, and skiing. It's a wonder Traverse City residents ever go inside.

These attractions draw visitors year round who explore the historic sites, shifting sand dunes, and islands and hike and ride the extensive state trail system. The National Cherry Festival held in Traverse City is one of Michigan's largest events. In winter, skiers hit the many slopes around the region.

The healthy stream of tourists boosts Traverse City's retail trade. Only two small cities have a higher rate of retail establishments. Only one micro has higher per capita retail sales. Traverse City's attractions are drawing people to stay, also. Population grew at four times the slow Michigan state growth and twice the national rate.

Traverse City incomes are considerably above the micro median, as is government spending on education, health care, and parks and recreation. It's not surprising, perhaps, that home prices and property taxes are also above those of the typical micro. Home prices are 29 percent above the micro median, but remain 13 percent below the national average. Property taxes are the eighth highest of all micros; one-and-a-half times the national average and two-and-a-half times the micro median.

Traverse City enjoys a level of public safety higher than even that of the typical small city. Educational rates are also high: 85 in 100 Traverse City adults are high school graduates, a rate considerably above the national average of 78 percent.

The ratio of medical specialists is the fifth highest among small cities; the ratio of doctors and of hospital beds is among the top 10 percent. Seven radio stations and two television stations provide local programming to the area; the rate of membership groups and social services is above the micro median. Traverse City's remote locale requires such a well-developed health-care and community network.

The many state forests and lakes in Michigan's Lower Peninsula restrict the number of highways in the area, but air service is plentiful. The airport, which accommodates large-jet service, is the fourth busiest among small cities.

6. Port Angeles, Washington

Few cities large or small can match the breathtaking location of Port Angeles. The micro is nestled below the towering peaks of the Olympic Mountains and before the Strait of Juan de Fuca. At its back door lie 1,400 square miles of mountains, lakes, glaciers, and rain forest in the Olympic National Park.

The U.S. Pacific Fleet docked at Port Angeles in the 1920s and early 1930s, and as many as 30,000 sailors once crowded the town's small streets. Times are quieter these days, but you can still get a bite to eat and catch a movie on a Saturday night. Port Angeles's restaurant and amusement establishment indexes are well above the micro median. Incomes in Port Angeles are within the top 25 percent of small cities. Crime rates are low, and the share of high school grads is high.

With the sea before it, and the mountains behind it, Port Angeles is relatively isolated by car. It has the second lowest highway availability index in micropolitan America. The local airport handles large jets, however, and Seattle is less than ninety miles away. Victoria, Canada, lies across the strait, accessible by ferry.

If the reference to a rain forest in the Olympic Ranges has you worried, never fear. The mountains act as a shield, limiting Port Angeles to a modest twenty-five inches of precipitation each year.

7. Sandusky, Ohio

Sandusky belongs to the list of top-ten micros that are water towns. Sandusky is a Great Lakes city, located on Lake Erie, and much of the city's economic and recreational life has always taken place on the waters and shores of the vast lake. Thrills have come easily in Sandusky for more than 125 years. The micro is home to Cedar Point Amusement Park, founded in 1870, which boasts the most roller coasters of any amusement park worldwide and draws three million visitors a year.

Lake Erie keeps Sandusky's summers moderate and pleasantly warm. July temperatures top out at 83 degrees on average. Incomes are the fourteenth highest among all small cities and grew at a rate three times that of the national average during the first half of the decade. Other indicators of Sandusky's healthy economy are high retail sales and many restaurants. The number of restaurants per 100,000 residents in Sandusky is 50 percent above that of the typical micro.

Sandusky breaks with Ohio small cities in an unfortunate way. While crime rates in other micros statewide are below the micro median, Sandusky's rate is 25 percent higher. Violent crime in Sandusky rates 38 percent above the median for small cities, but remains 39 percent below the national average.

Sandusky residents have easy access to metropolitan attractions. The cultural attractions, shopping, and sports of Cleveland are just sixty miles away, giving Sandusky one of the highest urban proximity scores among small cities.

8. Columbus, Indiana

Columbus is the small city built by big architects. The city features more than fifty public and private buildings designed by architects such as I. M. Pei, Eero Saarinen, and Richard Meier.

The micro offers the enviable combination of homes priced below the national average and personal incomes that top the national average. Columbus home prices are more than one-quarter below the national average; incomes are a nominal but noticeable 3 percent above the national average. Only six other small cities have higher median incomes. Columbus homeowners do receive a property tax bill that is 55 percent above the micro median, however.

No small city invests more highly in public health and hospitals than Columbus. Local government spending is twenty-two times the median for small cities and nine times the national average. Columbus's total score in the health category is within the top 15 percent of all micros.

Columbus's public safety score is also within the top 15 percent of small cities. The rate of violent crime is particularly low—just 38 percent of the national average. Columbus has ready access to the attractions of a major metro. A drive of less than one hour to Indianapolis places Columbus in a tie for fifth place in overall urban proximity.

9. Concord, New Hampshire

Concord was settled and doing business long before cities west of the Mississippi were even a gleam in settlers' eyes. Concord was founded in 1725 by colonists from Massachusetts; it became the state capital in 1808. New Hampshire's government continues to convene in the original chambers of the 1819 State House.

A wealth of colleges, libraries, museums, and even a planetarium have grown up in Concord with the passing of nearly 275 years. The micro has the fourth highest rate of arts and learning institutions among small cities. In addition to Concord's own cultural activities, Manchester is twenty miles away and Boston is just fifty-eight miles farther.

Incomes are high in Concord, 39 percent above the micro median. Only three other small cities have a higher income. Concord also has the fourth highest ratio of medical specialists, a reflection of a comprehensive regional health-care network that is centered in the city. The micro scores within the top ten for overall public safety. The total crime rate is nearly half that of the typical small city; the violent crime rate just one-third.

Housing does not come cheaply in Concord: home prices run 221 percent of micro median and 150 percent above the national average. Only four small cities have a median home cost higher than Concord's, only two have higher property taxes.

10. Mason City, Iowa

The vast northern Iowa landscape makes Mason City a natural home for buildings by Prairie School architects Frank Lloyd Wright and Walter Burley Griffin and Marion Mahoney Griffin. Mason City is also familiar on a musical note. Native son Meredith Wilson used Mason City as the setting for the popular 1957 Broadway musical *The Music Man.*

There's plenty to do in Mason City beyond a parade. The micro ties for second place in community assets. It scores in the top 5 percent for diversions, with a good selection of shopping and dining. Only five small cities have a greater share of restaurants and taverns. Two state parks border local Clear Lake.

Mason City offers the lowest housing prices among the top ten small cities. The price of a home in Mason City is 15 percent below the micro median and 42 percent below the national average. The city achieves a high rate of high school graduation and a large share of high school graduates without the influence of a major local college. Mason City commuters have the second shortest commute among small-city workers—nearly half that of the average U.S. commuter.

On the down side, it gets cold in Mason City. The average January low is just 3.5 degrees, clearly a bad habit picked up from nearby Minnesota. Only seven small cities have colder winter weather.

Regional and State Leaders

People have different tastes. It would be foolish to expect a stampede of newcomers to Mount Vernon, Washington, just because it ranks first among the nation's small cities. Some people simply don't want to live in the Pacific Northwest, with all due respect. Some will want to confine their search for a congenial small city to a particular region of the country, the East, say, to stay near family and friends. A few people may narrow their plans still further, limiting themselves to a single state.

It is easy to determine the best micropolitan areas in each of the regions and states, using the same point totals employed for the national list. The following tables list the top-scoring micros by region and state.

It is also possible to measure the distribution around the country of those small cities with the highest and lowest scores. All communities scoring 545 points or higher are designated as superior; those with scores below 445 are rated as inferior. There are nineteen micros that classify as superior, and twenty-two as inferior. This also approximately represents the top and bottom ten percent.

The East has the fewest states, and the fewest micropolitans, but four Eastern small cities have superior scores: Morgantown, West Virginia (ranked third nationwide); Ithaca, New York; Concord, New Hampshire; and Plattsburgh, New York. Three eastern micros rate as inferior.

The South has the most small cities. Seventy-seven micros (40 percent) are located within the thirteen-state region. Just two rate as superior: Rome, Georgia, and Frankfort, Kentucky. Eleven Southern small cities have inferior ratings.

Seven of the fifty-five Midwestern small cities are superior. Ames, Iowa (ranked second nationwide); Traverse City, Michigan; and Sandusky, Ohio, have the highest scores. No small cities in the Midwest have inferior ratings.

The West has six superior micros, four of them in Washington state. Mount Vernon, Washington (first in the nation); Port Angeles, Washington; and Wenatchee, Washington, lead the way. Eight of the West's small cities rate as inferior, four of them in New Mexico.

Best in Each Region

East	Rating Points
1. Morgantown, W.Va.	592
2. Ithaca, N.Y.	584
3. Concord, N.H.	563
4. Plattsburgh, N.Y.	547
5. Rutland, Vt.	539
6. Kingston, N.Y.	533
Olean, N.Y.	533
8. Augusta-Waterville, Maine	527
9. Watertown, N.Y.	524
10. Cortland, N.Y.	521
Keene, N.H.	521

South	Rating Points
1. Rome, Ga.	556
2. Frankfort, Ky.	547
3. Tupelo, Miss.	542
4. Winchester, Va.	541
5. Harrisonburg, Va.	535
La Grange, Ga.	535
7. Valdosta, Ga.	534
8. Cookeville, Tenn.	533
9. Milledgeville, Ga.	531
Stillwater, Okla.	531

Midwest	Rating Points
1. Ames, Iowa	602
2. Traverse City, Mich.	582
3. Sandusky, Ohio	568
4. Columbus, Ind.	565
5. Mason City, Iowa	558
6. Mankato, Minn.	553
7. Willmar, Minn.	546
8. Burlington, Iowa	544
9. Carbondale, Ill.	540
10. Mattoon-Charleston, Ill.	536

West	Rating Points
1. Mount Vernon, Wash.	605
2. Port Angeles, Wash.	570
3. Wenatchee, Wash.	557
4. Bozeman, Mont.	555
5. Bend, Ore.	551
Longview, Wash.	551
7. Albany-Corvallis, Ore.	540
8. Coeur d'Alene, Idaho	539
9. Missoula, Mont.	531
10. Rock Springs, Wyo.	525

Best in Each State

State	Top-Ranked Micropolitan Area	Rating Points	National Rank
Alabama	Auburn-Opelika	509	84
Alaska*	Fairbanks	442	174
Arizona	Prescott	505	91
Arkansas	Jonesboro	520	59
California	Arcata-Eureka	504	92
Connecticut*	Torrington	520	59
Florida	Key West	517	69
Georgia	Rome	556	12
Idaho	Coeur d'Alene	539	25
Illinois	Carbondale	540	23
Indiana	Columbus	565	8
Iowa	Ames	602	2
Kansas	Salina	534	30
Kentucky	Frankfort	547	17
Louisiana	Ruston	482	125
Maine	Augusta-Waterville	527	45
Maryland*	Salisbury	520	59
Michigan	Traverse City	582	5
Minnesota	Mankato	553	14
Mississippi	Tupelo	542	21
Missouri	Cape Girardeau-Sikeston	524	51
Montana	Bozeman	555	13
Nebraska*	Grand Island	467	149
Nevada	Carson City	515	72
New Hampshire	Concord	563	9
New Mexico	Roswell	481	129
New York	Ithaca	584	4
North Carolina	Statesville	519	64
North Dakota*	Minot	525	48
Ohio	Sandusky	568	7
Oklahoma	Stillwater	531	36
Oregon	Bend	551	15
Pennsylvania	New Castle	491	110
Rhode Island*	Newport	515	72
South Carolina	Greenwood	511	78
Tennessee	Cookeville	533	33
Texas	Paris	498	100
Utah	St. George	476	139

Best in Each State (continued)

State	Top-Ranked Micropolitan Area	Rating Points	National Rank
Vermont*	Rutland	539	25
Virginia	Winchester	541	22
Washington	Mount Vernon	605	1
West Virginia	Morgantown	592	3
Wisconsin	Stevens Point	517	69
Wyoming*	Rock Springs	525	48

*Only one micropolitan area in state.

Note: Six states do not have any micropolitan areas: Colorado, Delaware, Hawaii, Massachusetts, New Jersey, and South Dakota.

Individual Report Cards

You would be impetuous to select your new hometown or vacation spot solely on the basis of total points. You need to go beyond the numbers to find the community that will offer you the exact type of life you are seeking.

Let's say you have narrowed your list to Ames, Iowa, and Traverse City, Michigan. Ames seems the obvious choice, having a healthy leading edge in points of 602 to 582. But keep in mind that all ten sections carry equal weight in the total score. That's the fairest way to compile a national ranking for general use. But the performances in some sections may be more important to you than others.

Feel free to tinker with the numbers. If diversions and community assets are especially important categories to your way of thinking, double those scores. Traverse City now scores better than Ames. Perhaps you really don't care about either area's offerings in local diversions. Eliminate those scores for each, then refigure the totals. Ames now has an even clearer lead of 552 to 511.

It is also a good idea to do further research about the communities that interest you. Check the report cards on the following pages for a start. They summarize the overall scores and ranks, section totals, general information, and the strengths and weaknesses for each micropolitan area. Each assessment lets you know how the small town in question compares with the others. (A note of clarification: when a micropolitan is rated as "highest" or "lowest" in its state, this means highest or lowest among all the micropolitans in the state.) Further information is always available at your library or by calling local chambers of commerce. Many of the cities have Internet web sites with local information, visitors' guides, events calendars, and local links.

It's a big country. Happy hunting!

ALABAMA

Albertville

Points: 470
National Rank: 144
State Rank: 2 of 5

General Information
Components: Marshall County
Area Population: 76,802
Central City Population: 17,146
Location: Northeastern Georgia, between Gadsden and Huntsville
Nearest Metro Center: Gadsden, 22 miles

Strengths: Albertville ties for the highest overall score in housing among the nation's micros. It is near two metropolitan centers and scores well in public safety, with a particularly low rate of juvenile crime.

Weaknesses: Educational attainment is low throughout the area; Albertville has the second highest high school dropout rate among small cities. The area has no local paper and few local broadcast outlets.

Scores by Section	
Climate/Environment	68
Diversions	44
Economics	43
Education	12
Community Assets	25
Health Care	30
Housing	87
Public Safety	68
Transportation	17
Urban Proximity	76
Total Points	470

Auburn-Opelika

Points: 509
National Rank: 84
State Rank: 1 of 5

General Information
Components: Lee County
Area Population: 91,869
Central City Population: Auburn 35,862; Opelika 23,818
Location: East-central Alabama, near the Georgia border
Nearest Metro Center: Columbus, 32 miles

Strengths: Auburn-Opelika ranks first among Alabama small cities. It stands out in education, largely due to the influence of Auburn University. No other Alabama micro comes close to the high levels of education in Auburn-Opelika.

Weaknesses: Outside of college-related activities, there is little to do: Concentrations of stores, restaurants, community groups, and amusement places are low. Housing prices are far above those of the other Alabama micros.

Scores by Section	
Climate/Environment	65
Diversions	27
Economics	30
Education	56
Community Assets	31
Health Care	55
Housing	77
Public Safety	60
Transportation	36
Urban Proximity	72
Total Points	509

Cullman

Points: 469
National Rank: 146
State Rank: 3 of 5

General Information
Components: Cullman County
Area Population: 71,615
Central City Population: 18,081
Location: North-central Alabama, south of Decatur
Nearest Metro Center: Decatur, 32 miles

Strengths: Housing in Cullman is very affordable. Home prices are just 60 percent of the national average and the area boasts the lowest property taxes of any micro nationwide. Cullman has the lowest crime rates among Alabama small cities.

Weaknesses: The share of both high school and college graduates is very low. Cullman has the second highest dropout rate among the state's small cities. Only one other micro nationwide spends less per capita on local schools.

Scores by Section	
Climate/Environment	71
Diversions	26
Economics	32
Education	11
Community Assets	37
Health Care	36
Housing	85
Public Safety	69
Transportation	24
Urban Proximity	78
Total Points	469

Selma

Points: 442
National Rank: 174
State Rank: 5 of 5

General Information
Components: Dallas County
Area Population: 47,991
Central City Population: 24,647
Location: Central Alabama, west of Montgomery
Nearest Metro Center: Montgomery, 49 miles

Strengths: Selma boasts affordable housing and low property taxes. Like other Alabama micros, it also scores high points for a moderate winter climate and urban proximity.

Weaknesses: Selma's population has been slipping away, due in part to the poor economy. Incidences of crime are high in Selma: The city has the fifth highest total crime rate among the nation's small cities. Only two micros have a higher rate of violent crime.

Scores by Section	
Climate/Environment	64
Diversions	28
Economics	26
Education	28
Community Assets	49
Health Care	35
Housing	83
Public Safety	32
Transportation	36
Urban Proximity	61
Total Points	442

Talladega

Points: 461
National Rank: 158
State Rank: 4 of 5

General Information
Components: Talladega County
Area Population: 76,034
Central City Population: 19,184
Location: East-central Alabama, east of Birmingham
Nearest Metro Center: Anniston, 23 miles

Strengths: Talladega ties for first in housing among all micros, with some of the lowest prices, taxes, and energy needs. If you need to get out of your affordable house, Talladega is convenient to Anniston and Birmingham.

Weaknesses: Like its neighbors, Talladega scores poorly in education. The area has low levels of educational attainment and school financing. The local economy is weak, rating last among its neighbors.

Scores by Section	
Climate/Environment	62
Diversions	26
Economics	20
Education	15
Community Assets	34
Health Care	39
Housing	87
Public Safety	62
Transportation	32
Urban Proximity	84
Total Points	461

ALASKA

Fairbanks

Points: 442
National Rank: 174
State Rank: 1 of 1

General Information
Components: Fairbanks North Star Borough
Area Population: 84,711
Central City Population: 34,321
Location: Interior Alaska, northeast of Anchorage
Nearest Metro Center: Anchorage, 361 miles

Strengths: Fairbanks's boom of the 1980s has cooled, but the economy is still one of the strongest among small cities. There's plenty to do in Fairbanks and the educational level is high.

Weaknesses: Once you're there, you're there. Fairbanks is easily the most isolated micro. Income growth is stagnant after big gains in the previous decade. And the climate? January nights average 19 degrees below zero.

Scores by Section	
Climate/Environment	32
Diversions	59
Economics	50
Education	63
Community Assets	45
Health Care	37
Housing	45
Public Safety	55
Transportation	56
Urban Proximity	0
Total Points	442

ARIZONA

Prescott

Points: 505
National Rank: 91
State Rank: 1 of 2

General Information
Components: Yavapai County
Area Population: 127,942
Central City Population: 30,386
Location: Central Arizona, northwest of Phoenix
Nearest Metro Center: Flagstaff, 89 miles

Strengths: Prescott does not register an outstanding score in any one section, but it performs well across most of them. It scores best for its climate and urban proximity.

Weaknesses: Health care is a weak spot in Prescott, with a small selection of physicians and specialists. Local government spends little on community health.

Scores by Section	
Climate/Environment	65
Diversions	58
Economics	36
Education	40
Community Assets	51
Health Care	26
Housing	54
Public Safety	60
Transportation	53
Urban Proximity	62
Total Points	505

Sierra Vista

Points: 462
National Rank: 157
State Rank: 2 of 2

General Information
Components: Cochise County
Area Population: 107,446
Central City Population: 38,271
Location: Southeast Arizona, near the Mexican border
Nearest Metro Center: Tucson, 70 miles

Strengths: Sierra Vista has a good share of new housing and relatively low energy needs for heating and cooling, especially in Arizona. Public safety and transportation scores are above average.

Weaknesses: The area has the lowest health-care score of all micros. Availability of doctors and hospitals is very low, as is health funding. The local health network is challenged by a very high death rate.

Scores by Section	
Climate/Environment	57
Diversions	46
Economics	30
Education	39
Community Assets	38
Health Care	12
Housing	69
Public Safety	64
Transportation	62
Urban Proximity	45
Total Points	462

ARKANSAS

Blytheville

Points: 410
National Rank: 189
State Rank: 6 of 6

General Information
Components: Mississippi County
Area Population: 50,923
Central City Population: 17,335
Location: Northeastern Arkansas, near the Missouri border and the Mississippi River
Nearest Metro Center: Memphis, 68 miles

Strengths: Incomes in Blytheville grew impressively in the first part of the decade. The area had the third highest income growth of all small cities. The lights of Memphis are slightly more than an hour down the river.

Weaknesses: Local earnings still remain near the lowest among Arkansas small cities. Few broadcast outlets, museums, and membership groups give the area the second lowest score in community assets.

Scores by Section	
Climate/Environment	66
Diversions	29
Economics	39
Education	20
Community Assets	17
Health Care	24
Housing	79
Public Safety	32
Transportation	36
Urban Proximity	68
Total Points	410

El Dorado

Points: 475
National Rank: 140
State Rank: 3 of 6

General Information
Components: Union County
Area Population: 46,255
Central City Population: 23,879
Location: Extreme south-central Arkansas, near the Louisiana border
Nearest Metro Center: Monroe, La., 85 miles

Strengths: El Dorado ties for the most affordable housing among the state's small cities. Seventy-four percent of residents own their home—well above the national average.

Weaknesses: El Dorado has below-average educational and health resources. The area is relatively isolated from metropolitan areas and major highways.

Scores by Section	
Climate/Environment	63
Diversions	38
Economics	34
Education	27
Community Assets	59
Health Care	37
Housing	79
Public Safety	52
Transportation	39
Urban Proximity	47
Total Points	475

Hot Springs

General Information
Components: Garland County
Area Population: 79,792
Central City Population: 35,644
Location: Central Arkansas, southwest of Little Rock
Nearest Metro Center: Little Rock, 55 miles

Strengths: The famous Hot Springs National Park attracts large numbers of tourists, providing plenty of recreation establishments for residents as well. Hot Springs isn't given over to tourism completely. It has a high community assets rating.

Weaknesses: Hot Springs commuters have a long drive for micropolitan residents and just one major highway. Hot Springs has few medical specialists and a high share of terminal cases.

Points: 501
National Rank: 97
State Rank: 2 of 6

Scores by Section	
Climate/Environment	63
Diversions	59
Economics	38
Education	24
Community Assets	67
Health Care	29
Housing	70
Public Safety	57
Transportation	33
Urban Proximity	61
Total Points	501

Jonesboro

General Information
Components: Craighead County
Area Population: 73,447
Central City Population: 50,209
Location: Northeastern Arkansas, near the Missouri border
Nearest Metro Center: Memphis, Tenn., 66 miles

Strengths: Jonesboro bests other Arkansas small cities in health care, but it largely owes its first-place standing in the state to moderate scores in all sections, rather than outstanding scores in one or two.

Weaknesses: The Jonesboro area suffers from the same problems found across Arkansas. Its schools compare poorly to the national average and its transportation system is not well developed.

Points: 520
National Rank: 59
State Rank: 1 of 6

Scores by Section	
Climate/Environment	68
Diversions	35
Economics	51
Education	34
Community Assets	59
Health Care	56
Housing	78
Public Safety	55
Transportation	40
Urban Proximity	44
Total Points	520

Russellville

Points: 465
National Rank: 156
State Rank: 5 of 6

General Information
Components: Pope County
Area Population: 50,211
Central City Population: 23,243
Location: West-central Arkansas, east of Fort Smith
Nearest Metro Center: Little Rock, 76 miles

Strengths: The Russellville area offers a good stock of new, large houses at reasonable prices. National forests lie to the north and south, providing plenty of opportunity for outdoor recreation.

Weaknesses: No major roads other than Interstate 40 serve the area. The nearest regularly scheduled air service is more than an hour's drive away. Summer temperatures are the second highest among the state's small cities, averaging 94 degrees in July.

Scores by Section	
Climate/Environment	65
Diversions	38
Economics	37
Education	33
Community Assets	47
Health Care	32
Housing	80
Public Safety	59
Transportation	25
Urban Proximity	49
Total Points	465

Searcy

Points: 467
National Rank: 149
State Rank: 4 of 6

General Information
Components: White County
Area Population: 59,554
Central City Population: 18,074
Location: Central Arkansas, northeast of Little Rock
Nearest Metro Center: Little Rock, 44 miles

Strengths: Searcy boasts the best housing market among Arkansas micros and a high rate of homeownership. The area invests significantly in the local community hospital. The violent and juvenile crime rates are very low.

Weaknesses: The local economy is the weakest of the six Arkansas small cities, with the lowest wages, slow growth in income, and below-average retail sales. The share of local high school grads is considerably below the national average.

Scores by Section	
Climate/Environment	71
Diversions	29
Economics	30
Education	30
Community Assets	40
Health Care	42
Housing	83
Public Safety	64
Transportation	24
Urban Proximity	54
Total Points	467

CALIFORNIA

Arcata-Eureka

Points: 504
National Rank: 92
State Rank: 1 of 4

General Information
Components: Humboldt County
Area Population: 121,715
Central City Population: Arcata, 15,451; Eureka, 27,218
Location: Extreme northern California, along the Pacific coast
Nearest Metro Center: Redding, 158 miles

Strengths: The Arcata-Eureka climate is exceedingly moderate, with just 31 degrees separating the average July high from the average January low. The area has the highest number of radio, TV, and cable services among small cities.

Weaknesses: Arcata-Eureka is convenient to the beautiful and remote northern California coast, but the nearest metro is a long, hard drive over the mountains. Easy access to metropolitan benefits such as arts, shopping, and sports are forfeited in Arcata-Eureka.

Scores by Section	
Climate/Environment	82
Diversions	57
Economics	31
Education	54
Community Assets	60
Health Care	38
Housing	59
Public Safety	54
Transportation	49
Urban Proximity	20
Total Points	504

El Centro-Calexico-Brawley

Points: 434
National Rank: 181
State Rank: 3 of 4

General Information
Components: Imperial County
Area Population: 137,090
Central City Population: El Centro, 37,593; Calexico, 24,268; Brawley, 21,828
Location: Extreme southeastern California, along the Mexican border
Nearest Metro Center: San Diego, 117 miles

Strengths: The El Centro-Calexico-Brawley area has an abundance of local broadcast outlets. It has the largest share of new houses among the California micros.

Weaknesses: Personal income plummeted 17 percent in the first part of the decade, compared with a growth of nearly 6 percent for micros overall. The area is weak in education, diversions, and community assets.

Scores by Section	
Climate/Environment	36
Diversions	30
Economics	34
Education	36
Community Assets	32
Health Care	43
Housing	63
Public Safety	61
Transportation	52
Urban Proximity	47
Total Points	434

Hanford-Lemoore

Points: 405
National Rank: 190
State Rank: 4 of 4

General Information
Components: Kings County
Area Population: 110,867
Central City Population: Hanford, 33,979; Lemoore, 15,125
Location: Central California, south of Fresno
Nearest Metro Center: Visalia, 20 miles

Strengths: Housing in the Hanford-Lemoore area is newer and more affordable than in other California small cities. Fresno and Visalia are short freeway drives away.

Weaknesses: Hanford-Lemoore has relatively few restaurants, shops, and amusement places. There are also few local assets in the way of broadcast outlets and membership organizations.

Scores by Section	
Climate/Environment	34
Diversions	28
Economics	20
Education	30
Community Assets	18
Health Care	34
Housing	75
Public Safety	54
Transportation	49
Urban Proximity	63
Total Points	405

Hollister

Points: 452
National Rank: 166
State Rank: 2 of 4

General Information
Components: San Benito County
Area Population: 41,082
Central City Population: 21,998
Location: South-central California coast, below San Jose
Nearest Metro Center: Watsonville, 28 miles

Strengths: Hollister enjoys moderate coastal weather; the area has the fewest degree days among the nation's small cities. Monterey Bay and San Jose are nearby. So is Castroville, the self-proclaimed "Artichoke Capital of the World."

Weaknesses: Home prices in Hollister are the steepest of any micro—nearly four times the median value. There is little developed community life. The area offers only a minor economy and few diversions, assets, or health-care services.

Scores by Section	
Climate/Environment	73
Diversions	33
Economics	27
Education	38
Community Assets	19
Health Care	45
Housing	60
Public Safety	61
Transportation	18
Urban Proximity	78
Total Points	452

CONNECTICUT

Torrington

Points: 520
National Rank: 59
State Rank: 1 of 1

General Information
Components: Litchfield County
Area Population: 178,523
Central City Population: 33,789
Location: Northwest Connecticut, west of Hartford
Nearest Metro Center: Waterbury, 20 miles

Strengths: The Torrington area has a high share of arts and learning institutions. Waterbury is close by and the many cultural attractions of Hartford are an easy drive away.

Weaknesses: Torrington is not the Filene's Basement of small cities. A glance at the median personal income will tip you off. Torrington has the second highest home prices among small cities and one of the highest property taxes.

Scores by Section	
Climate/Environment	67
Diversions	40
Economics	36
Education	55
Community Assets	49
Health Care	30
Housing	32
Public Safety	78
Transportation	46
Urban Proximity	87
Total Points	520

FLORIDA

Key West

Points: 517
National Rank: 69
State Rank: 1 of 2

General Information
Components: Monroe County
Area Population: 81,796
Central City Population: 24,690
Location: The western tip of the Florida Keys
Nearest Metro Center: Miami, 161 miles

Strengths: No micro offers a wider array of things to do: Key West has the top score in the diversions section. The weather is usually pleasant. Only forty-four days climb above 90 degrees or drop below 32 degrees each year.

Weaknesses: Key West's spending on its schools is low, its dropout rate high. Isolation can be a problem—there is only one road back to the mainland. Key West's total crime rate is among the steepest of all micros.

Scores by Section	
Climate/Environment	71
Diversions	88
Economics	50
Education	36
Community Assets	53
Health Care	42
Housing	34
Public Safety	48
Transportation	49
Urban Proximity	46
Total Points	517

Vero Beach

Points: 511
National Rank: 78
State Rank: 2 of 2

General Information
Components: Indian River County
Area Population: 95,618
Central City Population: 18,138
Location: Central Florida's Atlantic coast, between Melbourne and Fort Pierce
Nearest Metro Center: Fort Pierce, 16 miles

Strengths: Vero Beach has a large share of new homes and the fewest degree days of any small city on the East Coast. Personal income is the highest among micros. Two metropolitan areas are within short drives.

Weaknesses: Although many are new, houses tend to be small in Vero Beach, and property taxes are high. The high school dropout problem is serious and investment in schools is below average.

Scores by Section	
Climate/Environment	59
Diversions	54
Economics	48
Education	30
Community Assets	52
Health Care	48
Housing	55
Public Safety	63
Transportation	41
Urban Proximity	61
Total Points	511

GEORGIA

Brunswick

Points: 527
National Rank: 45
State Rank: 6 of 12

General Information
Components: Glynn County
Area Population: 65,037
Central City Population: 17,725
Location: Extreme southeastern Georgia, on the Atlantic coast
Nearest Metro Center: Jacksonville, Fla., 71 miles

Strengths: Brunswick is a popular vacation destination, located on the south-Georgia coast, just off Interstate 95. The area has far and away the most dining, shopping, and recreational variety among Georgia small cities.

Weaknesses: Brunswick does not buck the low education levels of the state. It has the third highest dropout rate among Georgia micros and one of the lower levels of educational funding.

Scores by Section	
Climate/Environment	44
Diversions	61
Economics	46
Education	29
Community Assets	49
Health Care	62
Housing	75
Public Safety	54
Transportation	49
Urban Proximity	58
Total Points	527

Dalton

Points: 529
National Rank: 40
State Rank: 5 of 12

General Information
Components: Whitfield County
Area Population: 76,859
Central City Population: 22,378
Location: Extreme northwestern Georgia, near the Tennessee border
Nearest Metro Center: Chattanooga, Tenn., 28 miles

Strengths: Dalton is the self-proclaimed "carpet capital of the world," a title which brings with it one of Georgia's stronger small-city economies. Chattanooga is a short ride north. Dalton spends far above average on its community hospital and health services.

Weaknesses: Dalton, unfortunately, claims the highest dropout rate among the nation's small cities. Nearly 24 percent of high-school-age youth are not graduates and are not in school. Dalton's overall educational score is one of the lowest among all micros.

Scores by Section	
Climate/Environment	69
Diversions	34
Economics	46
Education	17
Community Assets	40
Health Care	58
Housing	70
Public Safety	64
Transportation	49
Urban Proximity	82
Total Points	529

Dublin

Points: 502
National Rank: 95
State Rank: 10 of 12

General Information
Components: Laurens County
Area Population: 42,264
Central City Population: 17,925
Location: South-central Georgia, southeast of Macon
Nearest Metro Center: Macon, 56 miles

Strengths: The Dublin area has the highest share of membership organizations and social services of any Georgia micro. It also has the most access to highways. Macon is an hour's drive away.

Weaknesses: Dublin shares the high dropout rates prevalent throughout much of the state. Its rate of 18.6 percent is the ninth highest among small cities. Few adult high school graduates and low school funding compound the problem.

Scores by Section	
Climate/Environment	70
Diversions	44
Economics	34
Education	21
Community Assets	44
Health Care	46
Housing	83
Public Safety	51
Transportation	46
Urban Proximity	63
Total Points	502

Gainesville

Points: 510
National Rank: 80
State Rank: 7 of 12

General Information
Components: Hall County
Area Population: 105,204
Central City Population: 19,476
Location: Northeastern Georgia, northeast of Atlanta
Nearest Metro Center: Athens, 39 miles

Strengths: Located on Lake Lanier and just twenty-five miles from the Chattahoochee National Forest, Gainesville also has access to many metropolitan attractions. The small city is fifty miles from the sports, shopping, and fine arts of Atlanta.

Weaknesses: Gainesville suffers the same high dropout rates common throughout much of the state. Other than the highway to Atlanta, Gainesville residents are limited in their choice of main roads. There is no local air service.

Scores by Section	
Climate/Environment	72
Diversions	30
Economics	43
Education	19
Community Assets	42
Health Care	48
Housing	74
Public Safety	69
Transportation	19
Urban Proximity	94
Total Points	510

Hinesville

Points: 400
National Rank: 192
State Rank: 12 of 12

General Information
Components: Liberty County
Area Population: 58,895
Central City Population: 27,009
Location: Southeastern Georgia, southwest of Savannah
Nearest Metro Center: Savannah, 41 miles

Strengths: Hinesville has one of the highest housing scores in Georgia, a state that leads the way in the housing section. Metropolitan Savannah as well as the Georgia coast are within an hour's drive, making for plenty of recreational choices.

Weaknesses: The predominance of Fort Stewart creates a transitory population, one that receives many of its services on base rather than in the community-at-large. As a result, Hinesville has few restaurants, diversions, or community assets.

Scores by Section	
Climate/Environment	67
Diversions	14
Economics	36
Education	28
Community Assets	12
Health Care	29
Housing	83
Public Safety	48
Transportation	37
Urban Proximity	46
Total Points	400

La Grange

Points: 535
National Rank: 28
State Rank: 2 of 12

General Information
Components: Troup County
Area Population: 57,560
Central City Population: 27,032
Location: West-central Georgia, southwest of Atlanta, near the Alabama border
Nearest Metro Center: Columbus, 45 miles

Strengths: La Grange ties for first place in the state for public safety, with an especially low juvenile arrest rate. The area is also convenient to the arts, shopping, and sports of Atlanta.

Weaknesses: Income gains and retail sales, although not far below average, lag behind those of other micros in the state. Overall, La Grange has the weakest economy of Georgia small cities.

Scores by Section	
Climate/Environment	67
Diversions	38
Economics	27
Education	24
Community Assets	42
Health Care	57
Housing	73
Public Safety	69
Transportation	48
Urban Proximity	90
Total Points	535

Milledgeville

Points: 531
National Rank: 36
State Rank: 4 of 12

General Information
Components: Baldwin County
Area Population: 41,334
Central City Population: 18,376
Location: Central Georgia, northeast of Macon
Nearest Metro Center: Macon, 29 miles

Strengths: The home of writer Flannery O'Connor boasts a good housing market, strong health care system, and easy metropolitan access. The rate of doctors per resident is high and Milledgeville invests highly in the community hospital. Macon is just down the road.

Weaknesses: The presence of Georgia College helps to bolster the local education environment, but Milledgeville still has significantly low educational attainment. And unless you raise peacocks as Flannery did, you may have to head to Macon for your entertainment.

Scores by Section	
Climate/Environment	71
Diversions	30
Economics	34
Education	28
Community Assets	37
Health Care	65
Housing	80
Public Safety	67
Transportation	47
Urban Proximity	72
Total Points	531

Rome

Points: 556
National Rank: 12
State Rank: 1 of 12

General Information
Components: Floyd County
Area Population: 83,268
Central City Population: 31,198
Location: Northwestern Georgia, northwest of Atlanta
Nearest Metro Center: Gadsden, Ala., 54 miles

Strengths: Rome's high scores in health care, community assets, and urban proximity land it in first place among Georgia micros. Rome has the highest health-care rating among all small cities, with top scores in both doctor and hospital bed availability.

Weaknesses: Rome's weaknesses are on the moderate side. It fails to rise far above Georgia's low educational standards. The choice of diversions is slightly below the median for other small cities.

Scores by Section	
Climate/Environment	68
Diversions	37
Economics	36
Education	31
Community Assets	50
Health Care	74
Housing	71
Public Safety	60
Transportation	40
Urban Proximity	89
Total Points	556

Statesboro

Points: 506
National Rank: 89
State Rank: 8 of 12

General Information
Components: Bulloch County
Area Population: 47,810
Central City Population: 18,291
Location: Southeastern Georgia, northwest of Savannah
Nearest Metro Center: Savannah, 54 miles

Strengths: Statesboro's educational level far outshines that of other small Georgia cities. The influence of Georgia Southern University is a major factor. The dropout rate so prominent in other state micros is just 5 percent in Statesboro.

Weaknesses: The area displays below-average community resources such as local broadcast outlets, newspaper penetration, and membership groups. Personal income is below the median for micros and significantly below the national average.

Scores by Section	
Climate/Environment	70
Diversions	46
Economics	33
Education	51
Community Assets	29
Health Care	48
Housing	81
Public Safety	58
Transportation	35
Urban Proximity	55
Total Points	506

Thomasville

Points: 504
National Rank: 92
State Rank: 9 of 12

General Information
Components: Thomas County
Area Population: 40,246
Central City Population: 18,394
Location: Extreme southern Georgia, near the Florida border
Nearest Metro Center: Tallahassee, Fla., 37 miles

Strengths: Georgia micros offer some of the best housing values among the nation's small cities. Thomasville exemplifies this, with affordably priced homes and low energy needs. Sixty-one percent of Thomasville houses have three or more bedrooms.

Weaknesses: Georgia cities, large and small, unfortunately are also likely to have low numbers of high school grads and school funding that is significantly below national averages. Thomasville is no exception.

Scores by Section	
Climate/Environment	65
Diversions	43
Economics	43
Education	26
Community Assets	51
Health Care	58
Housing	83
Public Safety	57
Transportation	28
Urban Proximity	50
Total Points	504

Valdosta

Points: 534
National Rank: 30
State Rank: 3 of 12

General Information
Components: Lowndes County
Area Population: 82,310
Central City Population: 44,787
Location: Extreme south-central Georgia, near the Florida border
Nearest Metro Center: Tallahassee, Fla., 78 miles

Strengths: Valdosta weighs in with a strong local health network and an attractive housing market. Spending on public health far outpaces the national average. Retail sales are the third highest among Georgia micros.

Weaknesses: Valdosta doesn't share the same level of urban proximity that some other Georgia metros enjoy. The nearest city for the fine arts or sports is Atlanta, 230 miles north.

Scores by Section	
Climate/Environment	71
Diversions	39
Economics	41
Education	35
Community Assets	42
Health Care	60
Housing	84
Public Safety	58
Transportation	51
Urban Proximity	53
Total Points	534

Waycross

Points: 493
National Rank: 107
State Rank: 11 of 12

General Information
Components: Ware, Pierce Counties
Area Population: 50,044
Central City Population: 17,568
Location: Extreme southeastern Georgia
Nearest Metro Center: Jacksonville, Fla., 76 miles

Strengths: The Waycross area ties for first in housing nationwide. The area has a large share of modern, roomy, and affordable houses. Property taxes in Waycross are enviably low.

Weaknesses: Waycross is one of the more isolated of the Georgia micros. The share of high school grads is below average and little college influence is felt from grads or college students.

Scores by Section	
Climate/Environment	64
Diversions	37
Economics	31
Education	20
Community Assets	57
Health Care	47
Housing	87
Public Safety	55
Transportation	40
Urban Proximity	55
Total Points	493

IDAHO

Coeur d'Alene

Points: 539
National Rank: 25
State Rank: 1 of 4

General Information
Components: Kootenai County
Area Population: 87,345
Central City Population: 28,457
Location: Western edge of the Idaho panhandle, near the Washington border
Nearest Metro Center: Spokane, Wash., 33 miles

Strengths: Coeur d'Alene is the only small city in Idaho with a claim to urban proximity. An interstate drive brings you to Spokane, Washington, in thirty-three miles. The Coeur d'Alene economy is the third strongest among small cities nationwide.

Weaknesses: Aside from the interstate and the airport in Spokane, getting around in more local ways is difficult in Coeur d'Alene. The area has few major roads, and many of them lead through and around the mountains. The micro is also weak in community assets.

Scores by Section	
Climate/Environment	66
Diversions	60
Economics	55
Education	46
Community Assets	38
Health Care	52
Housing	62
Public Safety	58
Transportation	43
Urban Proximity	59
Total Points	539

Idaho Falls

Points: 485
National Rank: 120
State Rank: 4 of 4

General Information
Components: Bonneville County
Area Population: 79,181
Central City Population: 49,928
Location: Southeastern Idaho, northeast of Pocatello
Nearest Metro Center: Salt Lake City, Utah, 203 miles

Strengths: Idaho Falls scores the highest among the four Idaho small cities in public safety. It has a particularly low violent crime rate and significant spending on police and fire protection. The area also has a high number of broadcast outlets.

Weaknesses: Despite the low overall crime rate, juvenile arrests are high in the Idaho Falls area. Temperature swings are wide. Summer highs reach into the upper 80s and the lows average 10 degrees in January. Idaho Falls is also the most remote of the state's micros.

Scores by Section	
Climate/Environment	42
Diversions	54
Economics	43
Education	49
Community Assets	57
Health Care	49
Housing	63
Public Safety	67
Transportation	51
Urban Proximity	10
Total Points	485

Pocatello

Points: 501
National Rank: 97
State Rank: 2 of 4

General Information
Components: Bannock, Power Counties
Area Population: 79,127
Central City Population: 49,634
Location: Southeastern Idaho, east of Boise
Nearest Metro Center: Salt Lake City, Utah, 160 miles

Strengths: Getting around is easy in Pocatello: The area has the second highest transportation score of any micro. Pocatello has regular commuter air service, as well as popular local bus service. Housing and health care are strong.

Weaknesses: Pocatello rates poorly in the climate/environment section, due in part to the wide temperature variations and to environmental pollution. The nearest metro is Salt Lake City, a long haul at 160 miles.

Scores by Section	
Climate/Environment	40
Diversions	48
Economics	42
Education	47
Community Assets	46
Health Care	62
Housing	66
Public Safety	60
Transportation	72
Urban Proximity	18
Total Points	501

Twin Falls

Points: 486
National Rank: 118
State Rank: 3 of 4

General Information
Components: Twin Falls County
Area Population: 58,619
Central City Population: 31,568
Location: South-central Idaho, southeast of Boise
Nearest Metro Center: Boise, 129 miles

Strengths: Twin Falls has a well-developed community network, especially in the area of local broadcast outlets. High investment in community health and a low rate of terminal cases (due to Twin Falls's young population) give the area a high score in health care.

Weaknesses: This is the hottest small city in Idaho. July days reach an average high of 91 degrees. Twin Falls is also isolated from metropolitan attractions. Boise is a 129-mile drive away. Education scores are the lowest among the state micros.

Scores by Section	
Climate/Environment	47
Diversions	55
Economics	38
Education	36
Community Assets	56
Health Care	67
Housing	62
Public Safety	56
Transportation	54
Urban Proximity	15
Total Points	486

ILLINOIS

Carbondale

Points: 540
National Rank: 23
State Rank: 1 of 8

General Information
Components: Jackson County
Area Population: 61,444
Central City Population: 27,201
Location: Extreme southern Illinois, southeast of Saint Louis
Nearest Metro Center: East St. Louis, 96 miles

Strengths: Carbondale has far and away the highest educational score among Illinois small cities, due in part to the presence of Southern Illinois University. Carbondale ties for sixth place in education among all micros.

Weaknesses: Incomes are lowest in Carbondale; the city lags behind other Illinois micros in overall economic vitality. The housing situation is reasonably good, but houses tend to be small; just 43 percent have three or more bedrooms.

Scores by Section	
Climate/Environment	69
Diversions	49
Economics	26
Education	68
Community Assets	48
Health Care	42
Housing	64
Public Safety	58
Transportation	45
Urban Proximity	71
Total Points	540

Danville

Points: 485
National Rank: 120
State Rank: 8 of 8

General Information
Components: Vermilion County
Area Population: 87,799
Central City Population: 33,289
Location: East-central Illinois, near the Indiana border
Nearest Metro Center: Champaign, 35 miles

Strengths: Danville features a relatively moderate climate, accessibility to interstate highways, a nearby metro area, and local commuter air service.

Weaknesses: Education is not a local priority. All the regional college influence is concentrated down the road at the University of Illinois, Champaign. The high school dropout rate is above average, the highest among Illinois micros.

Scores by Section	
Climate/Environment	70
Diversions	36
Economics	32
Education	30
Community Assets	41
Health Care	30
Housing	58
Public Safety	64
Transportation	49
Urban Proximity	75
Total Points	485

Freeport

Points: 489
National Rank: 112
State Rank: 6 of 8

General Information
Components: Stephenson County
Area Population: 49,015
Central City Population: 26,620
Location: Extreme northern Illinois, west of Rockford
Nearest Metro Center: Aurora, 29 miles

Strengths: Freeport scores well in public safety, with below-average crime rates and significant investment in the police and fire departments. The Rockford metropolitan area is approximately thirty miles away via a major highway.

Weaknesses: Personal income is higher in Freeport than in the other state micros, but like much of the state, income growth and retail sales are slow. Minor population growth over the first part of the decade also reflects Freeport's slow economy.

Scores by Section	
Climate/Environment	65
Diversions	37
Economics	32
Education	41
Community Assets	43
Health Care	35
Housing	57
Public Safety	66
Transportation	41
Urban Proximity	72
Total Points	489

Galesburg

Points: 516
National Rank: 71
State Rank: 4 of 8

General Information
Components: Knox County
Area Population: 56,287
Central City Population: 33,316
Location: West-central Illinois, northwest of Peoria
Nearest Metro Center: Davenport, Iowa, 48 miles

Strengths: Galesburg offers the fourth most-affordable housing of all the micros. Median home cost is 69 percent of the typical micropolitan home and just 47 percent of the average U.S. home.

Weaknesses: Slight declines in population hurt Galesburg's otherwise fair economic performance. A low share of college grads and local college influence dampens Galesburg's educational rating.

Scores by Section	
Climate/Environment	61
Diversions	59
Economics	28
Education	38
Community Assets	60
Health Care	38
Housing	56
Public Safety	61
Transportation	56
Urban Proximity	59
Total Points	516

Mattoon-Charleston

Points: 536
National Rank: 27
State Rank: 2 of 8

General Information
Components: Coles County
Area Population: 52,231
Central City Population: Mattoon 18,484; Charleston 20,560
Location: East-central Illinois, southeast of Decatur
Nearest Metro Center: Decatur, 44 miles

Strengths: Mattoon-Charleston ties for the sixth safest micro in the country. The total crime rate in the area is less than half that of the nation; the violent crime rate is a mere 12 percent. Mattoon-Charleston ranks second in education among the Illinois micros.

Weaknesses: Mattoon-Charleston's ratio of available community hospital beds is the lowest in micropolitan Illinois and local government spending on health is virtually nonexistent. Per capita income is slightly above average, but the third lowest among the state's eight micros.

Scores by Section	
Climate/Environment	70
Diversions	49
Economics	37
Education	54
Community Assets	51
Health Care	24
Housing	58
Public Safety	77
Transportation	50
Urban Proximity	66
Total Points	536

Ottawa

Points: 487
National Rank: 114
State Rank: 7 of 8

General Information
Components: La Salle County
Area Population: 109,415
Central City Population: 18,247
Location: North-central Illinois, southwest of Chicago
Nearest Metro Center: Joliet, 45 miles

Strengths: The fine arts, the restaurants, and the Bulls of Chicago are within ninety miles of Ottawa. And getting there is easy: No other state micro has better overall highway availability. Ottawa ties for second place in state small-city retail sales and for first in personal income.

Weaknesses: The area is lacking in medical specialists and local government spending on health is very low. Just 11 percent of Ottawa adults are college grads, the second lowest figure among Illinois micros.

Scores by Section	
Climate/Environment	56
Diversions	50
Economics	37
Education	31
Community Assets	40
Health Care	21
Housing	55
Public Safety	68
Transportation	43
Urban Proximity	86
Total Points	487

Quincy

Points: 525
National Rank: 48
State Rank: 3 of 8

General Information
Components: Adams County
Area Population: 67,769
Central City Population: 40,615
Location: West-central Illinois, on the Mississippi River
Nearest Metro Center: Springfield, 102 miles

Strengths: Quincy finishes first among small cities in community assets. The area has a wide selection of local television and radio stations, as well as community groups, libraries, museums, and other public institutions. No Illinois micro has a better ratio of doctors than Quincy.

Weaknesses: This is the most isolated micro in Illinois, the only one more than 100 miles from a metro center. The area is poorly served by major roads, compounding Quincy's isolation. Only one other state micro has a lower highway availability score.

Scores by Section	
Climate/Environment	63
Diversions	48
Economics	35
Education	39
Community Assets	75
Health Care	41
Housing	58
Public Safety	61
Transportation	54
Urban Proximity	51
Total Points	525

Sterling

Points: 491
National Rank: 110
State Rank: 5 of 8

General Information
Components: Whiteside County
Area Population: 60,381
Central City Population: 15,163
Location: Northwestern Illinois, southwest of Rockford
Nearest Metro Center: Rockford, 57 miles

Strengths: Sterling has a good supply of large homes and property taxes are the fourth lowest among Illinois small cities. Sterling can also claim low crime rates, with an especially low incidence of violent offenses.

Weaknesses: Personal income growth is slower in Sterling than in other Illinois small cities. Retail sales and the value of manufacturing productivity are also among the lowest of the eight small cities.

Scores by Section	
Climate/Environment	64
Diversions	40
Economics	26
Education	33
Community Assets	43
Health Care	45
Housing	62
Public Safety	65
Transportation	51
Urban Proximity	62
Total Points	491

INDIANA

Columbus

Points: 565
National Rank: 8
State Rank: 1 of 6

General Information
Components: Bartholomew County
Area Population: 67,042
Central City Population: 35,689
Location: South-central Indiana, south of Indianapolis
Nearest Metro Center: Bloomington, 39 miles

Strengths: The Columbus area offers the chance to earn a good living: Its per capita income tops the national average and ranks seventh among all micros. Income growth is healthy in Columbus, also; personal income has risen more than 11 percent—twice the micro median.

Weaknesses: Housing in Columbus is the most expensive among Indiana small cities and is slightly above the median for all micros. Property taxes are 55 percent higher than the micro median.

Scores by Section	
Climate/Environment	54
Diversions	43
Economics	49
Education	41
Community Assets	56
Health Care	56
Housing	63
Public Safety	65
Transportation	45
Urban Proximity	93
Total Points	565

Marion

Points: 477
National Rank: 137
State Rank: 5 of 6

General Information
Components: Grant County
Area Population: 73,858
Central City Population: 32,312
Location: East-central Indiana, northeast of Indianapolis
Nearest Metro Center: Kokomo, 32 miles

Strengths: Indianapolis is slightly more than an hour away on Interstate 69. Access to the metro's arts, shopping, and sports gives Marion its highest score: 89 of 100 points in the urban proximity section.

Weaknesses: The local health network is not well developed. Marion has the lowest score in health care among Indiana small cities. Population growth was effectively flat through the first half of the decade, showing a 0.4 percent decline.

Scores by Section	
Climate/Environment	61
Diversions	34
Economics	31
Education	36
Community Assets	56
Health Care	27
Housing	59
Public Safety	45
Transportation	39
Urban Proximity	89
Total Points	477

Michigan City-La Porte

Points: 471
National Rank: 142
State Rank: 6 of 6

General Information
Components: La Porte County
Area Population: 110,008
Central City Population: Michigan City, 33,899; La Porte, 22,913
Location: Extreme northwestern Indiana, between Chicago and South Bend
Nearest Metro Center: Gary, 25 miles

Strengths: Chicago is fifty-six miles from Michigan City-La Porte, helping the area to the second highest urban proximity score among all micropolitans. Getting to Chicago or elsewhere is easy: The area scores first among all micros in the highway index.

Weaknesses: The area is dealing with two potentially dangerous hazardous waste sites and failure to meet air quality standards. Michigan City-La Porte's rate of income growth is below the micro median, the lowest among Indiana micropolitans.

Scores by Section	
Climate/Environment	52
Diversions	32
Economics	32
Education	33
Community Assets	37
Health Care	33
Housing	60
Public Safety	44
Transportation	53
Urban Proximity	95
Total Points	471

New Castle

Points: 509
National Rank: 84
State Rank: 4 of 6

General Information
Components: Henry County
Area Population: 49,018
Central City Population: 18,716
Location: East-central Indiana, east of Indianapolis
Nearest Metro Center: Muncie, 20 miles

Strengths: An hour after stepping into your car in New Castle, you can be in downtown Indianapolis, forty-eight miles away. New Castle has the most affordable housing in micropolitan Indiana and the third most affordable in micropolitan America.

Weaknesses: New Castle commuters have one of the longest drives of all micro workers, equivalent to the national average. The area has a very low ratio of private-practice doctors (but a well-established community hospital) and a low share of diversions.

Scores by Section	
Climate/Environment	70
Diversions	28
Economics	34
Education	34
Community Assets	55
Health Care	36
Housing	63
Public Safety	65
Transportation	31
Urban Proximity	93
Total Points	509

Richmond

Points: 520
National Rank: 59
State Rank: 2 of 6

General Information
Components: Wayne County
Area Population: 72,557
Central City Population: 38,810
Location: Extreme east-central Indiana, east of Indianapolis
Nearest Metro Center: Dayton, Ohio, 41 miles

Strengths: The Richmond area's violent crime rate is the second lowest among Indiana small cities and its share of museums and learning institutions is the highest. Dayton is just forty-one miles away, Cincinnati sixty-two, and Indianapolis seventy-three.

Weaknesses: Richmond's educational performance is hampered by little college influence and little spending on local schools. The high school dropout rate is above the micro median and is the highest among Indiana small cities.

Scores by Section	
Climate/Environment	64
Diversions	38
Economics	35
Education	30
Community Assets	66
Health Care	34
Housing	58
Public Safety	61
Transportation	49
Urban Proximity	85
Total Points	520

Vincennes

Points: 510
National Rank: 80
State Rank: 3 of 6

General Information
Components: Knox County
Area Population: 40,240
Central City Population: 19,789
Location: Southwestern Indiana, on the Wabash River
Nearest Metro Center: Evansville, 54 miles

Strengths: Vincennes has the lowest high school dropout rate among the six Indiana micros. High rates of homeownership, newspaper readership, and local arts and learning institutions give Vincennes the second highest community assets rating among the state's micros.

Weaknesses: Vincennes has limited availability of amusement establishments and restaurants and taverns. Low highway and aviation availability depresses the area's transportation rating.

Scores by Section	
Climate/Environment	60
Diversions	39
Economics	33
Education	40
Community Assets	63
Health Care	53
Housing	55
Public Safety	70
Transportation	33
Urban Proximity	64
Total Points	510

IOWA

Ames

Points: 602
National Rank: 2
State Rank: 1 of 5

General Information
Components: Story County
Area Population: 74,478
Central City Population: 46,562
Location: Central Iowa, north of Des Moines
Nearest Metro Center: Des Moines, 28 miles

Strengths: Ames is a run-away winner among Iowa micros in education. The city has the highest share of high school graduates of any small city, the lowest share of dropouts, and the second highest share of college graduates. Ames also ties with Muscatine for the strongest small-city economy in the state.

Weaknesses: Housing prices are steep in Ames—41 percent above the median for small cities in the state. Utility bills can be high also because Ames has the second highest number of degree days among Iowa micros.

Scores by Section	
Climate/Environment	59
Diversions	50
Economics	50
Education	84
Community Assets	37
Health Care	64
Housing	54
Public Safety	65
Transportation	67
Urban Proximity	72
Total Points	602

Burlington

Points: 544
National Rank: 20
State Rank: 3 of 5

General Information
Components: Des Moines County
Area Population: 42,879
Central City Population: 27,573
Location: Extreme southeastern Iowa, on the Mississippi River
Nearest Metro Center: Iowa City, 78 miles

Strengths: Burlington is strong in its community resources: The area has the fourth highest rate of membership organizations. Homes prices and crime rates are the second lowest among state micros.

Weaknesses: Burlington is the most isolated of the Iowa micros, located seventy-eight miles from the nearest metro. Burlington residents have a 230-mile drive to reach Chicago, the nearest art and sports center. It's also a long drive to reach the interstate.

Scores by Section	
Climate/Environment	62
Diversions	55
Economics	37
Education	51
Community Assets	70
Health Care	45
Housing	50
Public Safety	69
Transportation	52
Urban Proximity	53
Total Points	544

Clinton

Points: 529
National Rank: 40
State Rank: 4 of 5

General Information
Components: Clinton County
Area Population: 50,983
Central City Population: 28,966
Location: Extreme east-central Iowa, on the Mississippi River
Nearest Metro Center: Davenport, 37 miles

Strengths: Clinton has the second lowest total crime rate of any micro and the lowest violent crime rate by far. The micro finishes first overall in the public safety section. Housing is the most affordable among Iowa small cities.

Weaknesses: Clinton has the second lowest health-care score among Iowa micros and the lowest personal income among Iowa small cities. Earnings in other micros are as much as 14 percent higher than in Clinton.

Scores by Section	
Climate/Environment	58
Diversions	53
Economics	39
Education	43
Community Assets	52
Health Care	36
Housing	53
Public Safety	85
Transportation	48
Urban Proximity	62
Total Points	529

Mason City

Points: 558
National Rank: 10
State Rank: 2 of 5

General Information
Components: Cerro Gordo County
Area Population: 46,518
Central City Population: 28,817
Location: North-central Iowa, northwest of Waterloo
Nearest Metro Center: Waterloo, 82 miles

Strengths: Mason City's availability of doctors is the fourth highest among all micros. The ratio of specialists and hospital beds is also advantageous. The area leads Iowa micros in entertainment availability.

Weaknesses: Mason City is the only Iowa micro without high scores in public safety. The total crime rate is 50 percent above the micro median and nearly 75 percent above the Iowa median.

Scores by Section	
Climate/Environment	51
Diversions	68
Economics	40
Education	53
Community Assets	74
Health Care	58
Housing	48
Public Safety	46
Transportation	61
Urban Proximity	59
Total Points	558

Muscatine

Points: 480
National Rank: 130
State Rank: 5 of 5

General Information
Components: Muscatine County
Area Population: 41,292
Central City Population: 23,936
Location: Extreme eastern Iowa, on the Mississippi River, southwest of Davenport
Nearest Metro Center: Davenport, 30 miles

Strengths: Muscatine has the highest per capita income of any Iowa micro. It is one of only ten micropolitans where personal incomes exceed the national average. Housing is affordable in Muscatine and a considerable share of houses contain three or more bedrooms.

Weaknesses: Muscatine has just one local radio station and no other local broadcast outlets. The area trails other Iowa micros when it comes to the availability of doctors, specialists, and hospital beds. Muscatine's ratio of doctors is one of the lowest among all micros.

Scores by Section	
Climate/Environment	55
Diversions	51
Economics	50
Education	40
Community Assets	39
Health Care	32
Housing	53
Public Safety	56
Transportation	43
Urban Proximity	61
Total Points	480

KANSAS

Hutchinson

Points: 478
National Rank: 133
State Rank: 3 of 3

General Information
Components: Reno County
Area Population: 62,653
Central City Population: 39,770
Location: South-central Kansas, northwest of Wichita
Nearest Metro Center: Wichita, 52 miles

Strengths: Hutchinson scores well in the community section, especially with a very high rate of subscription to the local daily paper. Housing in Hutchinson is the most affordable among the Kansas micros.

Weaknesses: Lack of major highways, public transit, and local passenger air service lead Hutchinson to score third in transportation among the three Kansas micros. Hutchinson also has the highest dropout rate of the three micros.

Scores by Section	
Climate/Environment	54
Diversions	49
Economics	30
Education	42
Community Assets	65
Health Care	32
Housing	53
Public Safety	61
Transportation	34
Urban Proximity	58
Total Points	478

Manhattan

Points: 496
National Rank: 104
State Rank: 2 of 3

General Information
Components: Riley, Pottawatomie Counties
Area Population: 86,818
Central City Population: 38,514
Location: Northeastern Kansas, northwest of Topeka
Nearest Metro Center: Topeka, 54 miles

Strengths: Manhattan has the fifth highest share of high school graduates and the seventh highest share of college graduates. Kansas State University provides a positive educational climate. Housing costs are reasonable and total crime is the lowest among the three state micros.

Weaknesses: The transient population of the university and, to some extent, Fort Riley, act to keep the share of owner-occupied housing down. Nearly half of houses are rented. The area is also weak in other community assets such as broadcast outlets and membership groups.

Scores by Section	
Climate/Environment	60
Diversions	37
Economics	32
Education	69
Community Assets	35
Health Care	36
Housing	61
Public Safety	56
Transportation	58
Urban Proximity	52
Total Points	496

Salina

Points: 534
National Rank: 30
State Rank: 1 of 3

General Information
Components: Saline County
Area Population: 49,301
Central City Population: 44,167
Location: Central Kansas, north of Wichita
Nearest Metro Center: Wichita, 90 miles

Strengths: Salina leads the Kansas micros in availability of both doctors and hospital beds. Salina has a newspaper subscription rate even higher than Hutchinson's. Personal income and retail sales are also the highest among the three Kansas micros.

Weaknesses: The total crime rate in the Salina area is one of the ten highest among small cities. Only two micros have a higher rate of juvenile arrest. Incomes have increased at a rate below that of the other Kansas micros.

Scores by Section	
Climate/Environment	57
Diversions	59
Economics	43
Education	46
Community Assets	69
Health Care	51
Housing	61
Public Safety	41
Transportation	54
Urban Proximity	53
Total Points	534

KENTUCKY

Bowling Green

Points: 523
National Rank: 54
State Rank: 3 of 5

General Information
Components: Warren County
Area Population: 83,027
Central City Population: 45,451
Location: South-central Kentucky, southwest of Louisville
Nearest Metro Center: Clarksville, Tenn., 61 miles

Strengths: The Bowling Green area has experienced a high rate of income growth, much higher than other Kentucky micros. The area has the lowest dropout rate in micropolitan Kentucky and the third highest local broadcast market of all micros.

Weaknesses: Although the area has good highway availability, transportation scores are low otherwise, particularly in public transit usage, highway investment, and aviation service.

Scores by Section	
Climate/Environment	67
Diversions	45
Economics	49
Education	41
Community Assets	55
Health Care	55
Housing	76
Public Safety	50
Transportation	35
Urban Proximity	50
Total Points	523

Frankfort

Points: 547
National Rank: 17
State Rank: 1 of 5

General Information
Components: Franklin County
Area Population: 45,603
Central City Population: 28,708
Location: Northern Kentucky, between Louisville and Lexington
Nearest Metro Center: Lexington, 23 miles

Strengths: Frankfort boasts the lowest property taxes in micropolitan Kentucky. It also has the closest metro proximity and the highest rate of museums, libraries, and other community arts and learning institutions.

Weaknesses: Frankfort has some of the lowest rates of amusement and recreation establishments among Kentucky micros. The area has an above-average dropout rate and below-average spending on schools.

Scores by Section	
Climate/Environment	71
Diversions	29
Economics	38
Education	34
Community Assets	63
Health Care	53
Housing	75
Public Safety	51
Transportation	48
Urban Proximity	85
Total Points	547

Madisonville

Points: 478
National Rank: 133
State Rank: 5 of 5

General Information
Components: Hopkins County
Area Population: 46,283
Central City Population: 18,846
Location: West-central Kentucky, south of Evansville, Ind.
Nearest Metro Center: Owensboro, 48 miles

Strengths: Madisonville has the least expensive housing of Kentucky micros: Home prices are 70 percent of the state's small-city median. The area also has a high ratio of doctors and hospital beds.

Weaknesses: Madisonville saw little income growth in the first half of the decade. The increase amounted to just one-fifth of the median for all micros. The area has the highest dropout rate of Kentucky small cities.

Scores by Section	
Climate/Environment	69
Diversions	38
Economics	24
Education	15
Community Assets	54
Health Care	57
Housing	74
Public Safety	60
Transportation	30
Urban Proximity	57
Total Points	478

Paducah

Points: 529
National Rank: 40
State Rank: 2 of 5

General Information
Components: McCracken County
Area Population: 64,708
Central City Population: 26,749
Location: Extreme western Kentucky, on the Ohio River
Nearest Metro Center: Clarksville, Tenn., 96 miles

Strengths: The highest small-city personal income in Kentucky goes to residents of Paducah. Property taxes are second lowest among state micros and community assets are strong.

Weaknesses: Paducah has the second highest violent crime rate—more than five times the micro median. A federal hazardous waste site in the area gives Paducah one of the highest rates of potential hazardous sites per 1,000 square miles.

Scores by Section	
Climate/Environment	54
Diversions	41
Economics	53
Education	31
Community Assets	70
Health Care	61
Housing	73
Public Safety	40
Transportation	53
Urban Proximity	53
Total Points	529

Radcliff-Elizabethtown

Points: 500
National Rank: 99
State Rank: 4 of 5

General Information
Components: Hardin County
Area Population: 90,401
Central City Population: Radcliff 19,879; Elizabethtown 20,361
Location: North-central Kentucky, south of Louisville
Nearest Metro Center: Louisville, 36 miles

Strengths: Fewer than 8 percent of houses in the Radcliff-Elizabethtown area predate 1940. The micro is the third closest of all micros to a retail hub (Louisville). Getting there is easy: The area ties for the seventh highest highway index among all micros.

Weaknesses: There is money in Radcliff-Elizabethtown, but most of it is in the vaults of Fort Knox. The micro has the lowest personal income of any Kentucky small city. It also spends the least on schools.

Scores by Section	
Climate/Environment	62
Diversions	24
Economics	32
Education	33
Community Assets	38
Health Care	41
Housing	79
Public Safety	67
Transportation	43
Urban Proximity	81
Total Points	500

LOUISIANA

Hammond

Points: 434
National Rank: 181
State Rank: 3 of 3

General Information
Components: Tangipahoa County
Area Population: 91,337
Central City Population: 17,654
Location: Southeastern Louisiana, east of Baton Rouge
Nearest Metro Center: Baton Rouge, 41 miles

Strengths: Hammond has Louisiana's highest urban proximity score; Baton Rouge and New Orleans are both less than an hour away. Property taxes are the third lowest among all small cities.

Weaknesses: Hammond has the lowest public safety score among all small cities. Its total crime and violent crime rates were exceptionally high for the year in question. Personal income is low in Hammond and high school dropout rates are high.

Scores by Section	
Climate/Environment	57
Diversions	24
Economics	39
Education	23
Community Assets	33
Health Care	44
Housing	85
Public Safety	28
Transportation	26
Urban Proximity	75
Total Points	434

New Iberia

Points: 468
National Rank: 147
State Rank: 2 of 3

General Information
Components: Iberia County
Area Population: 70,820
Central City Population: 33,658
Location: South-central Louisiana, south of Lafayette
Nearest Metro Center: Lafayette, 20 miles

Strengths: New Iberia invests well in local health and hospitals, with government spending three times the national average. Housing prices are low in New Iberia, as are property taxes and heating and cooling requirements.

Weaknesses: New Iberia has the eighth highest drop-out rate among all small cities. Fewer than 60 percent of adults are themselves high school graduates, far below the national average. The economy is the weakest of the three Louisiana micros.

Scores by Section	
Climate/Environment	62
Diversions	31
Economics	32
Education	17
Community Assets	36
Health Care	46
Housing	81
Public Safety	68
Transportation	33
Urban Proximity	62
Total Points	468

Ruston

Points: 482
National Rank: 125
State Rank: 1 of 3

General Information
Components: Lincoln County
Area Population: 43,112
Central City Population: 20,123
Location: North-central Louisiana, west of Monroe
Nearest Metro Center: Monroe, 31 miles

Strengths: Incomes are up dramatically in Ruston, with a growth rate higher than all but five other small cities. Education scores are far above the other Louisiana micros, due to influence of Grambling State University.

Weaknesses: Ruston has the seventh lowest score among the nation's micros in the diversions category. Despite the positive educational influence from the university, spending on local schools is low, as is spending on health care.

Scores by Section	
Climate/Environment	64
Diversions	24
Economics	39
Education	61
Community Assets	37
Health Care	35
Housing	79
Public Safety	61
Transportation	42
Urban Proximity	40
Total Points	482

MAINE

Augusta-Waterville

Points: 527
National Rank: 45
State Rank: 1 of 2

General Information
Components: Kennebec County
Area Population: 117,111
Central City Population: Augusta, 19,770; Waterville, 16,233
Location: South-central Maine, northeast of Lewiston
Nearest Metro Center: Lewiston, 30 miles

Strengths: Augusta-Waterville scores the second highest among micros for community resources, including a high number of local broadcast outlets and museums. Violent crime is low and tourism boosts retail sales.

Weaknesses: Incomes are above average in Augusta-Waterville, but declined a percentage point in the first half of the decade. Housing costs are 50 percent above the median for small cities. Like the rest of Maine, population growth has slowed to minimal.

Scores by Section	
Climate/Environment	62
Diversions	44
Economics	29
Education	46
Community Assets	74
Health Care	43
Housing	45
Public Safety	68
Transportation	50
Urban Proximity	66
Total Points	527

Biddeford-Saco

Points: 478
National Rank: 133
State Rank: 2 of 2

General Information
Components: York County
Area Population: 169,410
Central City Population: Biddeford, 20,416; Saco, 15,386
Location: Extreme southern Maine, southwest of Portland
Nearest Metro Center: Portland, 16 miles

Strengths: There's plenty to do in Biddeford-Saco. The area has the fifth highest rate of arts and learning institutions and above-average rates of amusement establishments, shopping, and restaurants. There is little violent crime.

Weaknesses: Housing costs are the sixth highest among small cities. Property taxes are twice the micro median. Doctor availability is below average and availability of specialists is just high enough to keep Biddeford-Saco off the bottom-ten list in that category.

Scores by Section	
Climate/Environment	63
Diversions	48
Economics	24
Education	46
Community Assets	53
Health Care	22
Housing	35
Public Safety	68
Transportation	37
Urban Proximity	82
Total Points	478

MARYLAND

Salisbury

Points: 520
National Rank: 59
State Rank: 1 of 1

General Information
Components: Wicomico County
Area Population: 78,469
Central City Population: 22,204
Location: Extreme southeastern Maryland, on the Delmarva peninsula
Nearest Metro Center: Wilmington, Del., 102 miles

Strengths: Homes are large and prices and property taxes are below the national average. The area's three local television and nine radio stations place Salisbury tenth among small cities in broadcast outlets.

Weaknesses: Crime is a problem in Salisbury. The area has the seventh highest violent crime rate of all small cities. The juvenile arrest rate is twice the micropolitan median. Salisbury is remote from arts, retail, and sports centers and scores low in the diversions section.

Scores by Section	
Climate/Environment	76
Diversions	37
Economics	37
Education	40
Community Assets	63
Health Care	55
Housing	72
Public Safety	42
Transportation	54
Urban Proximity	44
Total Points	520

MICHIGAN

Marquette

Points: 502
National Rank: 95
State Rank: 3 of 4

General Information
Components: Marquette County
Area Population: 70,156
Central City Population: 22,196
Location: The north shore of Michigan's Upper Peninsula, along Lake Superior
Nearest Metro Center: Green Bay, Wisc., 175 miles

Strengths: Marquette's violent crime rate is the lowest among the state's four micros. The area is second only to Traverse City when it comes to health-care availability. Marquette has the fifth lowest high school dropout rate of any small city.

Weaknesses: Winters are for the brave only, with an average nightly low of 4 degrees in January. The area is truly isolated. No micro east of the Mississippi is farther from its nearest metro center.

Scores by Section	
Climate/Environment	59
Diversions	51
Economics	32
Education	55
Community Assets	61
Health Care	57
Housing	49
Public Safety	60
Transportation	59
Urban Proximity	19
Total Points	502

Mount Pleasant

Points: 526
National Rank: 47
State Rank: 2 of 4

General Information
Components: Isabella County
Area Population: 55,545
Central City Population: 23,860
Location: Central Michigan, northwest of Saginaw
Nearest Metro Center: Saginaw, 53 miles

Strengths: Central Michigan University helps place Mount Pleasant in a tie for first place for education among Michigan small cities. The total crime rate is the second lowest in micropolitan Michigan.

Weaknesses: The Mount Pleasant area's per capita income is the lowest among Michigan's micros. So is its availability of community hospital beds and doctors.

Scores by Section	
Climate/Environment	65
Diversions	38
Economics	31
Education	61
Community Assets	43
Health Care	45
Housing	62
Public Safety	63
Transportation	51
Urban Proximity	67
Total Points	526

Owosso

Points: 457
National Rank: 163
State Rank: 4 of 4

General Information
Components: Shiawassee County
Area Population: 71,729
Central City Population: 16,619
Location: South-central Michigan, west of Flint
Nearest Metro Center: Flint, 25 miles

Strengths: Flint is just thirty minutes from Owosso; Lansing is forty-four miles away; much larger Detroit is eighty-two miles away. Housing prices are the second lowest and per capita incomes the second highest among Michigan small cities.

Weaknesses: The existence of few amusement establishments and restaurants place Owosso last among Michigan small cities in diversions. The area has the fifth lowest rate of retail establishments among all micros. Owosso commuters have one of the longest drives of all small-city residents.

Scores by Section	
Climate/Environment	67
Diversions	21
Economics	31
Education	37
Community Assets	37
Health Care	26
Housing	61
Public Safety	65
Transportation	28
Urban Proximity	84
Total Points	457

Traverse City

Points: 582
National Rank: 5
State Rank: 1 of 4

General Information
Components: Grand Traverse, Leelenau Counties
Area Population: 87,728
Central City Population: 15,696
Location: Northwestern portion of Michigan's Lower Peninsula, north of Grand Rapids
Nearest Metro Center: Muskegon, 134 miles

Strengths: Traverse City is one of the minority of small cities whose personal incomes rival the national average. Traverse City has the third highest rate of retail establishments and the second highest per capita retail sales of all micros. The area has one of the highest shares of high school graduates among all small cities and a strong health-care network.

Weaknesses: Traverse City's beautiful and remote setting places it far from the nearest metro: Muskegon is more than two hours away. Winters are the second coldest among the state's small cities. Just seven micropolitans have higher property taxes than Traverse City.

Scores by Section	
Climate/Environment	63
Diversions	71
Economics	57
Education	61
Community Assets	59
Health Care	68
Housing	48
Public Safety	65
Transportation	55
Urban Proximity	35
Total Points	582

MINNESOTA

Faribault

Points: 512
National Rank: 77
State Rank: 5 of 5

General Information
Components: Rice County
Area Population: 51,524
Central City Population: 17,890
Location: Southeastern Minnesota, south of Minneapolis
Nearest Metro Center: Minneapolis, 48 miles

Strengths: Faribault is less than an hour from the Twin Cities on Interstate 35. The easy access to Minneapolis's museums, stores, and stadiums places Faribault first among Minnesota small cities in overall metro proximity. Per capita health funding is the second highest among Minnesota micros.

Weaknesses: Faribault has a relatively short supply of shops and restaurants as well as medical specialists. This may make a trip into Minneapolis a necessity. Other than the north-south interstate, the local road network is limited.

Scores by Section	
Climate/Environment	46
Diversions	41
Economics	32
Education	51
Community Assets	47
Health Care	45
Housing	53
Public Safety	59
Transportation	46
Urban Proximity	92
Total Points	512

Mankato

Points: 553
National Rank: 14
State Rank: 1 of 5

General Information
Components: Blue Earth, Nicolett Counties
Area Population: 83,118
Central City Population: 31,404
Location: South-central Minnesota, southwest of Minneapolis
Nearest Metro Center: Minneapolis, 75 miles

Strengths: Mankato boasts one of the lowest high school dropout rates among the nation's small cities. Its funding for local highways is second only Willmar, both in the state and in the nation. Local commuter air service also contributes to Mankato's high score in transportation.

Weaknesses: As with other Minnesota small cities, a large share of Mankato's homes predate 1940. Likewise, the cold winters produce a high number of heating degree days. Property taxes are the second highest among the state's micros.

Scores by Section	
Climate/Environment	47
Diversions	52
Economics	37
Education	63
Community Assets	62
Health Care	34
Housing	52
Public Safety	69
Transportation	71
Urban Proximity	66
Total Points	553

Red Wing

Points: 529
National Rank: 40
State Rank: 3 of 5

General Information
Components: Goodhue County
Area Population: 42,039
Central City Population: 15,742
Location: Southeastern Minnesota, on the Mississippi River, southeast of Minneapolis
Nearest Metro Center: St. Paul, 50 miles

Strengths: Incomes in Red Wing top Minnesota small cities; they are among the highest for all micros. As with other Minnesota micros, crime rates are low. Red Wing has the second highest rate of membership and social service groups among all small cities.

Weaknesses: Property taxes are far above those of other Minnesota micros; they are the tenth highest among all micros. Regardless of high taxes, little money is invested in local health and hospitals. The area has a below-average ratio of hospital beds and medical specialists.

Scores by Section	
Climate/Environment	54
Diversions	61
Economics	38
Education	48
Community Assets	50
Health Care	29
Housing	42
Public Safety	75
Transportation	44
Urban Proximity	88
Total Points	529

Willmar

Points: 546
National Rank: 19
State Rank: 2 of 5

General Information
Components: Kandiyohi County
Area Population: 40,563
Central City Population: 18,497
Location: South-central Minnesota, southwest of St. Cloud
Nearest Metro Center: St. Cloud, 63 miles

Strengths: Willmar invests in itself. Funding for schools, roads, health, and hospitals is superior. Property taxes remain far below the national average. Willmar has the highest availability of shopping among Minnesota small cities, as well as the most modern housing stock.

Weaknesses: Furnaces run long and hard through the cold winters in all five Minnesota micros, but they run the most in Willmar, where the total heating and cooling degree days is the fifth highest among all small cities. Incomes are lower in Willmar than in three other state micros and population growth has been relatively slow.

Scores by Section	
Climate/Environment	50
Diversions	50
Economics	33
Education	51
Community Assets	59
Health Care	60
Housing	55
Public Safety	53
Transportation	54
Urban Proximity	81
Total Points	546

Winona

Points: 523
National Rank: 54
State Rank: 4 of 5

General Information
Components: Winona County
Area Population: 48,351
Central City Population: 25,630
Location: Extreme southeastern Minnesota, on the Mississippi River, east of Rochester
Nearest Metro Center: La Crosse, Wisc., 29 miles

Strengths: Winona has the fourth lowest violent crime rate among the nation's small cities. Metro attractions are within an easy drive. The Winona area offers a high rate of arts and learning institutions and an above-average rate of membership organizations and social services.

Weaknesses: Winona has one of the highest shares of older housing in micropolitan America. Among Minnesota micros, it is the one most remote from arts, retail, and sports centers.

Scores by Section	
Climate/Environment	55
Diversions	46
Economics	31
Education	55
Community Assets	62
Health Care	28
Housing	52
Public Safety	76
Transportation	58
Urban Proximity	60
Total Points	523

MISSISSIPPI

Cleveland

Points: 439
National Rank: 178
State Rank: 6 of 7 (tie)

General Information
Components: Bolivar County
Area Population: 41,596
Central City Population: 15,487
Location: West-central Mississippi
Nearest Metro Center: Memphis, 98 miles

Strengths: Cleveland has the lowest total crime rate of any small city; its rate of violent crime is the lowest among Mississippi micros. Cleveland also offers the lowest home prices in micropolitan Mississippi and the tenth lowest prices among all micros.

Weaknesses: It's a three-hundred-mile drive to New Orleans, the nearest regional arts center; four hundred miles to Dallas, the nearest sports center. Personal income in Cleveland is 22 percent below the small-city median. The area offers the fewest restaurants in all of micropolitan America.

Scores by Section	
Climate/Environment	63
Diversions	27
Economics	28
Education	27
Community Assets	39
Health Care	35
Housing	79
Public Safety	69
Transportation	39
Urban Proximity	33
Total Points	439

Columbus

Points: 510
National Rank: 80
State Rank: 3 of 7

General Information
Components: Lowndes County
Area Population: 60,759
Central City Population: 26,849
Location: East-central Mississippi, northeast of Jackson
Nearest Metro Center: Tuscaloosa, Ala., 61 miles

Strengths: Columbus offers the best mix of modern, large, and inexpensive housing among the seven Mississippi small cities. The area features some of the best health-care networks in micropolitan Mississippi, with a strong financial commitment to public health.

Weaknesses: Columbus incomes are lower than most other Mississippi micros and are failing to rise significantly. Income gains in Columbus trail those of other Mississippi small cities dramatically.

Scores by Section	
Climate/Environment	62
Diversions	35
Economics	31
Education	35
Community Assets	47
Health Care	58
Housing	83
Public Safety	69
Transportation	45
Urban Proximity	45
Total Points	510

Greenville

Points: 439
National Rank: 178
State Rank: 6 of 7 (tie)

General Information
Components: Washington County
Area Population: 66,786
Central City Population: 44,394
Location: West-central Mississippi, on the Mississippi River
Nearest Metro Center: Pine Bluff, Ark., 102 miles

Strengths: Housing prices are the second lowest among Mississippi micros and are half of the national average. Just 9 percent of homes predate 1940. Incomes are not the highest but have risen 15 percent, the second fastest growth among the state's micros.

Weaknesses: Greenville is approximately 100 miles from the nearest metro, without the aid of an interstate. It's nearly four times that far to get to a professional ball game. Greenville has relatively few high school grads and the highest dropout rate among Mississippi small cities.

Scores by Section	
Climate/Environment	65
Diversions	30
Economics	36
Education	18
Community Assets	35
Health Care	49
Housing	79
Public Safety	45
Transportation	52
Urban Proximity	30
Total Points	439

Laurel

Points: 482
National Rank: 125
State Rank: 4 of 7 (tie)

General Information
Components: Jones County
Area Population: 63,000
Central City Population: 19,357
Location: Southeastern Mississippi, southeast of Jackson
Nearest Metro Center: Hattiesburg, 33 miles

Strengths: Laurel's consistently high housing features earn it a narrow win in that section among Mississippi micros. The high school dropout rate is one of the lowest in the state. The Hattiesburg metro area is a short drive down Interstate 59.

Weaknesses: Incomes are below the median for small cities. Laurel's low retail sales and low value added by manufacture reflect a slow economy. Shopping and amusement establishments are relatively limited and restaurants are scarce.

Scores by Section	
Climate/Environment	63
Diversions	30
Economics	32
Education	31
Community Assets	44
Health Care	47
Housing	84
Public Safety	52
Transportation	51
Urban Proximity	48
Total Points	482

Meridian

Points: 518
National Rank: 66
State Rank: 2 of 7

General Information
Components: Lauderdale County
Area Population: 76,377
Central City Population: 42,608
Location: East-central Mississippi, east of Jackson
Nearest Metro Center: Jackson, 88 miles

Strengths: Nine radio stations and four television stations place Meridian fourth among small cities for local broadcast outlets. Good highway accessibility and aviation availability give Meridian the highest transportation rating among Mississippi small cities.

Weaknesses: The Meridian area may be well-served by highways, but it's still a long drive to regional centers for shopping and sports. Meridian requires its local television. The area is part of one of the smallest regional TV markets.

Scores by Section	
Climate/Environment	66
Diversions	40
Economics	36
Education	33
Community Assets	57
Health Care	55
Housing	78
Public Safety	58
Transportation	60
Urban Proximity	35
Total Points	518

Tupelo

Points: 542
National Rank: 21
State Rank: 1 of 7

General Information
Components: Lee County
Area Population: 70,760
Central City Population: 32,987
Location: Northeastern Mississippi, southeast of Memphis, Tenn.
Nearest Metro Center: Florence, Ala., 78 miles

Strengths: Tupelo has a strong economy, including the highest median income among Mississippi small cities and the ninth highest retail sales among all small cities (Elvis souvenirs, perhaps?). Tupelo also ranks fifth among all micros in hospital-bed availability and has the largest supply of new houses in micropolitan Mississippi.

Weaknesses: The high school dropout rate in Tupelo is high—the second highest among the state's micros. Housing is the most expensive among Mississippi's small cities, although no higher than the median for all small cities.

Scores by Section	
Climate/Environment	64
Diversions	46
Economics	48
Education	29
Community Assets	57
Health Care	58
Housing	78
Public Safety	63
Transportation	52
Urban Proximity	47
Total Points	542

Vicksburg

Points: 482
National Rank: 125
State Rank: 4 of 7 (tie)

General Information
Components: Warren County
Area Population: 49,076
Central City Population: 28,122
Location: Western Mississippi, west of Jackson
Nearest Metro Center: Jackson, 44 miles

Strengths: Personal income in Vicksburg is higher than the median for all small cities and income growth has been high. Vicksburg has the highest share of college grads of any Mississippi small city.

Weaknesses: The total crime rate in Vicksburg exceeds the micro median by more than half. Property taxes are higher in Vicksburg than in any other Mississippi micro and are higher than the median for all small cities.

Scores by Section	
Climate/Environment	67
Diversions	39
Economics	44
Education	34
Community Assets	43
Health Care	42
Housing	75
Public Safety	56
Transportation	42
Urban Proximity	40
Total Points	482

MISSOURI

Cape Girardeau-Sikeston

Points: 524
National Rank: 51
State Rank: 1 of 4

General Information
Components: Cape Girardeau, New Madrid, Scott Counties
Area Population: 125,289
Central City Population: Cape Girardeau 35,936; Sikeston 17,298
Location: Extreme southeastern Missouri
Nearest Metro Center: St. Louis, 126 miles

Strengths: Cape Girardeau-Sikeston's housing market ranks second among the four state micros. Local manufacturing and retail sectors both show above-average performances. The arts, shopping, and sports of St. Louis are approximately 120 miles north via Interstate 55.

Weaknesses: Hospital beds have limited availability in Cape Girardeau-Sikeston. Area governments invest little money in local health. The share of adults with a high school education is significantly below the national average.

Scores by Section	
Climate/Environment	61
Diversions	45
Economics	37
Education	30
Community Assets	59
Health Care	37
Housing	75
Public Safety	58
Transportation	58
Urban Proximity	64
Total Points	524

Jefferson City

Points: 523
National Rank: 54
State Rank: 2 of 4

General Information
Components: Cole, Callaway Counties
Area Population: 101,396
Central City Population: 36,930
Location: Central Missouri, south of Columbia
Nearest Metro Center: Columbia, 33 miles

Strengths: Jefferson City's total crime rate is low and personal incomes are the highest in micropolitan Missouri. The area has a good number of arts and learning institutions as well as membership organizations and social services.

Weaknesses: The ratio of doctors and hospital beds is low in Jefferson City. Winters are colder and heating needs higher than in other Missouri small cities. The local paper has little penetration; fewer than 3 percent of residents subscribe.

Scores by Section	
Climate/Environment	66
Diversions	38
Economics	36
Education	38
Community Assets	61
Health Care	31
Housing	70
Public Safety	70
Transportation	48
Urban Proximity	65
Total Points	523

Poplar Bluff

Points: 479
National Rank: 131
State Rank: 3 of 4

General Information
Components: Butler County
Area Population: 40,146
Central City Population: 17,327
Location: Extreme southeastern Missouri
Nearest Metro Center: St. Louis, 151 miles

Strengths: Popular Bluff offers the second lowest home prices among the nation's small cities. Property taxes are the fifth lowest. The stores are active: Retail sales are the highest of Missouri small cities.

Weaknesses: The micro has the seventh lowest share of high school graduates among the nation's micros and the sixth lowest share of college grads. Highway availability is limited and there is no local passenger air service.

Scores by Section	
Climate/Environment	67
Diversions	40
Economics	38
Education	14
Community Assets	53
Health Care	46
Housing	79
Public Safety	53
Transportation	35
Urban Proximity	54
Total Points	479

Warrensburg

Points: 467
National Rank: 149
State Rank: 4 of 4

General Information
Components: Johnson County
Area Population: 46,024
Central City Population: 16,639
Location: West-central Missouri, southeast of Kansas City
Nearest Metro Center: Kansas City, 36 miles

Strengths: Warrensburg boasts one of the lowest dropout rates among all micros. The share of high school and college grads is higher than the median for small cities. The metropolitan attractions of Kansas City are close at hand.

Weaknesses: Incomes are low in Warrensburg, the lowest among the state's small cities. The area also has the lowest highway index of the four Missouri micros. Warrensburg's total crime rate is the highest among the state's micros.

Scores by Section	
Climate/Environment	67
Diversions	28
Economics	20
Education	57
Community Assets	29
Health Care	32
Housing	70
Public Safety	58
Transportation	24
Urban Proximity	82
Total Points	467

MONTANA

Bozeman

Points: 555
National Rank: 13
State Rank: 1 of 3

General Information
Components: Gallatin County
Area Population: 57,811
Central City Population: 25,067
Location: South-central Montana, west of Billings
Nearest Metro Center: Billings, 140 miles

Scores by Section	
Climate/Environment	61
Diversions	83
Economics	51
Education	76
Community Assets	56
Health Care	39
Housing	51
Public Safety	72
Transportation	58
Urban Proximity	8
Total Points	555

Strengths: Bozeman is one of the fastest-growing small cities in the country, confirmation of its healthy economy. Retail sales are high, spurred by tourism, and income has risen quickly. Bozeman's residents have above-average educations, due, in part, to Montana State University. The area has the third highest rate of recreation and amusement opportunities among all micros and a low total crime rate.

Weaknesses: Bozeman's isolation is second only to Fairbanks, Alaska. It's a long drive to reach regional arts, retail, and sports centers. Housing is one-third more expensive than the median for small cities and the area racks up the fourth highest number of heating degree days. The ratio of hospital beds is low and the community invests little in health and hospitals.

Helena

Points: 484
National Rank: 122
State Rank: 3 of 3

General Information
Components: Lewis and Clark County
Area Population: 51,604
Central City Population: 26,339
Location: West-central Montana, southwest of Great Falls
Nearest Metro Center: Great Falls, 91 miles

Scores by Section	
Climate/Environment	45
Diversions	67
Economics	37
Education	52
Community Assets	71
Health Care	48
Housing	49
Public Safety	52
Transportation	51
Urban Proximity	12
Total Points	484

Strengths: Helena has the highest income among the Montana micros. The share of resident high school graduates is the sixth highest among small cities. Helena boasts a large number of membership organizations and arts and learning institutions. The area scores highly in the diversions section.

Weaknesses: Temperature ranges are wide in Helena, from the mid-80s in summer to single-digit lows in winter. The availability of hospital beds is far below the median for small cities. It's a six-hundred-mile drive to the nearest regional arts center.

Missoula

Points: 531
National Rank: 36
State Rank: 2 of 3

General Information
Components: Missoula County
Area Population: 85,689
Central City Population: 45,364
Location: Extreme western Montana, near the Idaho border
Nearest Metro Center: Great Falls, 166 miles

Strengths: Missoula has a high availability of doctors, specialists, and hospital beds. Retail sales are the highest among the state's micros. The area ties for fourth among small cities for local broadcast outlets and has the fifth highest ratio of restaurants.

Weaknesses: Missoula has the highest rate of total crime among the three Montana small cities. It also has a much higher rate of juvenile arrest. Houses in Missoula tend to be smaller and older than those in Bozeman and Helena. The micro is the most removed from the nearest metro of the three Montana micros.

Scores by Section	
Climate/Environment	47
Diversions	69
Economics	47
Education	64
Community Assets	61
Health Care	64
Housing	50
Public Safety	56
Transportation	59
Urban Proximity	14
Total Points	531

NEBRASKA

Grand Island

Points: 467
National Rank: 149
State Rank: 1 of 1

General Information
Components: Hall County
Area Population: 50,747
Central City Population: 41,147
Location: Central Nebraska, west of Lincoln
Nearest Metro Center: Lincoln, 98 miles

Strengths: Grand Island has a good selection of shops and amusement establishments. The share of high school graduates is high. The area has an above-average number of local TV and radio stations and the local paper is widely read.

Weaknesses: Grand Island ranks ninth highest among micros in juvenile arrests. The area is far removed from regional arts and sports centers. Annual temperatures range from an average daily high of 89 in summer to a daily low of 9 in the winter.

Scores by Section	
Climate/Environment	37
Diversions	64
Economics	42
Education	41
Community Assets	62
Health Care	34
Housing	56
Public Safety	41
Transportation	54
Urban Proximity	36
Total Points	467

NEVADA

Carson City

Points: 515
National Rank: 72
State Rank: 1 of 2

General Information
Components: Carson City (independent city)
Area Population: 45,117
Central City Population: 45,117
Location: Extreme west-central Nevada, south of Reno
Nearest Metro Center: Reno, 32 miles

Strengths: Carson City leads micropolitan America in per capita retail sales, far outstripping the small-city median. Carson City is one of the few small cities with a personal income higher than the national average. Only two micros have a larger selection of new homes.

Weaknesses: Housing is expensive, with the median price of a home in Carson City nearly twice that of the typical small city. The nearest cultural center is San Francisco, a 234-mile drive.

Scores by Section	
Climate/Environment	55
Diversions	54
Economics	54
Education	50
Community Assets	41
Health Care	54
Housing	65
Public Safety	55
Transportation	39
Urban Proximity	48
Total Points	515

Elko

Points: 466
National Rank: 153
State Rank: 2 of 2

General Information
Components: Elko County
Area Population: 40,463
Central City Population: 18,583
Location: Northeastern Nevada, on Interstate 80
Nearest Metro Center: Salt Lake City, Utah, 226 miles

Strengths: Elko is growing rapidly, at a rate four times that of small cities as a whole. Incomes are among the highest in micropolitan America. Elko invests highly in its schools, roads, and hospitals. Property taxes remain close to the micro median.

Weaknesses: Elko is remotely located, a long drive to the nearest metropolitan attractions. The area has just one local television station, few community organizations or social services, and below-average newspaper readership. Elko commuters have the second-longest drive among all small city workers.

Scores by Section	
Climate/Environment	43
Diversions	56
Economics	47
Education	39
Community Assets	27
Health Care	47
Housing	56
Public Safety	72
Transportation	59
Urban Proximity	20
Total Points	466

NEW HAMPSHIRE

Concord

Points: 563
National Rank: 9
State Rank: 1 of 2

General Information
Components: Merrimack County
Area Population: 121,939
Central City Population: 36,198
Location: Southern New Hampshire, north of Manchester
Nearest Metro Center: Manchester, 20 miles

Strengths: Not only is Manchester just twenty miles down the turnpike from Concord, but the bright lights of Boston are just fifty-eight miles beyond that. Only three micros have higher per capita incomes than Concord. The area is also well-off with local arts and learning institutions, broadcast outlets, and community groups. Crime is low.

Weaknesses: Housing prices run more than twice the typical micro. Property taxes are the third highest among small cities. Concord commuters have a drive considerably longer than the micropolitan median.

Scores by Section	
Climate/Environment	67
Diversions	41
Economics	42
Education	51
Community Assets	71
Health Care	49
Housing	32
Public Safety	75
Transportation	46
Urban Proximity	89
Total Points	563

Keene

Points: 521
National Rank: 57
State Rank: 2 of 2

General Information
Components: Cheshire County
Area Population: 70,800
Central City Population: 21,916
Location: Extreme southwestern New Hampshire, west of Manchester
Nearest Metro Center: Fitchburg, Mass., 37 miles

Strengths: Crime rates are low in Keene and juvenile crime is not a problem. The arts, shopping, and sports of Boston are within a two-hour drive.

Weaknesses: Despite its wealth, Keene spends surprisingly little on public health. The ratio of local medical specialists is low. Property taxes are higher than even in Concord—the second highest among all small cities.

Scores by Section	
Climate/Environment	68
Diversions	40
Economics	42
Education	52
Community Assets	59
Health Care	31
Housing	32
Public Safety	70
Transportation	39
Urban Proximity	88
Total Points	521

NEW MEXICO

Alamogordo

Points: 433
National Rank: 183
State Rank: 4 of 7 (tie)

General Information
Components: Otero County
Area Population: 54,306
Central City Population: 29,628
Location: South-central New Mexico, northeast of Las Cruces
Nearest Metro Center: Las Cruces, 69 miles

Strengths: Alamorgordo's residents have the highest educational attainment in micropolitan New Mexico; 81 percent are high school graduates. The area's housing ranks eleventh among U.S. micros, tied with Clovis, New Mexico.

Weaknesses: Alamogordo does poorly in the health care section; its ratio of doctor availability is low and its spending on public health and hospitals minimal. Highways are scarce.

Scores by Section	
Climate/Environment	52
Diversions	39
Economics	20
Education	40
Community Assets	34
Health Care	24
Housing	83
Public Safety	60
Transportation	37
Urban Proximity	44
Total Points	433

Carlsbad

Points: 478
National Rank: 133
State Rank: 2 of 7

General Information
Components: Eddy County
Area Population: 52,795
Central City Population: 26,974
Location: Extreme southeastern New Mexico, east of Las Cruces
Nearest Metro Center: Odessa, Tex., 142 miles

Strengths: A strong public transit system, good highway availability, and local passenger air service place Carlsbad within the top ten micros for transportation. The violent crime rate is the lowest among state micros. Housing is affordably priced and taxes are light.

Weaknesses: Carlsbad's availability of doctors, hospital beds, and medical specialists is well below national norms. Carlsbad is isolated, even for a vast state such as New Mexico. Only two New Mexico micros are farther from a metro center.

Scores by Section	
Climate/Environment	51
Diversions	41
Economics	27
Education	32
Community Assets	44
Health Care	31
Housing	80
Public Safety	79
Transportation	61
Urban Proximity	32
Total Points	478

Clovis

Points: 433
National Rank: 183
State Rank: 4 of 7 (tie)

General Information

Components: Curry County
Area Population: 47,910
Central City Population: 36,091
Location: Extreme east-central New Mexico, near the Texas border
Nearest Metro Center: Lubbock, Tex., 102 miles

Strengths: Property taxes in Clovis are the lowest in micropolitan New Mexico and the fifth lowest among all small cities. Clovis's share of high school grads is surpassed in the state only by Alamogordo. The local bus system is well-utilized.

Weaknesses: Like other New Mexico micros, Clovis lacks a well-developed health network. It also shares isolation with its state counterparts: The nearest arts and sports center is Dallas, 418 miles to the east.

Scores by Section	
Climate/Environment	56
Diversions	36
Economics	35
Education	39
Community Assets	42
Health Care	29
Housing	83
Public Safety	47
Transportation	47
Urban Proximity	19
Total Points	433

Farmington

Points: 416
National Rank: 188
State Rank: 7 of 7

General Information

Components: San Juan County
Area Population: 99,279
Central City Population: 38,169
Location: Extreme northwestern New Mexico, northwest of Santa Fe
Nearest Metro Center: Albuquerque, 182 miles

Strengths: No other New Mexico micro dedicates more of its budget to education than Farmington. Farmington also leads the state micros in modern housing: Fewer than 3 percent of houses predate 1940. The local airport offers large-jet service.

Weaknesses: Farmington's violent crime rate is twice the micropolitan median. The area experiences the same isolation and lack of adequate health care that troubles other New Mexico micros.

Scores by Section	
Climate/Environment	43
Diversions	47
Economics	34
Education	36
Community Assets	44
Health Care	27
Housing	70
Public Safety	61
Transportation	35
Urban Proximity	19
Total Points	416

Gallup

Points: 426
National Rank: 186
State Rank: 6 of 7

General Information
Components: McKinley County
Area Population: 65,493
Central City Population: 19,964
Location: Extreme western New Mexico, near the Arizona border
Nearest Metro Center: Albuquerque, 138 miles

Strengths: Gallup's economy is boosted by its high worker productivity. Value added by manufacture in Gallup rates the seventh highest among all small cities. Gallup spends the second highest amount per capita on education among New Mexico micros.

Weaknesses: Poverty is a serious problem in Gallup. Personal income equals just 60 percent of the median for all small cities. Gallup has a low percentage of high school graduates among the adult population but a relatively low dropout rate among youth.

Scores by Section	
Climate/Environment	49
Diversions	42
Economics	41
Education	31
Community Assets	38
Health Care	32
Housing	68
Public Safety	54
Transportation	43
Urban Proximity	28
Total Points	426

Hobbs

Points: 448
National Rank: 170
State Rank: 3 of 7

General Information
Components: Lea County
Area Population: 57,079
Central City Population: 29,712
Location: Extreme southeastern New Mexico, near the Texas border
Nearest Metro Center: Odessa, Tex., 86 miles

Strengths: Hobbs places sixth among the nation's small cities in overall housing value and housing prices are the lowest among New Mexico micros. Hobbs's isolation is partly countered by local commuter air service.

Weaknesses: Hobbs has the highest dropout rate among New Mexico's small cities. It also has the highest violent crime rate. Availability of doctors and specialists is the lowest of the state's seven micros.

Scores by Section	
Climate/Environment	57
Diversions	48
Economics	29
Education	23
Community Assets	48
Health Care	29
Housing	84
Public Safety	55
Transportation	46
Urban Proximity	29
Total Points	448

Roswell

Points: 481
National Rank: 129
State Rank: 1 of 7

General Information
Components: Chaves County
Area Population: 60,986
Central City Population: 47,395
Location: Southeastern New Mexico, northeast of Las Cruces
Nearest Metro Center: Lubbock, Tex., 173 miles

Strengths: Roswell scores second among New Mexico micros in transportation. The area features a short commute to work, high investment in the roads, and commuter air service. Housing is some of the most affordable in micropolitan America.

Weaknesses: Per capita income declined 1.3 percent in Roswell during the first half of the decade. Incomes are the third lowest among the state's micros. Roswell has the highest rate of total crime in micropolitan New Mexico.

Scores by Section	
Climate/Environment	53
Diversions	53
Economics	22
Education	31
Community Assets	55
Health Care	46
Housing	81
Public Safety	62
Transportation	55
Urban Proximity	23
Total Points	481

NEW YORK

Cortland

Points: 521
National Rank: 57
State Rank: 6 of 7

General Information
Components: Cortland County
Area Population: 49,287
Central City Population: 19,989
Location: Central New York, south of Syracuse
Nearest Metro Center: Syracuse, 34 miles

Strengths: Cortland places second in education among New York small cities, with high rates of high school graduates, college students, and high school completion. No one has to cook in Cortland. The city has the highest share of restaurants of any New York micro.

Weaknesses: Cortland has just three local radio stations and no local television. Interstate 81 is close at hand, but the area is served by few other highways.

Scores by Section	
Climate/Environment	66
Diversions	54
Economics	30
Education	56
Community Assets	51
Health Care	33
Housing	45
Public Safety	65
Transportation	56
Urban Proximity	65
Total Points	521

Gloversville

Points: 420
National Rank: 187
State Rank: 7 of 7

General Information
Components: Fulton County
Area Population: 54,419
Central City Population: 17,316
Location: Eastern New York, northwest of Albany
Nearest Metro Center: Albany, 50 miles

Strengths: Moderate July temperatures make for pleasant summer weather in Gloversville, which lies just below the southern boundaries of the vast Adirondack state parklands, providing residents with ample opportunities for outdoor recreation year-round. The income growth is also highest among the New York micros.

Weaknesses: New houses are the exception in Gloversville; half of homes were built prior to 1940. That's especially significant when you consider heating them through the long, cold upstate winters. Local health care availability is limited.

Scores by Section	
Climate/Environment	62
Diversions	33
Economics	22
Education	43
Community Assets	36
Health Care	24
Housing	39
Public Safety	54
Transportation	49
Urban Proximity	58
Total Points	420

Ithaca

Points: 584
National Rank: 4
State Rank: 1 of 7

General Information
Components: Tompkins County
Area Population: 96,309
Central City Population: 29,242
Location: South-central New York, northwest of Binghamton
Nearest Metro Center: Elmira, 28 miles

Strengths: Ithaca earns 89 of a possible 100 points in the education section, placing it first among small cities. Violent crime is far below even that of the low rate typical for small cities. Community life features many local museums, libraries, parks, and membership groups.

Weaknesses: The faces in the neighborhood change frequently in Ithaca. Nearly half of housing is rented, not uncommon for towns that host colleges and military bases. The total crime rate in Ithaca is the highest among New York micros; highway availability is second lowest.

Scores by Section	
Climate/Environment	73
Diversions	45
Economics	28
Education	89
Community Assets	50
Health Care	46
Housing	40
Public Safety	69
Transportation	69
Urban Proximity	75
Total Points	584

Kingston

Points: 533
National Rank: 33
State Rank: 3 of 7 (tie)

General Information
Components: Ulster County
Area Population: 168,442
Central City Population: 23,420
Location: Southeastern New York, northwest of Poughkeepsie
Nearest Metro Center: Poughkeepsie, 19 miles

Strengths: New York small cities spend far above the micro median on education. Kingston spends the most among them and the second-most among all small cities. The area has the second-largest share of college grads among New York micros and a low dropout rate.

Weaknesses: Kingston housing does not come cheaply. Prices are the seventh highest among all small cities, property taxes are fourth highest. Kingston incomes were hard hit by the recession of the early 1990s and even by mid-decade they remained 3.4 percent lower than when the decade began.

Scores by Section	
Climate/Environment	67
Diversions	44
Economics	25
Education	60
Community Assets	56
Health Care	35
Housing	36
Public Safety	67
Transportation	57
Urban Proximity	86
Total Points	533

Olean

Points: 533
National Rank: 33
State Rank: 3 of 7 (tie)

General Information
Components: Cattaraugus County
Area Population: 85,472
Central City Population: 17,039
Location: Southwestern New York, southeast of Buffalo
Nearest Metro Center: Buffalo, 73 miles

Strengths: Health care in Olean is second strongest among the state's small cities, with good availability of doctors, specialists, and hospital beds. Homes in Olean run just 53 percent of national prices, the lowest among New York micros.

Weaknesses: Incomes in Olean are the lowest among the seven New York micros and were effectively flat through the first half of the decade. Olean also has the lowest rate of amusement establishments in micropolitan New York.

Scores by Section	
Climate/Environment	64
Diversions	48
Economics	23
Education	51
Community Assets	58
Health Care	32
Housing	52
Public Safety	65
Transportation	58
Urban Proximity	82
Total Points	533

Plattsburgh

Points: 547
National Rank: 17
State Rank: 2 of 7

General Information
Components: Clinton County
Area Population: 86,525
Central City Population: 20,940
Location: Extreme northeastern New York, on Lake Champlain
Nearest Metro Center: Burlington, Vt., 32 miles

Strengths: Summer visitors to Lake Champlain boost Plattsburgh retail sales to the top of New York small cities. A high value added by manufacture makes Plattsburgh's manufacturing sector the tenth strongest among all small cities.

Weaknesses: Plattsburgh's far-northern location in the state earns it the highest number of heating degree days in micropolitan New York. Like the state as a whole, Plattsburgh is failing to attract newcomers. Population growth has slowed to an absolute minimum.

Scores by Section	
Climate/Environment	63
Diversions	46
Economics	38
Education	51
Community Assets	57
Health Care	44
Housing	54
Public Safety	67
Transportation	60
Urban Proximity	67
Total Points	547

Watertown

Points: 524
National Rank: 51
State Rank: 5 of 7

General Information
Components: Jefferson County
Area Population: 115,327
Central City Population: 27,869
Location: North-central New York, north of Syracuse
Nearest Metro Center: Syracuse, 74 miles

Strengths: Summer temperatures are kept to a pleasant 80 degrees by breezes off Lake Ontario. Watertown enjoys a high level of public safety, with the highest overall score among the state's micros in that category.

Weaknesses: Watertown doesn't share the low dropout rates of other New York micros, in fact, its rate is above the overall micro median. The micro is first stop for winter weather barreling out of Canada and across Lake Ontario.

Scores by Section	
Climate/Environment	66
Diversions	43
Economics	27
Education	45
Community Assets	63
Health Care	36
Housing	46
Public Safety	79
Transportation	73
Urban Proximity	46
Total Points	524

NORTH CAROLINA

Albemarle

Points: 446
National Rank: 171
State Rank: 10 of 11

General Information
Components: Stanly County
Area Population: 53,756
Central City Population: 17,240
Location: South-central North Carolina, northeast of Charlotte
Nearest Metro Center: Charlotte, 35 miles

Strengths: Albemarle is ideally located between a national forest and a regional arts, shopping, and sports center, convenient to both. Housing is among the most affordable in micropolitan America.

Weaknesses: Albemarle has the highest dropout rate of North Carolina micros. Few major roads crisscross the Albemarle area. Local incomes have declined, even as those in other North Carolina micros have risen.

Scores by Section	
Climate/Environment	75
Diversions	28
Economics	19
Education	27
Community Assets	41
Health Care	19
Housing	76
Public Safety	56
Transportation	12
Urban Proximity	93
Total Points	446

Eden

Points: 437
National Rank: 180
State Rank: 11 of 11

General Information
Components: Rockingham County
Area Population: 87,496
Central City Population: 15,808
Location: Extreme north-central North Carolina, north of Greensboro
Nearest Metro Center: Danville, Va., 26 miles

Strengths: Eden shares the strengths prominent among North Carolina micros: affordable housing and convenient access to metropolitan attractions.

Weaknesses: The economy is weak, with the lowest retail sales among the eleven small cities in the state. The area ties for second lowest in the state for local diversions.

Scores by Section	
Climate/Environment	77
Diversions	24
Economics	36
Education	18
Community Assets	35
Health Care	23
Housing	73
Public Safety	55
Transportation	21
Urban Proximity	75
Total Points	437

Havelock-New Bern

Points: 483
National Rank: 124
State Rank: 5 of 11

General Information
Components: Craven County
Area Population: 83,930
Central City Population: Havelock, 21,121; New Bern, 18,090
Location: Extreme east-central North Carolina, near the Atlantic coast
Nearest Metro Center: Jacksonville, 50 miles

Strengths: Havelock-New Bern offers a good selection of modern houses; few were constructed prior to 1940. The temperate coastal climate is the most moderate of North Carolina micros, keeping heating and cooling costs down. Health services and the share of high school graduates are high.

Weaknesses: The micro is convenient to the Pamlico Sound and Atlantic Ocean, but the farthest of any state micro from metropolitan attractions. Highway availability is limited and funding, as with most state micros, is very low.

Scores by Section	
Climate/Environment	66
Diversions	33
Economics	36
Education	37
Community Assets	36
Health Care	60
Housing	80
Public Safety	52
Transportation	38
Urban Proximity	45
Total Points	483

Henderson

Points: 458
National Rank: 162
State Rank: 7 of 11

General Information
Components: Vance County
Area Population: 40,457
Central City Population: 16,036
Location: North-central North Carolina, northeast of Durham
Nearest Metro Center: Raleigh, 36 miles

Strengths: Henderson has the second lowest property taxes among the state's micros (Lumberton levies $2 less per person). The climate rates ninth overall among all small cities.

Weaknesses: Henderson's rate of total crime is the second highest in micropolitan North Carolina; its spending on police protection among the lowest. Henderson and Statesville tie for the highest dropout rate.

Scores by Section	
Climate/Environment	77
Diversions	31
Economics	29
Education	23
Community Assets	39
Health Care	33
Housing	79
Public Safety	49
Transportation	28
Urban Proximity	70
Total Points	458

Kinston

Points: 467
National Rank: 149
State Rank: 6 of 11

General Information
Components: Lenoir County
Area Population: 58,656
Central City Population: 25,227
Location: East-central North Carolina, southeast of Goldsboro
Nearest Metro Center: Goldsboro, 27 miles

Strengths: Kinston is one of just two North Carolina small cities with commuter air service. The nearest metro area is half an hour's drive on the highway. Incomes are above the median value for all small cities.

Weaknesses: Past Goldsboro, it's a long drive to regional arts and sports centers. Charlotte is more than 200 miles away, and there is no direct route to it. Like many of North Carolina's small cities, levels of educational attainment are low.

Scores by Section	
Climate/Environment	71
Diversions	39
Economics	41
Education	27
Community Assets	37
Health Care	34
Housing	77
Public Safety	49
Transportation	36
Urban Proximity	56
Total Points	467

Lumberton

Points: 453
National Rank: 166
State Rank: 9 of 11

General Information
Components: Robeson County
Area Population: 110,754
Central City Population: 19,187
Location: Southeastern North Carolina, south of Fayetteville
Nearest Metro Center: Fayetteville, 34 miles

Strengths: Lumberton incomes are the lowest among the state's micros, but they are rising the fastest. Income growth in Lumberton is five times the national average. The overall housing market is the best among North Carolina micros.

Weaknesses: Only a small share of Lumberton residents are high school grads. Doctor availability is very low. No other state micro has a more limited choice of stores and restaurants.

Scores by Section	
Climate/Environment	75
Diversions	22
Economics	37
Education	25
Community Assets	33
Health Care	28
Housing	84
Public Safety	49
Transportation	31
Urban Proximity	69
Total Points	453

Roanoke Rapids

Points: 457
National Rank: 163
State Rank: 8 of 11

General Information
Components: Halifax County
Area Population: 57,275
Central City Population: 16,564
Location: Northeastern North Carolina, north of Rocky Mount
Nearest Metro Center: Rocky Mount, 44 miles

Strengths: Roanoke Rapids invests in its community health-care network at a rate nine times higher than the micro median. The city also invests well in its schools. Housing costs are the second lowest among the state's micros.

Weaknesses: Only two small cities have a lower share of high school graduates. Personal income is below the national micro median and is second lowest among the state's small cities.

Scores by Section	
Climate/Environment	72
Diversions	34
Economics	25
Education	22
Community Assets	37
Health Care	37
Housing	80
Public Safety	53
Transportation	31
Urban Proximity	66
Total Points	457

Sanford

Points: 518
National Rank: 66
State Rank: 2 of 11

General Information
Components: Lee County
Area Population: 44,907
Central City Population: 16,240
Location: Central North Carolina, southwest of Raleigh
Nearest Metro Center: Fayetteville, 36 miles

Strengths: Incomes in Sanford are the highest of any state micro and are considerably above the median for all micros. Sanford has the second highest share of high school grads in micropolitan North Carolina.

Weaknesses: Community health spending is low, as is the availability of hospital beds. The area is removed from the interstate and spends little on its own roads. The nearest airport is more than thirty miles away.

Scores by Section	
Climate/Environment	78
Diversions	43
Economics	51
Education	37
Community Assets	46
Health Care	34
Housing	79
Public Safety	53
Transportation	20
Urban Proximity	77
Total Points	518

Shelby

Points: 497
National Rank: 102
State Rank: 3 of 11

General Information
Components: Cleveland County
Area Population: 88,482
Central City Population: 15,788
Location: Southwestern North Carolina, west of Charlotte
Nearest Metro Center: Charlotte, 40 miles

Strengths: Shelby may have a limited number of local highways, but it has a short pipeline straight to the arts, shopping, and professional sports in Charlotte. It boasts affordable housing and the lowest rate of juvenile arrest in micropolitan North Carolina.

Weaknesses: Retail sales are the third lowest of the eleven state micros. Income growth is the second lowest in North Carolina, and below the median for all micros.

Scores by Section	
Climate/Environment	64
Diversions	24
Economics	27
Education	28
Community Assets	51
Health Care	49
Housing	79
Public Safety	55
Transportation	28
Urban Proximity	92
Total Points	497

Statesville

Points: 519
National Rank: 64
State Rank: 1 of 11

General Information
Components: Iredell County
Area Population: 100,706
Central City Population: 18,201
Location: West-central North Carolina, north of Charlotte
Nearest Metro Center: Hickory, 27 miles

Strengths: Statesville rates first among micros in urban proximity. Its total crime rate is the eighth lowest among all small cities and its violent crime rate is half that of the typical micro. Personal income is well above the micro median.

Weaknesses: Statesville also excels in high school dropouts; its rate ties for highest among North Carolina small cities. The area defers to Charlotte for its media. Statesville has no local television and below-average readership of the local paper.

Scores by Section	
Climate/Environment	68
Diversions	38
Economics	37
Education	21
Community Assets	41
Health Care	38
Housing	76
Public Safety	73
Transportation	31
Urban Proximity	96
Total Points	519

Wilson

Points: 496
National Rank: 104
State Rank: 4 of 11

General Information
Components: Wilson County
Area Population: 67,050
Central City Population: 38,847
Location: East-central North Carolina, east of Raleigh
Nearest Metro Center: Greenville, 18 miles

Strengths: Incomes in Wilson are the second highest among the state's eleven small cities. The manufacturing sector is strong, with a value added by manufacture that is the fifth highest among all micros.

Weaknesses: Crime is a problem in Wilson: The total crime rate is twice the micropolitan median; violent crime, three times. Wilson places last in public safety among North Carolina small cities.

Scores by Section	
Climate/Environment	75
Diversions	35
Economics	47
Education	30
Community Assets	38
Health Care	35
Housing	75
Public Safety	50
Transportation	42
Urban Proximity	69
Total Points	496

NORTH DAKOTA

Minot

Points: 525
National Rank: 48
State Rank: 1 of 1

General Information
Components: Ward County
Area Population: 57,903
Central City Population: 35,352
Location: North-central North Dakota, north of Bismarck
Nearest Metro Center: Bismarck, 111 miles

Strengths: Minot has a strong complement of local broadcast outlets: nine radio stations and four television stations. The micro ties for fourth place among all small cities in the category. Minot enjoys very low crime rates and plenty of local diversions.

Weaknesses: Minot is one of the most isolated micros. Winters are long and hard. The average January low dips below zero. Only Alaska amasses more heating degree days.

Scores by Section	
Climate/Environment	44
Diversions	66
Economics	42
Education	51
Community Assets	71
Health Care	56
Housing	58
Public Safety	61
Transportation	61
Urban Proximity	15
Total Points	525

OHIO

Ashland

Points: 528
National Rank: 44
State Rank: 4 of 14

General Information
Components: Ashland County
Area Population: 50,594
Central City Population: 21,112
Location: North-central Ohio, southwest of Cleveland
Nearest Metro Center: Mansfield, 14 miles

Strengths: The arts, shopping, and sports of Cleveland are just sixty-five miles away via the interstate. Three smaller metro centers are even closer. Ashland's violent crime rate is the third lowest among small cities.

Weaknesses: Like many of Ohio's small cities, Ashland's health care system is underdeveloped. Doctor availability is especially low. One-third of local houses are more than fifty years old.

Scores by Section	
Climate/Environment	73
Diversions	41
Economics	29
Education	39
Community Assets	48
Health Care	23
Housing	63
Public Safety	79
Transportation	41
Urban Proximity	92
Total Points	528

Athens

Points: 510
National Rank: 80
State Rank: 7 of 14

General Information
Components: Athens County
Area Population: 60,409
Central City Population: 21,020
Location: Southeastern Ohio, southeast of Columbus
Nearest Metro Center: Parkersburg, W.Va., 39 miles

Strengths: Athens has the lowest violent crime rate among Ohio micros and the ninth lowest among all micros nationwide. Athens leads Ohio small cities in share of college grads. The local high school dropout rate is the tenth lowest in micropolitan America.

Weaknesses: Athens also has other notable low rates: incomes and doctors. Incomes in Athens are the lowest of all Ohio micros and only one other micro nationwide has a lower ratio of private-practice doctors.

Scores by Section	
Climate/Environment	73
Diversions	35
Economics	25
Education	63
Community Assets	43
Health Care	28
Housing	61
Public Safety	66
Transportation	36
Urban Proximity	80
Total Points	510

Chillicothe

Points: 487
National Rank: 114
State Rank: 11 of 14

General Information
Components: Ross County
Area Population: 73,250
Central City Population: 22,297
Location: South-central Ohio, south of Columbus
Nearest Metro Center: Columbus, 46 miles

Strengths: Chillicothe has an above-average broadcast outlet index, the second highest in micropolitan Ohio. Property taxes are among the lowest of the state's small cities and are just 60 percent of the national average.

Weaknesses: Chillicothe has few college grads: The micro's rate is second lowest among Ohio small cities. The total crime rate is significant, the second highest among the state's micros. The city's spending on health care is slight.

Scores by Section	
Climate/Environment	74
Diversions	27
Economics	36
Education	30
Community Assets	55
Health Care	26
Housing	64
Public Safety	57
Transportation	30
Urban Proximity	88
Total Points	487

Findlay-Fostoria-Tiffin

Points: 531
National Rank: 36
State Rank: 3 of 14

General Information
Components: Seneca, Hancock Counties
Area Population: 128,164
Central City Population: Findlay 36,809; Fostoria 15,193; Tiffin 18,530
Location: Northwestern Ohio, south of Toledo
Nearest Metro Center: Toledo, 38 miles

Strengths: The tri-city micro boasts the highest share of high school grads among Ohio small cities, reflecting the local influence of two universities and a college. Income in Findlay-Fostoria-Tiffin is the second highest among micros statewide.

Weaknesses: Findlay-Fostoria-Tiffin is farther removed from regional arts and retail centers than are other Ohio micros. Housing is among the most expensive among small cities statewide.

Scores by Section	
Climate/Environment	71
Diversions	42
Economics	31
Education	42
Community Assets	59
Health Care	30
Housing	60
Public Safety	73
Transportation	47
Urban Proximity	76
Total Points	531

Fremont

Points: 493
National Rank: 107
State Rank: 9 of 14

General Information
Components: Sandusky County
Area Population: 62,738
Central City Population: 18,133
Location: North-central Ohio, southeast of Toledo
Nearest Metro Center: Toledo, 32 miles

Scores by Section	
Climate/Environment	72
Diversions	32
Economics	31
Education	39
Community Assets	48
Health Care	24
Housing	63
Public Safety	67
Transportation	37
Urban Proximity	80
Total Points	493

Strengths: Fremont's manufacturing sector is strong, with a value added by manufacture measure 50 percent higher than the micro median. The area has the second highest share of high school grads among micros statewide.

Weaknesses: The health-care network is weak, with poor availability of doctors and specialists and low spending on community health. Fremont isn't bustling in a way to attract newcomers. Its population growth of 1 percent is lower than the state average.

Marion

Points: 534
National Rank: 30
State Rank: 2 of 14

General Information
Components: Marion County
Area Population: 65,272
Central City Population: 34,611
Location: Central Ohio, north of Columbus
Nearest Metro Center: Mansfield, 39 miles

Scores by Section	
Climate/Environment	72
Diversions	29
Economics	37
Education	33
Community Assets	57
Health Care	41
Housing	65
Public Safety	77
Transportation	35
Urban Proximity	88
Total Points	534

Strengths: Maybe doctors lacking in other Ohio small cities have gravitated to Marion—the micro has an availability of general physicians and specialists far above micropolitan Ohio's norm. Housing is affordably priced and a large share of homes feature three or more bedrooms.

Weaknesses: Marion's ratio of retail stores is considerably below the average micro. Highway accessibility is limited and funding for local roads is below average. Local spending on schools is also light.

Mount Vernon

Points: 486
National Rank: 118
State Rank: 12 of 14

General Information
Components: Knox County
Area Population: 50,108
Central City Population: 15,036
Location: North-central Ohio, south of Mansfield
Nearest Metro Center: Mansfield, 25 miles

Strengths: Few teens leave school early in Mount Vernon: The city has the second lowest dropout rate in micropolitan Ohio. Homes are reasonably priced.

Weaknesses: Mount Vernon has the weakest retail sector of Ohio micros, with a low ratio of stores. Retail sales are corresponding low, significantly below the rest of the state's micros.

Scores by Section	
Climate/Environment	71
Diversions	31
Economics	33
Education	40
Community Assets	47
Health Care	22
Housing	65
Public Safety	65
Transportation	29
Urban Proximity	83
Total Points	486

New Philadelphia

Points: 514
National Rank: 75
State Rank: 6 of 14

General Information
Components: Tuscarawas County
Area Population: 86,585
Central City Population: 16,635
Location: East-central Ohio, south of Canton
Nearest Metro Center: Canton, 26 miles

Strengths: Retail sales in New Philadelphia are the second highest among Ohio's fourteen micros. Local high school dropout rates are the third lowest statewide; the total crime rate is the fourth lowest.

Weaknesses: New Philadelphia's overall health-care rating is the lowest in a state with low ratings. Only one other small city nationwide has a lower ratio of specialists. Investment in local health is 40 percent below the micro median.

Scores by Section	
Climate/Environment	61
Diversions	49
Economics	30
Education	29
Community Assets	67
Health Care	17
Housing	62
Public Safety	74
Transportation	37
Urban Proximity	88
Total Points	514

Norwalk

Points: 489
National Rank: 112
State Rank: 10 of 14

General Information
Components: Huron County
Area Population: 58,016
Central City Population: 15,204
Location: North-central Ohio, north of Mansfield
Nearest Metro Center: Mansfield, 36 miles

Strengths: Norwalk ties for fifth place in metro proximity nationally. A thirty-six-mile drive brings residents to Mansfield. A forty-eight-mile drive brings accessibility to the arts, shopping, and sports of Cleveland.

Weaknesses: Incomes have risen only slightly in Norwalk, the lowest increase among the fourteen Ohio small cities. As with other Ohio micros, doctor availability is low and investment in local health is minimal.

Scores by Section	
Climate/Environment	72
Diversions	31
Economics	27
Education	34
Community Assets	37
Health Care	26
Housing	63
Public Safety	68
Transportation	38
Urban Proximity	93
Total Points	489

Portsmouth

Points: 450
National Rank: 169
State Rank: 14 of 14

General Information
Components: Scioto County
Area Population: 81,113
Central City Population: 23,906
Location: Extreme south-central Ohio, south of Columbus
Nearest Metro Center: Huntington, W.Va., 49 miles

Strengths: With two television stations and six radio stations, Portsmouth has the highest number of broadcast outlets of any Ohio small city. Housing is the least expensive and its number of degree days the lowest.

Weaknesses: Fewer than 9 percent of Portsmouth residents are college grads, the lowest share among Ohio small cities. Personal income is second lowest among the state's micros. The area has the lowest highway index in the state and spends the least on its roads.

Scores by Section	
Climate/Environment	76
Diversions	28
Economics	25
Education	28
Community Assets	49
Health Care	19
Housing	67
Public Safety	60
Transportation	22
Urban Proximity	76
Total Points	450

Sandusky

Points: 568
National Rank: 7
State Rank: 1 of 14

General Information
Components: Erie County
Area Population: 78,046
Central City Population: 30,171
Location: Extreme north-central Ohio, west of Cleveland, on Lake Erie
Nearest Metro Center: Lorain, 33 miles

Strengths: Sandusky boasts a strong economy with the highest incomes and retail sales among Ohio small cities. The micro spends more on its schools than do other Ohio small cities and it spends the second most on community health care.

Weaknesses: Sandusky has the highest total crime rate of Ohio small cities; close to the national rate. Its violent crime rate is the second highest statewide. Sandusky doesn't offer as much elbow room; its population density is fourth highest among all micros.

Scores by Section	
Climate/Environment	73
Diversions	48
Economics	43
Education	42
Community Assets	64
Health Care	45
Housing	56
Public Safety	67
Transportation	40
Urban Proximity	90
Total Points	568

Sidney

Points: 479
National Rank: 131
State Rank: 13 of 14

General Information
Components: Shelby County
Area Population: 46,648
Central City Population: 19,426
Location: West-central Ohio, north of Dayton
Nearest Metro Center: Lima, 34 miles

Strengths: Sidney boasts the third lowest total crime rate of all small cities. The short drive to Dayton ranks Sidney third nationally in arts center proximity. Residents enjoy the shortest commute in micropolitan Ohio.

Weaknesses: Sidney has the second highest dropout rate among Ohio small cities. It also has the second lowest availability of doctors. Education-related spending is among the lowest for state micros.

Scores by Section	
Climate/Environment	73
Diversions	30
Economics	29
Education	29
Community Assets	39
Health Care	21
Housing	67
Public Safety	69
Transportation	37
Urban Proximity	85
Total Points	479

Wooster

Points: 518
National Rank: 66
State Rank: 5 of 14

General Information
Components: Wayne County
Area Population: 106,176
Central City Population: 23,421
Location: North-central Ohio, southwest of Akron
Nearest Metro Center: Canton, 32 miles

Strengths: Wooster has the fourth lowest total crime rate among all micros. Local governments spend the most of any Ohio small city on health. The micro is a part of the Cleveland television market, the thirteenth largest in the country.

Weaknesses: Shopping in Wooster can be tough: The micro ranks second to last in Ohio when it comes to its concentration of retail outlets. The high school dropout rate is the highest among Ohio micros.

Scores by Section	
Climate/Environment	74
Diversions	22
Economics	36
Education	34
Community Assets	41
Health Care	41
Housing	63
Public Safety	71
Transportation	46
Urban Proximity	90
Total Points	518

Zanesville

Points: 509
National Rank: 84
State Rank: 8 of 14

General Information
Components: Muskingum County
Area Population: 83,685
Central City Population: 27,282
Location: East-central Ohio, east of Columbus
Nearest Metro Center: Columbus, 56 miles

Strengths: Zanesville offers some of the most affordable housing in micropolitan Ohio. The availability of retail stores is second highest.

Weaknesses: Zanesville its considered its own national television market, but that distinction lands it in 204th place of 211 TV markets. Although only fifty-six miles from the nearest metro, Zanesville still finishes last in the state for urban proximity.

Scores by Section	
Climate/Environment	71
Diversions	41
Economics	33
Education	36
Community Assets	59
Health Care	43
Housing	63
Public Safety	60
Transportation	36
Urban Proximity	67
Total Points	509

OKLAHOMA

Ardmore

Points: 487
National Rank: 114
State Rank: 2 of 6

General Information
Components: Carter County
Area Population: 43,729
Central City Population: 23,596
Location: Extreme south-central Oklahoma, southeast of Oklahoma City
Nearest Metro Center: Sherman, Tex., 72 miles

Strengths: Ardmore has the eighth least expensive housing in micropolitan America. Availability of hospital beds is greater in Ardmore than in any other Oklahoma micro and personal income is also the state's highest.

Weaknesses: Ardmore's total crime rate is easily the highest among Oklahoma micros; the rate of violent crime, second highest. Temperature variability is drastic, swinging from a high of 96 degrees in summer to a low of 13 degrees in winter.

Scores by Section	
Climate/Environment	60
Diversions	45
Economics	36
Education	33
Community Assets	52
Health Care	28
Housing	79
Public Safety	47
Transportation	42
Urban Proximity	65
Total Points	487

Chickasha

Points: 454
National Rank: 165
State Rank: 6 of 6

General Information
Components: Grady County
Area Population: 43,068
Central City Population: 15,156
Location: South-central Oklahoma, southwest of Oklahoma City
Nearest Metro Center: Oklahoma City, 42 miles

Strengths: Chickasha claims Oklahoma's highest score in urban proximity. Oklahoma City is just an hour up the turnpike.

Weaknesses: Income in Chickasha is the second lowest among state micros and shopping availability is low. Only one micro nationwide spends less on parks and recreation.

Scores by Section	
Climate/Environment	64
Diversions	27
Economics	27
Education	30
Community Assets	40
Health Care	27
Housing	78
Public Safety	59
Transportation	29
Urban Proximity	73
Total Points	454

Duncan

Points: 461
National Rank: 158
State Rank: 5 of 6

General Information
Components: Stephens County
Area Population: 43,195
Central City Population: 22,168
Location: South-central Oklahoma, east of Lawton
Nearest Metro Center: Lawton, 33 miles

Strengths: Duncan offers the largest share of new housing in micropolitan Oklahoma. Prices and property taxes are reasonable. Personal income is the second highest among state micros.

Weaknesses: Just one micro nationwide has a lower total health-care score than Duncan. Highway availability is the lowest among the state's micros.

Scores by Section	
Climate/Environment	66
Diversions	36
Economics	26
Education	32
Community Assets	44
Health Care	15
Housing	80
Public Safety	62
Transportation	34
Urban Proximity	66
Total Points	461

McAlester

Points: 477
National Rank: 137
State Rank: 4 of 6

General Information
Components: Pittsburg County
Area Population: 42,721
Central City Population: 17,620
Location: Southeastern Oklahoma, south of Tulsa
Nearest Metro Center: Tulsa, 91 miles

Strengths: Housing in McAlester is the least expensive among the nation's 193 small cities. Property taxes are the lowest in the state.

Weaknesses: Low incomes match the low home prices in McAlester. Only eight micros nationwide have smaller personal incomes. McAlester's percentage of high school graduates is the lowest among the state's micros.

Scores by Section	
Climate/Environment	69
Diversions	32
Economics	20
Education	29
Community Assets	47
Health Care	45
Housing	78
Public Safety	65
Transportation	29
Urban Proximity	63
Total Points	477

Muskogee

Points: 484
National Rank: 122
State Rank: 3 of 6

General Information
Components: Muskogee County
Area Population: 69,295
Central City Population: 39,299
Location: East-central Oklahoma, southeast of Tulsa
Nearest Metro Center: Tulsa, 50 miles

Strengths: No Oklahoma micro bests Muskogee's ratio of doctors and medical specialists or the per capita value of its health-care funding. Muskogee also leads state micros in highway availability.

Weaknesses: Violent crime is prevalent in Muskogee. The rate is twice that of the median for all micros. Muskogee's rate of juvenile arrests is also prevalent, the highest among Oklahoma micros. Income growth has been slight.

Scores by Section	
Climate/Environment	71
Diversions	36
Economics	26
Education	32
Community Assets	47
Health Care	51
Housing	74
Public Safety	49
Transportation	33
Urban Proximity	65
Total Points	484

Stillwater

Points: 531
National Rank: 36
State Rank: 1 of 6

General Information
Components: Payne County
Area Population: 63,436
Central City Population: 37,514
Location: North-central Oklahoma, northeast of Oklahoma City
Nearest Metro Center: Oklahoma City, 64 miles

Strengths: Oklahoma State University is located in Stillwater, helping the area to the best education score among state micros and perhaps to the high diversion score, also. The micro has a high ratio of hospital beds and significant health funding.

Weaknesses: Home prices in Stillwater are the highest in micropolitan Oklahoma. It's a long haul to Dallas, the nearest arts and sports center. Stillwater winters are colder than other state micros, resulting in the highest number of annual degree days.

Scores by Section	
Climate/Environment	65
Diversions	46
Economics	30
Education	69
Community Assets	42
Health Care	50
Housing	68
Public Safety	63
Transportation	36
Urban Proximity	62
Total Points	531

OREGON

Albany-Corvallis

Points: 540
National Rank: 23
State Rank: 2 of 7

General Information
Components: Linn, Benton Counties
Area Population: 172,410
Central City Population: Albany, 31,785; Corvallis, 46,244
Location: West-central Oregon, south of Salem
Nearest Metro Center: Salem, 29 miles

Strengths: Moderate weather places the Albany-Corvallis area first in the climate section nationwide. The area is strong in education, particularly in Corvallis, where Oregon State University is a prominent local presence. Portland is just seventy-five miles away.

Weaknesses: Health care area-wide is underdeveloped, with a low ratio of private-practice doctors and specialists and the lowest ratio of community hospital beds among Oregon micros. The ratio of retail stores is also the lowest in micropolitan Oregon.

Scores by Section	
Climate/Environment	87
Diversions	40
Economics	40
Education	59
Community Assets	44
Health Care	35
Housing	64
Public Safety	60
Transportation	42
Urban Proximity	69
Total Points	540

Bend

Points: 551
National Rank: 15
State Rank: 1 of 7

General Information
Components: Deschutes County
Area Population: 91,089
Central City Population: 23,951
Location: Central Oregon, east of Eugene
Nearest Metro Center: Eugene, 127 miles

Strengths: Bend claims several top ratings among Oregon small cities. It has the highest share of high school grads, highest personal incomes, and highest per capita retail sales. The Bend area scores fourth among all micros in diversions.

Weaknesses: The Cascade Mountains separate Bend from Oregon's metro centers. The mountains also block coastal weather from Bend, resulting in colder temperatures and drier conditions. Highway availability is limited; housing is relatively expensive.

Scores by Section	
Climate/Environment	63
Diversions	73
Economics	51
Education	60
Community Assets	62
Health Care	52
Housing	53
Public Safety	66
Transportation	37
Urban Proximity	34
Total Points	551

Coos Bay

Points: 497
National Rank: 102
State Rank: 3 of 7

General Information
Components: Coos County
Area Population: 62,731
Central City Population: 15,508
Location: Southwestern Oregon, on the Pacific coast
Nearest Metro Center: Eugene, 115 miles

Strengths: Coos Bay's ratio of libraries and museums is among the highest in micropolitan America. The violent crime rate is the second lowest among state micros. Housing prices are reasonable and public health funding is eleven times the micro median.

Weaknesses: A southern seaside locale removes Coos Bay from metropolitan Oregon. The area rates lowest in urban proximity and highway availability. A view of the sea also guarantees Coos Bay the most precipitation of any Oregon small city.

Scores by Section	
Climate/Environment	68
Diversions	54
Economics	29
Education	42
Community Assets	65
Health Care	49
Housing	59
Public Safety	55
Transportation	38
Urban Proximity	38
Total Points	497

Grants Pass

Points: 443
National Rank: 172
State Rank: 7 of 7

General Information
Components: Josephine County
Area Population: 69,421
Central City Population: 19,328
Location: Extreme southwestern Oregon, northwest of Medford
Nearest Metro Center: Medford, 28 miles

Strengths: Grants Pass has a large share of modern housing and the lowest per capita property taxes of Oregon micros. Medford is just twenty-eight miles away. The rate of violent crime is below the median for all micros.

Weaknesses: Personal income in Grants Pass is the lowest and the slowest growing among Oregon micros. The high school dropout rate is far above the micro median. The area has a below-average availability of doctors and specialists and low health funding.

Scores by Section	
Climate/Environment	73
Diversions	50
Economics	32
Education	27
Community Assets	49
Health Care	27
Housing	64
Public Safety	52
Transportation	34
Urban Proximity	35
Total Points	443

Klamath Falls

Points: 468
National Rank: 147
State Rank: 5 of 7

General Information
Components: Klamath County
Area Population: 60,534
Central City Population: 18,827
Location: Extreme south-central Oregon, southeast of Medford
Nearest Metro Center: Medford, 76 miles

Strengths: Klamath Falls is well-supplied with local media and community membership groups. The total crime rate is low; the juvenile arrest rate is far below that of other small cities in the state. Housing prices are below the micro median.

Weaknesses: It's a long drive from Klamath Falls to the nearest retail hub and even farther to an arts center. Incomes are the second lowest in micropolitan Oregon. Local government spends the least on health care of any small city statewide.

Scores by Section	
Climate/Environment	59
Diversions	50
Economics	30
Education	36
Community Assets	57
Health Care	30
Housing	55
Public Safety	64
Transportation	59
Urban Proximity	28
Total Points	468

Pendleton

Points: 452
National Rank: 167
State Rank: 6 of 7

General Information
Components: Umatilla County
Area Population: 63,197
Central City Population: 15,694
Location: Extreme north-central Oregon, south of Kennewick, Wash.
Nearest Metro Center: Kennewick, Wash., 58 miles

Strengths: Pendleton boasts both the lowest housing prices and the lowest violent crime rate among Oregon micropolitans. The area is well-served by highways and the local airport provides large-jet service.

Weaknesses: Both personal income and income growth are below the median for small cities nationwide. The availability of medical specialists is the lowest among Oregon micros. The area lacks a local television station and has few local museums and libraries.

Scores by Section	
Climate/Environment	57
Diversions	51
Economics	29
Education	37
Community Assets	32
Health Care	29
Housing	63
Public Safety	59
Transportation	55
Urban Proximity	40
Total Points	452

Roseburg

General Information
Components: Douglas County
Area Population: 98,355
Central City Population: 17,653
Location: Southwestern Oregon, south of Eugene
Nearest Metro Center: Eugene, 71 miles

Strengths: Local government spending on education, health, and highways far outpaces that of the typical micro. Crime rates are low, especially for violent crime. Roseburg has the second lowest number of degree days among state micros.

Weaknesses: Roseburg's personal incomes and retail sales are low. The high school dropout rate is above that of the typical micro and college influence considerably below. The nearest regularly scheduled passenger air service is seventy-one miles away in Eugene.

Points: 470
National Rank: 144
State Rank: 4 of 7

Scores by Section	
Climate/Environment	72
Diversions	52
Economics	26
Education	34
Community Assets	47
Health Care	34
Housing	65
Public Safety	57
Transportation	38
Urban Proximity	45
Total Points	470

PENNSYLVANIA

Chambersburg

General Information
Components: Franklin County
Area Population: 125,959
Central City Population: 16,935
Location: Extreme south-central Pennsylvania, southwest of Harrisonburg
Nearest Metro Center: Hagerstown, Md., 21 miles

Strengths: The arts, retail, and sports hubs of Washington and Baltimore are both less than two hours by car from Chambersburg. Per capita income is the highest among the state's three micros and considerably above the micro median.

Weaknesses: The Chambersburg area has the lowest ratio of restaurants and taverns among the state's micros. Health care funding is just one-third the micro median. Five area hazardous waste sites give Chambersburg the third lowest score in that category.

Points: 441
National Rank: 176
State Rank: 2 of 3

Scores by Section	
Climate/Environment	54
Diversions	26
Economics	31
Education	29
Community Assets	45
Health Care	23
Housing	66
Public Safety	53
Transportation	28
Urban Proximity	86
Total Points	441

New Castle

Points: 491
National Rank: 110
State Rank: 1 of 3

General Information
Components: Lawrence County
Area Population: 96,639
Central City Population: 27,798
Location: Extreme west-central Pennsylvania, northwest of Pittsburgh
Nearest Metro Center: Youngstown, Ohio, 16 miles

Strengths: New Castle has the highest share of high school graduates and the lowest share of dropouts among Pennsylvania small cities. Pittsburgh is less than sixty miles away. Highway availability is among the best of all small cities.

Weaknesses: New Castle's share of shops and restaurants is below par for small cities. Income growth and population growth were slow in the first half of the 1990s. Availability of private-practice doctors and specialists is low.

Scores by Section	
Climate/Environment	75
Diversions	22
Economics	24
Education	36
Community Assets	44
Health Care	23
Housing	64
Public Safety	60
Transportation	48
Urban Proximity	95
Total Points	491

Pottsville

Points: 440
National Rank: 177
State Rank: 3 of 3

General Information
Components: Schuylkill County
Area Population: 154,063
Central City Population: 16,603
Location: East-central Pennsylvania, northwest of Reading
Nearest Metro Center: Reading, 35 miles

Strengths: Pottsville features one of the largest shares of large and affordably priced houses in micropolitan America. The rate of homeownership in Pottsville is the highest of all small cities. The violent crime rate is low.

Weaknesses: Pottsville also features the highest share of pre-1940 houses in micropolitan America. Local population grew just 1 percent in the first half of the decade. Few micros spend less on recreational funding.

Scores by Section	
Climate/Environment	58
Diversions	25
Economics	23
Education	24
Community Assets	54
Health Care	20
Housing	64
Public Safety	55
Transportation	37
Urban Proximity	80
Total Points	440

RHODE ISLAND

Newport

Points: 515
National Rank: 72
State Rank: 1 of 1

Scores by Section	
Climate/Environment	53
Diversions	57
Economics	43
Education	59
Community Assets	44
Health Care	30
Housing	30
Public Safety	76
Transportation	36
Urban Proximity	87
Total Points	515

General Information
Components: Newport County
Area Population: 83,689
Central City Population: 24,214
Location: Southeastern Rhode Island, on the Atlantic coast
Nearest Metro Center: Fall River, Mass., 22 miles

Strengths: Newport has the highest ratio of arts and learning institutions among small cities. Only three small cities have a higher share of college graduates than Newport; only five have higher personal incomes. Value added by manufacture is third highest.

Weaknesses: House prices and property taxes in Newport are among the most expensive in micropolitan America. Incomes declined slightly over the first half of the decade and residents trickled away at a much faster rate. Few small cities invest less money in public health.

SOUTH CAROLINA

Greenwood

Points: 511
National Rank: 78
State Rank: 1 of 2

Scores by Section	
Climate/Environment	73
Diversions	40
Economics	34
Education	33
Community Assets	50
Health Care	67
Housing	78
Public Safety	34
Transportation	26
Urban Proximity	76
Total Points	511

General Information
Components: Greenwood County
Area Population: 61,401
Central City Population: 23,163
Location: Northwestern South Carolina, southeast of Anderson
Nearest Metro Center: Anderson, 41 miles

Strengths: Greenwood housing costs are reasonable and property taxes are low. The ratio of doctors is far above the micro median. Spending on public health and hospitals is fourth highest among small cities.

Weaknesses: Violent crime is prevalent in Greenwood, with the fifth highest rate in micropolitan America. The area has a below-average share of high school grads and limited access to highways.

Hilton Head Island

Points: 503
National Rank: 94
State Rank: 2 of 2

General Information
Components: Beaufort County
Area Population: 97,230
Central City Population: 27,379
Location: Extreme southern South Carolina, on the Atlantic coast
Nearest Metro Center: Savannah, Ga., 31 miles

Strengths: Hilton Head boasts the strengths of a popular vacation spot: a high ratio of restaurants and diversions, new housing, high retail sales, and local air service. Educational levels are high; heating and cooling requirements are low.

Weaknesses: Hilton Head's rate of violent crime is more than three times that of the typical micro. Home prices are among the highest in micropolitan America. Regional arts and sports centers are a long drive away. The nearest retail hub is a 285-mile drive to Atlanta.

Scores by Section	
Climate/Environment	52
Diversions	72
Economics	45
Education	49
Community Assets	31
Health Care	55
Housing	62
Public Safety	44
Transportation	50
Urban Proximity	43
Total Points	503

TENNESSEE

Cleveland

Points: 494
National Rank: 106
State Rank: 3 of 5

General Information
Components: Bradley County
Area Population: 77,543
Central City Population: 33,718
Location: Southeastern Tennessee, northeast of Chattanooga
Nearest Metro Center: Chattanooga, 31 miles

Strengths: Cleveland's personal income and retail sales are the highest among Tennessee micros and above those of the typical small city. Close proximity to Chattanooga gives Cleveland the best access to air service of any state micro.

Weaknesses: Cleveland's dropout rate is one of the highest among small cities nationwide. The area has a low ratio of museums, libraries, and other cultural centers. Public transportation serves just 1 commuter in 1,000.

Scores by Section	
Climate/Environment	70
Diversions	26
Economics	41
Education	17
Community Assets	42
Health Care	53
Housing	79
Public Safety	59
Transportation	33
Urban Proximity	74
Total Points	494

Columbia

Points: 513
National Rank: 76
State Rank: 2 of 5

General Information
Components: Maury County
Area Population: 63,936
Central City Population: 34,907
Location: Central Tennessee, southwest of Nashville
Nearest Metro Center: Nashville, 44 miles

Strengths: Columbia is one of the fastest-growing micros in the country. Like other Tennessee micros it boasts affordable housing and a high share of newer, large units. Few small cities spend more per capita on public health.

Weaknesses: The rate of violent crime in Columbia is the highest of all the state's micros. The drive to work is considerably longer than the micro median. The drive to Atlanta—the nearest arts and sports hub—is longer still, at approximately 250 miles.

Scores by Section	
Climate/Environment	67
Diversions	38
Economics	48
Education	24
Community Assets	41
Health Care	57
Housing	75
Public Safety	66
Transportation	28
Urban Proximity	69
Total Points	513

Cookeville

Points: 533
National Rank: 33
State Rank: 1 of 5

General Information
Components: Putnam County
Area Population: 55,870
Central City Population: 25,884
Location: Central Tennessee, east of Nashville
Nearest Metro Center: Nashville, 76 miles

Strengths: Cookeville's ratio of college grads is the highest among the state's micros. It is the only Tennessee micro with a dropout rate below the micro median. Property taxes are nearly half that of the average small city; the total crime rate one-third less.

Weaknesses: Cookeville spends the least of any small city on education. The ratio of hospital beds is the lowest of any of the state's micros; the number of degree days is the highest. The nearest air service is in Nashville, seventy-six miles away.

Scores by Section	
Climate/Environment	66
Diversions	42
Economics	46
Education	33
Community Assets	48
Health Care	48
Housing	79
Public Safety	68
Transportation	36
Urban Proximity	67
Total Points	533

Morristown

Points: 482
National Rank: 125
State Rank: 4 of 5

General Information
Components: Hamblen County
Area Population: 52,376
Central City Population: 22,019
Location: Northeastern Tennessee, southwest of Johnson City
Nearest Metro Center: Knoxville, 41 miles

Strengths: Morristown shares the high scores in housing of other Tennessee small cities. It has an above-average ratio of membership organizations. Knoxville's array of retail shops is just forty-one miles away.

Weaknesses: Morristown has the lowest share of high school graduates among Tennessee small cities. The area has a relatively low share of private-practice doctors and spends very little on public health. Only one other small city has a higher population density.

Scores by Section	
Climate/Environment	76
Diversions	27
Economics	38
Education	17
Community Assets	53
Health Care	30
Housing	80
Public Safety	68
Transportation	29
Urban Proximity	64
Total Points	482

Tullahoma

Points: 472
National Rank: 141
State Rank: 5 of 5

General Information
Components: Coffee, Franklin Counties
Area Population: 78,851
Central City Population: 17,745
Location: South-central Tennessee, southeast of Nashville
Nearest Metro Center: Huntsville, Ala., 58 miles

Strengths: Tullahoma edges out other Tennessee micros for top slot in the competitive housing section. The Tullahoma area also has the best highway accessibility among the state's small cities.

Weaknesses: Tullahoma has the second highest total crime rate among all small cities. The supply of restaurants and amusement establishments is slightly below the micro median. The Tullahoma area has no local daily newspaper or local television station.

Scores by Section	
Climate/Environment	68
Diversions	36
Economics	35
Education	24
Community Assets	44
Health Care	28
Housing	84
Public Safety	51
Transportation	31
Urban Proximity	71
Total Points	472

TEXAS

Corsicana

Points: 487
National Rank: 114
State Rank: 3 of 8

General Information
Components: Navarro County
Area Population: 40,326
Central City Population: 22,906
Location: East-central Texas, southeast of Dallas
Nearest Metro Center: Dallas, 46 miles

Strengths: The arts, shopping, and sports of Dallas are just forty-six miles from Corsicana. Home prices are one-half of the national average and one-quarter of the micro median. Income growth is the highest among Texas's eight small cities.

Weaknesses: Corsicana spends little on public health and hospitals. The area has a below-average share of amusement places, restaurants, and shops. Commuters have the longest drive of Texas small-city workers.

Scores by Section	
Climate/Environment	69
Diversions	33
Economics	34
Education	34
Community Assets	40
Health Care	29
Housing	69
Public Safety	57
Transportation	29
Urban Proximity	93
Total Points	487

Del Rio

Points: 403
National Rank: 191
State Rank: 7 of 8

General Information
Components: Val Verde County
Area Population: 42,764
Central City Population: 35,371
Location: Southwestern Texas, on the Rio Grande, west of San Antonio
Nearest Metro Center: San Antonio, 150 miles

Strengths: Few Del Rio houses predate 1940 and prices are below the micro median. The area has the lowest violent crime rate among the eight Texas micros. Del Rio's availability of restaurants and taverns is the second highest statewide.

Weaknesses: Del Rio's share of high school grads is far below that of the typical micro. Incomes are low. Air service is 155 miles away, the greatest distance for any micro. Daily maximum temperatures in July average 99 degrees.

Scores by Section	
Climate/Environment	51
Diversions	34
Economics	23
Education	29
Community Assets	34
Health Care	43
Housing	71
Public Safety	52
Transportation	29
Urban Proximity	37
Total Points	403

Eagle Pass

Points: 371
National Rank: 193
State Rank: 8 of 8

General Information
Components: Maverick County
Area Population: 44,297
Central City Population: 24,926
Location: Southwestern Texas, on the Rio Grande, southwest of San Antonio
Nearest Metro Center: San Antonio, 154 miles

Strengths: Housing costs and property taxes in Eagle Pass are the lowest among the state's micros. Spending per capita on public health is far above the micro median. Incomes, which have a lot of catching up to do, are growing at twice the national average.

Weaknesses: Personal income in Eagle Pass is the lowest of all micros. Educational attainment is very slight. The area is the most isolated of the eight Texas micros, with drives of 150 to 400 miles to regional metro centers. Highway availability is limited.

Scores by Section	
Climate/Environment	51
Diversions	27
Economics	29
Education	19
Community Assets	31
Health Care	42
Housing	74
Public Safety	40
Transportation	30
Urban Proximity	28
Total Points	371

Huntsville

Points: 466
National Rank: 153
State Rank: 4 of 8

General Information
Components: Walker County
Area Population: 53,706
Central City Population: 28,995
Location: East-central Texas, north of Houston
Nearest Metro Center: Bryan, 56 miles

Strengths: Huntsville has the highest share of high school grads of any Texas micro and the only share to match the micro median, thanks largely to Sam Houston State University. The total crime rate and juvenile arrest rate are the lowest among the state's small cities.

Weaknesses: Shopping is limited; Huntsville has the fourth lowest ratio of retail establishments of all micros. Income growth has been the slowest of the eight Texas small cities. One interstate crosses the micro, but otherwise the area is underserved by highways.

Scores by Section	
Climate/Environment	67
Diversions	29
Economics	20
Education	46
Community Assets	30
Health Care	31
Housing	72
Public Safety	57
Transportation	27
Urban Proximity	87
Total Points	466

Lufkin

Points: 461
National Rank: 158
State Rank: 5 of 8

General Information
Components: Angelina County
Area Population: 74,826
Central City Population: 31,660
Location: Extreme east-central Texas, southeast of Tyler
Nearest Metro Center: Tyler, 83 miles

Strengths: Lufkin's housing is among the newest and largest in micropolitan Texas. Degree days are the second lowest. Lufkin has the second highest share of homeowners and the largest complement of broadcast outlets among Texas micros.

Weaknesses: Like most Texas small cities, Lufkin's share of high school graduates is below the micro median. Its percentage of dropouts is high. Income growth lags behind that of the typical small city. Highway availability is limited.

Scores by Section	
Climate/Environment	70
Diversions	29
Economics	31
Education	29
Community Assets	44
Health Care	43
Housing	77
Public Safety	46
Transportation	27
Urban Proximity	65
Total Points	461

Nacogdoches

Points: 493
National Rank: 107
State Rank: 2 of 8

General Information
Components: Nacogdoches County
Area Population: 56,072
Central City Population: 31,756
Location: Extreme east-central Texas, southeast of Tyler
Nearest Metro Center: Longview, 70 miles

Strengths: Nacogdoches has the lowest dropout rate of all Texas micros, due in part to the influence of Stephen F. Austin State University. Local government invests in health and hospitals at a rate eight times that of the typical micro.

Weaknesses: The Nacogdoches area shares many of the same weaknesses of the other Texas micros: below-average incomes, diversions, and community assets such as libraries, arts centers, and membership organizations.

Scores by Section	
Climate/Environment	69
Diversions	30
Economics	31
Education	51
Community Assets	32
Health Care	59
Housing	71
Public Safety	56
Transportation	31
Urban Proximity	63
Total Points	493

Palestine

Points: 443
National Rank: 172
State Rank: 6 of 8

General Information
Components: Anderson County
Area Population: 49,850
Central City Population: 18,300
Location: East-central Texas, southwest of Tyler
Nearest Metro Center: Tyler, 48 miles

Strengths: Palestine shares micropolitan Texas's high percentage of new houses and below-average housing costs. Dallas is a two-hour drive away, giving Palestine high marks in the urban proximity category. The total crime rate is the second lowest among the eight Texas micros.

Weaknesses: Retail sales and value added by manufacture are considerably below the micro median. Palestine has the third lowest rate of eating and drinking establishments of any small city. The share of college grads is second lowest among Texas micros.

Scores by Section	
Climate/Environment	70
Diversions	26
Economics	20
Education	22
Community Assets	40
Health Care	24
Housing	77
Public Safety	56
Transportation	27
Urban Proximity	81
Total Points	443

Paris

Points: 498
National Rank: 100
State Rank: 1 of 8

General Information
Components: Lamar County
Area Population: 44,924
Central City Population: 24,550
Location: Extreme northeastern Texas, northeast of Dallas
Nearest Metro Center: Sherman, 64 miles

Strengths: Paris has the highest per capita income of Texas small cities and the only one to top the micro median. Likewise, retail sales in Paris are the only ones in micropolitan Texas to surpass the micro median.

Weaknesses: Crime is more prevalent in Paris than in other Texas micros; the rate of violent crime is the fourth highest among all small cities. Highway accessibility is limited. The Paris area has the highest number of degree days in micropolitan Texas.

Scores by Section	
Climate/Environment	69
Diversions	38
Economics	40
Education	37
Community Assets	42
Health Care	46
Housing	73
Public Safety	40
Transportation	32
Urban Proximity	81
Total Points	498

UTAH

Logan

Points: 466
National Rank: 153
State Rank: 2 of 2

General Information
Components: Cache County
Area Population: 75,888
Central City Population: 36,078
Location: Extreme northern Utah, north of Salt Lake City
Nearest Metro Center: Salt Lake City, 79 miles

Strengths: Logan is strong in education, with the fourth highest share of high school grads and fifth highest share of college grads of any small city. Home prices are reasonable and property taxes are low. The violent crime rate is one of the lowest in micropolitan America.

Weaknesses: Logan has one of the lowest urban proximity scores among small cities. Highway availability is limited. Cold winters lead to a high number of degree days. The area has just one-third the ratio of membership organizations of the typical micro.

Scores by Section	
Climate/Environment	55
Diversions	36
Economics	32
Education	68
Community Assets	24
Health Care	37
Housing	64
Public Safety	66
Transportation	37
Urban Proximity	47
Total Points	466

St. George

Points: 476
National Rank: 139
State Rank: 1 of 2

General Information
Components: Washington County
Area Population: 65,231
Central City Population: 38,950
Location: Extreme southwestern Utah, near the Arizona border
Nearest Metro Center: Las Vegas, 117 miles

Strengths: St. George is the fastest-growing of all micros, and it has a large share of new houses to prove it. Only three other small cities spend more on parks and recreation. Of the two Utah micros, winters in St. George are by far the milder.

Weaknesses: Health-care services have yet to catch up with St. George's growth spurt; the ratio of doctors and specialists is low. The area is isolated from regional arts, retail, and shopping hubs. Among all small cities, only Logan, Utah, has fewer membership groups.

Scores by Section	
Climate/Environment	54
Diversions	58
Economics	52
Education	54
Community Assets	41
Health Care	25
Housing	70
Public Safety	48
Transportation	45
Urban Proximity	29
Total Points	476

VERMONT

Rutland

Points: 539
National Rank: 25
State Rank: 1 of 1

General Information
Components: Rutland County
Area Population: 62,495
Central City Population: 17,489
Location: Central Vermont, southeast of Burlington
Nearest Metro Center: Glens Falls, N.Y., 45 miles

Strengths: Restaurants and shopping are plentiful in Rutland. The area also has the second highest share of arts and learning institutions among small cities. Crime rates are low, especially juvenile arrest rates. Summer highs in Rutland don't stray far above 80 degrees.

Weaknesses: Housing in Rutland tends to be older and property taxes are high. Investment in health and hospitals is low. Population growth slowed to nearly a standstill in the first half of the decade. The nearest retail hub is a long 250-mile drive to New York City.

Scores by Section	
Climate/Environment	70
Diversions	72
Economics	34
Education	50
Community Assets	70
Health Care	34
Housing	37
Public Safety	65
Transportation	54
Urban Proximity	53
Total Points	539

VIRGINIA

Blacksburg-Radford-Christiansburg

Points: 507
National Rank: 88
State Rank: 4 of 5

General Information
Components: Montgomery, Pulaski Counties and Radford independent city
Area Population: 125,725
Central City Population: Blacksburg, 35,231; Radford, 15,789; Christiansburg, 17,532
Location: Southwestern Virginia, west of Roanoke
Nearest Metro Center: Roanoke, 30 miles

Strengths: The presence of both Virginia Tech University and Radford College contribute to the area's very low dropout rate and high college influence. Housing is the second most affordable of the five Virginia micros.

Weaknesses: Local incomes are considerably below the micro median and are the lowest of the Virginia small cities. Blacksburg-Radford-Christiansburg is the greatest distance from metro attractions of the state micros and has the lowest ratio of local retail stores.

Scores by Section	
Climate/Environment	79
Diversions	31
Economics	26
Education	57
Community Assets	28
Health Care	43
Housing	71
Public Safety	70
Transportation	50
Urban Proximity	52
Total Points	507

Harrisonburg

Points: 535
National Rank: 28
State Rank: 2 of 5

General Information

Components: Rockingham County and Harrisonburg independent city
Area Population: 94,398
Central City Population: 33,267
Location: West-central Virginia, northwest of Charlottesville
Nearest Metro Center: Charlottesville, 59 miles

Strengths: Harrisonburg's economy is the second strongest among the state's micros. The area has an above-average share of broadcast outlets, arts and learning institutions, and membership organizations. Crime rates are the lowest among Virginia small cities.

Weaknesses: As with other Virginia micros, Harrisonburg's investment in public health is far below the typical micro. Harrisonburg is more removed from metro centers than most of the state micros. The national television market is one of the smallest in the country.

Scores by Section	
Climate/Environment	75
Diversions	37
Economics	40
Education	41
Community Assets	61
Health Care	37
Housing	69
Public Safety	69
Transportation	48
Urban Proximity	58
Total Points	535

Martinsville

Points: 430
National Rank: 185
State Rank: 5 of 5

General Information

Components: Henry County and Martinsville independent city
Area Population: 72,479
Central City Population: 15,818
Location: Extreme south-central Virginia, south of Roanoke
Nearest Metro Center: Danville, 28 miles

Strengths: Of the five Virginia small cities, only Martinsville offers home prices below the micro median. Property taxes are the lowest in micropolitan Virginia and winter temperatures are the mildest.

Weaknesses: Martinsville incomes fell during the first half of the decade. Value added by manufacture is one-third below the micro median. The share of high school grads is among the lowest of all small cities; the share of dropouts among the highest.

Scores by Section	
Climate/Environment	72
Diversions	24
Economics	21
Education	11
Community Assets	46
Health Care	33
Housing	77
Public Safety	54
Transportation	30
Urban Proximity	62
Total Points	430

Staunton-Waynesboro

Points: 519
National Rank: 64
State Rank: 3 of 5

General Information

Components: Augusta County and Staunton, Waynesboro independent cities
Area Population: 102,491
Central City Population: Staunton, 24,840; Waynesboro, 18,749
Location: West-central Virginia, west of Charlottesville
Nearest Metro Center: Charlottesville, 38 miles

Strengths: Staunton-Waynesboro's share of high school graduates is the highest among the state's micros. Incomes are slightly above the micro median. The area offers a large percentage of houses with three or more bedrooms. Crime rates are low.

Weaknesses: Personal incomes declined in Staunton-Waynesboro between 1990 and 1994. The area has the lowest per capita retail sales of the Virginia small cities. The share of both resident college grads and college students is below the micro median.

Scores by Section	
Climate/Environment	76
Diversions	31
Economics	31
Education	29
Community Assets	57
Health Care	41
Housing	72
Public Safety	66
Transportation	43
Urban Proximity	73
Total Points	519

Winchester

Points: 541
National Rank: 22
State Rank: 1 of 5

General Information

Components: Frederick County and Winchester independent city
Area Population: 74,486
Central City Population: 23,796
Location: Extreme northwestern Virginia, northwest of Washington, D.C.
Nearest Metro Center: Hagerstown, Md., 41 miles

Strengths: Winchester boasts the highest incomes and highest retail sales among the Virginia micros, considerably above the micro medians. Winchester's supply of shops and restaurants also outpaces the typical small city. Funding for schools is high. The arts, shopping, and sports of Washington, D.C., are just seventy-one miles away. Doctors are readily available.

Weaknesses: Winchester home prices are the highest among the state's micros and far above the micro median. Incomes were effectively stagnant in the first half of the decade. Commutes are some of the longest in micropolitan America, highway funding some of the lowest.

Scores by Section	
Climate/Environment	70
Diversions	47
Economics	40
Education	36
Community Assets	48
Health Care	58
Housing	68
Public Safety	58
Transportation	28
Urban Proximity	88
Total Points	541

WASHINGTON

Aberdeen

Points: 520
National Rank: 59
State Rank: 6 of 6

General Information
Components: Grays Harbor County
Area Population: 66,701
Central City Population: 16,852
Location: Extreme western Washington, west of Olympia
Nearest Metro Center: Olympia, 47 miles

Strengths: Aberdeen housing is the most affordable of the Washington small cities. The area has the second highest ratio of amusement establishments and restaurants among state micros. Public transit is strong. Temperature variability is very low.

Weaknesses: Incomes and retail sales in Aberdeen are second lowest among the six Washington micros. The area has the lowest share of both high school and college graduates statewide. Few micros nationwide have a health-care network less developed. Precipitation is excessive.

Scores by Section	
Climate/Environment	69
Diversions	65
Economics	27
Education	32
Community Assets	46
Health Care	18
Housing	65
Public Safety	64
Transportation	53
Urban Proximity	81
Total Points	520

Longview

Points: 551
National Rank: 15
State Rank: 4 of 6

General Information
Components: Cowlitz County
Area Population: 87,463
Central City Population: 32,705
Location: Southwestern Washington, on the Columbia River
Nearest Metro Center: Vancouver, 44 miles

Strengths: Longview's moderate climate earns it the second highest overall score in that category. Investment in parks and recreation is third highest among small cities. The shopping and sports of Portland are an hour's drive away.

Weaknesses: The share of college grads is below the median for all micros. Spending on health care is the lowest of state micros and only half that of the typical small city. Longview ties for last place among all micros in local arts and learning institutions.

Scores by Section	
Climate/Environment	86
Diversions	62
Economics	36
Education	38
Community Assets	41
Health Care	31
Housing	68
Public Safety	64
Transportation	38
Urban Proximity	87
Total Points	551

Mount Vernon

Points: 605
National Rank: 1
State Rank: 1 of 6

General Information
Components: Skagit County
Area Population: 91,762
Central City Population: 20,680
Location: Northwestern Washington, south of Bellingham
Nearest Metro Center: Bellingham, 27 miles

Strengths: Mount Vernon has the largest share of high school grads among the Washington micros. Incomes and health funding are high. The metro attractions of Seattle are an hour's drive south. A moderate climate earns Mount Vernon the third highest overall climate/environment score.

Weaknesses: Housing expenses are high in Mount Vernon, with home prices 50 percent above the national micro median. Total crime rates are one-third above the micro median. Personal income rose less than 1 percent in the first half of the decade.

Scores by Section	
Climate/Environment	85
Diversions	62
Economics	49
Education	45
Community Assets	50
Health Care	57
Housing	63
Public Safety	61
Transportation	41
Urban Proximity	92
Total Points	605

Port Angeles

Points: 570
National Rank: 6
State Rank: 2 of 6

General Information
Components: Clallam County
Area Population: 61,784
Central City Population: 18,910
Location: The northern coast of Washington's Olympic peninsula, northwest of Seattle
Nearest Metro Center: Bremerton, 79 miles

Strengths: Port Angeles has the lowest total crime rate of Washington small cities and the second highest share of high school grads. Spending on health and hospitals far outpaces the micro median. The area airport is one of the few micropolitan airports to handle large jets.

Weaknesses: Only one other small city nationwide has less highway access than Port Angeles. Personal income declined nearly 1 percent in the first half of the decade. Local broadcast outlets are limited to two radio stations. Housing costs are far above the micro median.

Scores by Section	
Climate/Environment	79
Diversions	59
Economics	35
Education	37
Community Assets	42
Health Care	46
Housing	65
Public Safety	66
Transportation	59
Urban Proximity	82
Total Points	570

Walla Walla

Points: 524
National Rank: 51
State Rank: 5 of 6

General Information
Components: Walla Walla County
Area Population: 52,734
Central City Population: 29,189
Location: Southeastern Washington, southeast of Richland, near the Oregon border
Nearest Metro Center: Kennewick, 45 miles

Strengths: Walla Walla has a great name. It also has the largest share of college grads and medical specialists among Washington small cities. Housing costs are the second lowest of the state's micros. Spending on parks and recreation is three times the micro median.

Weaknesses: Walla Walla has several less desirable highs and lows. The area has the highest property taxes and highest total crime rate among Washington micros. Shopping and restaurants ratios are the lowest, as are incomes and retail sales.

Scores by Section	
Climate/Environment	63
Diversions	47
Economics	28
Education	55
Community Assets	51
Health Care	57
Housing	61
Public Safety	57
Transportation	58
Urban Proximity	47
Total Points	524

Wenatchee

Points: 557
National Rank: 11
State Rank: 3 of 6

General Information
Components: Chelan County
Area Population: 56,275
Central City Population: 23,310
Location: Central Washington, northeast of Yakima
Nearest Metro Center: Yakima, 105 miles

Strengths: Wenatchee incomes are among the highest of all small cities and some of the fastest growing. The area rates second among all small cities in overall recreation/amusement availability. Property taxes are below the micro median. The local airport offers large-jet service.

Weaknesses: Wenatchee's total crime rate is high and its rate of juvenile arrest is among the highest of all micros. The area has poor highway availability. Wide temperature variability and little precipitation earn Wenatchee the lowest overall climate score among the state's micros.

Scores by Section	
Climate/Environment	51
Diversions	86
Economics	48
Education	35
Community Assets	58
Health Care	52
Housing	58
Public Safety	48
Transportation	54
Urban Proximity	67
Total Points	557

WEST VIRGINIA

Beckley

Points: 471
National Rank: 142
State Rank: 3 of 4

General Information
Components: Raleigh County
Area Population: 78,132
Central City Population: 18,453
Location: Southern West Virginia, southeast of Charleston
Nearest Metro Center: Charleston, 59 miles

Strengths: Beckley has micropolitan West Virginia's best stock of new homes, as well as its largest percentage of homes with at least three bedrooms. Property taxes are the state's lowest; its ratios of doctors and specialists are the second highest.

Weaknesses: Beckley is isolated to an extent unmatched by West Virginia's three other micros: its urban proximity score is by far the state's lowest. Only 63 percent of Beckley's adults are high school grads. Crime rates are the highest among the state's small cities.

Scores by Section	
Climate/Environment	82
Diversions	28
Economics	33
Education	26
Community Assets	58
Health Care	48
Housing	73
Public Safety	53
Transportation	32
Urban Proximity	38
Total Points	471

Clarksburg

Points: 515
National Rank: 72
State Rank: 2 of 4

General Information
Components: Harrison County
Area Population: 70,770
Central City Population: 17,678
Location: North-central West Virginia, east of Parkersburg
Nearest Metro Center: Parkersburg, 74 miles

Strengths: Clarksburg's total crime rate is the lowest in micropolitan West Virginia. Its housing costs are considerably below the micro median. Seven radio and two television stations give Clarksburg micropolitan West Virginia's highest broadcast outlet score.

Weaknesses: Colder winters and hotter summers give Clarksburg a higher temperature variability than the three other state micros. Spending on both public health and local highways is one-third of the typical micro.

Scores by Section	
Climate/Environment	74
Diversions	34
Economics	37
Education	33
Community Assets	63
Health Care	32
Housing	64
Public Safety	72
Transportation	44
Urban Proximity	62
Total Points	515

Fairmont

Points: 459
National Rank: 161
State Rank: 4 of 4

General Information
Components: Marion County
Area Population: 58,109
Central City Population: 20,627
Location: North-central West Virginia, northeast of Parkersburg
Nearest Metro Center: Wheeling, 70 miles

Strengths: Fairmont housing costs are the lowest among West Virginia's small cities, 20 percent below the micro median. Fairmont has the lowest juvenile arrest rate of any small city. Pittsburgh is less than two hours via Interstate 79.

Weaknesses: The rate of hazardous waste sites and substandard air quality is relatively high in Fairmont. Spending on local highways is the second lowest among all small cities. Incomes are the lowest of the state's micros.

Scores by Section	
Climate/Environment	63
Diversions	27
Economics	26
Education	40
Community Assets	54
Health Care	24
Housing	62
Public Safety	71
Transportation	25
Urban Proximity	67
Total Points	459

Morgantown

Points: 592
National Rank: 3
State Rank: 1 of 4

General Information
Components: Monongalia County
Area Population: 78,013
Central City Population: 26,517
Location: Extreme north-central West Virginia, south of Pittsburgh, Pa.
Nearest Metro Center: Cumberland, 72 miles

Strengths: West Virginia University contributes to Morgantown's high educational scores. No other U.S. micro has a better ratio of doctors than Morgantown; only one micro has a better availability of specialists. Incomes are above the micro median. Pittsburgh is just seventy-seven miles away.

Weaknesses: Morgantown houses are the smallest and most expensive among the four state micros. Apart from the university, community assets such as museums, libraries, and membership organizations are limited.

Scores by Section	
Climate/Environment	66
Diversions	36
Economics	49
Education	61
Community Assets	46
Health Care	72
Housing	63
Public Safety	62
Transportation	54
Urban Proximity	83
Total Points	592

WISCONSIN

Fond du Lac

Points: 509
National Rank: 84
State Rank: 2 of 4

General Information
Components: Fond du Lac County
Area Population: 92,834
Central City Population: 39,340
Location: East-central Wisconsin, west of Sheboygan
Nearest Metro Center: Appleton, 38 miles

Strengths: Incomes in Fond du Lac are the highest among the state micros, considerably above the median for all small cities. Retail sales also outpace other state micros. Fond du Lac also has the highest ratio of doctors.

Weaknesses: Property taxes in Fond du Lac are the highest among Wisconsin small cities and exceed the micro median by 80 percent. Juvenile arrest rates are more than twice the micro median. The minimum daily temperature in January averages 7 degrees.

Scores by Section	
Climate/Environment	55
Diversions	41
Economics	39
Education	48
Community Assets	44
Health Care	37
Housing	52
Public Safety	59
Transportation	50
Urban Proximity	84
Total Points	509

Manitowoc

Points: 506
National Rank: 89
State Rank: 3 of 4

General Information
Components: Manitowoc County
Area Population: 82,077
Central City Population: 33,076
Location: The Lake Michigan coast, southeast of Green Bay
Nearest Metro Center: Sheboygan, 27 miles

Strengths: Home prices in Manitowoc are the least expensive among the Wisconsin micros. Crime rates are low, especially rates of violent crime. Highway funding is among the highest for all small cities. Milwaukee's museums, theaters, shopping, and sports are eighty-two miles away.

Weaknesses: Two hazardous waste sites and substandard air quality give Manitowac one of the lowest potential environmental danger scores in micropolitan America. Although total and violent crime rates are low, juvenile arrest rates in Manitowoc are the highest of any micro.

Scores by Section	
Climate/Environment	49
Diversions	40
Economics	31
Education	38
Community Assets	49
Health Care	31
Housing	56
Public Safety	70
Transportation	60
Urban Proximity	82
Total Points	506

Stevens Point

Points: 517
National Rank: 69
State Rank: 1 of 4

General Information
Components: Portgage County
Area Population: 64,123
Central City Population: 21,269
Location: Central Wisconsin, south of Wausau
Nearest Metro Center: Wausau, 34 miles

Strengths: Stevens Point's share of high school and college grads leads Wisconsin micros. The dropout rate is one of the lowest among all small cities. Value added by manufacture is the highest among the four state micros, as is the share of modern homes.

Weaknesses: Cold winters and warm summers give Stevens Point one of the highest total annual degree days of any micro. Just two radio stations earn the area one of the lowest broadcast outlet scores among all small cities. Home prices are the highest among micros statewide.

Scores by Section	
Climate/Environment	59
Diversions	49
Economics	38
Education	56
Community Assets	41
Health Care	37
Housing	56
Public Safety	66
Transportation	54
Urban Proximity	61
Total Points	517

Watertown

Points: 498
National Rank: 100
State Rank: 4 of 4

General Information
Components: Jefferson, Dodge Counties
Area Population: 150,906
Central City Population: 20,687
Location: Southeastern Wisconsin, northwest of Milwaukee
Nearest Metro Center: Waukesha, 34 miles

Strengths: Crime rates in Watertown are below the micro median; rates for violent crime are among the lowest of all micros. Only four other micros have better access to highways. The arts and shopping of Milwaukee are less than sixty miles away.

Weaknesses: Watertown has the lowest ratio of shops and stores of the four Wisconsin micros. The ratio of doctors and specialists also trails the other state micros. Retail sales are the lowest in micropolitan Wisconsin.

Scores by Section	
Climate/Environment	61
Diversions	44
Economics	33
Education	39
Community Assets	34
Health Care	21
Housing	55
Public Safety	64
Transportation	57
Urban Proximity	90
Total Points	498

WYOMING

Rock Springs

Points: 525
National Rank: 48
State Rank: 1 of 1

General Information
Components: Sweetwater County
Area Population: 40,792
Central City Population: 20,144
Location: Southwestern Wyoming, southwest of Casper
Nearest Metro Center: Salt Lake City, Utah, 172 miles

Strengths: The Rock Springs area is free with its pocketbook: it ranks first among all U.S. micros in spending on both education and parks and its spending on health care is eight times the micro median. Personal income is high and wide open spaces are plentiful.

Weaknesses: Paying for all of its services has a down side: Property taxes in Rock Springs are the highest of all small cities, nearly four times the micro median. Home prices are nearly one-third above median. Regional arts, retail, and sports centers are far away.

Scores by Section	
Climate/Environment	46
Diversions	68
Economics	58
Education	58
Community Assets	39
Health Care	48
Housing	48
Public Safety	71
Transportation	64
Urban Proximity	25
Total Points	525

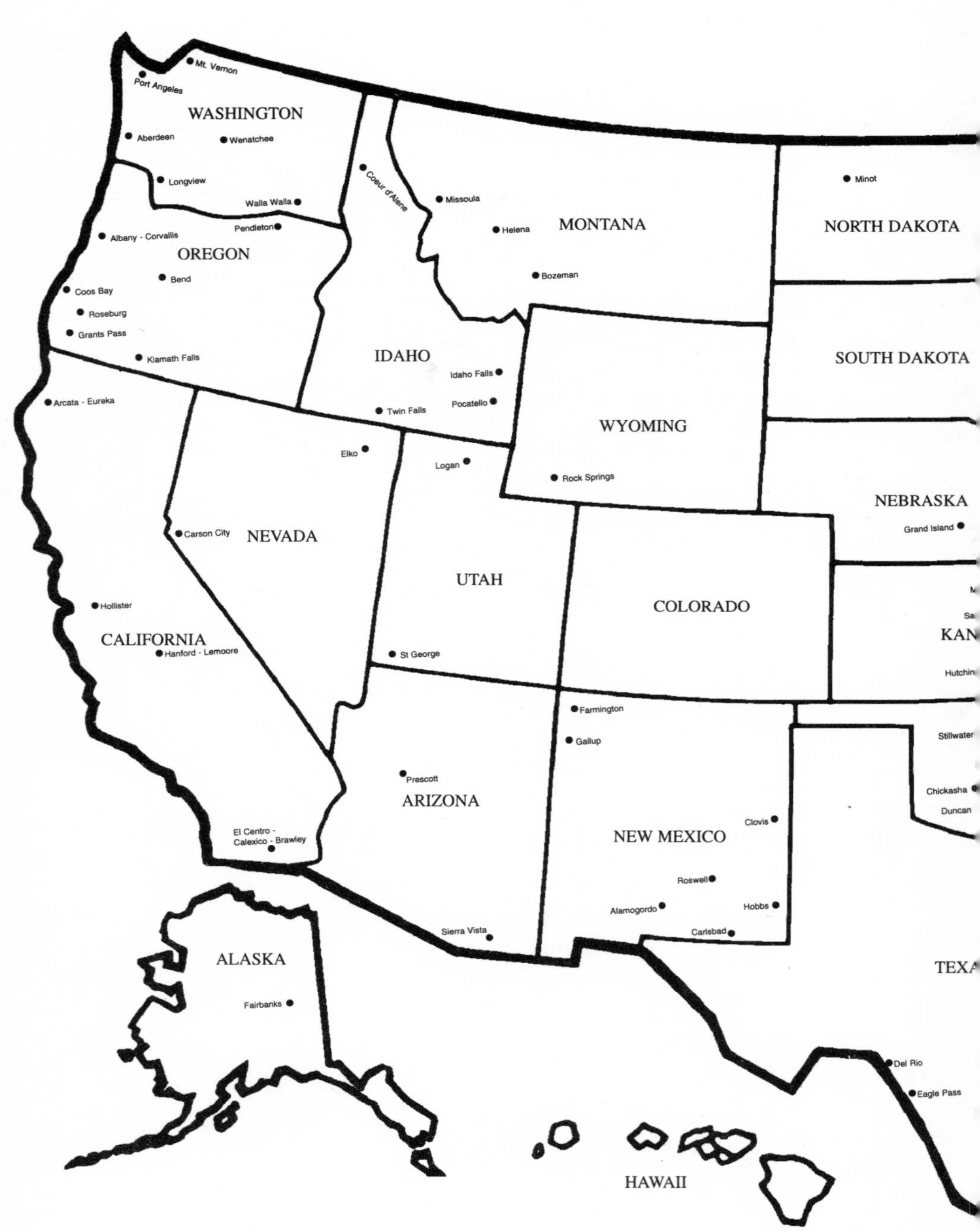

Mt. Vernon
Port Angeles
WASHINGTON
Aberdeen
Wenatchee
Longview
Walla Walla
Pendleton
Albany - Corvallis
OREGON
Bend
Coos Bay
Roseburg
Grants Pass
Klamath Falls
Coeur d'Alene
Missoula
Helena
MONTANA
Bozeman
Minot
NORTH DAKOTA
SOUTH DAKOTA
IDAHO
Idaho Falls
Pocatello
Twin Falls
Arcata - Eureka
WYOMING
Rock Springs
Elko
Logan
NEBRASKA
Grand Island
Carson City
NEVADA
UTAH
COLORADO
Hollister
CALIFORNIA
Hanford - Lemoore
St George
Farmington
Gallup
Stillwater
Prescott
ARIZONA
Chickasha
Duncan
Clovis
El Centro -
Calexico - Brawley
NEW MEXICO
Roswell
Alamogordo
Hobbs
Carlsbad
Sierra Vista
ALASKA
Fairbanks
Del Rio
Eagle Pass
HAWAII

America's 193 Micropolitan Areas